Fast and Able

Life Stories of Great Gloucester
Fishing Vessels

Fast and Able

Life Stories of Great Gloucester
Fishing Vessels

Gloucester 350th Anniversary Edition

Gordon W. Thomas

Edited by Paul B. Kenyon

Gloucester 350th Anniversary Celebration, Inc.
Gloucester, Massachusetts
1973

To the memory of
Captain Jeffrey F. Thomas

my father

a Gloucester fishing captain
who died at the wheel of
his schooner *Adventure*,
at sea, March 24, 1934

and to all those great heroes,
those sturdy, courageous toilers
of the deep

the Gloucester Fishermen

Contents

Foreword

The handsome schooner *Puritan*, designed for speed, was so tricky that she overran her course by twenty miles and sailed at twelve knots right over a Sable Island bar into shallow water where she died, only one hundred and one days afer launching.

The sturdy schooner *Effie M. Morrissey* was still sailing seventy-eight years after she was built. She was used for scientific voyaging in the Arctic Ocean, freighting and fishing.

Gordon Thomas has made it his life work— a labor of love largely—to collect and share authentic information of the great Gloucester vessels. His selection for this Gloucester 350th Anniversary book ranges in time from the schooner *Grace L. Fears*, 1874, to the 1930 schooner *Gertrude L. Thebaud*.

The *Fears* is known in the literature of the sea as the vessel from which Gloucester's superdoryman, Howard Blackburn, went astray in a winter snowstorm. He let his hands freeze around the oars, rowed for five days until he reached Newfoundland, and returned to Gloucester to prosper and sail alone across the Atlantic, twice.

The *Thebaud* caught haddock and halibut, was greeted in Washington by President Franklin Roosevelt, attracted crowds at the 1933 World's Fair in Chicago, raced the Canadian schooner *Bluenose* and was flagship of the Coast Guard's corsair fleet that patrolled the coast in World War II.

Six of the schooners in this book were sunk by German submarine action on both sides of the Atlantic. The fishermen, characteristically, piled into their dories and rowed to safety.

Gloucester schooners were able and rugged, but without engines they were sometimes overpowered by the elements. A third of those in this book were wrecked on rock or reef, sand or shoal, forced there by wind, fog, snowstorm, or ice. About a fifth of the vessels sank at sea, storm-battered or burdened beyond endurance in such latter-day uses as carrying salt from Europe to Canada.

But the real story here is the way the schooners lived: nearly half lasted ten to twenty years; five floated more than half a century. Fishing was always a hard life, but during the heyday of the Gloucester schooner there were unprecedented opportunities for crews and owners to earn well and enjoy a quality of life that involved challenge and the thrill of depending on their own resources in tune with or struggle against the elemental forces of nature.

PAUL B. KENYON *Editor*

Introduction

My great hope is that this book will help keep alive the memory of the glorious sailing vessels of Gloucester and their gallant crews.

I was born in Gloucester and grew up hearing about the vessels from my father, Captain Jeff Thomas, and playing on deck and in the rigging. I knew at first hand that fishing was a hard life. My father would not let me be a fisherman.

I also knew that Gloucester fishermen were more than equal to the challenge. They were courageous, sturdy and generous, and they lessened their burdens with a ready, grim humor.

Gloucester's fishing captains were the greatest mariners in the world. Without diplomas, without engines, without modern navigating equipment, they took vessels to all parts of the North Atlantic and brought them back. They were respected and liked by their men and were mainstays of their community. From the highliners to the least successful they were truly "Captains Courageous."

Gloucester schooners were superior to any other wooden schooners ever built. "Fast, able and handsome," they were famous all over the world. I have loved these vessels ever since I can remember.

About forty-five years ago, while I was looking at newspaper files in the Sawyer Free Library in Gloucester, the idea of a book about the sailing vessels took hold of me. Since then I have scanned the files of the *Gloucester Daily Times* and other old local and Boston newspapers, and studied records of United States, Canadian and British government agencies to glean facts about Gloucester vessels. I have corresponded with officials as far away as Lisbon, Portugal, and I have talked at length with oldtime skippers, crew members and others connected with the fisheries.

This fourth edition of *Fast and Able* includes seventy-six vessels, built during fifty-eight years, and highlights of the lives of some of the great captains and crewmen, the greatest designer and the greatest builder of Gloucester schooners. In connection with the life stories of the vessels I have reported all the names of men lost from them, so far as I have been able to determine. The vessels' stories are arranged in chronological order, alphabetically within each year.

Thirty-eight of the articles first appeared in the *Gloucester Daily Times*. These and the first edition of the book were under the title *Builders of Gloucester's Prosperity*. In some cases I have revised my articles on receipt of additional information.

The cover photograph shows the schooner *Oriole*, in the author's opinion perhaps the most beautiful of them all, in Gloucester Harbor (photograph by Herman W. Spooner).

I am grateful to many persons who have helped in compiling and publishing these stories of great Gloucester vessels. The late Roy L. Parsons, while editor of the *Gloucester Daily Times*, welcomed my suggestion that a series of articles be printed, helped with research and writing in the early stage, and provided the apt title of the first edition, *Builders of Gloucester's Prosperity*. The Cape Ann Savings Bank made it possible for the series to be issued in book form in 1952 under the auspices of the Gloucester Fishermen's Institute.

My thanks go out to others who have aided me, including the late John D. McLoud, former vessels manager of Gorton-Pew Fisheries Company, Ltd.; the late Captains Wylie Rudolph and Archie A. MacLeod of Gloucester and Samuel Walters of Fortune Bay, Newfoundland; the staff of the Sawyer Free Library, where I studied old newspaper files; the Cape Ann Historical Association; the William G. Brown Company, co-sponsor with the Fishermen's Institute of the second edition; and Historic Ships Associates, Boston, sponsor of a third edition.

I am proud that this fourth edition is part of the Gloucester 350th Anniversary Celebration of 1973. I greatly appreciate the cooperation of the Publications Committee of the Anniversary Celebration. Among those who have been particularly helpful are Julian Hatch, chairman of the anniversary celebration; Allen B. Sanderson, publications chairman; Paul B. Kenyon, who edited the first edition and collaborated again on this edition; and the Cape Ann Bank and Trust Company, which encouraged me in this work.

Fellow collectors of schooner lore who have shared their knowledge and judgment include Dana Story of Essex, son of the leading builder of Gloucester schooners, and R. Loren Graham of Swampscott, one of the founders of the Steamship Historical Society.

GORDON W. THOMAS

58 Central Street
Ipswich, Massachusetts
October 1972

Glossary

BALLOONER large jib topsail

BOOM spar at foot of sail

BOWSPRIT spar projecting over forward end of vessel

CAPELIN a small fish of the smelt family

CLOSEHAULED position of sails almost parallel with length of vessel so she can sail as near as possible into the wind

COMPANIONWAY entrance from deck to cabin below

FLITCHED HALIBUT halibut boned, then sliced and salted on the vessel

HAIL captain's estimate of weight of fish aboard

HIGHLINE having the best record for catching fish

HOVE DOWN vessel heeled so far over that she is almost capsized; on her beam ends

JUMBO fore staysail

KNOCKABOUT rig without a bowsprit

KNOTS speed in nautical miles (6,080 feet) per hour

SEINE a special net used to catch mackerel

SHACKING Gloucester term for trip in which fish caught early were salted, and the rest brought in fresh, iced

SHARE amount allotted from earnings to each man in crew

SHEER lengthwise upper profile of a vessel, usually beautifully curved

SHEET rope used to control position of boom and sail

STAYSAIL large "kite" set between main topmast head and foremast head

STOCK total amount paid for fish; operating expense and owners' proceeds are deducted from stock

TONS gross and net ton figures are technical measurements of cargo capacity in terms of space available

Perhaps never previously published, this photograph shows schooner *Grace L. Fears* being built at the David Alfred Story shipyard on Vincent Cove in downtown Gloucester. Such a massive bowsprit, here supported by noble trailboards, was sometimes called a widow-maker because fishermen had to work from such precarious positions when handling the jibs.

Grace L. Fears

HOWARD BLACKBURN ROWED TO SHORE AND FAME/1874–1897

Searching through my records, I decided to use the history of one of the older vessels of the era prior to our famous flying fishermen.

I chose the schooner *Grace L. Fears* because she was typical of the period, was always worked hard, fished under many great skippers, and was part of a legend, that of Howard Blackburn, Gloucester's greatest hero.

The *Grace L. Fears* was built by David Alfred Story at Pearce Street, Gloucester, and launched on July 2, 1874. The firm of Dennis and Ayer were her owners and Capt. Randall McDonald her skipper.

She was a fair sized vessel, typical of vessels of that time, with a heavy clipper bow, with trailboards and flying jibboom. She carried a large rig.

The *Fears* and schooner *Bunker Hill* were off the same mould. She was named after the sister of Albert Fears of Gloucester, a dealer in pigiron ballast.

The *Grace L. Fears* during her career was used in most all branches of the fishery, including halibuting, haddocking, Georges handlining, mackerel seining and Newfoundland herring voyages.

Many of our greatest skippers commanded the *Fears*. In 1874–78, Capt. Randall McDonald was her commander. Capt. Nat Greenleaf, 1881–82; Capt. Jim McKinnon, 1882; Capt. Alex Griffin, 1882; Capt. Tom Lee, 1883–85; Capt. John Campbell, 1885–88; Capt. Julius Van Amberg, 1891; Capt. Will Doane, 1891–92; Capt. Louis Johnson, 1893–94. Capt. Neil McPhee had the *Fears*, Georges handlining, in 1894–95.

Capt. Nat Greenleaf was probably the most successful of the *Fears*'s skippers. In March 1882 he landed 92,000 pounds halibut and 3,000 cod at Gloucester, stocking $6,016, with a share of $206. The vessel was gone five weeks.

Many folks today have the impression that the fishermen of the past made very little money and their vessels were slave ships. This was not so. There were many successful skippers and vessels and many fishermen shared well. Of course there were lean years and good years and money was made the hard way at great risk of life. This was the way Gloucester was built.

The *Grace Fears* had several owners. The Atlantic Halibut Co. was listed as the owner in 1882. In 1888 Pool, Gardner Co. were the owners. David I. Robinson was the owner in 1893–94. In December 1894 she was sold to Stockbridge and Co. for $2,700. The estate of Seth Stockbridge sold the *Fears* to Capt. Sol Rowe in March 1897 for $1,075.

The *Grace L. Fears* had her share of hard luck. While under command of Capt. Greenleaf, Charles Nelson and Lafayette Greenleaf, brother of the skipper, two of her crew, went astray in the fog on Grand Bank, August 10, 1881. They were picked up five days later by a French bark and landed at Savannah, Georgia. When they were rescued they had only one quart of water left.

Thomas Walsh, one of the crew, was lost off Burgeo, Newfoundland, on January 25, 1883.

On February 24, 1885, the *Fears* arrived at Gloucester from a Bank halibut trip. She reported very severe weather. Her cable was parted twice, losing two anchors and 140 fathoms of cable. She was obliged to lay to for nearly a week.

In August 1893 the *Fears* was struck by a gale on Brown's Bank. She ran for Liverpool, Nova Scotia, after springing aleak, with two foot of water over cabin and forecastle floor. On entering the harbor she ran ashore and filled with water. She was floated later and repaired.

On January 25, 1883, the *Grace L. Fears*, Capt. Alex Griffin, was fishing on Burgeo Bank. Two of her crew, Howard Blackburn and Thomas Welsh, went astray in the fog. The thrilling story of Blackburn's courageous attempt to save his dorymate's life has been expertly told by Joseph E. Garland, Gloucester author, in his book, *Lone Voyager*. I think without a doubt Howard Blackburn is Gloucester's greatest hero. Never in the annals of the sea has a man shown the courage, endurance and strength of this Gloucester fisherman, who rowed to shore after his hands froze around the oars.

The *Grace L. Fears* sailed on her last voyage on December 9, 1897. She was bound to Newfoundland for a herring cargo in command of Capt. John Aiken. She was sighted on the morning of December 17th by schooner *Columbia*, Capt. John Campbell, about thirty miles from St. Pierre, Miquelon. She was never seen again. She was supposed to have gone down in the gale that arose the following day. She carried a crew of seven.

Capt. John Aiken, fifty-six years old, was a native of Barrington, Nova Scotia. He left a widow and five children.

While glancing through the files of the *Gloucester Daily Times* of August 20, 1901, I found a very interesting article. It states that William DeWinter, nineteen years old, picked up a bottle on the beach to the westward of the Cut Bridge. It contained a message reading: "We are sinking in the *Grace L. Fears*. Whoever finds this, hand it to my wife. John Aiken, captain."

The article stated that the message was given to the captain's widow. I do not know if this story was true or not, but if so, the bottle had been afloat for four years.

Capt. Nathaniel Greenleaf died at Sailors Snug Harbor, Staten Island, New York, in March 1937 at the age of eighty-seven. Capt. Nat and his brother, Capt. William, were two of the greatest Down East fishermen. Capt. Nat was the king of the halibuters in the 1870's, 1880's and 1890's. He was a native of Westport, Maine. Some of his commands were schooners *Lizzie Greenleaf, Oresa, Grace L. Fears, Edward Perkins, Senator, Porter S. Roberts, Kineo, Harvard* and *Republic*.

Gross tons, 84; net tons, 81; length, 81 feet; breadth, 22 feet; depth, 8 feet.

One of the saddest sights on land or sea is a good vessel breaking up. Cape Cod surf and sand have broken the back of the *Elsie M. Smith.*

Elsie M. Smith

BREECHES BUOY SAVED THIRTEEN MEN / 1882–1904

Schooner *Elsie M. Smith* was one of the fast sailers in the "Down East" fleet and an exceptionally staunch and strong vessel.

The *Elsie M. Smith* was built by George Christensen of Kennebunk, Maine, in 1882 for the Abial M. Smith firm of Portland, Maine. She was built alongside of the fine schooner *Fanny Spurling*, also owned by the Smith firm.

The *Elsie M.* was a rugged vessel of medium size with a clipper bow and rigged with a flying jib boom. She carried a figurehead of an eagle, one of the very few fishing schooners carrying a figurehead. Later a pole bowsprit replaced the old flying jib boom.

During her Down East career she was commanded by Capt. Lincoln Jewett, one of the great sail carriers of the Maine coast, who later rose to fame as commander of the six-master *Eleanor Percy.* Very few craft could boast of victory over the *Elsie Smith* and Capt. Linc Jewett, especially in heavy weather.

In February, 1890, three vessels of the Abial Smith firm were sold to Albert P. Babson of Gloucester for $17,000. They were the *Elsie M. Smith, Fanny Spurling* and *Abbie M. Deering.* The *Elsie Smith* arrived in Gloucester in tow of the tug *Belknap* on February 17th.

During her Gloucester career the *Elsie M.* was commanded by several fine skippers. Capt. Colin McIntosh took over in May, 1890. Capt. Frank Deveau was skipper in February, 1895, and Capt. John Rust in May 1895. Capt. James Fiers was skipper in March, 1896. Capt. Frank Hall, one of our great mariners, took over seining in April, 1896, and remained in her several seasons.

In December, 1898, the *Elsie Smith* was sold to Capt. Otto Jensen of Gloucester. Capt. Jensen took the vessel to Newfoundland for herring cargoes that season of 1898–99. Capt. Fred Thompson, another great mariner, took over the *Elsie M.* in 1909 as his first command, using her shacking and halibuting. The last skipper of the *Smith* was Capt. Charles Nickerson.

The *Elsie Smith* had several narrow escapes from destruction. The winter of 1898–99 was a hard one for Cape Ann. On February 13, 1899 the Cape was hit by a heavy blizzard, almost equal to the great Portland breeze which occurred several months previous. The *Elsie M. Smith*, which had been chartered by Capt. Frank Hall, had just returned from Newfoundland with a herring cargo and was lying in the stream off the steamboat wharf. The drifting ice and heavy wind carried her ashore during the night on to Rocky Neck, just westward of the C. F. Wonson and Co. wharf. She lay stern on with her bow hove down. Schooner *Ellen Gleason*, Capt. Walter Whittey, was securely fastened to William Dennett's wharf at the Fort, but at high tide she broke away and drove up on the Rocky Neck shore about 100 yards to the westward of the *Elsie Smith*.

The next day after the storm subsided, the tugs *Startle, Eveleth* and *Joe Call* worked on the *Smith* and attempted to float her without success. The frozen herring in her cabin was then lightened and she was hauled off quite easily at high tide that night. The lighter *Abbott Coffin* pumped her out and she was put on Burnham's ways for repairs. The *Ellen Gleason* was floated several days later. This was the same breeze in which Capt. Jack Greenlaw of the schooner *Annie Greenlaw* was washed overboard to his death off Cape Cod.

The *Elsie M.* had another narrow escape on August 1, 1901, when on a shacking trip in command of Capt. Fred Thompson she ran into three fathoms of water on the North East Bar of Sable Island, but by the skillful efforts of Capt. Thompson they managed to get clear. Incidentally, on this trip a pair of walrus tusks were hauled up in the trawls by Hugh McKinnon and Harry Gibbs.

Allan J. Larry or Leary, one of the crew of the *Elsie Smith*, was drowned by the capsizing of his dory on LaHave Bank on December 4, 1894. His dorymate, Dominic Newhouse, clung to the overturned dory and was rescued. The drowned man was a native of Philadelphia, Pa. and 35 years old. This was his first trip in the vessel.

The life of the *Elsie Smith* was ended on the sands of Cape Cod in February, 1902. Two of the crew were drowned. Three were snatched from death in the surf and 13 others were taken from the wreck in a breeches buoy by a life-saving crew.

The vessel, in command of Capt. Charles Nickerson, stranded on Orleans Bar during a blinding snowstorm on the night of February 13. When the vessel struck, five of the crew attempted to reach shore through the angry surf in two dories. Had these five men remained on the vessel, they would have been saved, as were their 13 mates, in the breeches buoy. Silvine Doucette and his brother, Dean, were drowned in the icy waters. Louis Surrette, Fred Amero and James Rogers were pulled from the surf in an almost exhausted condition by the crew of the Orleans and Old Harbor Lifesaving Station. Meanwhile, Capts. Doane and Charles of the lifesaving crews had planted their sand anchors, and at the first shot had sent a line over the vessel's jib stay. It was made fast in the fore rigging about 10 feet below the mast head, and soon the breeches buoy was sent off to the craft. Within an hour from that time 13 men had been safely landed.

The *Elsie M.* was a total loss. At the time of the disaster she was bound to Boston from the South Channel with a fare of fresh fish. She hit the beach with terrific force and the great seas soon began to pound her to pieces. The next day she looked a pitiful sight as she lay on the bar, her back broken and some of the sails still set. Her value was placed at $8,000.

Crew members rescued in the breeches buoy included Capt. Charles L. Nickerson, William Wiliams, Nelson Hickman, Amillie Doucette, John Clement, Fred Dogget, John Murphy, Paul McLean, Arthur Kaegs, William Surrette, William Ackerman, Michael Drew and Lauris Doucett. They were all cared for at the Orleans and Old Harbor station.

The drowned men, Silvine and Dean Doucette, were natives of Tusket, Nova Scotia.

Capt. Otto Jensen, last owner of the *Elsie Smith*, passed away at his home in Lubec, Maine, in February, 1940. Capt. Otto, a native of Denmark, was one of our fine mariners in the days of sail.

Gross tons, 113; net tons, 107; length, 93.5 feet; breadth, 24 feet; depth, 9.1 feet.

Businesslike as she sails out of Boston Harbor is the *Horace B. Parker*, one of the top moneymakers of her time.

Horace B. Parker

TEN TIMES HER COST IN SIX YEARS / 1888–1907?

In 1888, two vessels were built for Gloucester firms and named for members of the Parker, Holmes Shoe Co. of Boston, They were schooner *Horace B. Parker* for the Capt. John Chisholm firm, and schooner *Edwin B. Holmes* for the Ben Low Co. The vessels were very successful, and were the top leaders of their day.

A glance at their records for their first six years afloat gives the *Horace Parker* a stock of $139,481 haddocking (1888 to 1894) *Edwin B. Holmes*, $105,556 Georges (1888 to 1894), a total stock of $245,037. Their total building cost was only $20,000. This was big money in those days.

This is the story of the more famous of these vessels, schooner *Horace B. Parker*, named for the senior member of this well known Boston firm. She was commanded by Capt. William H. Thomas, one of the greatest fresh fishing skippers who ever sailed from Gloucester. She

5

was built by Tarr and James Yard at Essex, launched on July 24, 1888, and towed around to Gloucester by the tug *Emma S. Bradford*.

The *Parker* was a fine, sturdy schooner built of white oak, and copper fastened. She was built on contract at a cost of $10,000. Capt. George (Mel) McClain of Rockport was her designer, and she was built off the model of the famous fisherman *I. J. Merritt, Jr.* Capt. John Chisholm and Capt. Billy Thomas, my uncle, were the owners. The length of her forecastle was 26 feet. She had a clipper bow, with square mast heads (round mast heads were not carried on fishermen at that time). The crews of the *Horace B. Parker* were mainly Arichat Frenchmen. They were sturdy men and great fishermen, and they came from Capt. Billy's birthplace in Cape Breton.

Schooner *Horace B. Parker* was fitted for haddocking at Gloucester. She arrived at Boston with her maiden fare on October 15, 1888, hailing for 20,000 lbs. cod, 4000 lbs. haddock. (Sailing news of fishermen was vague way back in the 80's. No record can be found of the *Parker* sailing on her maiden trip.)

From the time she was built, the *Horace B. Parker*, in command of Capt. Thomas, was a money maker. Under his guidance she was always used haddocking and shacking. Her total stock for 14 years, up to the time she was sold by Capt. Thomas, was $292,000. One of her best years was 1899, when she was high line of the haddockers with a stock of $25,441.

The *Parker* could step along with the best sailers of the fleet, and Capt. Billy, one of Gloucester's great sail carriers, drove her all the way. In a brush with the schooner *Leader*, from Georges to Boston, in September, 1891, she beat that fast vessel home by about an hour.

Only four men were ever lost from the *Parker*. On March 7, 1896, Simon Landry was washed from the bowsprit on Georges and drowned. The jib was being furled when a heavy sea hit the vessel. Landry was 32 years old and a native of Arichat, Cape Breton.

Thomas Landry fell from the main boom and drowned on La Have Bank January 10, 1897. He was a native of Arichat and was 24 years old.

On May 18, 1899, my uncle, Capt. John Thomas, and Lawrence Smith, two of the crew of the *Horace B. Parker*, were drowned on Western Bank. It was a fine clear day. Capt. Billy couldn't see the sail of his brother's dory and suspected something was wrong, so a flag was set in the rigging calling the crew in. The vessel got under way and found the overturned dory, but nothing was seen of the occupants. The dory plug had been hauled clean through the bottom of the dory, showing the desperate struggle the men must have put up. Capt. John Thomas was a native of Arichat, Cape Breton, and was 37 years old. He was formerly in com-

mand of the schooners *Essex* and *Quickstep*. Lawrence Smith was 40 years old and a native of Arichat, Nova Scotia.

Many incidents took place in the life of the *Horace B. Parker*. On December 20, 1890, she came upon the battered, sinking hulk of the Canadian ship *Eurydice* of St. John, New Brunswick, badly battered and leaking after meeting successions of gales. The pumps were not sufficient to keep the water down and the crew resorted to bailing with buckets. Capt. William Brown and his crew of 17 men were taken off the sinking ship by the *Parker's* crew with great difficulty. Heavy seas were running and the weather was intensely cold. The rescued men were fearfully frost bitten. Capt. Brown of the wrecked ship reported that he had spoken to two schooners, but neither responded to his distress signals. They were mighty happy when they sighted a Gloucester fisherman, which proved to be the *Horace B. Parker*. They knew that help was near. The doomed ship sank four hours after the rescue. The rescued men were landed at Shelburne, Nova Scotia.

In April, 1892, the Canadian government presented a gold watch to Capt. Thomas and $10 each to the *Parker's* crew of 19 in recognition of their heroic deed. The crew list of the *Parker* at that time: Thomas Shields, Simon Landry, Angus Cameron, Michael Foley, Lawrence Smith, Thomas Martin, Joseph Ryan, Patrick Daniels, William Clew, John White, Charles Veno, Edward Kippen, Morris Thomas (my uncle), Nicholas Hickman, Henry Wolf, Thomas Burns, Andrew Hanson, John Winthrop and Robert Dexter.

In March, 1891, Capt. Thomas received a beautiful pair of marine glasses from the French government, in recognition of the rescue of two of the crew of the French schooner *Josephine*, who went astray from their vessel. They were adrift four days and nights, and when found by the *Parker* 40 miles southeast of Scaterie, they were lying exhausted in the bottom of their dory. They were taken on board with great difficulty. The marine glasses were on exhibition at Thompson's Jewelry store in Gloucester.

The *Horace Parker* stranded on Oak Island bar, Crescent Beach (Revere Beach) on February 11, 1894. She was bound to Boston from Georges with 60,000 pounds fresh fish, when she lost her bearings in a dense fog. The craft was floated unassisted and repaired at Gloucester. Her keelson was gone and the stern post was started.

Tragedy overtook the *Parker* in 1895. At 3:40 a.m. on January 5, she rammed and sank the Boston pilot boat, *D. J. Lawlor* (No. 3) about eight miles north of Minot's Light. Four of the *Lawlor's* crew were drowned and only one, the cook, was saved. A heavy sea was running at the time and there was a dense vapor. The temperature was near zero. Both vessels were bound to Boston. The *Parker* was coming from the South Channel with a trip and the pilot boat was returning from her Cape Shore station. The doomed craft was struck about the middle of her port side and went down quickly in 37 fathoms of water. The lost men were asleep in the cabin at the time of the crash. The *Parker* spent the next day looking for survivors, but nothing was seen but a floating bucket. The *Horace B.* lost her bowsprit and fore rigging. The value of the *D. J. Lawlor* was put at $10,000. She was built in 1892 and was considered the best heavy weather boat in the pilot service. When the *Parker* reached Boston, Capt. Thomas visited the pilot's office and expressed his regrets.

On opening day of the new Gloucester Fresh Fish Co., December 6, 1897, the *Horace B. Parker* was there with a trip of fish. This was a great event in Gloucester. All flags in the city were flying. There was a parade and fireworks. This new company opened against the Boston market paying 25 cents a hundred-weight higher than the latter. Hon. David I. Robinson was manager. Schooners *Lizzie B. Adams*, *Viking*, *A. S. Caswell*, and *Norman Fisher* were also there with trips. Schooner *Norman Fisher* was flying her flag at half mast, to the memory of her skipper, Capt. Harvey Anderson, one of our great mariners, who was washed overboard and drowned a few days before.

The *Horace B. Parker* rode out the Portland Breeze of 1898 on the northeast part of Georges. Capt. Thomas reported the gale not too severe. She didn't drift off the bank during the blow.

Capt. Billy sold the *Horace Parker* to Capt. Jerry Gayton and Capt. Jesse Morton in December, 1902. Her phenomenal stock of $292,000 under Capt. Thomas had never been equalled up to that time. In 1903 and 1904 Capt. Gayton

took her salt banking, and in 1905–06–07 she sailed under Capt. Jesse Morton in this same fishery.

The *Horace B. Parker* wound up her career out of Gloucester in December, 1907, when she was sold to the French at St. Pierre, Miquelon, for fishing on Grand Bank. Many Gloucestermen were sold to St. Pierre about that time, among them the *Edwin B. Holmes* (sister of the *Horace Parker*), in 1905. The *Horace B. Parker* was renamed *Eugene Robert*, and this was the last I ever heard of her.

Capt. William H. Thomas died of a heart attack in Gloucester, June 29, 1925. He was manager of the Gloucester Cold Storage at the time. Capt. Billy was a native of Arichat, Cape Breton. He was of French and Welsh descent. At the time of his death he was 67 years old. He was one of the greatest skippers out of Gloucester. He was well known wherever fish was bought and sold on the North Atlantic coast. A fisherman of the first water, a man combining the qualities of hustling and judgment, and an honored and respected citizen. A glance at this great skipper's record and talks with many old fishermen still with us, place Capt. William Thomas as the greatest skipper in the fresh fishery who ever sailed out of Gloucester. It was considered an honor to sail with him. Some of the finest fishermen sailed under him. Men of his character, courage and ability are the men who built this port. A skipper for 32 years, he commanded many fine vessels including the *Dido*, *Mystic*, *Horace B. Parker*, *Elmer E. Gray*, *Monarch* and *Thomas S. Gorton*. He retired from the sea in 1916. His total stock in 32 years was a little short of $900,000. Capt. Billy was the leader of them all.

Gross tons, 98; net tons, 62; length, 89.4 feet; breadth, 23.6 feet; depth, 9.7 feet.

This is the kind of documentary photograph Ernest L. Blatchford took as a leading member of the Cape Ann Camera Club and manager of the New England Fish Co., Duncan Point, Gloucester. The *Golden Hope* could be bound for Newfoundland to bring back a cargo of herring.

Golden Hope

FLYING JIB BOOMS AND SQUARE
MASTHEADS/1890–1904

Schooner *Golden Hope*, a real old timer with a beautiful name, made her debut in the twilight of the flying jib booms and square mastheads. She was one of the last vessels in the Gloucester fleet with this rig.

Schooner *Golden Hope* was a medium-sized vessel built by Arthur D. Story at Essex during the winter of 1889–90 and launched in January, 1890, for George Dennis and Capt. Alex (Little Alex) McEachern of Gloucester. She was taken off the model of the famous schooner *I. J. Merritt, Jr.* and was rigged with square mastheads and a long flying jib boom. Later the jib boom was taken off, leaving only the stump bowsprit.

Many famous Gloucester fishing schooners joined the fleet with the *Golden Hope* in 1890, including the schooners *Oliver Wendell Holmes*, (she carried one of the longest names out of Gloucester), *Nannie C. Bohlin*, *Penobscot*, *Lottie S. Haskins*, *Lucille*, *Parthia*, *Eliza B. Campbell*, *W. E. Morrissey*, *Volunteer*, *Shenandoah*, *Norumbega*, *Maggie E. Wells* and *Susan L. Hodge*. What a glorious fleet! Many of these craft were destined in the years to come, to carry the name and fame of Gloucester across the North Atlantic.

The *Golden Hope* sailed on her maiden trip to Fortune Bay, Newfoundland, for a herring cargo, on January 29, 1890 in command of Capt. Alex McEachern. She arrived on March 17, 1890 in ballast, having been unable to secure a fare.

Capt. McEachern turned his attention to salt fishing and in the *Golden Hope* firmly established his reputation as one of Gloucester's finest mariners. He remained as skipper of the *Golden Hope* salt fishing summers, making Newfoundland herring trips during the winter months until October 1891 when he took over his new schooner *Maggie and May*, named for his two daughters.

Capt. Frank Seeley took the *Golden Hope* to Newfoundland for a herring cargo in December, 1891. Capt. Will Cluett had her seining in 1894.

The *Golden Hope* was sold in April, 1894 to the D. B. Smith firm of Gloucester. Capt. Harry Gardner took the vessel on a Greenland flitched halibut trip in May 1895. Capt. Will Goodwin had her salt banking during the season of 1896. Capt. Douglass McLean took over seining in 1897 and remained as skipper until 1900, seining, haddocking, and cod fishing. The *Golden Hope* was commanded by Capt. J. D. Morrissey

during the fall of 1900. Capt. Walter Whittey had her shacking in the summer of 1901. Capt. Douglass McLean again took the *Golden Hope* seining during 1902–03. Capt. Charles Stewart had her seining in the summer of 1904.

Capt. Jack Morash took her to the Cape Shore in the fall of 1904. Shortly after the "Portland Breeze" of November, 1898, the *Golden Hope* in command of Capt. Douglass McLean came upon the abandoned Nova Scotian schooner *Annie G.* off Cape Sable, Nova Scotia. The helpless, crewless craft was drifting about at the mercy of the elements. Capt. McLean and some of his crew boarded the derelict. One body was found in the cabin. Shortly after, another vessel picked up the *Annie G.* and towed her into Clark's Harbor, Nova Scotia.

On Sept. 15, 1904 the *Golden Hope*, while on a Cape Shore seining trip in command of Capt. Jack Morash, stranded on Indian Beach; at the entrance to North Sydney, Cape Breton. The crew was taken off by the tug *Iona*. The vessel was floated the next day with little damage. Ten years before the *Golden Hope* had run ashore in the very same place.

Loss of life in the *Golden Hope* was very small. On July 16, 1904 Charles Bohan fell overboard and drowned off Eastern Point, Gloucester. Bohan was sitting on the rail aft and lost his balance, falling into the sea. A dory was quickly put over but no trace of him could be found. He was a native of Gloucester and 42 years old.

The end came to the *Golden Hope* in 1904. On November 21 the *Golden Hope*, in command of Capt. Joachim Murray, sailed from the Bay of Islands, Newfoundland, for Gloucester with a full cargo of herring. Early the next morning she was struck by a heavy gale and began to leak. The craft was headed for shore but soon her deck was awash. When about 35 miles from Wood Island, her crew decided to take to the dories. They hardly cleared the vessel's side when she plunged forward and sank like a plummet. The men struggled against the fierce gale for 30 hours before reaching land.

The crew of the *Golden Hope* at the time of her loss were Capt. Joachim Murray, Michael Smith, John Gamradt, Daniel Maher, John Holder, John McIntosh. The shipwrecked men arrived home on December 1, 1904.

Capt. Alex McEachern, first skipper of the *Golden Hope*, lost his life with eight of his crew in the schooner *Maggie and May*, when that vessel was run down on La Have Bank in August 1908 by the German schoolship *Freya*. Little Alex, as he was affectionately known, was one of our leading mariners; smart, capable, and a real builder of Gloucester's prosperity. He was a leader in the salt fishery and the Newfoundland herring trade. His untimely death cut short a brilliant future. His commands included the *Mascot, Golden Hope,* and *Maggie and May*. He was a native of River Inhabitants, Cape Breton, and was 48 years old.

Capt. Douglass S. McLean passed away at West Gloucester in February 1935 at the age of sixty-eight years. He was a native of Halifax, an able mariner of wide experience, a fine all around fisherman, at his best in the mackerel fishery. He commanded freight steamers in the Merchant Marine during World War I. Some of his commands in the fisheries were the schooners *Annie C. Hall, Hazel Oneita, Lucinda I. Lowell, Golden Hope, Madonna, Victor, Pinta* and *Grace Darling*.

Capt. John Morash died at Boston in November 1966 at the age of eighty-five. He was a native of Chester, Nova Scotia. He and his brothers Jim and Elkanah, and Jim's son Carroll, were excellent engineers. They knew the gasoline and Diesel oil engines from A to Z. Some of Jack's commands were schooners *Golden Hope, Good Luck, Alice and Mildred,* and *Leretha*.

Gross tons, 107; net tons, 102; length, 89 feet; breadth, 24 feet; depth, 9.5 feet.

In the official book about Gloucester's 250th Anniversary Celebration in 1892 this picture appears, along with reports of the *Nannie C. Bohlin's* splendid performance. She finished second in the big Anniversary Race . . . "the race that blew." The man is Captain Thomas Bohlin.

Nannie C. Bohlin

CONNOLLY WROTE: "THE MAN NEVER LIVED WHO COULD MAKE THE *NANNIE* QUIT" / 1890–1909

"I drove her an' I drove her an' I drove her. Could I make her quit? The man never lived who could make the *Nannie* quit." These famous words of Capt. Tommie Bohlin, quoted from *The Book of the Gloucester Fishermen* by James B. Connolly, typify this great skipper and vessel. Schooner *Nannie C. Bohlin* was one of the most famous fishing schooners that ever sailed out of Gloucester. She is the famous *Nannie O.* of Connolly's great classic of the sea, *Out of Gloucester*. Years ago, after reading the book over and over again, I vowed that some day I would write a history of these glorious vessels, and their men. The following is my version of one of the greatest, the *Nannie C. Bohlin*.

She was built during the summer and fall of 1890 by John Bishop at Vincent Cove, Gloucester, and launched in October 28, 1890. A long, low, sleeky vessel with a clipper bow, long bowsprit and lofty rig, she was taken from the lines of the famous schooner *Fredonia*, which was an Edward Burgess design. The *Nannie C.* was owned by the firm of William H. Jordan and her skipper was Capt. Thomas Bohlin. She was named for the daughter of Capt. Bohlin. Later, in January, 1897, Capt. Bohlin purchased the Jordan interest in the vessel, making him the sole owner.

The *Bohlin* at the time of her launching was one of the largest vessels out of Gloucester. She was one of the first fishermen to be equipped with round mastheads. Up to the time of the schooner *Fredonia*, 1889, all fishermen had square mastheads. The length of her forecastle was 30 feet, which was the longest of any vessel at that time.

Capt. Thomas Bohlin was one of the great halibuters. Previous to the building of the *Bohlin* he had lost his fine schooner *Norseman*, a vessel only a year old, in the Magdalen Islands.

The *Nannie C. Bohlin* sailed on her maiden trip halibuting on November 25, 1890, in command of Capt. Bohlin. She arrived back in Gloucester on December 31, 1890, with a fare of 15,000 halibut. The trip was sold to the Atlantic Halibut Co.

Halibuting was usually the *Bohlin's* business, and during the course of her career she landed plenty of these large flat denizens of the deep. She also did a little seining and shacking under Capt. Tommie. In September, 1892 she made two halibut trips in 30 days. The first trip, gone 14 days, was 17,000 lbs. halibut, stocking $2,180 and the second trip, gone 16 days, was a fare of 42,000 lbs. of halibut, stocking $2,922.

The skippers of the *Nannie Bohlin* were few. Capt. Tommie was in command during most of her career, but in 1897 he paid a visit to his old home in Norway and Capt. Albert Chandler took over the helm. In December, 1899, Capt. Norman A. Ross, one of her crew, was the *Bohlin's* skipper, when Capt. Tommie took a rest ashore. Capt. Tom Somers had her haddocking the fall of 1903 and the winter of 1903–04. In Sept. 1904 Capt. Antone Courant was master.

Incidents in the life of this great vessel were many. Some of the most important follow: The *Nannie C. Bohlin* was a participant in the great anniversary race off Gloucester in August, 1892. The *Nannie* had stiff competition, as she sailed against the fastest vessels in the fleet, schooners *Ethel B. Jacobs*, *Grayling*, *Joseph Rowe* and *Harry L. Belden*. The race was sailed in a heavy gale, and all the vessels with the exception of the *Harry L. Belden* had a tough time of it, because of the removal of ballast before the race. Nevertheless, the *Nannie* made a splendid showing, finishing second to the *Belden*. This was the greatest race ever sailed by fishermen. Fine pictures of the *Nannie Bohlin* and *Harry L. Belden* on chinaware and plaques were on sale at S. S. Hartwell's store in Gloucester at the time.

Incidentally, during the 250th Anniversary of Gloucester, the Gloucester Fishermen's Institute was established at 8 Duncan Street, a permanent memorial to the fishermen. Rev. F. C. Charlton was the first chaplain.

On April 3, 1892 the *Nannie Bohlin* arrived in Gloucester from Burgeo Bank with 30,000 lbs. halibut. She reported that on March 12, at daylight, while bowling along by the wind, under full sail, she was struck by a squall and hove down. The watch were on deck, and the man at the wheel threw the wheel down. The vessel lay flat on the water with her sails half under. One of the crew walked on her side from the wheel box to the forerigging. The men in the cabin couldn't get out. The crew in the forecastle were soon on deck, and one of them let go the head sails and the vessel soon came up.

On June 13, 1893 the *Nannie Bohlin*, in command of Capt. Bohlin, sailed from Gloucester on an experimental cruise to Norway to search for mackerel. The tug Charlie towed her down the harbor. With her flags flying she presented a handsome appearance as she sailed out past Eastern Point. Crowds lined the wharves and she was saluted by the tugs *Startle*, *Emma S. Bradford* and *Joe Call*.

The *Bohlin* took on porgies at Newport and sailed from there on June 22, arriving at Stavanger, Norway, July 13, 1893, after a fine passage of 21 days. While lying in port at Norway, she was viewed by hundreds. She fished on two banks, 120 to 160 miles off the Norwegian coast. Just as the fish showed, the wind started up and blew north and northwest for a month, spoiling the chances of getting a trip. However, she did better than the fleet of 200 native vessels. The *Nannie C.* sailed for home on September 8, with 59 bbls. mackerel. It was a stormy trip, but Capt. Tommie drove her all the way, making the passage of about 4,700 miles in 22 days for an average of 212 miles per day. On the last leg, she made Cape Sable to anchorage at Gloucester in 14½ hours. The British cup challenger *Valkyrie* on her way to America at about this time to race for the America's Cup, made her passage of 800 miles less in 30 days. The *Nannie* on this passage lost two jibs and the mainsail, but new spare sails were bent on. This is the passage that inspired Connolly's *Tommie Ohlsen's Western Passage*.

On June 9, 1894 at 7 p.m. the *Nannie Bohlin* was off Cape Sable, Nova Scotia. She dropped anchor in Gloucester at noon of June 10, making the run of 230 miles in 17 hours. It seemed the harder it blew the faster the *Nannie* flew.

On October 31, 1894 a queer looking craft was observed coming around Eastern Point. She was sloop rigged, had dories on deck and her topmast was housed. That much was all right, but it was her size which puzzled everybody. She was very large. Soon it was discovered that the craft was none other than the *Nannie Bohlin*, with her foremast carried away close to the deck. She had lost her foremast off Sable Island and her ingenious skipper had rigged her up in good shape. A stay was rigged from the mainmast head to the heel of the foremast. The jumbo was set. It was a big job to clear the wreckage, but in 24 hours everything was in fair shape again and the vessel started for home. As she sailed up the harbor, she showed her heels to many of the crack craft, which were coming up at the same time.

The *Nannie Bohlin* probably carried away more spars and topmasts than any vessel from this port. It is said that she carried away five sets of spars. Capt. Bohlin was a sail carrier of the first order and he drove the *Nannie* unmercifully.

The *Nannie C. Bohlin* arrived in Gloucester on July 28, 1897 in command of Capt. Albert Chandler (Capt. Bohlin was on a visit to Norway) with a small fare of halibut. The vessel had sailed on this trip completely around Newfoundland in an unsuccessful search for halibut. She had visited White Bay, and came down through the Straits of Belle Isle. The hardy mariners of the olden days searched far and wide for their fish.

Loss of life was fairly heavy in the *Nannie C.*

George Baker, a native of Cape Island, Nova Scotia, was drowned by the capsizing of his dory on the banks February 22, 1891.

John Mouleson (Happy Jack) 35 years old and a native of Tusket Head, Nova Scotia, was washed overboard in a gale on Quero Bank on March 18, 1893.

Joseph McEachern and Knute Kloster drowned when their dory capsized on the banks, April 3, 1894. Koster, a Norwegian, was one of the survivors of the Gloucester schooner *Susan L. Hodge*, that foundered on January 19 of that same year.

Enoch Johnson, 30 years old and a native of Sweden, was knocked overboard by the jumbo boom, and drowned 90 miles west of Sable Island on December 3, 1899. The craft at the time was going 13½ knots. Johnson had intended to make this his last trip before going home to Sweden.

Henry Harmon, 35, a native of Sweden, died of a heart attack on board on Grand Bank August 25, 1901. He was buried at Louisburg, Cape Breton.

Time was running out for the old *Nannie C.* Capt. Bohlin had met with reverses and in August, 1904 the grand old schooner was sold at public auction to the D. B. Smith Co. of Gloucester for $3,250. I can well imagine how this old skipper felt the day he had to part with the *Nannie C.*

In March, 1905, the *Nannie C. Bohlin* was sold by the Smith firm to Capt. Manuel Cancea of Providence, Rhode Island, for use in the Cape Verde trade. She left Gloucester for the last time on March 10, 1905, when she sailed to New Bedford.

The *Nannie C.*, in command of Capt. Cancea arrived at Cape Verde in December, 1906, reporting the loss of two of her crew on the way across. She had been hit by a giant sea, which swept five of her crew overboard. Three were saved and two drowned.

The end of the *Nannie C.* came in 1909. She had been used in the Cape Verde packet trade

several years, and was then sold to Joseph Messina of Pensacola, Florida. In October, 1909, the *Nannie C. Bohlin*, in command of Capt. N. H. Borden, stranded on· Tortugas in a heavy northeast gale. She was bound from Pensacola to Bahia with a cargo of lumber. The old *Nannie* became water logged and was a total loss. Tugs tried to float her, but the vessel would not budge. The only things saved were the sails and personal belongings. Just four years after leaving her beloved birthplace, the *Nannie C. Bohlin* died on the reefs of Tortugas.

Capt. Thomas Bohlin passed away on December 3, 1910. He was traveling in a motor boat from Goose Arm, where his command, the schooner *Constellation*, was loading frozen herring, to Birchy Cove, Bay of Islands, Newfoundland, for medical treatment. He was a native of Norway and 55 years old. Capt. Bohlin was one of the great Sea Kings of Gloucester, a great halibuter and one of the greatest sail carriers out of this port. He took his first command, the schooner *Elisha Cromwell*, in 1885, and then the *James A. Garfield, Herbert M. Rogers, John G. Whittier, Norseman, Nannie C. Bohlin, Oriole* and *Constellation*.

The *Nannie C. Bohlin* suited the captain and in this craft he achieved his greatest reputation. In her he displayed his powers to the fullest extent. He knew his craft and could tell to the last fraction of an inch what she could stand. Added to this he was a great navigator and his knowledge aided him in making those driving, dead of winter passages. He was modest, mild mannered and reticent in speaking of himself. He was short of stature, thick set and had great strength. It was said he possessed the strongest pair of hands in Gloucester, Capt. Bohlin was famed in song and story, the hero of numberless sea tales, most of them based on actual fact. He was immortalized by James B. Connolly in his great stories of the Gloucester fishermen, the most famous of these being *Tommie Ohlsen's Western Passage*.

In 1905, Capt. Bohlin was engaged to sail the schooner *Fleur De Lys* in the great ocean race across the Atlantic. Although the little *Fleur De Lys* was no match for the larger yachts, Capt. Tommie drove her, and made a splendid showing. For several years after, Capt. Tommie was sailing master of the *Fleur De Lys*.

Capt. Bohlin was greatly admired and respected by the Newfoundlanders. His dealings with them were always fair.

The wonderful endurance of this man was demonstrated about two years before his death, on a Christmas morning. Capt. Bohlin trudged seven miles in Newfoundland snow, waist deep, laden with $5,000 in gold, silver, and paper, wearing a pair of heavy rubber boots and carrying a precious accumulation of clean clothes. A young mail carrier who went along to guide him to the spot on the shore where the motorboat was to take him off to his schooner, had to beg to be allowed to stop for a rest. At the end of the seven miles, not knowing how he was to get down a 12 foot embankment at the bottom of which the boat waited, he lay down and rolled. He landed against a fence with laundry, money and boots intact; rose and waded through yards of slush to climb into his boat. Men of Capt. Bohlin's character are the men who brought fame to this great seaport of ours.

Gross tons, 131; net tons, 124; length, 110.2 feet; breadth, 23.5 feet; depth, 11.2 feet.

Caviare

A SCHOONER BY ANOTHER NAME
FLOATS AT SOUTH STREET
SEAPORT / 1891–1916

The *Caviare* was built by Willard A. Burnham at South Essex and launched in August, 1891. Her owners were Nagle and Powers of Gloucester, who conducted a bait and fresh fish business at Fort Wharf, located in the Fort section of Gloucester. This locality in those days was inhabited mostly by Irish and later became the Italian section of the city.

The *Caviare* was a pretty little craft with a clipper bow and was designed by the foremost designer of fishermen at that time, Capt. G. Melvin McClain of Rockport. *Caviare* was built for the shore fishery and her first skipper was Capt. Frank Stevens.

The vessels used in the shore fishery were usually of the smaller type. Quick trips, short stays in port and they were always on the go. They set their trawls from single dories (one man to a dory) and fished the nearby banks from Georges to Brown's off the southern tip of Nova Scotia.

The *Caviare* arrived at Boston with her maiden trip of 20,000 lbs. fresh fish on September 16, 1891. She became a money maker and never lost a man while fishing out of Gloucester.

In August, 1892, during Gloucester's 250th Anniversary celebration, a fishermen's race was sailed off the old port. The fast little *Caviare* was entered in the second class (60 to 80 feet, waterline). The race was sailed in a howling northeast gale and has always been known as the greatest race ever sailed by fishermen. Several craft were damaged and forced to quit, but *Caviare*, expertly sailed by Capt. Stevens, finished second in her class behind the fleet *Lottie Haskins*, another McClain-designed vessel. The big plumb stemmed schooner *Harry L. Belden* was the winner in the first class.

A random glance through the files of the *Gloucester Times* of 1894 found the *Caviare* landing many big trips and up among the leaders of the shore fleet.

Caviare's life nearly came to an end when she stranded during a northeast snow storm at Wood End, Cape Cod, January 22, 1902. Capt. Charles O'Neil and his crew escaped to shore only a few yards away. The vessel was left high and dry by the ebbing tide. The next day, the crew, with the help of Capt. George Bickers and his life saving crew from the Wood End Station, and the aid of the big ocean tug *International*, made an attempt to float the vessel. A heavy hawser was made fast around the vessel's masts. The tug pulled her over on her side and she was towed, sideways, seaward and then afloat. She was anchored in Provincetown Harbor, leaking, but not hurt badly. Up to that time, not many vessels had been salvaged from that shore in the midst of a gale.

The owners of the southern red snapper fishing fleets were great admirers of the New England schooners, and many of the smaller craft were sold for that fishery during the late years of the 19th century and the early years of the present. Big prices were paid, and *Caviare* was sold in 1903 to the E. E. Saunders Co. of Pensacola, Florida, largest of the Gulf operators.

Ice, fog, snow and gales of the North Atlantic were behind the *Caviare*. Ahead were long, hard years of squalls and vicious hurricanes in the Gulf of Mexico.

In August, 1916, the vessel sank in a hurricane and her name was stricken from the United States register. She was salvaged, however, but did not appear again in the register until 1923 under the name of *Mystic C.* Thomas Welles had taken over the Saunders fleet and the vessel was named after his home town of Mystic, Connecticut. The *Mystic C.* was rebuilt at Baypoint, Florida, in 1923. An auxiliary engine was installed and she again became a snapper fisherman in the Gulf.

The little vessel survived many long hard years in the Gulf and in 1966 with only four vessels remaining, the Welles fleet was disbanded. The *Caviare* was sold to Historic Ships Associates. She was sailed from Pensacola to Fairhaven, Massachusetts, where she was restored as nearly as possible to the days when she sailed out of Gloucester as the *Caviare*. On July 20th, under the able command of Capt. Paul Dunn, the *Caviare* sailed home again, after an absence of 64 years, to begin a new life as a memorial to all Gloucester fishermen.

The vessel was moored at East Gloucester, where she was used as a museum and memorial. Expected interest did not take place, however, and the little vessel was sold to the South Street Seaport Museum in New York City in September 1968.

Her new owners were suspicious that she was not the *Caviare*, and research was con-

A smart little fisherman going fishing. The *Caviare* seems to be doing nicely with her four lowers set. Dories are nested on deck.

ducted to try and find out her true identity.

Records were found in Pensacola that proved the vessel was the little Beverly, Massachusetts, shore-fishing schooner *Lottie G. Howard*, built by A. D. Story in Essex in 1893. So ended the mystery.

I had my own suspicions from the start. In my records the *Caviare* had gone down in 1916 in the Gulf of Mexico. I didn't think she would be worth an attempt at salvage.

As it has turned out, the Historic Ships Associates who brought the vessel to Gloucester were given wrong information. They should be commended for their interest and enthusiasm in bringing back one of our old fishing schooners—and a Mel McClain one at that!

So ends the story of *Cavaire*. She almost came back from the dead. Her epitaph: Schooner *Caviare*, lost in hurricane on Alacran Reef, Gulf of Mexico, July 7, 1916.

If ever a man deserves a place in the Valhalla of Fishermen, it is the great mariner and designer, Capt. George Melvin McClain of Rockport, Massachusetts. Capt. Mel, as he was always known, was in my estimation the greatest designer of clipper-bowed fishing schooners. He created beauty, speed and stability in the fleet. His vessels were "fast and able."

His ideas were sharply criticized at the time by the so-called experts, but Capt. Mel had forgotten more than any of them ever knew. He based his theory on the fact that a deeper vessel, properly ballasted, was the safest. To save lives, his desire was to get away from shoal-draft vessels, and in 1886 he produced the schooner *I. J. Merritt, Jr.* The sharper and deeper vessel was so successful, over one hundred schooners were taken off her model.

In 1890, McClain designed the schooner *Lottie Haskins*, named for his daughter. She was a smaller type vessel, and many vessels were taken off her lines, including the *Caviare*.

The larger *Marguerite Haskins* came out in 1893, and this speedy vessel was the forerunner of many of the handsome schooners of the 1890's. The *Marguerite Haskins* was named for his granddaughter.

Prior to 1855, there were a great many vessels from Gloucester lost at sea with all hands, but since the McClain model began to predominate, these occurrences were less frequent, and up to 1900 only one of his models was lost with all on board. This was theh schooner *Mildred V. Lee*, which doubtless went ashore on Sable Island, Nova Scotia, in 1895.

A terrifying experience took place aboard the McClain-designed schooner *Helen G. Wells* on Grand Bank in November, 1897. The vessel was struck by a giant sea, the watch on deck jumped below and the craft was hove down, rolled completely over and then righted herself. She was almost a complete wreck, not a man was lost and she lived to tell the tale.

In Mel McClain's own words, "It makes no difference, shoal or deep, when a monster sea strikes fair, down goes the vessel on her beam ends. Then comes the test; if she is well designed, well built, and properly ballasted, up she comes again, if otherwise, sad is her fate."

There was nothing more handsome afloat than a McClain-designed clipper-bowed schooner under sail.

Besides being a designer, Capt. Mel was also a successful skipper. As late as 1909, he was mackerel seining in his own creation, the schooner *Good Luck*, a round-bowed vessel which proved to be his last design.

Some of McClain's most famous vessels were the schooners *I. J. Merritt, Jr., Helen Miller Gould, Lottie S. Haskins, Marguerite Haskins, Caviare, Rienzi, Leader, Clara R. Harwood, Clara M. Littlefield, Lewis H. Giles, Senator Lodge, Gladiator, Mildred V. Lee, Susan L. Hodge, Niagara, Fortuna, Elsie F. Rowe, Golden Rod, Helen G. Wells, Grayling, Sheffield, Yosemite,* and *Good Luck.*

Capt. Mel passed away at Sailors's Snug Harbor, Staten Island, New York. He was a native of Bremen, Maine.

Capt. Frank Stevens passed away at East Braintree, Massachusetts, in December, 1935, at the age of 72. Capt. Frank, a native of Lanesville, Massachusetts, was one of the very few native-born skippers of that period. He was a smart fisherman, especially on the Cape Shore, and was always up among the highliners. He served in the U. S. Navy during World War I and also in the Merchant Marine as an officer. *Gross tons, 62; net tons, 59; length, 74.3 feet; breadth, 20.7 feet; depth 8.7 feet.*

Probably on her maiden trip is the *Grayling*, under full sail, American flag at the peak of the main, two seineboats in tow.

Grayling

WEATHERED THE PORTLAND BREEZE /
1891–1911

Schooner *Grayling* was one of the finest schooners of her day. She was built during the time when the fleet was fast changing from the old Georges type of vessel to the fine yacht-like vessels that were to bring fame and glory to Gloucester. She was one of the last vessels to see the steamer Portland, that went down in Massachusetts Bay in the great "Breeze" (named after her) of November 26, 1898.

The *Grayling* was built during the winter and spring of 1890–91 by Tarr and James in Essex and launched on May 8, 1891. She was towed around to Gloucester by the tug *Startle*, Capt. Linnekin, who made the record time of six hours (round trip). On the *Grayling* were 25 passengers. The new *Grayling* lay at Walen's wharf, where she was visited by many people.

Schooner *Grayling* was owned by the William H. Jordan firm, three-fourths, and Capt. Charles H. Harty, one-fourth. She was a medium-sized schooner, clipper bowed with a lofty rig and long bowsprit. The length of her forecastle was 28 feet. She was designed by the great Cape Ann designer, Capt. George (Mel) McLain and was one of his greatest masterpieces.

This fine designer drew the lines of more Gloucester fishermen of the 90's than any other person, and he was a pioneer in the development of the clipper type of fisherman.

The *Grayling*, like many of the vessels of that day, was named after a famous schooner yacht. The word is the name of a fresh water salmon-like fish, native to North America.

Schooner *Grayling* was one of the fastest fishermen of her day, and she had plenty of competition in the schooners *Ethel B. Jacobs*, *Nannie C. Bohlin*, *Senator Lodge*, *Harvard*, *Susan L. Hodge*, *Joseph Rowe*, *Harry L. Belden*, and that great light wind sailer, the *Marguerite Haskins*. Several years before his death, Capt. Rueben Cameron told me that the *Grayling* was the fastest vessel he was ever in, although the *Joseph Rowe* was the most able.

The *Grayling* sailed on her maiden trip to the Cape Shore for mackerel, in command of Capt. Harty on May 20, 1891. She arrived in Gloucester with her first fare of 209 barrels of mackerel on June 22, 1891. On her maiden trip she had a brush with the crack *Ethel B. Jacobs*, Capt. Sol Jacobs, and gave her a close race. On this trip she reported that the Cape Shore was alive with small mackerel which, however, did not show except in very calm weather.

A new experiment was tried in the seining season of 1893. Two steam seine boats were built at the Higgins and Gifford (seine boat builders) yard at Gloucester for Capt. Harty of the *Grayling* and Capt. Hans Joyce of the big down east steamer, *Novelty*. The *Grayling's* seine boat was named *Shark* and the steamer *Novelty's* boat called the *Cormorant*. They were 50 feet overall. There was a house over the machinery amidships, which consisted of a 40 horsepower Mason Compound engine. A 25-foot mast was carried forward. While trying out the *Shark*, off the mouth of Gloucester Harbor on June 24, 1893 (with no intention of getting mackerel) she caught 18 barrels of mackerel, which were sold at the Fort, and the next day 13 barrels were taken. Capt. Harty had Capt. Joyce along as a guest on this trial. The loud noise of the steam engine apparently didn't frighten the fish. Although the *Grayling* used the seineboat *Shark* during the 1893 season, it was not used thereafter.

In July, 1892, William H. Jordan offered to race his schooners *Grayling*, *Fredonia*, *Joseph Rowe* and *Nannie C. Bohlin*. $5,000 for an ocean race or $1,000 for a bay race.

The *Grayling* was a contestant in the great 250th Anniversary Race off Gloucester in August, 1892. In command of Capt. Harty, she was forced to withdraw halfway over the course, due to her not being in proper trim to meet the heavy weather conditions of the day. The *Grayling* no doubt, if properly trimmed, would have made a good showing.

The *Grayling* in her early days was used for seining summers, and for Newfoundland

herring voyages in the winter months. Capt. Harty remained in command, seining, from 1891 through 1895. Capt. Ben McGray was her skipper during the winter of 1894–95 haddocking. In 1896 Capt. Hugh Quinlan took over a few trips. She was then taken over by Capt. Reuben Cameron and that great all round skipper had her seining, haddocking and on Newfoundland herring trips, until the seining season of 1905. In 1904, the *Grayling* in command of Capt. Cameron was highline of the seiners, stocking $21,547 with a share of $475.

Capt. Anson Leaman was her seining skipper in 1905–06 and Capt. Joe Smith, another of the mackerel "killers," was skipper during 1907-08-09. Capt. Axel Laeger took over in April, 1910, for fletched halibuting and remained in her to the end, Georges handlining and fletched halibuting.

An interesting item appeared in the *Gloucester Times* on September 28, 1893: "The harbor presented a sight this morning. Fully 50 sail of seiners are in port on account of the rough weather outside. The fleet have been fishing off the Point. Some of the most famous vessels noetd in this fleet were the *Grayling*, *Ethel B. Jacobs*, *Lottie Gardner*, *Harvard*, *Joseph Rowe*, *Senator Lodge*, *Miranda*, *Marguerite Haskins*, *Fredonia*, *Hattie Graham*, *Harry L. Belden* and *Roulette*."

On December 15, 1896, the *Grayling* had been fishing on Liscomb Ridges, and she started home. The next day she was struck by a heavy gale. She was forced to run before it, with only a reefed foresail. When about 25 miles south of Cape Sable, with only the watch, Joseph Brown and Henry Atwood, on deck (Brown was lashed to the wheel and Atwood standing near him) a giant sea, mast head high, rose up astern. It was so high, one could see right under it. Brown saw it and shouted to Atwood to grab something and Atwood threw his arms around the main boom. The wave fell on deck, sweeping everything before it. Capt. Cameron, in the cabin, rushed for the deck, but was forced back by the rush of water. When he finally made deck, an awful sight greeted him. Brown had been hit by the sea, thrown against the wheel and killed. Atwood, who had been clinging to the boom, was swept overboard when the boom broke, and then swept back again. The boom, and gaffs, dories and mainsail were gone. The hatches, companionways and taffrail were smashed. Capt. Cameron said that if the vessel had not been under sail and running before it, the sea would have carried vessel and crew to the bottom.

Joseph Brown, the man killed, was a native of Gloucester and 33 years old. His was the only death in the life of the *Grayling*.

On the night of the Portland Breeze, November 26, 1898, the *Grayling*, Capt. Reuben Cameron, fought the gale while running for Gloucester and experienced its fullest violence.

(My father, Capt. Jeff Thomas, was one of her crew.) At about 11 that night when about 12 miles off Thacher's a big white steamer, undoubtedly the *Portland*, was sighted. The *Grayling* was very close to the steamer, and she probably was all right at the time, as the *Grayling*, crossing the steamer's bow, showed her signal torch to warn the steamer and the steamer returned the signal, to show she saw the schooner, at the same time shifting her course a little to be sure to clear. Schooner *Florence E. Stream*, Capt. Frank Stream, also saw the steamer at about the same time, in this vicinity. The *Grayling* came through this gale without damage.

The loss of the steamer *Portland* that night, with 176 lives, was needless. Both Capt. Cameron and my father, at the time, wondered why she had not put into Gloucester for harbor and safety. The Portland Breeze was freakish. Some of the Gloucester fleet out that night were considerably damaged and others hardly touched. The *Grayling* had fared much worse two years before off Cape Sable.

Much has been written of the famous Portland Breeze and many have claimed to have been the last to see the *Portland*. (It seems as if every fisherman in Gloucester was out that night.) But there is no doubt in my mind, after examining the records, that the crews of the *Grayling* and *Florence Stream* were the last people on earth to see this steamer before her destruction.

At about 11 p.m. on February 21, 1911, the schooner *Grayling*, Capt. Axel Laeger, for some unknown reason, crashed into the auxiliary schooner *Sylvia Nunan*, Capt. Tom Holbrook, of Cape Porpoise, Maine, two miles off Thacher's Island.

The *Nunan*, bound to Cape Porpoise to fit out, was sliding right along under sail and power when she was hit on the starboard bow by the *Grayling*, bound for Gloucester. The bow of the larger *Grayling* opened up a huge hole in the *Nunan*. The *Nunan's* crew, with the exception of John Goodick, quickly climbed aboard the *Grayling*. John Goodick had been penned in the peak of the forecastle by the bow of the *Grayling*. With presence of mind he crawled through the hole made by the collision and just as the *Nunan* was settling and his mates thought he was gone, up over the bow of the *Grayling* popped the head of Goodick. This is one of the most narrow escapes recorded in the history of the fisheries.

The *Nunan* sank just three minutes after the crew left her. Nothing was saved. The *Grayling* lost her bobstay and head stays, and several stanchions were split.

The end of the *Grayling* came in July, 1911. She left Gloucester in command of Capt. Laeger on a fletched halibut voyage, on April 27, 1911. Finding it impossible to fish off Labrador, because of heavy field ice, she sailed for the Greenland grounds.

On July 11, while in Davis Strait, about 40 miles from Holsteinborg, Greenland, a gale sprang up, and she headed for shore. She anchored in a small cove, but as her stern swung around, she bid up on a sunken reef. The impact drove the rudder clean through the stern, while the stove in the cabin, with its fire, upset. The craft began to fill with water and at the same time caught fire. Although in July, the temperature at the time was freezing and the surrounding coast was covered with ice and snow. The crew left in their eight dories, landed on an uninhabited island, and camped for the night. Fires were lighted and a meal cooked, consisting of wild birds, and provisions saved from the ship. Not knowing the name of the island, they called it Grayling Island. All night they had to stay awake to keep warm and the next day started down the coast in their dories, reaching Holsteinborg, 40 miles away. They reached Gloucester on August 22, 1911.

The *Grayling's* crew at the time of her loss: Capt. Axel Laeger, Eric Erickson (cook), Foster Oxner, Charles Malmberg, Hans Schubert, John (White) Thompson, Peter Jefferies, William Dahl, Samuel Hatfield, Albion Bachman, Carl Carlson, Fred Dodt, Wallace McKay, Peter Schink, Charles Clauson, Walter R. Vannah, Samuel Smith, August Letman.

Capt. Reuben Cameron, one of the greatest mariners out of Gloucester, passed away on January 18, 1950, at the age of 86. He was a native of Clark's Harbor, Nova Scotia. Some of our great skippers served under Capt. Reub. He was an all around skipper, but was at his best in the seining game. Some of his commands were the *Joseph Rowe*, *Grayling*, *Marguerite Haskins*, *Stilletto*, *Mary E. Harty* and *Esperanto*.

Gross tons, 121; net tons, 115; length, 97.8 feet; breadth, 24.4 feet; depth, 10.4 feet. Original spar measurements: mainmast, 77 feet (deck to cap); foremast, 69 feet; main boom, 67 feet; bowsprit, 30.5 feet (outboard).

End of a hard life: the wreck of the *Hattie Graham* on Baline Rock, Cape Breton, Nova Scotia.

Hattie Graham

NEVER USED DORIES FOR FISHING /
1891–1909

In February, 1891, Capt. Joe Graham lost his fine new schooner *Senator Morgan* at Cow Bay, near Halifax, Nova Scotia. The following March the keel of a new vessel for Capt. Graham was laid by Moses Adams in Essex. The new craft was a fine, large clipper bowed vessel of the *Fredonia* model. She was named after the daughter of Capt. Graham. At the time of her launching she was the deepest two-masted fishing schooner built at Essex.

The *Hattie Graham* was launched June, 1891, and fitted at Gloucester. She sailed on her maiden voyage to the Cape Shore for mackerel on July 28, 1891, in command of Capt. Graham, one of the great mackerel "killers" of that time. She arrived back in Gloucester on September 8, 1891, with 200 bbls. mackerel, taken on the Maine coast.

The *Hattie Graham* was one of the very few vessels in the Gloucester fleet that never used dories for fishing. For the *Hattie Graham*, it was seining summers and Newfoundland herring voyages during the winter months. Capt. Graham remained in command until the seining season of 1899, when she was taken over by Capt. John Seavey, great Down East mackerel skipper. Capt. Seavey had the *Graham* until 1904 when Capt. Sargent took over seining. Capt. Charles Stewart had her seining during 1905.

Capt. Jerry Cook was her seining skipper during 1906, Capt. Gilbert Gallant seining 1907, Capt. Roy Kimball seining 1908 and Capt. Bill Foley seining in 1909.

The *Hattie Graham* had many narrow escapes from destruction. In May, 1897, while the vessel was bound for New York with a trip of mackerel, in command of Capt. Graham, an unknown steamer brushed by her in the night, nearly sending her to the bottom. The big steamer rushed by, chafing the vessel's side, carrying away her staysail and tearing her mainsail from head to foot. The quick action of the *Graham's* helmsman by throwing her wheel hard down saved the vessel from certain destruction.

On January 31, 1898, Cape Ann was struck by the worst storm and gale in 59 years. About 25 vessels and boats were ashore at one time in the harbor. The *Hattie Graham* was one of the victims. Schooners *Vesta*, *Martha Bradley* and *Eleanor Eaton* broke adrift from Sylvanus Smith's wharf and drifted down the harbor, colliding with the schooners. *Hattie M. Graham*, *Nereid* and the Eastport, Maine, schooner, *Sarah Nightingale*.

Together the six vessels drifted onto the Rocky Neck shore. The *Graham* landed on the rocky beach east of the copper paint factory, where the schooners *John M. Keen*, *Lawrence A. Munroe*, and the stone sloop *Riverside*, were also ashore.

The next day she was floated by tugs, leaking badly. While hauling out at Tarr's Railways on Rocky Neck, some of the blocks under her slipped off, gave way and the vessel literally slid under the wharf and down on her starboard side, almost completely broadside up. Her spars lay directly across the pier. The wrecking lighter *Bull of Boston* was engaged to right her, but in order to get chains under her quarter it was necessary to cut through the wharf 40 feet. She was finally raised and put on the ways on February 5th.

The Newfoundland herring trade was hazardous and gruelling and the *Hattie Graham* had her share of rough usage in this risky business. In March, 1899, the crew of the *Graham* in command of Capt. Alex Bushie were forced to cut a channel through ice some 18 inches thick at Placentia Bay, Newfoundland, before the craft could get under way for home.

In February, 1900, while bound home from Placentia Bay, in command of Capt. George Hamor, she was struck by a gale on the Cape Shore and was forced into Pubnico, Nova Scotia, leaking, 300 strokes an hour. She later sailed for Yarmouth, Nova Scotia, where repairs were made. On leaving that port, she was struck by another gale which forced her into Boothbay, Maine. She finally arrived in Gloucester, leaking badly, February 8th. Her cargo consisted of 390 bbls. frozen herring and 1285 boxes frozen squid.

In January, 1905, in command of Capt. Bill Greenleaf, the *Hattie M. Graham* sailed from the Bay of Islands, Newfoundland, for Gloucester with a cargo of herring. Soon after leaving she ran into a gale, and was forced back into the bay where she was imprisoned in the ice the remainder of the winter. Schooners *Arabia*, *Lewis H. Giles* and *Annie M. Parker*, were also caught at the same time and forced to spend the winter in the ice. The *Hattie Graham*, in command of Capt. Charles Stewart, who had been sent down to bring her back, arrived home on May 17, 1905, hailing for 600 bbls. frozen herring. She was towed to Rockport and her cargo put in the freezer there.

Fortunately, no lives were lost in the *Hattie Graham*. On October 8, 1894 the *Hattie Graham*, in command of Capt. Graham, arrived in Gloucester with the lumber schooner *Alice T. Bordman* of Calais, Maine, in tow. The *Bordman* was picked up on October 6, seventy-five miles east by south of Highland Light, waterlogged and abandoned. Capt. Graham put nine of his men aboard the derelict and they got underway for home, arriving without mishap. On arrival at Gloucester it was learned that the *Bordman's* crew had been rescued by a steamer shortly before the *Graham* had come along.

The *Hattie M. Graham* was sold to Capt. Tom Hodge of Gloucester in May, 1904.

On the night of July 11, 1907, the Gloucester Cold Storage Co. plant on Rogers Street was swept by fire. The *Hattie Graham* was lying at the head of the wharf at the time, and everyone thought she was doomed. She was in the path of the sparks. Her foretopsail caught fire. The masthead was badly burned and she lost her foretopsail, jib and staysail. Her mainsail was also badly burned. It was a close one for the *Graham*.

The end came June 15, 1909. In command of Capt. William Foley the vessel ran ashore on Bauline Rock, near Louisburg, Cape Breton, during a thick fog. Laden with 250 barrels salt mackerel, she was making in toward land and trying to locate Scateri whistle when she bid up on the submerged ledge. Her crew left in the seineboat and reached shore safely. A few days later the craft was mostly under water. The only things saved were the seine and seineboat. The scene of the disaster was one of the roughest points along the Cape Breton coast.

Capt. Joseph Graham passed away at Watertown in August, 1939, at the age of eighty-one. Joe was one of the great mackerel killers of the past; a fine, capable and respected skipper. He commanded many fine vessels, including the schooners *Senator Morgan*, *George F. Edmunds*, *Lizzie W. Hannum*, *Evelyn L. Smith*, *Speculator*, *Mooween*, *George Parker*, *Grace Otis*, and *Ramona*. He was a native of Jonesport, Maine.

Capt. William Foley, last skipper of the *Hattie M. Graham*, passed away in Gloucester after a lingering illness, January 27, 1922, at the age of sixty-six. He was another of the fine mariners out of Gloucester in the glorious days of sail. Some of his commands were the *Annie C. Hall*, *Squanto* and *Hattie Graham*.

Gross tons, 140; net tons, 105; length, 108.3 feet; breadth, 24.3 feet; depth, 11 feet.

A deckload of happy people helps make the trial trip of the *Mildred V. Lee* a festive occasion. She was one of the early "flying fishermen."

Mildred V. Lee

THEY CALLED HER THE WHITE BEAUTY /
1891–1895

Schooner *Mildred V. Lee*, known when she made her debut as the "white beauty," was one of the prettiest vessels out of Gloucester in the old days of sail and a vessel whose story is both prosperity and disaster.

The *Mildred V. Lee* was built during the winter and spring of 1891 by James and Tarr in Essex for her skipper, Capt. William T. (Tom) Lee and the firm of Gardner and Parsons of Gloucester. The Lee was built alongside the schooner *Grayling* and was launched on the night of June 19, 1891.

The *Mildred V. Lee* was a beautiful vessel of medium size with a clipper bow, long pole bowsprit and a good spread of canvas. She was from a new design by Capt. George Mel McClain of Rockport and was one of the first of the fine graceful vessels that were to become famous as the "flying fishermen." She was painted white when new, but changed to black in October, 1891. In September, 1892 her color became green, but again was changed to black in June, 1893. The firm of E. L. Rowe and Sons made the sails and Charles H. Andrews the spars for the new craft. She was named for the daughter of Capt. Lee.

The trial of the *Mildred V.* was sailed on July 9, 1891. In tow of the tug *Startle* she was pulled into the stream with some 175 guests, almost half of them ladies, on board. Off the point she was dropped by the tug and the beautiful craft was on her own. Soon the fine schooner *Susan L. Hodge*, Capt. John Diggins, was seen coming around the point all in trim for a brush.

The older schooner *Rattler* also joined in the race. At the end of five miles the *Lee* was ahead. A little later the *Hodge* passed ahead. Then the vessels started for home and the fun began. There were many about this time who wished they hadn't come. When nearing the point, the big schooner yacht *Peerless* fell in and joined the race, but she wasn't in it with the flying fishermen. The vessels then began to beat up the harbor and the *Susan Hodge* won by about two vessel lengths. It was a tough race from start to finish although there were too many people on board the *Lee* to allow her to be handled properly. The *Hodge* also carried a party. Capt. William Gibbs handled the wheel of the *Lee*.

The *Mildred V. Lee* sailed on her maiden trip halibuting in command of Capt. Tom Lee on July 11, 1891. The outer harbor presented a pretty sight that morning as several vessels got under way together and stood across the harbor all in a line in the following order: *Nellie N. Rowe, Winona, Susan L. Hodge* and *Norumbega.* The *Mildred V. Lee* came down the harbor in tow of the tug *Emma S. Bradford.* The *Susan L. Hodge* dropped out and waited for the *Lee* and as she passed, Capt. Diggins gave the new "white beauty" a salute. After sailing about the harbor for a while, the two craft headed to the eastward.

Capt. Tom Hodgdon of the schooner *Ralph F. Hodgdon* reported seeing schooners *Mildred V. Lee* and *Susan L. Hodge* on the morning of July 12th, 20 miles off Cape Sable, with the *Hodge* leading by about three miles. Capt. Hodgdon said that both vessels were going along at a high rate of speed.

The *Mildred Lee* arrived home with her maiden fare of 18,000 halibut on August 15, 1891. She was always used in the halibut fishery and was a money maker right from the start, stocking $21,704 in her first year. On October 12, 1891, she landed 20,000 lbs. halibut at Gloucester, stocking $4,100, having been gone only 17 days. On February 1, 1892 she landed 40,000 lbs. halibut, stocking $4,360 and sharing $130. She was out 18 days on this trip and baited at Portsmouth, New Hampshire.

Incidentally, on this trip a peculiar fish was brought in by the *Lee*. It was nearly oval in shape, 3½ feet long, 2½ feet wide and weighed 112 lbs. The fish was taken on LaHave Bank on a trawl in 300 fathoms of water and nothing like it was landed in Gloucester before. The fish was photographed by Walter Gardner. It was later pronounced as an opah or sunfish by the Smithsonian Institution.

The flag on the *Mildred Lee* was lowered for the loss of two of her crew in 1893. James Veno was washed overboard and drowned while taking in sail on April 12, 1893. The vessel took an ugly roll, the sea washing over the rail and taking Veno with it. He swam and caught hold of the logline to which he clung for a minute. Suddenly the line parted, and a dory was quickly put over, but before he could be reached, sank from sight. He was a native of Arichat, Cape Breton, and 25 years old.

John McKenzie, one of the *Lee's* crew died November 9, 1893, at Halifax, Nova Scotia, where he had been landed sick.

The *Mildred Lee* was undoubtedly a tender vessel. This fault probably was the cause of her tragic loss. In December, 1892, she came very near going down. The vessel arrived at Halifax in December, 1892, in a battered condition. She reported that she had been struck by a squall while hove to on the banks. A giant wave rose over the bow and broke clear over her, sweeping her deck clean. Every dory was smashed, main and fore gaffs broken and the mainboom and mainsail gone. Her ballast had shifted. She was repaired at Halifax.

On January 30, 1895, the schooner *Mildred V. Lee* sailed from Gloucester on a halibut trip to Grand Bank. She and her fine crew of 16 men never returned to port. A great gale swept the western North Atlantic on February 8th of that year. Many vessels in Gloucester Harbor and all along the coast were damaged. Schooner *Clara F. Friend* was lost with all her crew off Liverpool, Nova Scotia. Capt. Caleb Hines of the schooner *Reub L. Richardson* was washed overboard and drowned on the passage home from Newfoundland.

It has always been believed that the *Mildred V. Lee* was lost in this gale. On February 19th, the schooner *Henry M. Stanley*, Capt. Adolph Burman, picked up the cabin house of a vessel floating upside down in the water on Quero Bank. It was seen at once that it was part of a fishing schooner. Hanging on the outside of the stateroom partition was a nickel clock. Beside this, a number of halibut hooks were found in the house, which proved to the crew of the *Stanley* that the piece of wreckage belonged to a halibut catcher. The clock, of Seth Thomas make, was brought home to Gloucester. The cabin house and clock no doubt belonged to the *Mildred V. Lee*.

Days and months passed, but not a word was heard from the *Mildred V. Lee*. On May 8, 1895, her owners sadly admitted she would never return. On that day the following beautiful poem appeared in the *Gloucester Times*, written by Arthur L. Millett:

"Given up." The sad sad words are whispered
   low, when hope is past,
When weeks are sped and naught is heard,
No tidings of the missing craft.
Where is the craft so brave?
Did she go down mid gale and gloom,
Mid blinding snows and mountain wave?
Is Sable Island's strand her tomb?
Where are her crew and captain true?
Alas! theirs is a sailor's grave,
Deep down they sleep beneath the blue,
Their requiem, the swelling wave.
Ah! well; tis not for us to know
Upon what shoal or in what gale,
Til He, who rules all here below,
Shall draw away the misty veil.

In June, 1895 schooner *Senator*, Capt. Jerome McDonald, picked up a floating spar. All of the crew thought it belonged to the *Mildred V. Lee*. It was found near the spot where the cabin house was found by the *Henry M. Stanley*. The mast was identified by the rigging, iron work and masthead. It had been in the water some time, causing it to turn red. Capt. McDonald thought the *Lee* had been hit by a sea and hove down and went to the bottom, the spar coming up when the wreck broke up on the bottom.

The crew list of the *Mildred V. Lee*: Capt. William T. Lee, a native of Edgecomb, Maine; Asa Swain, Canso, Nova Scotia; Thomas Clausen, Sweden; John Chisholm, Judique, Cape Breton; George Grant, Burgeo, Newfoundland; Thomas and Richard Williams (brothers), of Bay of Bulls, Newfoundland; Wallace Grindle, North Brookfield, Maine; Patrick Faha Furmose, Newfoundland; Michael Connelly, Toads Cove, Newfoundland; Lawrence King, St. Mary's Newfoundland; Charles Johnson, Sweden; John Simmonson, Sweden; Fenwick Williams, Bay of Bulls, Newfoundland; John Carey, Newfoundland.

Gross tons, 108; net tons, 102; length, 97 feet; breadth, 23 feet; depth, 10.4 feet.

Resolute

The strange looking craft in the accompanying photo, looking very much like an English yacht sailing off the English coast, was a real Gloucester fisherman, the yawl *Resolute*, first American beam trawler, and forerunner of the present day draggers.

The *Resolute* was built by Arthur D. Story in Essex, during the summer and fall of 1891 and launched on October 3, 1891, for Ben Low and Capt. Alfred Bradford of Gloucester. She was towed around to Gloucester by the tug *Emma S. Bradford*.

The *Resolute* was built from a model by Charles O. Story of Essex and from designs by the U. S. Fish Commission. She was exactly like the English fishermen of that time. It was quite a task getting the *Resolute* ready for sea. Crowds of people visited Ben Low's wharf to watch every detail of the preparation.

The yawl *Resolute* was a plumb stemmed, straight-sided vessel with a long pole bowsprit. The crosstrees were very long. The rigging was done by George Esterbrook and the finishing by Hugh Bishop.

The *Resolute* had no houses and no break in her deck. Access to the cabin and forecastle was by means of rolling companion ways.

She carried a boom or beam, with a trawl or drag attached. When the vessel was fishing, her boom was lowered over the side and she began her dragging operation. *Resolute's* sails were of extra heavy duck. They were baggy and loose fitting (English fashion).

The machinery for operating the trawl was below the deck. This consisted of an English steam engine with a boiler well aft. Five tons of coal were carried. Her sails were hoisted by steam. When the trawl was hauled, the end of the mainboom was hauled up and the whole mainsail was hoisted half way up the mast, out of the way. Extra fishing gear was carried for replacements. A crew of eight men including the captain and cook manned the vessel. Her capacity was 100,000 pounds of fish.

The *Resolute* sailed on her maiden trip, beam trawling, on November 12, 1891, in command of Capt. Alfred Bradford. Crowds lined the wharves as the tug *Startle* towed her down the harbor. Various were the opinions passed upon her. She created more discussion and difference of opinion than any other vessel out of this port up to that time. She looked odd indeed with her short jigger mast and little spanker sail. Hope was high for *Resolute's* owners in the new venture.

The *Resolute* arrived at Gloucester with her maiden fare on November 28, 1891, 23,000 pounds of fresh fish. On her second trip she landed about 26,000 pounds of fresh fish, which consisted of 17,000 pounds of haddock, 2,000 pounds of cod, 2,000 pounds of hake, 4,000 pounds of plaice, 1,000 pounds of lemon sole, 1,000 pounds of brill, 200 pounds of halibut and 500 pounds of English turbot.

On her third trip she arrived in Gloucester December 29, 1891, with a small fare of 7,000 pounds of fresh fish. On this trip while dragging in the channel, her trawl caught on an obstruction, which snapped the boom tram. The net was torn almost to shreds. Her crew said that in England when an accident occurred it did not hinder them much as they did not have to return to port for repairs. Everything needed was supplied by a steamer that brought supplies and carried the catches of the fleet to market.

Resolute arrived in Gloucester from Georges on her fourth trip on February 8, 1892, with 20,000 pounds of haddock and sole. She was out 25 days, striking foul weather.

This proved to be the last of beam trawling for *Resolute*. Her owners had had enough. The *Resolute* was considered too light for this kind of fishing. She sailed March 12, 1892, on a fresh and salt trip to the eastward and arrived back in Gloucester on May 17, with 45,000 pounds of cod and 200 pounds of halibut.

In October, 1892, she arrived from the Labrador coast with 150,000 lbs. of cod. She was then changed over to schooner rig at Burnham Brothers' railways.

Capt. James H. Goodwin took command of *Resolute* under her new rig. This, incidentally, was his first command.

In February, 1894, the *Resolute*, while on a halibut trip in command of Capt. Thomas Thompson, lost four of her crew in a heavy squall on Quero Bank. They were Alexander Stewart and Tracy Preston, from Nova Scotia, William Ferguson, from Finland, and Augustus Christensen, native of Sweden. On October 21, 1894, James Hanley and Patrick Londrigan, natives of Newfoundland, went astray.

The end came to *Resolute* on February 9, 1896, when in command of Capt. John MacDonald on a halibut trip, she stranded at Little Lorraine, Cape Breton. It was a thick fog with a rough sea. The vessel was trying to make Louisburg harbor. She struck a rock, listed over and began to break up. One of the crew was drowned when a dory capsized. The rest of the crew of 15 reached shore. The vessel carried no cargo at the time. Her value was $8000.

Capt. Alfred Bradford, *Resolute's* first skipper, was a native of England. He moved to British Columbia in 1902 and died there in April, 1932.

Capt. Thomas Thompson, who once commanded *Resolute*, was also a native of England. He was lost with his 19-year-old son in the small boat *Percy*, out of Block Island in January, 1900.

Capt. James H. Goodwin, another of *Resolute's* commanders, was swept to his death from the schooner *Agnes* on western bank during a heavy gale in March, 1906. He was a native of Sand Point, Straits of Canso.

Ben Low, owner of the *Resolute*, died of a heart attack while on a business trip in New York in February, 1894. He had started in business with his brother, David, in 1854, and at the time of his death was the owner of a fine fleet of vessels, including the schooners *Eliza Parkhurst* and *John E. McKenzie*. The firm was later taken over by Hugh Parkhurst.

Gross tons, 95; net tons, 90; length, 85 feet; breadth, 22 feet; depth, 9.6 feet; Mainmast, 73 feet; jigger mast, 55 feet.

Yosemite

EIGHT MEN SURVIVED ON RIGGING AND ROCK / 1891–1897

The Gloucester schooner *Yosemite* was one of the finest vessels of her time, built in 1891 by Arthur D. Story at Essex for Fred L. Davis and Capt. John McFarland of Gloucester.

In December, 1896 she sailed to Placentia Bay, Newfoundland, in command of Capt. John (Shortscope) McKinnon to pick up a herring cargo for her owners. On January 26, 1897, a dispatch was received by Fred L. Davis from Lockeport, Nova Scotia, which read: "Schooner *Yosemite* total wreck. Cook and one man drowned. Captain has leg broken. Struck south end of Ram Island Thursday night." The full details of the disaster were not received until several days later. It was a sea story seldom equalled in harrowing details.

The disaster occurred at 7:15 on Thursday, January 21st. The vessel at the time, homeward bound, was running under reefed foresail and jumbo, in a heavy southeast gale and blinding snowstorm. All hands were on deck and the vessel was scudding fully 12 knots when without warning she brought up suddenly—she had struck a ledge.

In an instant the staunch craft was at the mercy of the waves and all hands were forced to flee to the rigging for their lives. Not once, after the vessel struck, did anybody go below and after the rigging was gained, no man again trod the *Yosemite's* deck.

The seas washed the vessel farther on the rocks and swung her around, broadside to a ledge. For fully an hour the men were in the rigging. Clinging to the fore rigging were Capt. McKinnon, cook Joseph Ferry and Philip Fiander. The rest of the crew were in the main rigging.

When the *Yosemite* struck, nearly the whole bottom went out of her, and in an hour she broke squarely in two. Then without warning the mainmast went, taking with it most of the foremast.

Then came the struggle for life, the fight with the sea to gain a foothold on a rock which was close by. This was finally accomplished. The cook, Joe Ferry, was missing. He had evidently been killed when the foremast broke and he was never seen again. Capt. McKinnon's leg was badly injured and Fiander had both legs broken below the knee.

Both his boots and oil pants were gone. He had evidently been caught in the wreckage and had literally pulled out of them in his efforts to gain the rock.

Although on the rock, the men were far from safe, as it was high tide and the seas broke entirely over it, threatening with each succeeding wave to wash them off to their doom. Then began anew the battle for life. They secured bits of timber, or wood which floated up from the wreck and thrust them into crevices. Then with ropes they secured themselves to these improvised stakes and held on.

Imagine the scene if you can. On a rock not 17 feet in circumference, in the midst of a terrible gale and blinding snowstorm with waves dashing over them and above all, the darkness of night, nine men clinging to ropes and driftwood for life. Nothing in sight, so dark they could not even distinguish each other, the captain with his leg hurt, Fiander with both legs broken, with the thoughts of one of their number drowned, these brave fellows uttered no protests but hung on through the long hours of the night, hoping that the morning would bring rescue.

When daylight dawned, they found themselves on this rock and between them and the island, which they recognized as Ram Island, was another ledge which was bare at low water: They knew that Ram Island was 1½ miles from the Nova Scotian mainland.

At 10 a.m. of the 22nd, Phillip Fiander, who had borne his terrible suffering courageously, died.

All day they watched patiently, hoping that the log line would come within reach, so that with it one of them could swim to the next

Even the author, lifelong collector that he is, has no photograph of the schooner *Yosemite*. Instead, he shares one of his favorites, a picture of "the gang standing by for a squall."

ledge and haul a heavier rope and thus save all hands.

About the middle of the afternoon Capt. McKinnon called the mate Pat Rose to his side and whispered, "Another night means death, Pat; you know that." Pat nodded solemnly. He did not say a word, but he crawled to the edge of the rock, carefully noting the action of the waves, the eddies of the tide and possibility of landing place on the other side of the leaping water. Then he arose, stripped himself to his underclothes. He stood straight up, shaking with the result of 20 hours of exposure. His freezing legs scarcely supported him. "It's no use, boys," he said simply "to stay here and die. I'll take the chances for you." He leaped into the waves and struck out for the opposite ledge. His companions watched his course with fearful anxiety.

Rose was an exceptionally strong man and expert swimmer and after a hard battle reached the ledge about 4 o'clock. From this ledge, he could wade to the island and his comrades saw him running along shore toward the fish houses, looking for a boat or some human being to assist him. Fully half a mile he ran in his underclothes and then came back and waded out to the inside ledge. He shouted to his mates that he could find no aid and that their only chance was to swim.

As if by an act of Providence, the log line which had all day eluded their grasp, now came within reach. John Hickey, one of the men on the rock, grasped and promptly made it fast to himself and bravely plunged into the

sea. As he neared the other ledge, Rose met him and helped him to land.

Then the stouter rope was hauled over and made fast, and on this the men came hand over hand, and then waded to the island and made their way to one of the fish houses to shelter themselves. They placed a coat on a pole to let the people on shore know that some had survived the wreck and to come to their rescue.

In the hut, an old stove and kindling were found but no stove pipe. Under the stove they found four matches, only one of which was good. With this they started a fire and endured the smoke all night. Morning found them all smoke blind and unable to see the people who came from shore to rescue them.

The people on shore had seen the signal, but so rough was the sea then that it was impossible to launch a boat to go to the island. Think of it! Too rough to launch a boat, yet Pat Rose and John Hickey had boldly plunged into the waves to save their comrades if possible. Oh, the bravery of Gloucester fishermen! Spartans were not made of sterner stuff.

The American consul at Shelburne was notified, medical attendance was secured and everything possible was done to make them comfortable. All were more or less ill.

On January 25th the body of Phillip Fiander was taken from the rock where it had lain since the wreck. Much difficulty was experienced by the rescuing party, as the body was frozen into a crevice of the rock. The remains were interred in the Methodist burying ground at Little Harbor, Nova Scotia. He was 27 years old and a native of St. Jaques, Newfoundland. Hero Pat Rose was one of the rescuing party that recovered Fiander's body.

Only small pieces of the *Yosemite's* bow could be seen on the rock. Nothing but broken fragments of the hull came ashore.

The crew of the *Yosemite* who spent those fearful hours on the rock off Ram Island were Capt. John McKinnon, Mate Pat Rose, James Somers, Horatio Beck, Stephen Cole, John Hickey, Walter Pike, and Hugh McEachern.

If ever any men deserved a place in the Sailors Valhalla it was Pat Rose and the heroes of the *Yosemite*, Gloucester fishermen.

Capt. John (Shortscope) McKinnon lost his life four years later when his vessel, the *Eliza H. Parkhurst*, was lost with all hands on a Newfoundland herring passage.

Gross tons, 121; net tons, 115; length, 97.8 feet; breadth, 23.2 feet; depth, 11.5 feet.

Fortuna

TWO OF THE SAME NAME LOST IN TWO YEARS / 1893–1896

A story of disaster and tragedy concerns an oldtime vessel of the Gloucester fleet, or rather two of them. There were two *Fortunas*, one following the other in about a year. They were named for the Goddess of Fortune but were treated unkindly by the fickle lady of fate.

During the spring and summer of 1893, John Bishop built a vessel at Vincent Cove for Capt. Augustus G. Hall and Fred L. Davis. She was off the lines of the *Lewis H. Giles*, a medium size, clipper bow vessel. Capt. Jack Greenlaw had done well in the schooner *Fredonia* and he was given command of the fine new schooner.

After her launching she was given the name of *Fortuna*, after the famous schooner yacht owed by Commodore Henry Hovey of Freshwater Cove. Mr. Hovey owned the fine estate that later was to become John Hays Hammond's home at Lookout Hill. The schooner yacht *Fortuna* used to moor off the estate. The forecastle of the fisherman *Fortuna* had berths for 16 men. Her cabin was finished with white ash and rock maple, with one stateroom.

The trial trip of the *Fortuna* on September 4, 1893, was a gala affair. The day was fine with a good breeze. The vessel anchored off the ferry landing and took on six seineboat loads of men, women and children. With Capt. John Collins at the wheel, the *Fortuna* started on a cruise to Boston, went as far as Fort Independence in Boston Harbor, and then started on her return trip.

The *Fortuna* sailed on her maiden trip, haddocking, on September 9, 1893, in command of Capt. Jack Greenlaw and arrived back in Boston on September 18 with a fine fare, stocking $1,200.

The *Fortuna*'s life was short. While she was fishing in the Channel on February 12, 1894, a heavy snow storm set in and the schooner headed for safety at Provincetown. In trying to round the cape under her four lower sails she struck on the outer bar, a quarter of a mile east of Race Point Light. Heavy seas began breaking over her. The crew started to leave the vessel in dories. One dory containing four men upset and James McLean and Abram Brow (a bridegroom of two weeks) were drowned. Capt. Greenlaw, at the risk of his own life, helped save the other members of the capsized dory. One of these, a small boy named Fred Lawrence, was held up in the water by the skipper until other members of the crew helped in his rescue.

At the time of the vessel's stranding it was low water and she began to break up. After a desperate struggle, the Coast Guard crew from Race Point succeeded in rescuing the survivors.

After the loss of the *Fortuna*, a new vessel was immediately ordered for Capt. Greenlaw. In the meantime, he took the schooner *Richard Steele* on a few trips haddocking.

The second *Fortuna* was launched at the John Bishop Yard at Vincent Cove on June 5, 1894. Over 500 people attended her launching. Capt. Jack Greenlaw, Capt. Gus Hall, and Fred L. Davis each owned a third of the schooner. She was built along the same lines as her predecessor, only with a foot less beam—a handsome vessel with a clipper bow.

Her trial trip was sailed on June 18, 1894. The new vessel was lying in the stream off of the Ferry Slip. The tug *Startle* and the ferryboat *Little Giant* brought nearly 300 people on board. An enjoyable sail to Boston and return was experienced. The wind was both light and fresh. A delightful fish chowder was served on board. In Broad Sound, Boston Harbor, the training ship *Enterprise* was met and passed. Off Fort Independence, she easily beat the pilot boat *Columbia* (2) and on the return trip she again met and beat the *Columbia*. The return trip home was made in three hours. Capt. Greenlaw was the proud owner of a new easy chair for his cabin presented to him by his fiancee, Miss Annie Powers of Gloucester.

The *Fortuna* sailed on her maiden trip haddocking June 21, 1894. She arrived in Gloucester on July 9, 1894, with 27,000 lbs. of fresh fish. On this trip a new type of dory, equipped with air tanks and supposed to be unsinkable, was tried out. On Lahave Bank on June 28 this dory capsized and John Doyle was drowned. He had clung to the dory for three hours but exhaustion forced him to release his hold. His dory-mate was saved.

Capt. Greenlaw did very well with the new *Fortuna* for two years but again the Goddess of Fortune frowned upon him. On January 13, 1896, the schooner, while running off before the wind, on a clear moonless night was rammed by the fruit steamer *Barnstable*, six miles off Cape Cod. The only men on the schooner's deck at the time were Capt. Greenlaw at the wheel and the watch forward. The lookout on the steamer could not see the schooner's lights as they were obscured by the sails. The vessel was struck amidship and the steamer's bow sliced through her and blocked the forecastle's companion way, preventing the men below from escaping. Nine men went to their deaths. Arthur Nunan, the cook, helped save several lives by opening the bulkhead into the fore hold. The captain of the steamer kept the prow of the steamer into the hole and slowly forced the doomed schooner ahead. By doing this the 14 survivors were able to climb the

Picking the bones of the *Fortuna* a few days after she struck the beach near Race Point, Cape Cod.

bow of the steamer to safety. The last man had hardly reached the deck of the steamer when the vessel plunged to the bottom.

The vessel was almost completely cut in two. It was a strange coincidence, that the second *Fortuna* was lost within a few miles of her namesake. Her survivors were landed at Boston by the steamer. Value of the schooner was $11,000.

Capt. Jack Greenlaw took command of a new vessel, the *Annie Greenlaw*, named for his wife, in 1896. On February 12, 1899, just five years to the day after the loss of the first *Fortuna*, he was swept to his death when struck by the mainsail in a howling snowstorm off of Cape Cod. The waters of Cape Cod had finally claimed this able mariner.

Capt. Greenlaw was one of Gloucester's finest skippers, well liked by his men and very successful. A native of Deer Isle, Maine, he was 39 at the time of his death.

All the tragic events in Capt. Greenlaw's life took place within this same locality, off Cape Cod.

Fortuna, 1893: gross tons, 123; net tons, 117; length, 98.9 feet; breadth, 25 feet; depth, 10.2 feet.
Fortuna, 1894: gross tons, 125; net tons, 125; length, 98.3 feet; breadth, 24 feet; depth, 10.2 feet.

Iced up, but safe in port, is the *Georgie Campbell*. The author's father, Captain Jeff Thomas, pounded ice just before he succumbed to a heart attack in his schooner *Adventure*, at sea.

Georgie Campbell

ICE WRECKED HER ON A REEF / 1893–1914

Capt. Johnnie Campbell's fine vessel, the *Georgie Campbell*, was one of the all-sail halibuters.

Capt. Campbell, who was one of the leaders in the halibut fishery, sold his interest in the schooner *Eliza Campbell* (named for his wife) to the Hodge and Pool Co. in March, 1893. Immediately a new vessel was started for him by Moses Adams at Essex. The new schooner was built off the older *Campbell's* lines and was named after Capt. Campbell's young son, Georgie.

The *Georgie Campbell* was launched at the Adams Yard on May 18, 1893. She was a fine medium sized, clipper bowed schooner, with a good spread of canvas. On June 6 of that year, the new vessel, in command of her owner, Capt. John Campbell, rounded Eastern Point, bound to the eastward on her maiden halibut trip. On board were the family of Capt. Campbell, including the vessel's namesake, who enjoyed a fine trip to Georgetown, Prince Edward Island, where they were to spend a summer's vacation on that beautiful island. Capt. Johnnie, after landing his family, headed the new vessel to sea, but the craft sprang a leak soon after and she was forced to put into Port Hawkesbury for repairs.

The *Georgie Campbell* arrived home in Gloucester with her maiden fare of 20,000 lbs. halibut, 10,000 lbs. cod on July 10, 1893.

While under Capt. Campbell's command, the *Georgie* was ashore at Canso, Nova Scotia, in February, 1895, but was floated shortly after, with little damage.

Capt. Campbell remained as skipper of the vessel, halibuting, until the winter of 1895–96 when Capt. Ed Cosgrove took her to Newfoundland for a herring cargo. Capt. Sam Colson, crack halibuter, took over the wheel in the spring of 1898 and remained in command until 1902. The *Campbell* changed over to salt banking in the spring of 1904 under the command of Capt. Bowman Spinney. The season of 1905, it was again salt banking under a new skipper, Capt. Albert Hubbard. In 1907 Capt. Robert Wilson took the *Campbell* salt banking.

Capt. Tom Flannagan took over command in 1908, salt banking, and remained as skipper through 1912. During the winter seasons, the *Campbell* made many voyages to Newfoundland for herring cargos. Capt. John Marshall took her to Newfoundland in the season of 1900–01, Capt. Wilson Cahoon in 1904–05, Capt. Albert Hubbard in 1905–06.

Many interesting things happened to the sturdy *Georgie Campbell* during her career. In the old days of sail, the fishing vessels took quite a beating during the hard winter months. It was a common occurrence to see one of these vessels arriving in the harbor almost completely covered with ice, causing the folks ashore to wonder how the vessels ever made port. The *Georgie Campbell* had one of the worst cases of icing up that had occurred up to that time. On February 27, 1900, in command of Capt. Sam Colson, the *Campbell* tied up at the Atlantic Halibut Co. wharf with 17,000 lbs. halibut and looking very much like a floating iceberg. Spectators who looked her over agreed that she was one of the worst cases that had ever come in the harbor. Ice formed from flying spray, which turned to ice almost before it had struck the craft. The ice enlarged the rigging and other parts to many times their normal size, while the decks were encrusted with a thick mass, the dories being frozen solid. The Campbell's sides were coated with a regular armor of ice. Her bowsprit looked like a long icicle. Ernest Blatchford was right on the job with his camera, at the time, and snapped an excellent photo of the *Georgie Campbell*.

On December 31 of the same year, 1900, the *Campbell*, in command of Capt. John Marshall, again proved an interesting sight as she sailed up the harbor. This time she was one of the deepest laden vessels to arrive in Gloucester up to that time. Twenty-seven days out of the Bay of Islands, Newfoundland, hailing for 1650 barrels herring, the *Campbell* cleared only a plank and a half out of the water in the waist, as she was made fast to the wharf. Capt. Marshall favored the vessel on the voyage home, because she was so deep. Those daring skippers used to take plenty of chances!

A most interesting occurrence involving the *Georgie Campbell* took place during the first week of August, 1901. During the week, 1,221,000 lbs. salt fish and 280,000 fresh fish was landed at the Fred L. Davis Wharf in Gloucester. Schooner *Georgie Campbell*, 200,000 lbs. salt fish; schooner *Mabel D. Hines*, 290,000 lbs. salt fish; *Maggie and May*, 304,- 000 lbs. salt fish; *John L. Nicholson* 225,000 lbs. salt fish; *Agnes*, 35,000 salt fish, 60,000 fresh cod; *Oregon*, 23,000 salt (part of trip); *Annie Greenlaw*, 7,000 salt cod (part of trip); *Braganza*, 60,000 fresh fish; *Oliver F. Kilham*, 40,000 fresh fish; *Harvester*, 120,000 fresh fish.

Six of the firm vessels including the *Campbell*, also fitted out at the wharf, which was one of the busiest in the city.

Fortunately not many lives were lost in the *Georgia Campbell*. Alex Johnson, one of the crew, died at St. Pierre as the result of a fall from a cliff while the vessel was at that port.

Daniel Bowes was washed overboard and drowned during a heavy breeze on Quero Bank on October 18, 1895. Capt. John Campbell was skipper at the time.

Alexander Collins and John Fortune went astray in the fog, from the *Georgie Campbell* off Sable Island on April 7, 1911, and were never heard from. Their overturned dory was later picked up by the schooner *Arcadia*. Collins was 30 years old and a native of Prince Edward Island. Fortune, 19 years old, was a native of Arichat, Cape Breton. This was Fortune's first trip. Capt. Tom Flannagan was the *Campbell's* skipper at the time.

Two more of the *Campbell's* crew came very nearly never seeing Gloucester again. Tom Grady and Duncan Chisholm went astray from the vessel, 140 miles off Funk Island, Newfoundland, during a dense fog on July 29, 1898. They suffered terribly from hunger and were obliged to eat raw fish that were in the bottom of their dory. They were rescued, very exhausted, by the British bark *Flying Foam*, which was bound to Labrador. They were landed at Black Tickle, an isolated port of Labrador, where they remained for 26 days in this dreary spot. Finally, the mail steamer *Leopard* picked them up and landed them in St. Johns, Newfoundland.

The end of the grand old *Georgie Campbell* came in January, 1914. The F. L. Davis Co., owner of the *Campbell*, sent the vessel in command of Capt. Jack McKeoughan, to Newfoundland for a herring cargo on December 6, 1913. She arrived at the Bay of Islands on December 30 and proceeded to North Arm on January 3, 1914. She started loading the next day and completed her cargo on January 8, too late, however, to escape the ice driven into the bay. January 24th found her anchored in six fathoms of water on the west side of Wood's Island, after several unsuccessful attempts to leave for home. At 11 o'clock that night, the ice began to run and carried the *Campbell* from her anchorage and drove her ashore on a reef of rocks. At 3 o'clock next morning the vessel heeled over and filled with water so rapidly that all hands took to the dories. The next day found the *Georgie Campbell* lying in a bad position, and full of water up to the hatches. She proved a total loss and Gloucester was minus another of the great vessels that had made her famous.

Capt. John Campbell, original skipper of the *Georgie Campbell*, passed away in Gloucester on February 20, 1937, at the age of 85. Capt. John was one of the big "killers" in the halibut fishery, back in the 80's and 90's. Tall, raw-boned and one of the great skippers in the glorious days of sail. He commanded many fine vessels including the *Hattie Chester*, *Carthage*, *Grace L. Fears*, *Eliza B. Campbell*, *Georgie Campbell*, *Argo*, *Preceptor*, *Columbia* (old), *J. J. Flaherty* and many others. He discovered a famous fishing spot, located eastward of Quero Bank, called "Johnnie Campbell's Spot." Capt. Campbell was a native of Little Harbor, Souris, Prince Edward Island.

John George Campbell, namesake of the vessel, died at Denver, Colorado, November 2, 1952.

Capt. Bowman Spinney, one of the *Georgie Campbell's* skippers, was accidentally killed in a fall from T-wharf to the deck of the schooner *Manhasset* at Boston on October 15, 1907. He was 42 years old and a native of Yarmouth, County, Nova Scotia.

Capt. Thomas Flannagan, skipper of the *Georgie Campbell* for many years, died at Chelsea Hospital on November 8, 1932. He was a native of Maxwell, England and 65 years old. Capt. Tom was one of the most beloved fishermen out of Gloucester. He was one of the few survivors of the schooner *Rex* disaster in 1925.

Gross tons, 111; net tons, 78; length, 94.8 feet; breadth, 24.3 feet; depth, 10 feet. Spars: mainmast (deck to cap), 66 feet; foremast, 63 feet; maintopmast, 38 feet; foretopmast, 30 feet; mainboom, 65 feet; main gaff, 37 feet; bowsprit (outboard), 29 feet; mast heads, 10 feet.

She was tender, was the *Helen G. Wells*, but she had what it took in the ultimate showdown. She was the only schooner that the author knows of that rolled over in a complete circle and lived. A burn mark the size and shape of a lid from the hot stove was a sight to see on the cabin ceiling for years.

Helen G. Wells

HOVE DOWN, SHE RIGHTED HERSELF / 1893–1915?

Schooner *Helen G. Wells* was a famous Gloucester fishing vessel; a vessel in which her fine skipper and owner met untimely death; a vessel that when hove down at sea turned bottom up but righted herself and brought the crew safely back to port to tell the tale.

Schooner *Helen G. Wells* was built during the winter and spring of 1893 at Tom Irving's yard on Vincent Street, Gloucester. She was built for her skipper, Capt. William Wells, one of the finest skippers out of Gloucester in the 1890's.

The *Helen G. Wells* was launched April 19, 1893. About 300 spectators watched as she gracefully slid into the water of Vincent Cove.

The trial trip was held on May 10. The tug *Charlie*, Capt. Charles T. Heberle, towed her down the harbor. On board were a number of vessel owners, skippers, and her designer, Capt. G. Melvin McClain, who watched her every movement with pride. All spoke well of her, and comments on her good looks and fine turn of speed were heard on every hand. The

Wells was out two hours in the bay when she was forced to return to port when the wind died out. She pulled in at the Perkins salt wharf to land her passengers.

Schooner *Helen G. Wells* was a handsome vessel of the clipper bow type designed by Capt. McClain of Rockport. Schooners *Marguerite Haskins* and *Miranda*, built the same year, were of the same model. She was named for the daughter of Capt. Wells.

The *Helen G. Wells*, in command of Capt. Wells, sailed on her maiden trip, halibuting, May 11, 1893. She arrived in Gloucester with her maiden fare of 25,000 pounds halibut June 8, 1893.

Four of the crew went astray in fog on Grand Bank June 28, 1896. George Upham and Herbert Foley, after being astray for four days, were picked up by the British schooner *Dorothy* and landed at St. John's, Newfoundland. Philip Merchant, a native of Arichat, Cape Breton, and John Thomas, a native of Halifax, were never seen again. These two men were the first ever lost by Capt. Wells in his twenty-four years as a skipper.

On February 1, 1897, the *Helen G. Wells* arrived at T Wharf, Boston, with her colors at half-mast for the loss of her skipper, Capt. William Wells. The vessel had fished one day when she encountered the terrible gale of January 28, 1897, and had to run before it. All that night the gale continued, and the vessel was run under the shortest of sail. At 1 p.m. January 29, Simon Muise, who was at the wheel, was knocked down by a sea. Fortunately he did not go overboard, as he was lashed to the wheel. Capt. Wells rushed to his assistance and as he did so another sea, larger than the first, smashed on board and swept Capt. Wells overboard. He was never seen again. The same sea swept the vessel's deck completely, taking dories, gurry kids (containers on deck) and everything movable, besides breaking the main boom.

Capt. Bill Wells was one of the most capable skippers of the halibut fleet. Of Capt. Wells nothing but good can be said. Quiet, kind and unassuming. As a master mariner he was a careful navigator and a first class fisherman. He had been a skipper for twenty-four years. His commands included the schooners *Elisha Crowell*, *Dido*, *Mary J. Wells*, *Bessie M. Wells*, *Maggie E. Wells* and *Helen G. Wells*.

One of the saddest thoughts connected with Capt. Wells' loss was the fact that he left a family of eight orphans, their mother having passed away two years previously. Leo Wells, one of the captain's sons, later became a Gloucester fishing skipper. Capt. Bill Wells was a native of Guysboro, Nova Scotia, forty-eight years old.

In that same gale of January 28, 1897, Capt. John (Long John) McDonald of the schooner *James G. Blaine* was swept overboard with one of his crew and drowned.

After the death of Capt. Wells the *Helen G. Wells* was taken over by the Gardner and Parsons firm and Capt. Joachim Murray was the skipper.

The *Helen Wells*, in command of Capt. Murray, sailed from Gloucester October 29, 1897, on a halibut trip. From the start the weather was bad and no fishing was done. On November 10 the vessel, lying at anchor on Green Bank, was struck by a heavy northwest gale. The cable parted and the vessel hove to under a three-reefed foresail. Shortly after midnight a huge sea broke over the vessel, striking her amidships on the port side and turning her right over till she rested nearly bottom up, in which position she remained for a short time. She was lying to, under riding sails, with all her canvas furled except a jib and a single-reefed foresail.

Two men were on watch, and when they saw the huge comber coming they jumped for the cabin to escape being carried overboard. Just as the second man's head vanished below a torrent of water poured down the open hatch. Seven men were now in the cabin and eleven in the forecastle. As the vessel was upset they were tossed out of their bunks and around the decks like ninepins. All thought their time had come and struggled fiercely in the dark, battling with the water that threatened every moment to drown them.

The crew could form no idea what happened, but the condition of the cabin and forecastle seemed to indicate she had turned completely over. Jack Barnable was first out of the cabin, and although the vessel lay on her beam ends, he seized the wheel and succeeded in righting her, and keeping her before the seas.

Capt. Murray was washed out of his room and back again twice before he could reach a place of safety.

In the forecastle Axel Johnson was hurled against the bulkwark and his hip seriously hurt. Ernest Nickerson was thrown from his bunk and got a cut in his head two inches long. Every man on board was cut and bruised more or less.

Nickerson, the first man out of the forecastle, found that all the cable—three hundred fathoms—ranged on deck had been washed out of its place and hurled through the foresail; was then hanging out over the side of the craft, tending to keep her down. He seized an axe, cut away, and this lightened her considerably. While they were clearing away the wreckage she was boarded by another sea that swept Jim Murphy away from the wheel, sent him high in the air, and dropped him down on the cabin. After the vessel was fairly off before it, the crew had a chance to look around and see what devastation the storm had wrought to their craft. Everything was soaking wet, both clothing and food. The two stoves had been broken up by the upset. When she turned bottom up, every drop of water in her tanks ran out. Conspicuously stuck up on the ceiling was a large lump of butter. For many years afterward the print of the cover of the galley stove could be seen on the ceiling.

The decks were swept clean; not a splinter was left of the eight dories. The fore boom, gaff and sail were gone, the mainsail and gaff likewise, the main boom, a spar as round as a man's body, broken in six pieces; halyards, stays and booms, main topmast, head sails and other gear stripped as clean as if she had been in riggers' hands. She looked a regular derelict.

The pump gear was carried away and she had to be bailed out by hand. The hull, despite the awful strain, did not leak a drop. The salvation of the vessel and her crew was the fact that her ice and ballast were safely stowed and did not shift when she upset.

On the 12th the storm abated and then under a ragged and torn headsail the *Wells* was headed for St. John's, Newfoundland. Off shore a tug got her and towed her in. She was said to be in the worst condition of any vessel that ever entered St. John's up to that time. The *Wells* was repaired at St. John's. She arrived home in Gloucester December 6, 1897.

Her recovery from the awful blow of the sea and the escape of her crew is one of those inexplicable things which some call Providence and which our brave fishermen term as luck.

The crew of the *Wells* when she was hove down included Capt. Joachim Murray, Peter Pero, cook, D. Dalton, Garret O'Reilly, J. Powers, H. Wagg, John Kennedy, Bernard Carter, William Johnson, Jack Barnable, W. Bateman, J. Murphy, W. Grady, James Hodneault, D. Anderson, F. Brewer, E. Nickerson and Alex Johnson.

Capt. Mel McClain once stated, "It makes no difference, shoal or deep, when a monster sea strikes fair, down goes the vessel on her beam ends. Then comes the test; if she is well designed, well built, and properly ballasted, up she comes again; if otherwise, sad is her fate."

Capt. Lem Firth told me that when he was in the *Helen Wells* she was a good vessel, stiff, and a fair sailer, but when she wet her rails you would never know what was going to happen.

On September 11, 1897, the *Helen G. Wells*, in command of Capt. Joachim Murray, arrived in Gloucester with 40,000 pounds halibut. Within a period of three days over 570,000 pounds halibut were landed, all from Baccalieu Bank: *Joseph Rowe*, Capt. Clayton Morrissey, 45,000 pounds; *Eliza Parkhurst*, Capt. Little Dan McDonald, 70,000 pounds; *Atalanta*, Capt. Dick Wadding, 100,000 pounds; *Pinta*, Capt. Jim Hayes, 60,000 pounds; *Gladiator*, Capt. Lem Spinney, 60,000 pounds; *Masconomo*, Capt. Bob Porper, 50,000 pounds; *Judique*, 85,000 pounds; and *Arbutus*, 70,000

pounds. In addition, the schooner *Josie M. Calderwood*, Capt. Walter Trowbridge, was in with 115,000 pounds flitched halibut.

Capt. Joe Cusick had the *Helen Wells* halibuting in 1898–99; Capt. George Marr, halibuting in 1900. Capt. Albert Larkin took her as his first command in 1902 and remained in her in 1903. Capt. Cusick again had the *Wells* in the spring of 1904, salt fishing, while he was waiting for his new vessel, the *Independence II*, to be built.

On April 5, 1904, the *Helen G. Wells* in command of Capt. Cusick arrived in Gloucester from the Peak with 140,000 pounds salt cod. This was the earliest bank trip on record. She had been gone only thirty-nine days.

Capt. Gus Hamor was skipper of the *Wells* seining in 1904–05. Capt. Lem Firth was seining skipper in 1906, and this was his first command. In 1907 Capt. Ed McClean was seining skipper. In 1908 Capt. Nat Greenleaf took over.

In 1909 the *Wells* was taken over by the Gorton-Pew Fisheries Co. when the Gardner and Parsons firm went out of business.

Under the Gorton-Pew ownership her skippers were as follows. In 1910 Capt. Ed Hiltz had her dory handling. In 1911 Capt. Jack Hackett, salt banking, and Capt. James (Coalhod Jim) McDonald, salt banking. In 1912 Capt. Alex Surrett took her Rip fishing and in the fall, Capt. Simon Theriault went pollocking. In 1913 Capt. Alex Surrett, Rip fishing, and that fall again Capt. Simon Theriault took her pollocking. In 1914, Capt. Surrett, Rip fishing. That fall, Capt. Jim McDonald took her on a North Bay seining trip. In 1915, Capt. Surrett, Rip fishing.

On October 2, 1912, the *Helen Wells* in command of Capt. Alex Surrett rescued the crew of four of the sinking Nova Scotian schooner *Ethel*, twenty-five miles off Sable Island, Nova Scotia. It was a brilliant rescue, performed in mountainous seas.

Capt. Surrett got to the weather of the sinking vessel and set loose a dory with a long line. After several ineffectual attempts the scheme succeeded and the crew of the *Ethel* made the necessary jump. The *Ethel* stayed afloat just an hour after the rescue. She was bound from New York to Halifax with 200 tons coal. The rescued men were landed at Pubnico, Nova Scotia.

The *Helen Wells* in command of Capt. Jack Hackett sailed to Newfoundland for a cargo of salt cod on December 13, 1911. She dragged ashore in a gale at Sandy Point, Bay of St. George, Newfoundland, in the middle of January, 1912. Owing to the peculiar locality where she struck it was impossible for repairs to be made until spring. She arrived home in Gloucester on June 26, 1912, with 150,000 pounds salt cod. She had been gone six months.

The gallant little *Helen Wells* was sold by

the Gorton-Pew company to Havana, Cuba, in December, 1915, for $3,600. This was the last I ever heard of her.

Thomas Irving, builder of the *Helen G. Wells*, passed away in Gloucester October 15, 1927, at the age of eighty-five. He was a native of Gloucester and came from old Revolutionary stock. Many fine vessels were sent down the ways by this great shipbuilder, including the schooners *Clara Harwood, Leader, Shefeyld, Viking, Mabel R. Bennett, Eliza H. Parkhurst, Helen G. Wells* and *Slade Gorton*.

Tom Irving was probably the greatest of all fisherman-model vessel builders; truly a master craftsman.

Capt. Joachim Murray died in Europe October 26, 1917. He was serving as boatswain's mate in the U.S. Naval Reserve. Capt. Murray was the first Gloucester man to die in overseas duty taking an active part in the war with Germany. He was a native of Newfoundland, fifty-five years old.

Mrs. Helen G. Wells Cahill died at Brighton, Massachusetts, in November, 1962, at the age of seventy-three.

Gross tons, 95; net tons, 66; length, 91.2 feet; breadth, 24.8 feet; depth, 9.4 feet.

Indiana

SHE BEAT STEAMER—TRAIN TIME / 1893–1916?

Schooner *Indiana* was one of our finest vessels and biggest producers in the 1890's; record holder of the fastest round trip Gloucester-Newfoundland herring voyage.

The *Indiana* was built during the winter and spring of 1893 at the Tarr and James Yard in Essex and launched in May of that year. The new vessel was owned by Andrew Leighton of Gloucester. Capt. Sewall Smith, crack skipper in the fresh fishery was her skipper.

The *Indiana* was a handsome clipper bowed vessel modeled off the famous schooner *Fredonia*, an Edward Burgess creation. She was named for the state of Indiana.

The trial trip was sailed on August 11, 1893 and it was a gala affair. Two hundred eleven guests jammed every inch of space on the vessel. This was probably the greatest crowd of people that ever sailed on a trial trip of a Gloucester fisherman. As the *Indiana* in tow of the tug *Startle*, moved slowly from the wharf, those on board sang "Farewell, Farewell My Own True Love." Just ahead of the new craft was Mr. Leighton's schooner *Gloriana*, Capt. Frank Lorenzo, which was bound to the fishing grounds.

The trip was marred by fog and lack of wind; and the *Indiana* with Capt. John Collins at the wheel was forced to turn for home when about 10 miles off Eastern Point. Everyone on board had a wonderful time, however, and a delightful fish chowder was served.

Some of the noted persons on this trip were Andrew Leighton, the owner; John James and Washington Tarr, the builders; Hugh Bishop, noted vessel builder; Benjamin Cook and Edward Tuck, sailmakers for the *Indiana*; and Howard Blackburn, one of Gloucester's greatest heroes.

The *Indiana's* new suit of sails, made by Cook and Tuck, set beautifully.

The *Indiana*, Capt. Sewall Smith, arrived at Boston with her maiden fare of 35,000 lbs. fresh fish on August 23, 1893. The bewhiskered Capt. Sewall Smith, a native of Mount Desert, Maine, was one of the topnotchers in the offshore fisheries. He had made a splendid record in the schooner *Gloriana* during 1891–92 and he kept up his reputation in the *Indiana*. During her first year, she landed 1,605,000 lbs. fish, stocking $24,388, with a share of $441 per man.

On June 25, 1894, the *Indiana* arrived at Boston with 100,000 lbs. fresh hake and 28,000

Standing-room-only on the *Indiana*, shown under full sail on her trial trip.

mixed fish. This was the largest fare of hake landed at T Wharf up to that time.

Capt. Smith was again highline in 1896 when he landed 1,571,000 lbs. fish, stocking $24,123 and sharing $503. This was big money in the haddock fishery in those days.

Capt. Smith remained in the *Indiana* until 1901. She was commanded by many fine mariners. Capt. John Anderson had her haddocking in 1902. Capt. Lov Hodgdon, haddocking in 1902. Capt. Steve Black and Oliver Thomas haddocking in 1904. Capts. Nat Greenleaf and Tom Cromwell seining in 1906. Capt. Ambrose Fleet seining in 1907.

The *Indiana* was sold by the Leightons to Capt. Almon Malloch (Al Miller), famous skipper, in April, 1907. From then on to her final sale, she was used in the mackerel fishery summers and to Newfoundland for herring cargoes during the winter months with Capt. Malloch himself usually in command.

In January, 1910, the *Indiana* broke the round trip record to Newfoundland. The craft left Gloucester on January 19th, in command of Capt. Al Malloch. She loaded at the Bay of Islands, and sailed on the return trip in command of the mate Jack McKeoughan, arriving back in Gloucester on February 5. The whole trip took only 17 days, which record has never been broken.

Capt. McKeoughan's homeward trip in the *Indiana* ranks with the very best. She was just 88 hours from Webald to Thacher's Island and but for having to heave to in a gale and snowstorm off Thatcher's on February 4th, for about 11 hours, would have made a passage never equalled or ever approached. As it was, passages from Bay of Islands inside of four days were few and far between.

Capt. Malloch sent the *Indiana* home in charge of his mate McKeoughan and started to come home by steamer and rail; so as to be in Gloucester ahead of the vessel. The vessel beat him by about four days. His friends jokingly remarked to him, "Well Al, if you wanted to get home in a hurry you should have come along in the vessel."

The *Indiana* completed her third herring trip of that season when she arrived in Gloucester on April 27, 1910, with 1500 bbls. herring, and her decks almost awash.

A successful skipper on a herring voyage had to drive a vessel from start to finish for time meant money, and quick trips were sure to find a good market. Capt. Al Malloch was one of the best in this branch of the fishery.

Capt. Rufus McKay took the *Indiana* to the Cape Shore for mackerel during the summer of 1910.

In November, 1910, Leslie Malloch, son of the skipper, took the *Indiana* to Newfoundland. Leslie was one of Gloucester's first and finest vessel engineers.

The *Indiana* was a fairly fast vessel. In September, 1893, while in command of Capt. Sewall Smith, she beat the crack Boston pilotboat *Varuna* (No. 6) out of Boston Harbor.

A story, almost without parallel, involved two of the crew of the *Indiana* in August, 1904. The *Indiana*, Capt. Oliver Thomas, was fishing off Sable Island, and the crew went out to haul their trawls. The fog shut down quickly, and the dory with Peter Grady and Cornelius Connolly was unable to find the vessel. They started to row for land and became confused and finally became so weak from want of food and water that their blistered hands could not hold an oar. Their strength gradually left them and after a while they sank into the bottom of the dory in exhaustion and despair. The weather continued thick and they drifted with the current, helpless as two babes. On toward the Newfoundland Coast the dory with its half dead occupants drifted, and on the eleventh day adrift they were picked up more dead than alive by the British schooner *Hydrangea*. They were in pitiable condition and the tenderest care was given them by men of the *Hydrangea*.

In the 11 days the dory made a drift of 200 miles, being within 40 miles of Miquelon when picked up. The men were landed at Sydney, Cape Breton, where they slowly recovered. They had only a half gallon of fresh water and not a morsel of food for 11 days.

I believe this is the longest period astray of any Gloucester fisherman.

The *Indiana* was lucky on loss of life. Sandy Powler was struck by the foreboom and knocked into the sea and drowned, while the vessel was jibing 30 miles east of Thacher's June 24, 1894. He was an Italian by birth, 53 years old and left a widow and six children.

The *Indiana's* fishing career came to an end in October, 1913, when Capt. Malloch sold the craft to New Bedford parties for use in the Cape Verde trade. In 1916 she was transferred to Portuguese registry. Ed Frelick, one of our fine old fishermen, used to sail to Newfoundland with Capt. Malloch in the *Indiana*. Ed once told me that on one of the homeward passages the mainsail of the *Indiana* was hoisted 13 times.

Capt. Almon Malloch, better known as Al Miller, died at Sailor's Snug Harbor, New York, in December, 1933. He was a native of Buxton, Maine, and was 76 years old. Al Miller was one of the greatest mariners sailing out of Gloucester. His reputation as a fisherman, sail carrier, and driver was known along the entire coast. He was a crack seiner and one of the best in the Newfoundland herring trade.

When I asked my father, Capt. Jeff Thomas, who he thought was the greatest sail carrier out of Gloucester, without hesitation he replied "Al Miller." I thought this was quite a tribute to come from a man who was an outstanding sail carrier himself. It was usually a bad beating to the vessel that came in contact with the big schooner *Edna Wallace Hopper* with Al Miller at the wheel. Some of his best known commands were schooners *Margaret Mather*, *Edna Wallace Hopper*, *Alert*, *Indiana*, *Squanto* and *Minna N.*

Gross tons, 122; net tons, 88; length, 106 feet; breadth, 24.4 feet; depth, 10.6 feet.

Drying sails at the old Halibut Wharf; the *Atalanta*.

Atalanta

HALIBUT WAS HER SPECIALTY/1894–1921?

Schooner *Atalanta*, named after a famous steam yacht built in 1883, and a fleet-footed maiden of Greek mythology who defied her suitors to catch her, was one of the greatest producers of halibut out of Gloucester. She became a grand old lady of the North Atlantic, always commanded by a great mariner, Capt. Richard Wadding.

Built by Moses Adams at Essex, she was launched in June, 1894, and towed to Gloucester by the tug *Startle*, Capt. Osborne P. Linnekin, on the 26th.

The *Atalanta* was a medium sized, fine-lined vessel with a clipper bow and long bowsprit, off the model of schooner *Susan L. Hodge*. Hodge and Pool were the original owners of *Atalanta*. After the firm went out of business Capt. Wadding bought the schooner.

Outward bound on her trial trip July 12, 1894, with 100 persons on board, the *Atalanta* dipped her ensign in salute to the U. S. S. *New York* and U. S. S. *Atlanta*, in the outer harbor. Right away the *Atalanta* was in a race with schooner *Helen G. Wells*, skippered by Capt. William Wells, to Minot's Light and return. The *Atalanta* was leading when the vessels turned, then the *Wells* forged ahead. Off Norman's Woe, the *Atalanta* shot ahead and she was the first to dock. Hundreds of summer people watched the impromptu race from the Magnolia shore.

The *Atalanta* arrived home August 13, 1894, from her maiden trip, with 15,000 pounds of halibut, caught on LaHave Bank. In the next 17 months the vessel stocked $30,121. On October 22, 1895, she hailed for 85,000 pounds of halibut taken on Green Bank. In 1896 she was high line of the halibuters, with a stock of $22,894, and landings of 424,347 pounds.

Among her big trips were: July 3, 1896, from Grand Bank, with 96,000 pounds of halibut, stocking $2527, sharing $61.05 (what a difference such a fare would mean today!); August 10, 1896, from New Seattle Bank with 80,000 pounds halibut, stocking $3433, sharing $86.

She brought the biggest trip and the biggest stock of the season of 1898, with 84,000 pounds from Baccalieu Bank, landed August 17, stocking $4800. On September 21, 1898, she arrived from Baccalieu with 90,000 pounds, stocking $4500 and sharing $119 for each of her crew of 20. On May 31, 1899, Capt. Dick brought the *Atalanta* in with 100,000 pounds of halibut taken off the Bay of Islands, Newfoundland, stocking $2904 and sharing $63.

In 1903 Capt. Wadding went mackerel seining, in 1905 he went salt banking and in 1910 he tried his hand at dory hand lining. But Wadding and *Atalanta* were best at halibuting. In 1911 Gorton-Pew Fisheries Co. took over the vessel's affairs and she was sent fletched halibuting summers and to Newfoundland for herring cargoes winters. In 1912 she stocked $9400 in fletched halibut. She brought 110,000 pounds of fletched halibut from Baccalieu October 4, 1915, stocking $9289 and sharing $215. She made the last fletched halibuting trip out of Gloucester, sailing May 4, 1916 and returning September 15 with a small fare of 40,000 pounds fletched halibut and 25,000 pounds of salt cod, stocking $4941.

The *Atalanta* had her share of mishaps. She was caught in the ice at North Arm, Bay of Islands, and frozen in for the winter of 1903–04. Previously, in December of 1903, she lost her bowsprit and sustained damage to fore-rigging and planking when a Canadian vessel broke adrift in a gale and came down on the Gloucester schooner. While lying at anchor on Quero Bank January 27, 1897, the *Atalanta* was rammed by the Gloucester schooner *Lizzie Griffin*. The *Griffin* was jogging and bore down on the *Atalanta*, changing course too late to avoid snapping off the boom. In 1908 she lost her rudder on Grand Bank, sailing home with a jury rudder made of boards and cable by the crew, arriving March 23 with 35,000 pounds of halibut.

She ran ashore at Arichat, Cape Breton, in June, 1908, when she misstayed while tacking up and down the harbor waiting for a landed dory. She struck a reef, but was floated at high water, little damaged.

More welcome was a voyage in December, 1910; round trip Gloucester to Bonne Bay, Newfoundland, and return with 1200 barrels of herring in eighteen days, just one day short of the record made the previous season by another vessel.

The *Atalanta*, during 23 years out of Gloucester, probably fished every bank in the western North Atlantic. Baccalieu, northeast of Newfoundland and the northernmost bank frequented by Gloucestermen, probably saw more of the *Atalanta* than any other vessel. She was a good sailer, and Capt. Wadding drove her for all she was worth. On passage home from the Bay of Islands with herring in December, 1915, the *Atalanta* beat the Gloucester schooner *John Hays Hammond* and the fast Canadian schooner *Muriel Walters*.

Capt. Dick parted company with his great vessel in October, 1917, when she was sold to Alexander Schwartz. The following month she was sold to New Bedford parties for use in the Cape Verde packet trade. She was transferred to Portuguese registry in 1921 and this is the last I ever heard of the old *Atalanta*.

Loss of life was heavy during the *Atalanta's* fishing career. Ten fine fishermen went to watery graves.

William Boudrou, twenty-eight, native of Arichat, Cape Breton, was washed off the main boom February 15, 1896.

Patrick Quinlan, thirty-five, native of Newfoundland, and Joseph McIsaac, thirty-two, went astray on the "Funks" July 30, 1898.

On December 5, 1898, while taking in the mainsail, a big sea broke under the *Atalanta's* quarter. She rolled down and the mainsail came back, sweeping James Burke, thirty, John Devine, twenty-eight, Oscar Anderson, thirty-three, Dan Sampson and Michael O'Brien into the sea. O'Brien grabbed a rope hanging off the main boom pennant and hauled himself back. Sampson caught the main boom tackle, trailing overboard, and climbed back. The rest were never seen again. It was thought that perhaps one or more grabbed the log line, as the log disappeared. Burke was a native of St. John's, Newfoundland. Devine was born in St. Mary's, Newfoundland. Anderson came from Finland.

In May, 1898, Chris Neilsen and Reub Myett,

two of the crew of *Atalanta*, went astray on Baccalieu Bank. They were picked up eight days later and landed at St. John's, Newfoundland. Little Chris had been astray for four days in 1892 when he was a member of the crew of schooner *Lizzie Stanwood*.

Oliver Lahey, thirty-six, a native of Fortune, Newfoundland, fell overboard and drowned off Sable Island February 13, 1901. Albert Smith, thirty-five, native of Sweden, fell overboard and drowned October 20, 1905, while on a passage to Newfoundland. William R. De Coste, twenty-seven, native of Harbor Bouchie, Nova Scotia, and Frederick Burke, twenty-eight, from Prince Edward Island, went astray on Western Bank December 8, 1908.

Capt. Wadding died at Sailors Snug Harbor, Staten Island, New York, in May, 1927, at the age of seventy years. This sturdy, quiet Englishman will go down in the history of the Gloucester fisheries as the last flitched halibuter. Other commands included schooners *Caroline Vought* and *Blanche*.

Moses Adams, a native of West Gloucester, was one of the leading shipbuilders of Essex, where he sent about a hundred vessels down the ways, including *Ethel B. Jacobs, Fredonia, Harry L. Belden, I. J. Merritt, Jr., Elsie F. Rowe, James G. Blaine, Charles Levi Woodbury, Masconomo,* and *George F. Edmunds.*

Adams started with Arthur D. Story in 1877 and went on his own in 1880. He was the first man to introduce machinery in Essex yards. He died at Essex July 16, 1894, fifty-six years of age.

Capt. Samuel Pool, one of the early owners of *Atalanta*, was a native of South Bristol, Maine. He was associated with the Gloucester Fresh Fish Co. and later with the Atlantic Halibut Co.

The flitched halibut trade, of which the *Atalanta* was the last survivor, was at one time one of Gloucester's leading branches of the fisheries. The vessels engaged were known as the "Farthest North Squadron" of the fishing fleet, their constant and sole company for four or five months being great bergs and fields of swift-moving ice.

The vessels usually fished on Baccalieu Bank and followed the bank up to the Labrador Coast and Hudson Strait. Occasionally, vessels fished on the Greenland grounds.

Years ago, so great was the demand for smoked halibut that a large number of vessels engaged in what was called halibut flitching. In the early days of the trade, about 1870, halibut was abundant on the banks, and large trips were taken. The halibut taken in northern waters have no equal. So many vessels were engaged in the flitched halibut business that, together with the large fleet of fresh halibut catchers, they so depleted the banks that the fishermen had to seek new fields.

On board one of these flitched halibuters were enough food and provisions to stock a good-sized store, and it was needed, too, for eighteen or twenty big strong healthy men have robust appetites in these northern latitudes.

The Atlantic Halibut building was one of the best known landmarks in Gloucester Harbor. It was erected in 1883 for the Atlantic Halibut Co. In 1904 it became the American Halibut Co. From December 1897 to December 1899 it was the Gloucester Fresh Fish Co. The plant was destroyed by fire in October 1953.

Gross tons, 104; net tons, 99; length, 93 feet; breadth, 23.5 feet; depth, 10 feet.

This is the only picture known to the author showing the great *Effie M. Morrissey* as a fisherman. She was often pictured as an Arctic exploration vessel and Cape Verde packet.

Effie M. Morrissey

FOUR CAREERS IN SEVENTY-EIGHT YEARS/1893–

This is the story of the *Effie M. Morrissey*, one of the most famous two-masted schooners in the world, and one of the staunchest ever built.

The *Morrissey* lived four whole lives and sailed under three flags. Her first life was as a fisherman out of Gloucester. Her second as a fisherman out of Digby, Nova Scotia, for years. Her third as an Arctic exploration vessel under the British flag, and her fourth as a Cape Verde packet under the Portuguese flag.

The *Effie M. Morrissey* was built by Willard Burnham at Essex during the winter of 1893–94 and was launched on February 1, 1894. The tug *Startle* towed her around to Gloucester to fit for sea.

The *Morrissey* was built for the John F. Wonson Co. of Gloucester and Capt. William E. Morrissey. She was named for Capt. Morrissey's daughter. A medium-sized clipper bow vessel taken off the model of the schooner *Mabel D. Hines*, she was the last vessel built for the John F. Wonson firm.

The *Effie M. Morrissey* sailed on her maiden trip salt banking, in command of Capt. William E. Morrissey, March 14, 1894. She arrived back in Gloucester on July 28, 1894 with a fine fare of 250,000 salt cod. The trip was sold to the C. W. Wonson Co. On November 8 of the same year she brought 320,000 pounds of salt cod from Grand Banks.

The *Morrissey* sailed under Capt. Morrissey about a year, but in April, 1895, on one of her banking trips, he was taken ill and the vessel was taken over by his son, Clayton, who was only 19 years old, and one of her crew at the time. This was Clayton's first command, and he remained in the *Morrissey* the remainder of that year, making two salt bank trips. Capt. Clayton took the *Morrissey* to Newfoundland in the winter of 1895–96 but he brought the schooner *Procyon* back. The *Morrissey* returned to Gloucester, under another skipper on January 25, 1896, with 860 barrels herring from Placentia Bay. The cargo was taken to New York.

In the season of 1897 and 1898 the *Effie M.* was in the seining game. During the Portland Breeze in November 1898 the *Effie Morrissey* went ashore in Smith's Cove, Gloucester. She had broken adrift from John F. Wonson's wharf together with schooners *Meteor*, *Reporter*, *Marguerite* and *Belle Franklin*. The

Morrissey was floated later, with little damage. Capt. John McInnis took her to Newfoundland for herring in the winter of 1898–99 and on her return, the cargo was sold to New York and she was sailed there by Capt. Rod McIntosh.

The season of 1899 found the *Morrissey* in command of Capt. John McInnis, who had her dory handlining. Capt. Josh Stanley was her next skipper and from September 1900 to September 1901 he stocked $30,000 with a share of $780 per man. This was a magnificent year's work in the haddock fishery at that time.

Capt. Stanley gave up the *Morrissey* in September 1901, as his new schooner *Lizzie M. Stanley* was nearly ready. Capt. Henry Atwood was the *Morrissey's* next skipper and he had her shacking and haddocking for about a year. In 1903 Capt. William Harding had her salt banking.

The *Effie Morrissey* was sold to Capt. Ansel Snow of Digby, Nova Scotia in March 1905. This ended her first life.

After the sale to her new owner, she was kept under American registry, but sailed out of Digby, Nova Scotia, with a Canadian crew.

On July 5, 1908, the *Morrissey* arrived at Gloucester with 200,000 pounds shack, caught in the Bay of Fundy. This was her first visit in three years.

In 1909 Capt. Ansel Snow, her owner, was also skipper.

Capt. Miller was her skipper in 1911 and she was landing her fares at Portland, Maine.

In 1913, Capt. William Ryder of Port Wade, Nova Scotia and Capt. Harry Ross were her skippers.

In 1914 the *Effie M.* ended her second life when she was sold to Harold Bartlett of Brigus, Newfoundland. She was then changed to British registry.

In January, 1917, the *Morrissey* stranded on Petrie Ledges off Sydney, Cape Breton, but was floated. Later Capt. Bartlett sold the *Morrissey* to his brother Capt. Bob Bartlett of Arctic and sealing fame.

In 1926 the *Morrissey* was sheathed with greenheart from Central America. A Diesel engine was installed and she was made ready for voyages into the Arctic. That year she cruised to Greenland and since then has made voyages to Arctic waters, bringing back many scientific findings such as animals, birds, plants and marine life. She has carried many famous men in the scientific field on her many voyages to the North.

In 1932 Capt. Bob took a party to Cape York in the Arctic Ocean to erect a monument to the memory of Adm. Robert E. Peary, discoverer of the North Pole. Capt. Bob was one of the admiral's closest friends and he had been commander of Peary's S. S. *Roosevelt* at the time of the Pole discovery. Many books of the *Morrissey*'s trips to the Arctic have been written and she well deserves all the praise and fame that have been given her. A great tribute to her builders at Essex, where no finer wooden vessels were ever built.

The *Effie M.* came back to her old home in 1944 and was tied up for the winter at the old Reed and Gamage wharf in East Gloucester.

Capt. Bob Bartlett died in New York in 1946 and the *Effie M. Morrissey* was sold to New York parties to be used as a freighter. She was then painted white. At Flushing, N.Y., in December, 1947 she caught afire and was scuttled. It was thought she would be a total loss, but she was raised and sold to parties in New Bedford for the Cape Verde packet trade in April, 1948. This was the beginning of the fourth life of the old *Effie M.*

Her engine was taken out and the old schooner was renamed *Ernestina,* and she was transferred to the Portuguese flag in March of 1949. Still in service, she arrived in Providence, R. I., in September, 1964, to pick up a cargo for the Islands.

Time was running out for the old *Effie Morrissey,* as the trade in which she was engaged is a gruelling one. Vessels used in the Cape Verde packet trade generally do not last long. The heavy gales of the Atlantic and the shores of the Western Islands take a heavy toll of ships.

Capt. William E. Morrissey, one of Glouces-

ter's great skippers, passed away at his home, Pubnico, Nova Scotia, on January 28, 1913, at the age of 68. He had retired several years before to run a hotel in Pubnico. He was the father of Capts. Clayton and William Morrissey and a brother of Capts. Fred, James (Del), and David Morrissey, a great line of fishing skippers.

Willard Burnham, builder of the *Effie Morrissey,* died at Essex in March, 1919 at the age of 77. A native of Essex, he established a yard with Don Poland at Gloucester, and went to Essex after a few years, where he built many fine vessels, including the *Riegal, Procyon, Caviare, Hazel Oneita, W. E. Morrissey* and *Oliver Wendell Holmes.* Many vessels of the John F. Wonson firm were built by Mr. Burnham.

Capt. Bob Bartlett, who brought great fame to the *Effie M. Morrissey,* passed away in New York, in April, 1946 at the age of 70. A famous Arctic explorer, author and lecturer, he was a native of Brigus, Newfoundland, and came from a great family of sealing skippers.

Edward Rapp, 22, a native of Shelburne, Nova Scotia, was washed overboard on Grand Bank, November 13, 1899.

There seems to be confusion as to who really built the *Effie Morrissey.* The *Gloucester Daily Times* at the time said she was built by Willard Burnham. Some Essex folks claim she was built at the James yard.

Whoever built her did a great job. She was still afloat in the Cape Verde Islands in 1972, so far as I could determine.

Gross tons, 120; length, 93.6 feet; breadth, 23.8 feet; depth, 10.2 feet. Mainmast, overall, 76 feet; foremast, 74 feet; main boom, 68 feet; main gaff, 35 feet.

When she was sixty-one years old the former *Effie M. Morrissey* looked like this, renamed the *Ernestine*, hailing from Fogo, Cape Verde Islands, tied up in Providence, Rhode Island.

Patches in the heavy canvas sails hint at the
battering the *Ralph Russell* took. Jib topsail
is about to be hoisted.

Ralph Russell

HANDLINING ON THE CAPE COD
RIPS / 1894–1919?

Schooner *Ralph Russell* was a pretty little
vessel of 73 tons, built during the winter and
spring of 1894 by Tom Irving at Vincent Cove,
Gloucester, and launched April 18. She was of
the clipper bow type designed by Capt. G.
Melvin McClain of Rockport. She was owned
by the D. B. Smith Co.

The *Ralph Russell* was a splendid handlining vessel. Many schooners were built off
her model, including the *Alice M. Parsons,
George E. Lane, Jr., Pauline, Hattie L. Trask*
and *A. S. Caswell.*

The trial trip May 2, 1894, was a gala affair.
Many lady and gentleman guests enjoyed a fine
sail on Massachusetts Bay. The tug *Charlie,*
Capt. Charles T. Heberle, towed the craft down
the harbor. She was let go near Eastern Point
and in a fresh southwest breeze stood out
across the bay.

Nearing Halfway Rock, those on board were
treated to a beautiful marine spectacle, falling
in with fully a dozen vessels of the haddocking
fleet bound down from Boston with their fish.
They had all left T Wharf at the same time
and were having a fine race, with all sail set.

Well to the windward with a comfortable
lead was the fast *Braganza.* Close up with her
and to leeward were the schooners *John E. Mc-
Kenzie, Ramona, Essex, Sylvia Nunan, Clara
M. Littlefield* and others. As the new craft

sailed through the fleet she was greeted with cheers. The *Ralph Russell* returned about 4:30 p.m. and presented a pretty picture as she bowled up the harbor with all sail set. On her trial she was sailed by Capts. Richard Cunningham and Nathaniel Smith.

No one seemed to enjoy the trip more than four-year-old Master Ralph Russell Smith, for whom the schooner was named and whose picture decorated the cabin wall. Ralph Russell was the son of Benjamin A. Smith, junior partner of the firm.

The sails were made by Samuel V. Colby. She was rigged by Purdy Bros., painted by J. B. Maguire; iron work was done by Charles A. Marr.

The *Ralph Russell* sailed on her maiden trip, Georges handlining, in command of Capt. Robert Brideson, May 8, 1894. She arrived at Gloucester May 29 with 25,000 pounds cod and 800 pounds halibut.

Capt. Louis Johnson took over command in January, 1895. Capt. Fred Crawford, one of the old Georges handlining skippers, had command in 1897. Capt. William Corkum had her seining in 1899.

Capt. Jerry Cook took over in 1900 and remained in her several years, haddocking and seining. Capt. Cook did well during the seining season of 1901. On June 26 he arrived in Gloucester with 185 barrels salt mackerel and 100 barrels fresh mackerel. The trip was taken off South Shoal Lightship and was sold to Frank Stanwood for 10 cents each for large, and 6 cents each for medium. Mackerel was sold by count in those days.

On August 16, 1901, she got a 100-barrel haul off the Isles of Shoals.

While in command of Capt. Jerry Cook the *Ralph Russell* rescued the crew of a sinking coaster. On February 6, 1902, the schooner came upon the three-master *Annie E. Rickerson*, 45 miles east by north of Thacher's. The sinking vessel, loaded with lumber, was bound from St. John, New Brunswick, to New Haven, Connecticut, and had been struck by heavy gales. Her crew had been constantly at the pumps for over twenty-four hours. Seven foot of water was in the hold.

Capt. Cook saw her signal of distress and put over three dories, himself going in the last one. The coaster's crew of six men were safely taken off. Before leaving they set the wreck on fire as she was a menace to navigation. The shipwrecked men were landed at Gloucester.

In the fall of 1905 Capt. Owen Whitten had the *Ralph Russell*, pollocking. The season of 1906 Capt. Allan Dolman took her Rip fishing.

When the D. B. Smith Co. was consolidated into the Gorton-Pew Fisheries Co. in 1906, schooner *Ralph Russell* came under their ownership. From then on the vessel was used as a handline Rip fisherman in the spring and summer, and hauled up during the winter months.

Capt. Adolphus Amirault, father of Capt.

Brad Amirault of the dragger *Catherine Amirault* in later years, was the *Ralph Russell's* skipper from 1909 to 1912, Rip fishing, with the exception of the fall of 1909, when Capt. Ed Peterson took her pollocking.

Capt. Leander Phalen took over command in 1912 and remained in the vessel until 1919, Rip fishing. Her stock for 1910 was $11,417. In 1917 she stocked $15,761; in 1918, $12,143.

Rip fishing was one of the most important branches of the fisheries. Vessels of the *Ralph Russell* type and size were generally used, and men fished with hand lines from the deck, using heavy leads.

The name was derived from the place where they usually fished: the Rips off Cape Cod. The vessels anchored, as there was not much room to drift, and there was always a heavy tide running.

Fishermen have told me when they used to go to Edgartown for bait they passed these Rip fishermen with their lines strung way out astern because of the heavy tides.

The *Ralph Russell* bid farewell to Gloucester in October of 1919 when she and the schooners *William H. Rider* and *Pauline* were sold to Cuba for use in the snapper fishery in southern waters.

Capt. Robert P. Brideson, first skipper of the *Ralph Russell*, died in Gloucester October 16, 1930, at eighty-four. A native of the Isle of Man, he was one of the few English skippers in the fleet.

Capt. Jerry Cook died in Gloucester November 2, 1928, at fifty-six. He was a native of Shelburne, Nova Scotia. He was one of the great mariners, one of the best liked skippers out of Gloucester: smart, capable and always hustling. His commands included schooners *Pythian*, *Talisman*, *Nourmahal*, *Ralph Russell*, *Smuggler* (built for him), *J. J. Flaherty*, *Ingomar* and *Saladin*.

Capt. Jerry established a record in 1904 when he completed three Newfoundland herring trips in sixty-six days. During World War I he was an ensign in the United States Naval Reserve. After the war he entered the lightering and stevedore business. He was one of the early commanders of Capt. Lester S. Wass Post No. 3, American Legion.

Ralph Russell Smith died in Gloucester in April 1958 at sixty-eight. He was a native of Gloucester, long connected with the fisheries, and one of Gloucester's greatest yachtsmen. He was the owner's representative on board the schooner *Esperanto* in the International Fishermen's Races in 1920.

Gross tons, 73; net tons, 48; length, 83 feet; breadth, 22 feet; depth, 8.5 feet. Original spars: mainmast, deck to cap, 60 feet; foremast, deck to cap, 54.5 feet; main topmast, 34 feet; fore topmast, 27 feet; main gaff, 32 feet; fore boom, 24.5 feet; bowsprit, outboard, 26 feet; main boom, 57 feet; mastheads, 8 feet.

Probably as nice a picture as anyone ever got of a fishing vessel, in the author's opinion. Aboard the *Admiral Dewey* men work on the bowsprit, dories are nested upside down. At right, "Pure Ale" sign marks brewery that produced Amber Ale on the Gloucester waterfront.

Admiral Dewey

One of the producers in the Chisholm fleet at the turn of the century was schooner *Admiral Dewey*, an Essex-built vessel, fairly good sized, not very fast but on rugged lines which made her able for long voyages to the great water to the northward.

The *Dewey*, built during the strenuous Spanish-American War days, was named for the famous Admiral George Dewey who rose to fame as commander of the United States fleet which defeated the Spanish armada in Manila Bay. Only a few oldtimers remember the *Dewey's* skipper, Capt. Jim Hayes, whose name was legion among the halibut catchers of the old days and who was always a highliner or close to the top in his game.

She was launched at the Tarr and James yard, Essex, on Friday, July 22, 1898, for Capt. John Chisholm. Capt. Hayes was also a part owner. There was little fanfare and the launching was briefly announced by the mere statement of fact that she was over, towed around from Essex by tug *Eveleth*, and would be commanded fresh halibuting by Capt. James Hayes. The nation was at war with Spain. Gloucester was in the headlines through the famous gunboat of the name, U. S. S. *Gloucester*, which was the potent factor in the defeat of Cervera's squadron at Santiago. Work was hustled in preparation of this new vessel and in less than three weeks, on Wednesday, August 10, 1898, the spanking new schooner *Admiral Dewey*, Capt. Jim Hayes, was towed down the harbor, sailed out around Eastern Point and set course to the east and northward on her maiden voyage, fresh halibuting.

Forty-one days later, schooner *Admiral Dewey* returned with the first fare of 50,000 pounds of fresh halibut, caught on Baccalieu Bank, in latitude 52.21, longitude 51, which the chart shows is pretty well northward of Grand Bank and almost east of the Straits of Belle Isle. That was a long haul, 800 to 1000 miles, a customary jaunt for Gloucester's fresh halibuters of that period. The maiden trip stocked $2630 and the share was $66.23.

Contemporary with the *Admiral Dewey* were the *Nannie C. Bohlin, Monitor, Norma, Argo, Gladiator, Emma* and *Helen, Eliza B. Campbell, American, Senator, Judique, Arthur D. Story, Sarah E. Lee* and others, all halibuters. The *Bohlin* and *Lee* were spoken on Baccalieu on the maiden trip.

The *Dewey* lived a long and useful life, making many long but usually successful trips in the pursuit of halibut, mostly fresh, but frequently during the summer, fletched trips. One trip lasted three months, when the craft was out of sight of land and vessels in the far reaches of the Atlantic.

Capt. Hayes' career was cut short in the spring of 1910 when he was landed ill at Newfoundland, where he died. His body was sent to Halifax, Nova Scotia, his native land, for burial. Charles Olson took over command of the ship and finished the trip.

The *Dewey* was sold to S. Tibbo, Grand Bank, Newfoundland, in January, 1911, and continued in the business of fishing for years after. Under British registry the *Dewey* returned to Gloucester at least twice, November 19, 1918, with a cargo of salt cod and again in January, 1926, also with salt cod.

Like most ships, schooner *Admiral Dewey* came to an untimely end, on September 10, 1932. The craft parted chains during an east-northeast gale in Miquelon Roads, was driven ashore and became a total loss. Capt. Tom Hardy was her commander at the time.

In the fine Blatchford photo of the *Admiral Dewey* can be seen the big wooden stock anchor on her port bow. These anchors were a very important part of a vessel's equipment. They could mean life or death to her crew.

The fisherman anchors were made by the famous Cape Ann Anchor Works at Gloucester from 1844 to 1917. They were made in parts, using old horseshoes, pig iron, etc., for material, and the parts were forged together.

The oldtime wood stock anchors had immense holding power and they could not foul easily. In the early days as high as 400 anchors were sold in a month. They were in demand along the entire Atlantic and Gulf coasts.

The *Admiral Dewey's* anchors weighed around 700 pounds each. She carried two. The 14-foot wooden stocks could be taken out and the anchors stowed on deck. About 400 or 500 fathoms of cable were carried by the *Dewey*.

For years the price of these anchors was six cents per pound. The wooden stocks cost about $4 each.

In the old days the crew would heave in the anchor, two men holding the cable, two men coiling and quite a gang at the windlass brakes. Later, hoisting engines were used.

Gross tons, 111; length, 92 feet; breadth, 24.3 feet; depth, 10.3 feet. Mainmast, deck to cap, 86 feet; foremast, 63 feet; main boom, 65 feet; bowsprit, outboard, 32 feet, later cut to 29.5 feet; main masthead, 10 feet.

Dauntless

ONE OF THE FINEST EVER BUILT /
1899–1957

The schooner *Dauntless* merits recognition as one of the finest fishing schooners ever built.

She was launched at the Tarr and James yard in Essex on January 11, 1899 for Capt. Charles C. Young of Gloucester. It is said that Tarr and James never built a poor vessel. *Dauntless* certainly proved that she was one of their finest.

She was off the *Arbitrator* model, an original Washington Tarr design, and a medium sized, clipper bow vessel, with beautiful lines. She was named after the schooner yacht *Dauntless*, a famous ocean racer.

The *Dauntless* sailed on her maiden trip halibuting January 31, 1899 in command of her owner, returning March 6, 1899 from Quero Bank with 25,000 pounds of halibut. During that March, severe gales struck the fleet and many craft came limping home battered by the elements. The new schooner *Dauntless* did not even lose a rope yarn. Her crew praised her highly.

Capt. Young took the *Dauntless* halibuting during the spring and summer of 1900 and to Newfoundland in December for a cargo of herring. One of her crew was washed overboard and drowned on the way down. In 1901, Capt. Young had her seining. On December 30, 1901, she arrived from Bay of Islands with 1,200 barrels of herring, gone only 25 days on the whole trip.

During the winter of 1902–03, the *Dauntless* was frozen in at Newfoundland with seven other American fishermen.

The *Dauntless* during her entire career in Gloucester was owned by Capt. Young, who lost his life in a fire at his camp on Vine Street, Gloucester, in June, 1932.

During 1903–04, Capt. William Publicover returned to sea and made two Newfoundland trips. On December 25, 1904, under his command, *Dauntless* arrived in Gloucester with a full cargo of salt herring, 80,000 in count. Capt. Publicover, one of Gloucester's finest cooks, had made many trips with Capt. Jack Greenlaw. Capt. Publicover was owner and manager of one of Gloucester's finest hotels, the Rockaway.

On July 12 of 1907, during heavy fog on Georges, the French liner *LaProvence* cut off the stern of the schooner's seine boat that was being towed on a short painter. This was the same dense fog in which the seining schooner *Natalie B. Nickerson* of Boothbay and the Boston swordfisherman *Shepherd King* were run down and sunk while fishing in Cape Cod waters, fortunately without loss of life.

Many fine skippers commanded the *Dauntless*, including Capt. Merrill Day, seining, 1904 and 1905; Capt. S. Campbell Peart, seining, 1906; Capt. Alfred Thorpe of Newfoundland in 1907; Capt. Tom Downie, seining, 1907; Capt. Don Mac Cuish, Newfoundland for herring, 1907; Capt. John Matheson, seining, 1908–09; Capt. Ambrose Fleet, seining, 1910; Capt. Wesley Farmer, seining, 1911.

On January 3, 1909 the *Dauntless* sailed from the Bay Islands in company with the schooners *Ralph L. Hall* and *Lottie G. Merchant*. All three vessels left within an hour of each other. On January 11, the *Dauntless* dropped anchor in Gloucester, with the other two schooners only a few minutes behind. This was pretty close sailing.

In 1911 the *Dauntless*, under command of Capt. John Glynn, came near to leaving her bones in the Bay of Islands. In trying to make Lark Harbor she was struck by a sudden puff of wind, laying the schooner flat on the water with one side under. She slowly righted herself and made port. Again the *Dauntless* proved her staunchness.

In March, 1912, the fine little *Dauntless* was sold by Capt. Young to Capt. C. Rose of Jersey Harbor, Newfoundland. In 1919, she was banking out of Grand Bank, Newfoundland, and owned by G. Harris.

The *Dauntless*, with her rig cut down and fitted with auxiliary power, was in the Newfoundland coastal trade under Capt. Jones. At that time it was said her hull was as good as the day she was built. Capt. Chesley Walters of the Newfoundland motor vessel *Garnish Queen*, when I talked with him on a trip to Gloucester, told me he made a trip across the Atlantic in the *Dauntless* in 1935 and she behaved wonderfully. However, the mastless hulk of the *Dauntless* was hauled up on a beach at Harbor Grace, Newfoundland, in 1957, to fall to pieces.

Capt. Young, Gloucester owner of the *Dauntless*, was a native of Denmark. He was an authority on the Newfoundland herring fishery. At one time he represented the John Chisholm interests there. In 1910 he was selected by Congressman A. P. Gardner to go to The Hague to arbitrate the fish question between the U. S. and Canada. He was 69 when he died, in 1932.

Gross tons, 111; net tons, 77; length, 91 feet; breadth, 24.2 feet; depth, 10.2 feet. Original spar measurements: mainmast (deck to map), 68 feet; foremast, 64 feet; main topmast, 40 feet; fore topmast, 35.5 feet; main boom, 65 feet; main gaff, 36 feet; bowsprit (outboard), 31 feet; mainmast head, 10 feet.

In Rip fishing, a specialty of the *Lucinda I. Lowell*, men handled baited lines from the deck of the schooner, standing at special rails.

Lucinda I. Lowell

HER BIG TRIPS WERE THE TALK OF THE WATERFRONT / 1899–1966

Schooner *Lucinda I. Lowell* was built during the spring and summer of 1899 by Arthur D. Story in Essex. She was launched in August of that year, and was towed around to Gloucester to await a purchaser. The new craft was sold to the D. B. Smith Co. of Gloucester and given the name of *Lucinda I. Lowell* after a member of the Lowell family of Amesbury, famous dory builders.

Incidentally, the firm of Hiram Lowell and Son at Amesbury Point built 23,000 dories from 1871 to 1897. With an average length of 18 feet each, this made more than 80 miles of boats.

The *Lucinda Lowell* was a fine, able, medium sized vessel of clipper bow type, taken off the model of the schooner *Esther Anita*. At the time of her advent she was considered one of the finest vessels in the fleet. Capt. Antone (Tony) Courant, veteran Portuguese, and one of the finest mariners out of Gloucester, was given command of the new craft.

The *Lucinda I. Lowell* in command of Capt. Courant arrived in Gloucester with her maiden fare on October 5, 1899 from Western Bank. She hailed for 150,000 lbs. fresh cod, which was one of the largest shack trips that had been brought in.

Capt. Tony's big trips in the *Lowell* were the talk of the waterfront. On March 30, 1900, she arrived from the Peak with 173,000 lbs. cod, breaking the record of the schooner *Talisman* made a few years previously. The *Lowell's* stock on this trip was $1,800, with a share of $40 each.

On April 24, 1900, Capt. Tony broke his own record when he brought the *Lowell* into Gloucester with 178,000 lbs. cod, also caught on the Peak. This was the largest fare of fresh fish landed up to that time in the history of the North American fisheries. Capt. Courant broke this record in the schooner *Gossip* in May, 1901, when he landed over 200,000 lbs. fresh fish.

When the *Lowell* arrived with this second big trip, she was said to have been the deepest fish laden craft that ever entered Gloucester. On this trip she stocked $1820 and the crew shared $48 each. Just think of it, two mammoth trips and the crew sharing only $88 each! The Lucinda *Lowell's* total stock in her first 13 months was $28,000.

Capt. Courant left the *Lucinda Lowell* in November, 1900 to take over the new schooner *Gossip*. The *Lowell's* new skipper was Capt. Douglass McLean, who remained until the winter of 1901–02, haddocking and seining.

Capt. Roderick (Rod) McNeil was the next skipper of the *Lowell*, remaining in her until 1905, haddocking, halibuting, shacking and salt banking. While under Capt. McNeil's command, disaster overtook the craft on December 5, 1902. On her way home from Newfoundland with 1250 bbls. salt herring, a sudden gale struck her, breaking her rudder, and Capt. McNeil, unable to clear the coast, let go the anchors but she continued to drag. The masts were cut away to ease the vessel and the mate, George Roberts, was killed by a falling spar. The vessel dragged ashore and struck on a ledge of rocks off Cranberry Light, Canso, Nova Scotia. Heavy seas began to break over her. A dory was put over and Peter Fougere, one of the crew, jumped in, but a sea swept the dory away. He was never seen again. The survivors, suffering terribly from the cold were taken off by the tug *Active*. The *Lowell* was later floated and towed into Canso. She arrived in Gloucester in tow of the Halifax tug *F. W. Roebling* on December 31, 1902.

George Roberts was 48 years old and a native of Maine. Peter Fougere was 32 years old and a native of St. Peter, Cape Breton.

Capt. Douglass McLean again took command in 1905, fresh cod fishing on the Peak. During February of that year, the *Lowell* was driven ashore by ice at Sandy Point, Shelburne, Nova Scotia. She was floated within a week with little damage. She was taken to Liverpool, Nova Scotia, for repairs. The following March she weathered beautifully 15 successive days of gales, sometimes of almost hurricane force. During one of these gales Capt. McLean nearly lost his life when he was swept overboard by a big sea and washed right back onto the vessel again.

Capt. Tom Benham had the *Lucinda Lowell* cod and pollock seining off Sable Island in 1906. Capt. Maurice Fogarty had her halibuting in her in 1907. Capt. Jim McHenry had her flitched halibuting and deck hand lining in 1908. On August 19, 1908 he landed 90,000 lbs. flitched halibut at Gloucester. They were caught on Baccalieu Bank.

On January 27, 1908, in command of Capt. Tom Benham, she arrived from Jordan River, Nova Scotia, with 400 bbls. salt herring.

During the season of 1909, Capt. Simeon Hirtle had her dory handlining.

In command of Capt. Jack Burton, the *Lowell*

arrived in Gloucester on November 26, 1909 with 1200 bbls. herring from Newfoundland, being the first of the fleet to arrive home that season.

Capt. Will Larkin was the skipper in 1910, salt banking.

Capts. Charles Wilson and Simon Theriault were the skippers in 1912. While in command of Capt. Wilson one of her crew, Robert Frazier was found dead in his bunk on October 10, 1912 while the vessel was at Provincetown for bait. He was 62 years old and a native of Harbor Bushee, Nova Scotia.

Capt. Dan McCuish was the *Lowell's* skipper halibuting in 1913. On May 27th of that year, she arrived in Gloucester with two French fishermen, members of the French salt banker *Juliette*, who were rescued on Quero Bank the previous week, after being astray a day and a half. They were sent to their homes in France by the French consul.

Capt. Oscar Lyons was the next skipper of the *Lucinda Lowell*, using her drifting during the seasons of 1914–15 and 1916. Capt. Lyons was one of the high liners of the drifters.

An interesting incident occurred on May 22, 1916, when Capt. Lyons and his crew picked up 10,000 feet of lumber, lost from a coaster, off Highland Light, Cape Cod.

The *Lucinda Lowell* was taken over by the Gorton-Pew Co. in 1906 when that firm was established. In 1916, she was transferred to the Manes Fishing Co., a subsidiary of Gorton-Pew. During that year she sailed to Norway in command of Capt. Fred Thompson, to engage in fishing in European waters. In August, 1916, she was seized, with the schooners *Lizzie Griffin* and *Maxine Elliott*, by a British warship and taken to the Shetland Islands where they were searched for contraband. All the vessels were later released.

The *Lucinda I. Lowell* was last registered in Lloyd's 1927, as the auxiliary schooner *Taakeheimen* of Bobo, Norway.

She was wrecked in ice in June, 1966. The crew was landed at Reykjavik, Iceland.

Capt. Antone Courant, first skipper of the *Lucinda I. Lowell*, died at eighty-five September 18, 1934. Capt. Tony was not only one of the greatest Portuguese skippers, but one of the greatest mariners who ever sailed past Eastern Point. For years he hammered at and broke records in the fresh fishery. Short and stocky in stature; courageous, capable and respected in virtue; a real sea dog of the North Atlantic. Capt. Tony never lost a man and experienced only one shipwreck, when his schooner *Smuggler* was lost on Cape Cod in December, 1895. After he retired from fishing, he was employed as night watchman at his old firm of D. B. Smith Co. During my youth I spent many happy evenings with Capt. Tony on the old Smith Wharf.

His commands included the schooners *William Wellington*, *Smuggler*, (built 1877), *Nellie G. Thurston*, *A. S. Caswell*, *Lucinda I. Lowell*, *Gossip*, and the new *Smuggler* built in 1902. He was a native of Fayal, Azores.

Capt. Roderick H. McNeil passed away at Sailors Snug Harbor, New York, on April 27, 1947, at the age of 88. Capt. McNeil, affectionately known as "Rod the Shacker," was another of our great mariners in the days of sail. Smart, well liked, and a good fisherman, Rod the Shacker never had any difficulty shipping a good crew. His commands include the schooners *Richard Steele*, *Lucinda I. Lowell*, *Titania*, *Henry N. Woods*, *S. F. Maker* and many others. The last 20 years of his life were spent at Sailors Snug Harbor. He was a native of McKinnon's Bay, Cape Breton.

In the days of the *Lucinda Lowell*, the distances to be sailed and the size of the vessel were never thought of. The crew knew what they had to face and they were equal to the task. Rather than filleting machines and larger boats, what the old port of Gloucester needs is men of the calibre of Capts. Tony Courant and Rod McNeil.

Gross tons, 110; net tons, 77; length, 93 feet; breadth, 24 feet; depth, 9.7 feet.

Niagara

THE MOST PHOTOGRAPHED VESSEL / 1899–1910

On postcards and pilot cracker boxes appeared pictures of this typical schooner, the *Niagara*. Photographs of her are rare now.

Schooner *Niagara*. Mention of her name brings back memories of our glorious past. The *Niagara* was probably the most photographed vessel of our fleet, back in the early part of the century. Chosen as a typical Gloucester fishing schooner, she adorned many advertisements and souvenir books of Cape Ann. Her sketch appeared for many years in the *Gloucester Times*, advertising the annual vessel list, published by Procter Brothers. Her picture also was used on the label of the famous Hubbard pilot crackers.

The *Niagara* was a fine, able vessel with a clipper bow, taken from a new model by Capt. George (Mel) McClain of Rockport. She was owned by Samuel C. Pool and Sons of Gloucester and was used most of her career in the halibut fishery. Many top notch halibut skippers commanded her. The *Niagara* was named after the famous American steam yacht of that name.

The keel of the *Niagara* was laid at the James and Tarr yard, Essex, in January 1899. She slid into the waters of Essex River on May 1, 1899. The tug *Startle* towed her to Gloucester to fit for sea.

The *Niagara* sailed on her maiden trip halibuting in command of Capt. Jack Carroll, one of our famous mariners, on May 27, 1899. A crowd gathered on Atlantic wharf to see the new "Queen" off. A party of invited guests took the trip down the harbor in tow of the tug *Eveleth*. In the outer harbor the guests were taken off by the tug and then Robert Phelps took photos of the vessel as she rounded Eastern Point, bound to the eastward.

The *Niagara* returned to Gloucester on June 22, 1899 with her maiden fare of 70,000 lbs. halibut which were taken off Bonne Bay, Newfoundland. This was a splendid catch to start the new craft off, but prices were low and the vessel stocked only $1959 with a share of $45 per man. She had been absent 24 days on the trip. Schooner *Georgie Campbell*, Capt. Sam Colson and schooner *Alva*, Capt. Jack McKay also arrived on that day hailing for 50,000 lbs. halibut which were caught in the same vicinity.

The *Niagara* arrived home with her second trip on July 31, 1899, hailing for 60,000 halibut caught on Baccalieu Bank. The share on this trip was $82. Capt. Carroll certainly knew where the halibut were! Incidentally this second trip was taken out at the New England Fish Co. in the remarkable time of five hours, all by hand.

Capt. Carroll remained in command of the *Niagara* until June, 1901, when he took over the new schooner *Massachusetts*. Capt. Adelbert (Del) Nickerson, another of our great halibuters, was the next skipper of the *Niagara*, remaining at the helm until September 1903. Capt. Del kept up his fine reputation in the *Niagara*, landing many large trips of halibut, One of his splendid fares was landed on August 25, 1903, consisting of 70,000 lbs. halibut caught on Baccalieu Bank.

Capt. Del was also a great sail carrier and one of his fast passages occurred in November 1901. The *Niagara* started from the eastern edge of Grand Bank in a fresh northeast breeze which turned into a roaring gale. With her helmsman lashed to the wheel during most of the passage the vessel made Gloucester in 82 hours.

Capt. Dan (Little Dan) McDonald took over command of the *Niagara* halibuting in September 1903. Capt. Gus Swinson took over in 1904 and remained as skipper through 1905–06 and part of 1907, landing many fine trips of halibut. Capt. Dick Wadding was skipper in November 1907. During 1908, Captains Fred Thompson and Tom Mason were skippers halibuting. Capt. Fred Thompson finished the season of 1908, high up among the halibut leaders, stocking $20,301.

Capt. Jim Bowie took over halibuting in March, 1909 and in the fall of that year, Capt. Charles Wilson was her skipper. The *Niagara's* last skipper was Capt. Melvin (Roaring Mel) Kilpatrick, who took over in November 1909 and lost her the following spring.

The *Niagara's* flag was half masted eight times during her career for the loss of eight of her crew. Thomas Doody and George Campbell went astray on Quero Bank on April 6, 1900 and were never heard of again. Doody was 31 years old, a native of Kettle Island, Newfoundland. Campbell, 50 years old, was a native of Nova Scotia. Capt. Jack Carroll was skipper at the time.

William McCreigh was washed from the main boom and drowned while taking in the mainsail off Cape Sable, Nova Scotia, on January 24, 1901. He was a native of Salmonear, Newfoundland and was 34 years old. Capt. Jack Carroll was the Niagara's skipper.

On December 9, 1904, Isaac Olson and Carl Danielson were drowned when their dory was run down by the vessel off Cape Sable, Nova Scotia. During a sudden snow squall, the Niagara, jogging about while the men were on their trawls, crashed into the dory, capsizing it and spilling the men into the water. Because of their heavy clothing, they were unable to grasp the bobstay and soon sank from sight. The unfortunate men were natives of Finland. Capt. Gus Swinson was skipper at the time.

Joseph Myers died in the hospital at Vineyard Haven on May 28, 1906 from a broken neck resulting from a fall received in Gloucester previous to the vessel's sailing. Myers was landed at Vineyard Haven in a paralyzed condition and death followed soon after. He was a native of Germany and was 44 years old. Gus Swinson was skipper.

John Edward Anderson lost his footing, fell overboard and drowned off Eastern Point on April 8, 1907, while the craft was bound out. A dory was put out but Anderson sank from sight. He was a native of Oland in the Baltic Sea and was 32 years of age. Gus Swinson was skipper.

Charles Peterson was washed overboard and drowned on Quero, April 19, 1908. He was 43 years old, a native of Denmark. Fred Thompson was skipper.

The end of the Niagara came on April 27, 1910. The vessel in command of Capt. Mel Kilpatrick was making for Canso, Nova Scotia, for bait, and during a dense fog struck on Wash Ball Shoal, southeast of Cranberry Island light, Canso, Nova Scotia. The doomed vessel began to pound badly and the crew left in their dories, rowing four miles to Canso. When they left the vessel, the water was over the forecastle floor. The next day all that showed of the wreck was four feet of the topmasts sticking out of water. She later broke in two, part of the hull sinking in deep water and the other part driven up on the beach.

A partial list of the crew at the time were Capt. Mel Kilpatrick, Capt. Jim McHenry (one of crew), Joseph Johnson, Norman Smith, Andrew Tennyson, Andrew Nelson, Fred Wennerberg, Thomas Simmons, James Cavanaugh, Thomas Williams, Charles Atkins, Albert Somes, Sylvester Mitchell, Peter Phalen and L. E. Johnson.

Capt. John Carroll, first skipper of the Niagara, passed away at Sailors Snug Harbor, Staten Island, New York, March 19, 1939 at the age of 71.

Capt. Carroll was one of our greatest halibuters and commanded many fine vessels, including the Gladstone, Carrier Dove, Lizzie Greenleaf, Oresa, Alva, Arbutus, Niagara and Massachusetts. In 1910 he went to the Pacific coast and engaged in the halibut fishery for 10 years, later returning to Gloucester. He also served as mate on several coast-wise steamers. He was a native of Fortune Harbor, Newfoundland.

Capt. Adelbert Nickerson also was one of our great halibuters. Few skippers landed any more halibut than Capt. Del. He commanded many vessels while 30 years as master, including schooners Puritan, Eliza Campbell, Mayflower, Niagara, Tacoma, Senator and Agnes. Capt. Del went south to engage in the snapper fishery and was lost with all hands in the schooner Chicopee in the great August gale in 1915 in the Gulf of Mexico. He was a native of Argyle, Nova Scotia.

Capt. Augustus Swinson was swept overboard to his death while a member of the crew of schooner Kineo, Capt. John G. Stream, on Georges, March 9, 1908. His commands included schooners Lizzie B. Adams, Blanche, Niagara and Harvard. He was a native of Sweden.

Capts. Jack Carroll, Del Nickerson and Gus Swinson—three great skippers—Newfoundlander, Nova Scotian and Swede. Strong, able and courageous men. Men who knew what they were doing and where they were going. Men who were admired and respected by their crews. Men who were leaders in the hardest branch of the fisheries, halibuting. Men who were a credit to their native and adopted lands. Builders of Gloucester.

Gross tons, 112; net tons, 78; length, 97.3 feet; breadth, 25.5 feet; depth, 10 feet. Original spar measurments: mainmast, 71.5 feet (deck to cap); foremast, 64 feet; main topmast, 41 feet; main gaff, 37 feet; mainboom, 65 feet; bowsprit (outboard), 27 feet.

Helen Miller Gould

FIRST TO SWITCH TO POWER / 1900–1901

Schooner *Helen Miller Gould* was the first large Gloucester fisherman to be fitted with auxiliary engines and really marked the beginning of the transition from sail to power for the Gloucester fleet. Under Capt. Solomon Jacobs, the *Gould* was a stupendous moneymaker in the 18 months of her short life.

Capt. G. Melvin McClain of Rockport was the designer. She had fine lines and a clipper bow. The schooner was built by John Bishop at the Vincent Cove yard, Gloucester, in the winter of 1899–1900 for Capt. Jacobs and was launched on March 29, 1900 at a spectacular affair before an estimated crowd of 3000 people. On board when the craft slipped into the water were Capt. Jacobs, Capt. Mel McClain, Capt. Thaddeus Morgan, Capt. Joseph Cusick and many others. The skipper's daughter, Miss Ethel Jacobs, broke the traditional bottle of wine and christened the vessel.

The *Gould* had a 150 h.p. Globe engine, said to be the largest in the country at the time. This drove her at eight knots. A 35 h.p. Globe was installed at first as the big plant was not ready. Dick Smith, a Negro, was the first engineer.

She was named for the famous daughter of Jay Gould, New York financier. No time was lost in equipping the *Gould* for sea, and on April 11, 1900, there was a trial trip, Gloucester to Beverly and return with about 200 guests.

The *Gould* sailed the following day, April 12, in pursuit of the wily mackerel.

Less than a month from the day of the launching, the *Helen Miller Gould* was at New York with the maiden fare of 200 barrels of fresh mackerel, handled by George T. Moon and Cheseboro Brothers and sold for 9 and 10 cents each. The *Gould* was highline seiner in 1900 with a stock of $40,660 and a share of $863, a record stock and share for seining up to that time.

On September 3, 1900, Capt. Jacobs brought the *Helen Miller Gould* home with 720 barrels of mackerel (470 salt and 250 fresh). Dories and the deck were full of mackerel from windlass to the wheel.

The mackerel season of 1901 was a repetition of the big year of 1900. On April 8, 1901, Capt. Jacobs, in the *Gould*, landed the first mackerel of the season at Fortress Munroe, Va., a fare of 35 bbls.

The marvelous career of the *Gould* was cut short as this splendid vessel was destroyed by fire on October 25, 1901 at North Sydney, Nova Scotia. The craft was on a fall Cape Shore seining trip at the time. The blaze started by a leak in the gasoline apparatus and danger from explosion of the gasoline tanks prevented any attempt to save the vessel. The crew were saved but lost all their personal belongings. Value of the *Gould* was put at $22,000.

Mrs. Helen Miller Gould Shepherd died in 1938.

Gross tons, 149; net tons, 99; length, 117 feet; breadth, 25.4 feet; depth, 10 feet. Mainmast, 80 feet overall; mainboom, 70 feet; main gaff, 42 feet; bowsprit, 28 feet (outboard).

Look, ma, no sails. . . . The *Helen Miller Gould* tries out her engine. Her foresail is ready for hoisting.

On her maiden trip, who'd have dreamed
that the *Monarch* would become a downtown restaurant and a rumrunner.

Monarch

RESTAURANT AND RUM-RUNNER /
1900–1932?

Schooner *Monarch* is best remembered by many Gloucester folks as this port's original floating restaurant.

One of the John Chisholm fleet, she was launched in January, 1900, at the Tarr and James yard, Essex.

The photo shows her in outer Gloucester harbor on her maiden trip, haddocking, starting February 1, 1900, under command of Capt. Sewall Smith.

Designed from the *Fredonia* and *Indiana* models with a clipper bow, but with the long bowsprit typical of the era, she was used in seining and halibuting, as well as haddocking, and made many trips to Newfoundland during the fall and winter in the salt herring branch.

A number of skippers who attained fame in the heyday of seining craft commanded the *Monarch.* They included Capts. William H. Thomas, John F. Vautier, Norman A. Ross, John J. Matheson, Dan Brady, Robertson (Strings) Giffin and Iver Carlson, the latter one of her last Gloucester skippers in the halibut branch in 1918.

On a seining trip under command of Capt. Vautier in May, 1909, *Monarch* struck the sunken wreck of the fourmasted schooner *Jennie Lippert*, lost in December 1908 with most of her crew on Winter Quarter shoal. *Monarch* ripped off 20 feet of her keel and shoe.

While hauled up at the Chisholm slip, foot of Water Street, during 1912, 1913 and 1914, Gus Quinn, one of the most famous cooks of his day, lived aboard. He conceived the idea of noon "mug-ups" for a few nearby workers. The "mug-up" business expanded and the spacious *Monarch* forecastle became the noon gathering place for many, many people.

Gus Quinn was a hustler, hard worker, a great cook. No one ever left his friendly forecastle with anything but a full stomach. It was fishermen's style, the forecastle table covered with dishes heaped high with tempting viands, not the least of them Quinn's hot biscuits and home-made bread. Seems to me the charge was a quarter. What a quarter's worth!

In 1922, Gorton-Pew Fisheries Co., Ltd., which acquired the vessel about 1916, sold her to British registry and she was registered out of Nassau, Bahama Islands (1924). The craft was renamed the *George Francis* and was used as a rum runner. In 1928–30, Lloyd's registered the craft from Cuba. She disappeared from the register in 1932.

The craft took a cargo of salt fish to Greece in 1919, sailing from here November 22, 1919, in command of Capt. Larsen, returning March 24, 1920.

A 100-horsepower Standard gas engine was installed in 1907, with exhaust pipes on both sides, the first such installation. Leslie Malloch was engineer four years. He got 9½ knots out of her, towing two seineboats.

Freeman A. Munroe, 27, a native of Whitehead, Nova Scotia, drowned August 1, 1918, when he was washed from the bowsprit on LaHave Bank. Six men including the skipper, Iver Carlson, were on the bowsprit taking in the sail. Capt. Carlson and a man named Gillon also were swept off. Carlson and Gillon were rescued, but Munroe was never seen again.

Gross tons, 127; net tons, 93; length, 103 feet; breadth, 24.8 feet; depth, 10.8 feet. Mainmast, deck to cap, 71 feet; foremast, 64 feet; main topmast, 40 feet; main gaff, 39 feet; bowsprit, outboard, original, 31 feet.

Rob Roy

NEW LOOK FOR A NEW CENTURY / 1900–1918

Schooner *Rob Roy*, when launched in April, 1900, showed a radical departure in design of fishing vessels hereabouts. She was cut away forward and had a spoon bow, short foremast and short bowsprit.

She was designed by B. B. Crowninshield, noted Boston yacht designer, and built at Essex by Arthur D. Story for George Steele of Gloucester. Her maiden trip ended at Boston October 20, 1900, when she hailed for 28,000 pounds of fresh fish. Capt. Julius Anderson was her first skipper, transferring in 1902 to the *Robert and Arthur*.

Not a very fast vessel, *Rob Roy* was used in practically all branches of the fishery: seining, haddocking, shacking, drifting, Georges handling, halibuting and fletched halibuting. Her best earnings were while seining, under Capt. Lemuel R. Firth, stocking $15,145 in 1913, $18,779 in 1914, $26,658 in 1915 and $43,269 in 1916. Capt. Peter Strescino did well in 1918, stocking $37,540 single dory fishing.

On December 8, 1908, the *Rob Roy*, Capt. William Clark, rescued the crew of the sinking coaster *Modoc*, 46 miles southwest of Matinicus Rock, Maine.

Capt. Patsy Vale took her to Greenland, fletched halibuting, in 1911. While in the Gorton-Pew fleet she was commanded also by Capts. Fred Carritt, William Clark, Jack McKeoughan, Dan McKay, John Glynn, John Carrigan, John McInnis and Freeman Crowell.

Two 27-horsepower Wolverine gasoline engines were installed in 1913. On July 14, 1914, with Lem Firth in command, the *Rob Roy* picked up the 17-man crew of the schooner *Galatea*, lost on Rose and Crown Shoal.

The *Rob Roy*, in command of Capt. Freeman Crowell, was sunk by German U-boat 156 off Seal Island, Nova Scotia, August 13, 1918, in company with the *Annie Perry* and the *Muriel* of Boston.

George Steele was one of the foremost vessel owners in Gloucester. He was always eager to promote new design in the fleet which could bring greater speed in getting to market and reducing the great loss of human lives.

His schooners *James Steele* and *Richard Steele* in 1891 and the *Rob Roy* in 1900 were great improvements over their predecessors.

Steele's place of business was on Rogers Street in Gloucester in 1857 and remained there until 1905, when the firm was taken over by his sons Howard and James under the firm name of H. and J. Steele. In October 1907 the firm went out of business and the fleet was sold to the Gorton-Pew company. The Steele wharf was sold to Davis Brothers in 1909.

George Steele passed away in Gloucester on November 10, 1906. He was 78, and a native of Gloucester. He was one of Cape Ann's greatest insurance agents, with marine insurance a specialty.

Some of the Steele vessels were schooners *Monmouth, Carthage, Plymouth Rock, Zenobia, Braganza, Almeida, Dido, Ramona, Vera, Olga, Latona, James Steele, Richard Steele* and *Rob Roy*.

Gross tons, 111; length, 96 feet; breadth, 23.6 feet; depth, 10.6 feet; sail area, 6,000 square yards. Mainmast, 82 feet (overall); foremast, 70 feet; main boom, 64 feet; main topmast, 40 feet; bowsprit, 23 feet outboard.

For her size, the *Annie M. Parker* could carry a lot of fish.

Annie M. Parker

LAST OF THE PLUMBSTEMMERS /
1901–1924

In the late 1880's there were a great many "plumbstemmed" fishing schooners. With the advent of the sharp clipper bow and round bow vessel in the 90's the popularity of the straight-stemmers waned. However, in 1901 two schooners of this model were built in the Arthur D. Story yard in Essex, the *George Parker* and the *Annie M. Parker*, both for the George Parker firm in Boston. These two "plumbstemmers," identical in size and rig, proved to be the last of their type built for the New England fisheries.

The *George Parker* was launched on May 22, 1901, and sailed on a fletched halibut trip that summer in command of Capt. Albert Flygare of Gloucester. The *George Parker* was sold to Hugh Parkhurst of Gloucester in April, 1904 to replace schooner *Rival*, that had been lost that spring. She sailed out of Gloucester until March, 1912, when she was sold to Newfoundland parties, and she was lost at sea the following June.

The *Annie M. Parker* was launched at the Story yard on September 17, 1901. She was fitted at Gloucester and sailed to Newfoundland on a herring voyage October 5, 1901, under the able command of Capt. Charles Flygare, one of Gloucester's finest skippers. (Two sister ships on their maiden trips in command of two brothers.)

On her homeward passage she was buffeted by gales, and when crossing the Gulf of St. Lawrence, her deck load of herring was washed overboard. She arrived at Boston on December 6, 1901 just two months from the date of her sailing. In coming up the harbor she grounded, but was easily floated at high tide, and towed to T Wharf to discharge her cargo of 1800 bbls. of salt herring.

In the summer of 1902, the *Parker* went seining in command of Capt. Jack O'Brien and he remained in her for the next several years. While on a Newfoundland herring voyage in January, 1904 under Capt. O'Brien, she was caught in the ice at the Bay of St. George, Newfoundland, and remained there until the following May when the ice broke up and she was released.

In January, 1905 she was again nipped in the ice, this time at the Bay of Islands, and remained there all winter in company with the schooners *Arabia, Lewis H. Giles*, and *Hattie Graham*. Capt. Douglass McLean took her seining in 1906.

The *Annie M.* came under Gloucester ownership in 1906, when she was acquired by the Gorton-Pew company.

Capt. Angus Hines was her next commander and for several years took her dory handlining and Newfoundland herring voyages. At one time when the *Parker* lost her rudder, Capt. Hines sailed her home, with the use of her sails only.

In 1911 Capt. C. Hiram Forbes took the *Parker* salt banking.

A strange and tragic incident happened to the *Annie M. Parker* on the night of November 1, 1913. She was homeward bound from a salt fishing trip, under command of Capt. Vincent Nelson.

The vessel had been struck by gales and was blown far off her course, when suddenly she struck on the treacherous Rose and Crown Shoals, 12 miles east of Sankatv Head, Nantucket. Heavy seas breaking over the vessel swept the cook to his death. Capt. Nelson and three of his crew were drowned, when the dory they were using in an attempt to leave the vessel was swamped. The 10 remaining members of the crew succeeded in leaving the vessel in dories.

The *Parker*'s time had not come yet, for she floated off and on November 3 was sighted by the British steamer *Astrakhan* 60 miles east of South Shoals Lightship.

The sails on the schooner were set and she was traveling about five miles an hour, but no sign of life was observed by the officers of the steamer. They decided to investigate, and a boat was sent over in command of the mate. It was fully an hour before the vessel could be caught and boarded. The sight that greeted the Britishers was a strange one, and it looked as if there was another *Mary Celeste*, a real phantom ship. The newly baked bread was still in the oven, the clock was ticking in the cabin, four dories were left in the starboard nest, the other four in the port nest were gone, showing that the vessel had been abandoned in a hurry. The vessel herself appeared only slightly damaged.

The British flag was hoisted, and she sailed for port under her prize crew. She was picked up by the cutter *Greshan* and towed to New Bedford, 12 hours before her survivors reached port. The survivors, including Capt. Nelson's young son, were picked up by the coaster *Tifton* and landed at Portland, Maine.

Everett A. Sawyer, who became a Gloucester fireman, was on the *Parker* this trip. He was the last to leave the vessel, as he had returned below to get some personal belongings. Everett was a youth of 17 at that time.

The *Parker* was only slightly damaged and returned to Gloucester later, having been released on bond furnished by the owners.

Those drowned were Capt. Nelson, 50, native of Pubnico, Nova Scotia; Leslie Fletcher, 27, native of Argyle, Nova Scotia; Ross Worthen, 24, from Pubnico, and Theophilus Landry, 30, native of Arichat, Cape Breton.

Capt. Hiram Forbes again took over the helm of the *Annie M. Parker* in 1914 and sailed in her several years salt fishing. Capt. Albert Flygare also commanded her.

On September 6, 1916 she arrived from Wood's Island, Newfoundland, with her freighted cargo of 500,000 lbs. of salt cod, 8,000 lbs. of dry cod and 8 barrels of capelin for the Gorton-Pew Company.

Another casualty was Ambrose Frizell, 30, native of Nova Scotia, washed overboard November 15, 1916, during passage to Greece.

The *Parker*, although under 100 feet in length, was burdensome and could carry a great amount of fish. The parting of the ways came for the *Annie M.* in 1920 when her own-ers, the Gorton-Pew Fisheries Company, sold her to the Holletts of Burin, Newfoundland.

In January, 1924, she was abandoned at sea, while homeward bound to Newfoundland from Cadiz, Spain, with a cargo of salt. Her crew were rescued by the steamer *Grooteneyk*.

Capt. Charles Flygare, who died in Gloucester March 9, 1911, was one of the port's top-notchers in fletched halibuting and Georges handlining. He was also an expert rigger. Some of his commands were the *Hattie E. Worcester*, *Henry M. Stanley*, *Puritan*, *Arbutus* and *Jennie B. Hodgdon*. He was a native of Sweden.

Capt. Hiram Forbes, who was born in Yarmouth County, Nova Scotia, sailed out of Gloucester over 35 years, retiring about 1916. Among his commands were the *Everett Steele*, *John L. Nicholson, American, W. E. Morrissey*, and *Catherine Burke*. He died at his home in Argyle, Nova Scotia, February 13, 1927.

Gross tons, 133; net tons, 100; length, 97 feet; breadth, 25.3 feet; depth, 10.5 feet. Mainmast, 75 feet (deck to cap); foremast, 67 feet; main topmast, 40 feet; fore topmast, 34 feet; main boom, 70 feet; main gaff, 40.5 feet; bowsprit, 32 feet (outboard); mainmast head, 10.5 feet.

Ooops . . . and only a mile or two from her home wharf! But the *Independence* floated again.

Independence

BIG, HANDSOME AND SHORT-LIVED /
1901–1903

The unusual photograph that illustrates this vessel may never again be approached in subject. It shows schooner *Independence*, the first of two vessels with that name, built at the turn of the century, high and dry on Black Rocks in the outer harbor, off Tarr & Wonson's factory at Rocky Neck.

While beating up the harbor on January 9, 1902, *Independence* luffed to keep clear of a coaster that was in her way. The schooner failed to answer her helm and piled up on the rocks almost her full length, knocking over a spindle buoy. At the time, tide was ebbing and the vessel was left high and dry with the bow high in the air. On the next high tide *Independence* was pulled off by tugs *Startle*, *Eveleth* and *Priscilla*.

Schooner *Independence* was built at the Tarr and James yard, Essex, during the winter of 1900–1901 and launched April 29, 1901 for the Gardner and Parsons firm, Gloucester. Tug *Eveleth* towed her around to Gloucester to fit for sea.

The *Independence* was off the model of the Boston schooner *Francis Whalen*, which was an Arthur Binney design and similar to the schooners *Aloha* and *Edna Wallace Hopper* that were built at that time.

Independence was a big, handsome vessel with a clipper bow and named after the big Tom Lawson sloop yacht *Independence.*

The *Independence* sailed on her maiden trip salt banking May 13, 1901 in command of Capt. Joseph Cusick. She arrived back in Gloucester from Grand Bank on September 22, 1901 with the largest salt fare of the season, 375,000 lbs. of salt cod, stocking $9,353.00 with the share of $195 to $241. It was one of the largest maiden trips on record. On this trip she reported speaking the schooners *Georgie Campbell* and *Helen F. Whitten* on Misanie Bank.

Capt. Joe Cusick, a native of St. Lawrence, Newfoundland, was one of the finest of the younger skippers sailing out of Gloucester. He was a driver and a hustler and nothing daunted him. He had many fast passages in the *Corsair* and *Dreadnaught* from the Gardner and Parsons firm.

In November, 1901, *Independence* arrived at Gloucester from Bay of Islands, Newfoundland, in five and a half days, with 1600 barrels of herring.

On November 20, 1902, *Independence* arrived from Bay of Islands with 1700 barrels of herring. She made the passage in 84 hours, a distance of 780 miles, beating the whole fleet home.

Casualties of the *Independence* included four men who went astray July 4, 1902, while fishing 120 miles off Newfoundland. They were William McDonald, 34, native of East Boston; Charles Olsen, 42, native of Sweden; Bert Dunbar, 38, native of Maine; and James Nocton, 45, native of Guysboro, Nova Scotia.

The vessel arrived in Gloucester July 23, 1902, from the Funks, both topmasts having been carried away on the homeward trip.

Four more men lost from the first *Independence* were the following, swept overboard by the mainsail off Bacaru, Nova Scotia, April 16, 1903: Bernard Welsh, 35, native of Bay of Bulls, Newfoundland; Bernard Carter, 25, native of Newfoundland; Ernest Connors, 28, of Lawn, Newfoundland; and John Oliver, 21, of Little Canso, Nova Scotia.

The first *Independence* made a fast trip from Scaterie in October, 1903, leaving the banks on the ninth and arriving off Gloucester on the eleventh, making an average of 12 knots. Off Gloucester she lost her main and foresails, and anchored until Capt. Charles T. Heberle towed her into the harbor with the tug *Priscilla.* The vessel had been gone five months; she hailed for 300,000 pounds of salt cod.

The career of *Independence* was cut short when she was lost in 1903. She sailed from Bay of Islands with a cargo of herring for Gloucester on December 25, 1903 in command of William Malone, as her regular skipper, Capt. Cusick, remained in Newfoundland to represent the herring interest of Gardner and Parsons. On December 27, she stranded at

Schooner Pond, near Glace Bay, Cape Breton, in a heavy northeast gale. The vessel struck a ledge near high rocky bluffs. Her hull was pushed close to a forty-foot cliff. Her port side was chafed off and she was badly hogged. The crew was saved but the vessel and cargo were a total loss. The value of the vessel was $18,000.

The Gardner and Parsons firm immediately engaged Tarr and James to build a new vessel for Capt. Cusick. Named *Independence II,* she was built during the winter and spring of 1903–1904 and launched June 25, 1904.

Independence II was off the lines of the old *Independence,* but was a larger vessel, a beautiful clipper bowed schooner and very fast in heavy weather. It took a lot of wind to drive the *Independence II.*

She sailed on her maiden trip salt banking on July 11, 1904 in command of Capt. Cusick. On October 15, 1904 she arrived in Gloucester with her maiden fare of 230,000 lbs. of salt cod from Grand Bank, in company with the *Arkona,* Capt. Harry Gardner. Capt. Cusick had sailed in command of four new vessels within five years for the Gardner and Parsons firm, schooner *Corsair* in November, 1899; schooner *Dreadnaught,* in April, 1900; schooner *Independence, I,* 1901 and *Independence II,* 1904.

Capt. Cusick's career came to a tragic ending on December 29, 1906 when he died of pneumonia at Birchy Cove, Newfoundland. Capt. Cusick, a native of St. Lawrence, Newfoundland, had spent most of his youth at St. Pierre. At the time of his death he was in charge of the herring interests for Gardner and Parsons. His body was brought to Gloucester. He was only 40 years old.

In the spring of 1907 Capt. Jack O'Brien had *Independence II* seining.

In 1908 *Independence II* was sold to a Mr. Adams of Swan Island in the West Indies, for the cocoanut trade. Capt. George Hamor sailed her to her new owners.

In the meantime the Gardner and Parsons firm went out of business in May, 1909. This company at one time was one of the finest firms in Gloucester. William Gardner and William Parsons dissolved from the Atlantic Halibut Company and started a new firm of their own in January, 1902. They were located at the Andrew Leighton wharf. Many fine vessels were owned by this company, including the *Dreadnaught, Corsair, Helen G. Wells, Alice M. Parsons, Illinois,* and others.

In May, 1910 the Cunningham and Thompson Co. purchased *Independence II* and Capt. Mel McClain was sent down to bring her home. She had been running from Mobile, Alabama, to Honduras and it was said she was one of the finest schooners sailing in the Gulf of Mexico.

Capt. George H. Peeples took the *Independence II* on a Newfoundland herring voyage in November, 1910.

Capt. John McInnis took over command of *Independence II* in 1911 and sailed in her seining and salt fishing until December, 1913 when she was taken to Newfoundland by Capt. James Fralick. Captain Newman Wharton had her salt banking in 1914 and his brother Capt. Lew Wharton, salt banking in 1915.

While under command of Capt. McInnis on July 13, 1911 she was run down and cut down to the water's edge by the steam trawler *Ripple* in a dense fog off Chatham. A big hole in the starboard bow was patched up and she was towed home by the trawler. Capt. Ralph Webber in schooner *Clintonia* heard the crash a mile away and investigated.

Independence II was sold to J. Hiscock of Brigus, Newfoundland, in March, 1916. In January, 1917 she was abandoned north of St. Vincent, Cape Verde Islands. Her crew in command of Capt. Barrett landed at Lisbon, Portugal. At the time she was carrying a cargo of salt from Santa Pola for St. John's, Newfoundland.

Lewis George, 33, a native of Carbonear, Newfoundland, died of a heart attack off Sable Island, April 2, 1905, while a member of the crew of the second *Independence*.

Independence I: gross tons, 137; net tons, 102; length, 107.7 feet; breadth, 25.2 feet; depth, 11.2 feet.

Independence II: gross tons, 145; net tons, 109; length, 111 feet; breadth, 25.4 feet; depth, 11.8 feet; mainmast, deck to cap, 73.5 feet; foremast, 65 feet; main topmast, 41 feet; fore topmast, 39 feet; main boom, 75 feet; main gaff, 43 feet; bowsprit, outboard, 33 feet, cut to 27 feet; main mast head, 11 feet.

That photographer-manager, Ernest Blatchford, who watched the ships go by, left us
this pictorial poem showing the *Monitor*
leaving the inner harbor.

Monitor

SHE RESCUED THE CAPTAIN'S BROTHER / 1901–1917

One of the best of the old Gloucester fishing schooners was Capt. Jerome McDonald's big *Monitor*.

The *Monitor*, the third vessel of that name owned by Capt. McDonald, was one of the crack vessels of the early 1900's and commanded by many of our finest skippers, mostly in the halibut and mackerel fisheries.

The first *Monitor* was built at Essex in 1885 and lost at Point May, Newfoundland, the following year. The second *Monitor* was launched in August, 1886 at Essex. She was sold to P. Whorff of Provincetown in 1901, being the first vessel sold out of Gloucester in the new century. The Gorton-Pew Fisheries Company purchased the second *Monitor* when the Whorff firm went out of business. In 1914 she ran ashore at Codroy, Newfoundland, and was refloated in May, 1915. She was then sold to the Bay of Islands, Newfoundland. In January, 1918, she was sent to the bottom by the Germans, off the Canary Islands. She had sailed from the African coast with a load of wood.

The third and last *Monitor* was built during the spring and summer of 1901, and launched on July 18 of that year. Like most of the McDonald fleet, she was built by James and Tarr in Essex. The *Monitor* was built alongside of the schooners *Electric Flash* and *Arkona*.

She was towed around to Gloucester by the tug *Startle*. Ten minutes after she was made fast to Burnham shears, her foremast was stepped. She had reached Gloucester at 5 p.m. on July 18, and at 7 p.m. both spars were in place and standing rigging was on her.

The *Monitor* was a large, handsome vessel of the clipper bow type, taken off the model of the schooner *Preceptor*. She was named after Capt. Jerome McDonald's previous *Monitors*. Capt. McDonald liked the name as he believed it lucky. All of the McDonald fleet had "or" on the end of their names. Another McDonald marker was the end of the mainbooms painted black.

The *Monitor* sailed on her maiden trip halibuting on July 29, 1901, just 11 days after her launching. Capt. McDonald himself going in command of the fine new craft.

The *Monitor* arrived in Boston with her maiden fare of 40,000 lbs. fresh halibut, 4,000 lbs. flitched halibut on September 10, 1901, stocking $3000. She was six weeks out and had taken the trip in 15 sets.

She was bothered by ice the entire trip. The *Monitor* sailed as far north as 58 degrees latitude, three whole degrees farther toward the frozen pole than ever a fresh halibut vessel

had been before. She was well into Dover Strait.

The *Monitor*, during her career, was commanded by many of Gloucester's finest skippers. Capt. Jim Bowie halibuting in 1902. Capt. Jim Goodwin had her halibuting in 1902–03. Capt. Fred Carritt took her seining in 1904. The winter of 1904–05, Capt. Forman Spinney had her haddocking; Capt. Ben Spurling seining in 1905. Capt. Jim McShara took her halibuting in the winter of 1905–06; Capt. Joe Lyle seining in 1906. Capt. Jack McKay took over halibuting early in 1907 and remained in her until 1911. Capt. George Marr took over in 1911 and remained in the *Monitor*, halibuting until her sale in 1916.

By a strange coincidence, three of the McDonald fleet all left Gloucester together on August 30, 1902. All three were bound to the eastward halibuting, schooner *Monitor*, Capt. Jerome McDonald, schooner *Senator*, Capt. Jim Bowie, and the *Preceptor*, Capt. Jim Goodwin. A fine race was sailed, the *Monitor* being the first to reach the fishing grounds. About a month later, the same three vessels arrived in Boston on the same day.

The *Monitor* was a lucky vessel. She was a great producer, she suffered no mishaps and according to my records only two men were lost from her.

Jacob Jennings or Jenson was drowned on Baccalieu Bank on July 27, 1908 by the capsizing of his dory. His dorymate was saved. He was a native of Harbor Breton, Newfoundland, and 26 years old. Capt. Jack McKay was skipper at the time.

Joseph Devol was washed from the mainboom and drowned on Grand Bank on November 1, 1913. He was 23 years old and a native of Newfoundland. Capt. George Marr was skipper at the time of the accident.

On February 15, 1905 the Boston schooner *Manhasset*, Capt. George Roberts, arrived at Boston and reported the loss of two of her crew, John Barry and James Lambert, who went astray on Georges on February 6.

A sad feature connected with the loss of the two men was that one of them, John Barry, was to have been married on February 18th.

On February 23 the *Monitor*, Capt. Forman Spinney, arrived at Boston with the two lost men. Capt. Spinney reported he had picked up the men after they had been adrift 28 hours, suffering terrible exposure in heavy zero weather. Thanks to the *Monitor* and Capt. Spinney, John Barry came home for his wedding after all.

In 1908, the *Monitor* again came to the rescue. On March 4, 1908, the *Monitor* in command of Capt. Jack McKay sailed from Gloucester on a halibut trip to the southern edge of Grand Bank, 1,000 miles away. Soon after leaving Capt. McKay had a feeling something was wrong. Something seemed to tell him that he must get to his destination in a hurry and he drove the *Monitor* for all she was worth. On reaching the bank, the schooner *Cavalier*, Capt. Bob Porper, was sighted with her dories all out on their gear. Billy McKay, brother of Capt. Jack, was one of the *Cavalier's* crew, so that when the vessel was sighted, the *Monitor* ran down the line of dories looking for Billy, so that Capt. Jack could have a chat with him.

Suddenly from the *Monitor* an overturned dory was sighted and Capt. Jack made all possible haste to reach the little craft. When they arrived on the scene, they found Billy McKay and his dory mate Milton Aiken clinging for their lives. It was almost all over with "Little Billy" McKay as his strength was about gone and he could hold on only a few minutes longer. The men were taken on board the *Monitor* where they were tenderly cared for.

It seemed as if Capt. McKay was guided by an unseen power, that he would make a 1,000 mile dash to snatch his brother from the jaws of death.

Young Willie McKay, son of Capt. Jack, was a passenger on this eventful trip. Young Willie made many, many trips to the banks with his father.

The *Monitor* was a fast, able vessel, especially in heavy weather. Capt. Wylie Rudolph told me that once when he was in the *Monitor* with Capt. Jack McKay, this great vessel made 70 miles in 6 hours in a heavy breeze. This was pretty good sailing and Capt. Jack could drive her.

The *Monitor*, like many of our fine vessels, was sold during World War I. Philip Templemen of Bonavista, Newfoundland purchased the craft in June 1916 for $14,000. Her life

under the Union Jack was short, however. After discharging a cargo of salt fish in Italy, she sailed for Cadiz, Spain to take on a cargo of salt for Newfoundland. About 40 miles off Monte Carlo on April 25, 1917 the *Monitor* was shelled by a German submarine. The crew left in their dories and landed at Monte Carlo. The Germans boarded the doomed *Monitor* and ransacked her for food and stores and then sank her with time bombs.

At the time of her loss she was commanded by Capt. Joe Legg and carried a crew of seven men.

Capt. Jerome McDonald sailed on his last voyage on March 12, 1917 at the age of 71. Capt. Jerome, known by the fishermen as the "Grand Bank Horse," was one of the greatest halibut skippers out of Gloucester. This rugged Prince Edward Islander was a giant in size and deed. Well liked, respected and owner of some of the finest vessels out of this port, including the three *Monitors*, *Elector*, *Gladiator*, *Senator*, *Preceptor*, and *Catherine Burke*.

Many fine skippers sailed from the McDonald firm, including Capts. Jim Goodwin, Jim McShara, Jim Bowie, Miles Somers, Forman Spinney, Lemuel Spinney, Jack McKay, Little Dan McDonald, George Marr, and many others.

Capt. Jerome, while skipper of the schooner *G. P. Whitman* in 1876, landed a trip of 140,000 lbs. fresh halibut. This was the largest fresh halibut trip ever landed in New England.

Capt. Jerome toward the latter part of his career used to make a trip annually in one of his vessels. His last trip was made in the schooner *Catherine Burke* in 1915.

Capt. Jerome will take his place as one of the leaders of the fishing industry in the glorious days of sail.

Gross tons, 137; net tons, 100; length, 109 feet; breadth, 25.4 feet; depth, 10.8 feet. Original spars: mainmast, deck to cap, 74 feet; foremast, 64 feet; main boom, 72 feet; main gaff, 43 feet; fore boom, 30 feet; bowsprit, outboard, 29 feet; mastheads, 11 feet.

Sadie M. Nunan

ALMOST A FLOATING MUSEUM / 1901–1958

Schooner *Sadie M. Nunan* was built in 1901 by Charles Hodgdon at East Boothbay, Maine, for Capt. Frank Nunan, one of the famous Nunans of Cape Porpoise, Maine. She was a handsome little vessel with a clipper toothpick bow and ample sail spread. She was named after the two-year-old daughter of Capt. Nunan.

The new craft sailed from Cape Porpoise, on her maiden trip, shore fishing in command of her owner, Capt. Frank Nunan on October 1, 1901. She arrived at Boston's T wharf with her first fare of 70,000 lbs. fresh fish, one week later on October 8th. From that time until Capt. Frank gave her up, the *Sadie M.* was certainly a lucky vessel. A glance at some of her records easily shows, that this vessel was among the topnotchers. Most all of her fish were landed at Boston.

From her maiden trip in October, 1901, to August 20, 1902, her crew shared $1007. From October 16, 1902 to October 7, 1903, she stocked $29,237 and the crew shared $1305. During this period she carried 12 single dories and landed 67 trips at Boston.

Capt. Nunan while in command of the *Sadie M.*, kept her going every minute. He landed three trips in four days, shore fishing in April, 1904. In February, 1907, three trips were landed in six days, fishing, her crew sharing $110 per man.

From September 14, 1907 to April 28, 1908 her crew of 16 men shared $1006 each.

With Capt. Frank Nunan at the helm, the *Sadie M.* was used shore fishing and swordfishing. On July 19, 1915, the *Sadie M.* arrived at Boston with 18 other swordfishermen, including such well known vessels as the *Topsail Girl, Rose Standish, Elva Spurling, Mertis Perry, Florida,* etc. A total of 1124 swordfish was landed that day. (Quite a change from the situation today). The price paid was 8 cents per pound.

Capt. Nunan gave up command of the *Sadie M.* in 1908 when he took over his new schooner *Elizabeth Nunan.* Various skippers then commanded the *Sadie M.* Capt. George Nunan, a nephew of Capt. Frank, was skipper in 1914.

Capt. Herbert Thompson had her haddocking in 1915. In 1914, a 60 horsepower gasoline engine was installed and her registry changed to Portland, Maine.

The *Sadie M. Nunan* was sold to Capt. Fred Bickford in May, 1918. Capt. Bickford also used the vessel on the shore and swordfishing. On a swordfish trip landed at Boston in 1918, Capt. Bickford's crew shared $461. On August 8, 1919 Capt. Bickford landed 147 swordfish at Boston, stocking $7700 and sharing $580 per man. The *Sadie M.* was high line of the swordfish fleet that year.

The *Sadie Nunan* was sold in 1921 to Philip P. Manta and her registry was changed to Boston. Various skippers commanded the *Sadie M.* while owned by Manta. Capt. "Pete" Hepson had her rig fishing in 1926. Capt. Alonzo Townsend took her halibuting in March, 1932, after the vessel had been hauled up all winter at Frank Smith's wharf in Gloucester. Other skippers of the *Nunan* were Capts. Manuel Goulart, Frank Gaspa (Vardee), Gus D'Entremont, Billy Forbes, Bill Devine and her last, Capt. Frank Fonseca (Big Frank) who had her haddocking in 1937.

The *Sadie M.,* besides being lucky at making money, was lucky in keeping free of serious accidents. Her worst misfortune happened in December, 1903, when she ran ashore near her home port of Cape Porpoise. The weather was bad at the time and it was feared the vessel would be a total loss. Capt. Frank Nunan secured the services of Gloucester's Capt. Charles Heberle and his tug *Priscilla,* and the *Sadie M.* was pulled off and grounded in shallow water, thanks to Heberle's great work. I discussed this episode with Capt. Heberle and he remembered quite clearly the facts and Capt. Nunan's plea to try and save her as she was such a "lucky vessel."

In June, 1911, the *Sadie Nunan* while bound for Gloucester from Boston, grounded on Norman's Woe but was floated easily with the damage. In May, 1916, in a storm, a heavy sea hit her and swept over eight of her dories.

Several of the *Sadie Nunan's* crew lost their lives. While in command of Capt. Frank Nunan, on October 20, 1907, Nick McKenney's dory capsized. He was found nearly unconscious, hanging to the bottom of the dory. He was taken on board the vessel, but failed to rally as he was so far gone and died soon after. He was a native of Cape Porpoise.

A few weeks later on November 13, 1907, Charles Gerry in some way lost his balance and fell overboard and drowned off Eastern Point, Gloucester, while the vessel was bound to market. Gerry was also a native of Cape Porpoise.

Thomas Kennedy drowned when his dory capsized on Jeffries Bank on November 1, 1920. He was a native of Newfoundland and 30 years old. Capt. Fred Bickford was skipper at the time.

While owned by Manta the gasoline engine

was removed and a sixty-horsepower crude oil engine was installed by Charlie Williams and Henry Burgess at Gloucester. Charlie also served as engineer in the *Sadie M.* at one time.

In April 1938, after rounding out thirty-seven years of fishing, the *Sadie Nunan* was sold by Manta through the agency of Marian Cooney to Ewing Parra, a young Argentinian. He intended to take the schooner on a world cruise, and her name was changed to *Expedition*. Repairs were made at Gloucester, including a new bowsprit, etc. The old *Sadie M.* never made the cruise, as Parra left Gloucester one day and never came back.

For years after Parra's disappearance the *Nunan* was taken care of by Joseph Mellow, lobster dealer. He used her for a short time as a party fishing boat and then for several years she was tied up at various Gloucester wharves.

Upkeep of the vessel was too much for Mellow, and the old craft was in bad shape. On August 16, 1952, she was sold at sheriff's sale to the Gloucester Museum Corporation to be used as a museum and memorial to the fishermen.

Little interest was shown in restoring the *Sadie M.* (her original name was given back to her by the museum people) and she was eventually sold to a quahog fisherman at Gloucester. After awhile she was moved to East Gloucester, where one day she rolled over on her side.

On the night of August 17, 1957, she was badly damaged in a fire that swept the Gloucester Yacht Yard at East Gloucester. Her spars were snapped off and the hull badly charred.

I was one of the little group that believed the little vessel would make a fine memorial. She was the last clipper-bowed vessel in these parts and she was pretty, well built, and had quite a history.

It was not to be, however. Money was scarce, and folks were not interested. The vessel was doomed. In March 1958 the remains of the *Sadie Nunan* were burned, to rid the harbor of a worthless hulk.

Captain Frank Nunan, first owner and skipper, passed away at his home in Cape Porpoise, Maine, on February 8, 1945, at the age of seventy-three. He was the son of Capt. Richard Nunan and was one of the greatest fishing skippers of the Maine coast. Well liked, capable, smart and a great producer in the days of sail.

Mrs. Sadie M. Nunan Sinnett, namesake of the vessel, resided later in South Boston.

I am indebted to Mrs. Helen Ward Nunan of Cape Porpoise, Maine, for information used in this article. I met this charming lady on my first visit to her quaint little town. Mrs. Nunan informed me that she used to write poetry for the *Gloucester Daily Times* about fifty years ago. When I left Mrs. Nunan and Cape Porpoise I knew that all that had ever been said of them was true. Wonderful folks, the Nunans of Cape Porpoise. Helen Ward Nunan passed away at Cape Porpoise April 6, 1956, at the age of eighty-five.

Gross tons, 73; net tons, 36; length, 81 feet; breadth, 21.4 feet; depth, 9.2 feet. Spar measurements (a slightly loftier rig was carried in her sailing days): mainmast 63 feet (deck to cap) foremast, 58 feet; mainboom, 51 feet (cut to 47 feet); main gaff, 29 feet (cut to 27); forebom, 21 feet; fore gaff, 21 feet; bowsprit, 19 feet (outboard); masthead, 9 feet.

Baiting up the hooks on lines to be coiled in tubs and used by fishermen in the single dories nested on the deck of the *Sadie M. Nunan.* The schooner survived her years at sea but succumbed to neglect in port.

What it was all about: the big *Tattler* bringing in a big fare.

Tattler

LARGEST MAINSAIL, LARGEST TRIP / 1901–1918

This story is about the largest two-masted fishing schooner out of Gloucester, one of the largest carriers and one of the really big producers of the days of sail. Yes, it's the *Tattler*, a ship that was as famous as the industry itself during the first dozen years of the present century, and usually commanded by a skipper whose name was legend wherever fisherfolks congregated, Capt. Alden Geele. *Tattler* landed millions of pounds of fish in Gloucester.

Tattler was a Story product, Arthur D. that is, at the famed Essex yard and was built during the spring of 1901 for D. B. Smith company. She was launched on June 22, 1901 and was named like most of the D. B. Smith vessels of that era, such as *Gossip*, *Flirt*, *Romance*, *Teazer*, *Althlete*. She was off the schooner *Flaherty* model from an original Laurence Jensen design with a clipper bow.

This vessel had the largest masts in circumference and the largest mainsail in yardage, of all Gloucester fishermen. As was customary in those days, no time was lost in getting a new vessel fitted for sea and 10 days after the launching, schooner *Tattler* sailed on her maiden trip, salt banking, under command of Capt. Jesse Morton.

Shortly afterward, Capt. Geele took command and smashed all records in dory handline fishing.

In the season of 1905, she seined for pollock and cod on Sable Island Bank (Capt. Geele tried this new venture in 1904 in schooner *Maxine Elliott*) and arrived in Gloucester, June 30, 1905 with 430,000 lbs. salt pollock and 40,000 lbs. salt cod.

On August 30, 1908, she arrived from Quero Bank with 430,000 lbs. salt cod.

In 1909, she brought in 479,433 lbs. salt cod, stocking $15,277 with a high line share of $342. This was the largest trip and biggest stock in this branch of fishing up to that time.

In 1912, in two trips, she stocked $15,481 with a share of $319. On March 8, 1913 she arrived from a six months trip to the Virgin Rocks and Labrador Coast with 400,000 lbs. salt cod.

On September 19, 1915 she arrived at Gloucester with 478,365 lbs. salt cod, $16,534 stock, which broke her previous record of 1909.

In 1916, on September 6, Capt. Geele sailed the *Tattler* into Gloucester with a record breaking trip of 500,000 lbs. salt cod, stocking $21,000 with a high line share of $533. This proved to be the largest trip and stock ever made in the dory hand line fishery. The *Tattler*, although built for a carrier instead of a fast sailer, did some pretty good sailing.

In the winter seasons she made many voyages to Newfoundland for herring cargoes, under command of Capts. Geele, Paddy Shea, Lew Wharton, Albert Hudder, John Belong and Antone Courant.

She made the passage from Bay of Islands, Newfoundland, to Gloucester in six days, in January, 1904, with Capt. Lew Wharton in command. In January, 1914, with Capt. Paddy Shea at the wheel, she repeated this performance, arriving with 1875 barrels of salt herring for Gorton-Pew Fisheries Co. In 1917, with Newfoundland paying high prices for Glouces-vessels, she was sold by Gorton-Pew Co. to Campbell and Mckay of St. John's, Newfoundland.

This grand vessel finally went to her last resting place when she was abandoned March 15, 1918 in Latitude 40°30' N. and Longitude 56°30' W. while on a voyage from Turk's Island, British West Indies, to Newfoundland with a cargo of salt. Her crew was rescued. At the time, while being British owned, she was still under American registry.

An interesting incident occurred to the *Tattler* on November 26, 1911, while returning from a dory handline trip from the Virgin Rocks. In a dense fog, she grounded on a sand spit at the entrance to the Essex River. She floated off shortly after, but when the fog cleared it was seen that had she struck 20 feet to the westward, she would have sailed right up the Essex River.

Gross tons, 172; net tons, 136; length, 113.9 feet; breadth, 25.8 feet; depth, 12 feet. Spar measurements out of existence.

Tall ship, Gloucester style: the *Theodore Roosevelt*, her topmasts towering above wharf buildings as her sails dry after a rain.

Theodore Roosevelt

FIRST VESSEL BUILT AT PAVILION
BEACH / 1901–1921

Schooner *Theodore Roosevelt* was built by Leonard B. MacKenzie at Pavilion Beach, and launched unnamed August 31, 1901. The vessel stuck in the sand, but was floated by the tugs *Startle* and *Priscilla*. Later she was sold to Fred L. Davis and named *Theodore Roosevelt* after the 26th President of the United States, who began his term in that year of 1901.

The *Roosevelt* was the first vessel to be built by Mr. MacKenzie at Pavilion Beach. His yard was located on the southern side of the beach, to the southward of the old Surfside Hotel.

The *Roosevelt* was probably designed by Mr. MacKenzie and was a fine, medium-sized vessel of the clipper bow type. She sailed on her maiden trip to Newfoundland for a cargo of herring in command of Capt. George H. Peeples, and arrived back in Gloucester from Bay of Islands, Newfoundland on December 6, 1901 with 1450 barrels of herring. The maiden voyage of the *Roosevelt* was a stormy one. On Cashes, she was hit by a heavy sea, which broke her main boom.

On that same voyage, the *Theodore Roosevelt* left Bay of Islands on November 25, 1901 in company with the schooner *Eliza H. Parkhurst*, Capt. John D. (Shortscope) McKinnon. Both vessels, owned by the same firm, decided to race to Gloucester. The new *Roosevelt* gradually drew ahead and when off Red Island, the *Parkhurst* could be just made out astern. This was the last ever seen of the *Eliza Parkhurst*. Nothing to this day has ever been heard of her and her crew. That night a heavy southeast gale sprang up. On December 26, 1901, her owners, Fred L. Davis and Capt. Alex McEachern, gave her up. In the *Gloucester Times* on that date the following sad announcement appeared: "Sch. Eliza H. Parkhurst will never return. She has been lost with all hands. The brave and hardy men who formed her crew have met a sailor's fate—death in the water— the sea their shroud, the angry waves chanting their Requiem." Words to this effect appeared in the local paper quite often in those days. Many fine vessels and brave men sailed from this port and never returned.

Capt. Daniel McDonald (Little Dan) took the *Roosevelt* halibuting in 1902 and later in that year Capt. James McHenry took over command and remained in her until 1909. Halibuting was Capt. McHenry's game.

An interesting incident occurred to the *Roosevelt* on January 5, 1905, while in command of Capt. McHenry, when 106 miles off Thacher's, she fell in with the disabled Canadian brig *Ohio*, flying a distress signal. The craft was badly iced and in bad shape. Several of her crew were frost bitten. Her crew, including Capt. Rupert Wry, 27 years old, his wife, two mates, cook and four seamen, were taken aboard the *Roosevelt*. Capt. McHenry hoped to save the brig and he put a prize crew of eight of his own men aboard the battered vessel. They were in charge of Sylvester Thompson. Both vessels headed for Cape Ann and arrived home on January 6. The brig anchored on Pancake Ground. They made it just in time as that night the heaviest gale of the winter set in. The brig, loaded with lumber, was bound to New York from Kingsport, Nova Scotia. She was 325 tons and owned in St. John, New Brunswick. The brig was claimed as salvage by the *Roosevelt* owners, and she was sold at auction to Louisburg, Cape Breton parties in May, 1905.

In 1908, Capt. Jack O'Brien took the *Roosevelt* seining. In 1909 Capt. Billy (Young Billy) Morrissey went salt banking in her.

In the spring of 1913, Capt. Joe Graham went seining.

On October 31, 1913 the *Theodore Roosevelt*, in command of Capt. James Bowie, ran ashore at Trout Cove, Nova Scotia. She was loading green salt cod for Davis Brothers and at the time had 100,000 pounds on board. The vessel was given up as a total loss. The Nova Scotians, however, floated the vessel and she was sold by the underwriters for $300 to A. Boutilier of Digby, Nova Scotia. She was renamed *Lila Boutilier* and she arrived at Digby, Nova Scotia with her first fare under the British flag on September 21, 1914. Capt. Arthur Casey was her skipper and she had a fare of 100,000 pounds of fresh fish.

The *Lila Boutilier* fished out of Digby for some time and she was then sold to Newfoundland. In 1921 she was owned by Charles Steer of St. John's, Newfoundland.

On December 3, 1921, the *Lila Boutilier*, our old *Theodore Roosevelt*, was lost in the Atlantic. She had finally joined *Eliza H. Parkhurst*, the vessel she had left behind on her maiden trip, 20 years before.

Capt. George H. Peeples died on board of his little schooner *Albert D. Willard* on May 6, 1927, while unloading mackerel at New York. A fine giant of a man, and one of Gloucester's great skippers. From 1910 to 1920 he was president of the Master Mariners' Association and for nearly 50 years a fisherman.

John Stobing, 38, native of Heligoland Island, Germany, and Robert Leonard, 35, native of East Boston, went astray on Green Bank February 4, 1908. Stobing left a widow and nine children.

Morris Muise, 18, native of Surrett's Island, Nova Scotia, drowned at Pubnico, Nova Scotia, October 27, 1910, after falling overboard.

Leonard B. MacKenzie, the builder, moved to Essex in 1912, and died there on July 25, 1915, at the age of 49. A native of Essex and the son of another great shipbuilder, Mr. MacKenzie built many fine vessels on Pavilion Beach, Gloucester, including the *Ralph L. Hall*, in 1901 (model of the Roosevelt), the *Betha and Pearl* in 1902, *Faustina*, in 1902, *Quonnapowitt* in 1903, *Mystery* in 1904, *Emily Sears* in 1906.

Gross tons, 125; net tons, 90; length, 104.6 feet; breadth, 24.5 feet; depth, 10.6 feet.

Alice M. Jacobs

A STEAMER FOR SOL JACOBS / 1902–1903

This is the story of a Gloucester fishing steamer, built for and commanded by the "King" of the mackerel seiners, Capt. *Sol Jacobs*. She was the *Alice M. Jacobs*, a wooden ship 141 feet, 7 inches long, built by Arthur D. Story in Essex during the winter of 1901–02.

Steam power at this time was in its infancy in the Gloucester fleet. The *Jacobs* was the first large fishing steamer built for local parties, and at the time of her launching the only big steamer used for seining. She was not, however, the first to be used in the mackerel fishing.

Capt. Frank Foster of Gloucester in 1885 chartered the steamer *William Floyd* of Greenport, Long Island, New York. She was a vessel of 86 tons and was the first steamer ever fitted at Gloucester for seining. Also in 1885 the big steamer *Novelty*, Capt. Hans Joyce of Portland, 197 tons (this steamer carried 52 men, four seines and three seine boats), the steamer *Mabel Bird*, of Portland, 130 tons, and the steamer *Nellie E. Rawson* of New Bedford, 73 tons, were all used as seiners. Porgy steamers occasionally seined for mackerel. It was stated in the local papers at that time that steamers would not drive out sail, as they were too costly to run.

On the loss of Capt. Jacob's fine auxiliary schooner *Helen Miller Gould* in 1901, a new vessel was started for him. This one was to be a steamer named *Alice M. Jacobs*, after Capt. Jacobs' younger daughter. She was launched at 11:15 a.m. on March 11, 1902. The launching was very successful; the heeled style (over on one side) being used. Before a large gathering of about 1,000 people, Albert Jacobs, young son of the skipper, christened the new craft with wine, and 40 guests enjoyed the initial dip into the Essex River. The Gloucester tug *Priscilla*, Capt. Charles T. Heberle (grand old towboat skipper, who died Sept. 23, 1956 at the age of 94.), immediately took the *Jacobs* in tow for her trip around the Cape to Gloucester.

This was a gala launching day for the Cape Ann folks. Right after the launching of the *Alice Jacobs*, the crowd went over to the Oxner and Story yard in South Essex to witness the launching of the first knockabout fisherman, schooner *Helen B. Thomas*, and at Gloucester on that day the Boston schooner *Manhassett* was launched at Hugh Bishop's yard.

One hour after the *Alice M. Jacobs* arrived in Gloucester the afternoon of March 11, her spars were stepped and she was taken in tow for Boston, where her machinery was installed.

Always trying something new, Captain Sol Jacobs had the first big steam-powered fishing vessel built. The *Alice M. Jacobs* is returning to the inner harbor after her trial trip.

The *Alice Jacobs* resembled an ocean going tug. Her keel, stem and stern post were of white oak; the frames were of white oak and hackmatack; the outboard planking and ceiling were yellow pine; and the deck, white pine. Forward was a large forecastle and galley, with accommodations for 26 men. From the forecastle bulkhead to the machinery bulkhead was the main hold, about 50 feet long. Abaft the machinery space was the cabin, with accommodations for the officers. She carried about 40 tons of ice, and her coal bunkers had a capacity of 100 tons. Her main engines were of the vertical inverted compound type, with 300 indicated horsepower.

Her sail plan was modest, with pole masts, intended principally for steadying purposes or "laying to" while fishing. She was designed by Richard F. and William T. Keough of East Boston, famous steam boat designers; the machinery by Bertelson and Peterson of East Boston.

The fine craft was equipped with a dynamo and was electrically lighted throughout. She had a powerful steam windlass.

The captain of the vessel was, of course, Capt. Jacobs. All hands numbered 21 men.

The trial trip of the new steamer was made on April 15, 1902. It was a perfect day and guests enjoyed the cruise. The *Jacobs* left the pier in East Boston where her engine had been installed, and she was saluted by many craft of

all descriptions as she proudly steamed down Boston Harbor. Off Half Way Rock, the custom house gasoline boat *Dreamer* that came up to meet her turned around, but couldn't keep up with her, and was left far astern. The engine of the *Jacobs* was opened up off Half Way Rock, and to Ten Pound Island she made 11 knots. Capt. Jacobs and the entire party were pleased with the showing.

She made the run to Gloucester in three hours, arriving at 4:15 p.m. Crowds lined the wharves as she steamed up the harbor.

The *Alice Jacobs* sailed on her maiden trip at 7:45 p.m. on April 7, 1902. She was bound to the south'ard for mackerel. A stop was made at Woods Hole for water. Capt. Jacobs was delighted with her performance. She arrived at Fulton Market, New York with her maiden fare of 90 bbls. of mackerel, nine days later on April 26th.

Capt. Sol started right in like the "killer" he was and broke all mackerel records that season, stocking $41,000. This broke his own record of $39,700, made the previous season in the auxiliary schooner *Helen Miller Gould*.

Incidentally, in May 1902, cruising with the *Alice Jacobs* off Isaacs Harbor, Nova Scotia, were 50 American seiners. The Canadian cutter *Acadia* was watching them closely to see that they didn't take fish within the three mile limit.

The *Alice M.* drew a lot of attention her first season afloat, as she steamed through the fleet, searching for mackerel. On September 14, 1902, she fell in with the disabled passenger steamer *Cape Cod* (this steamer was built by A. D. Story at Essex in 1900). The helpless steamer had lost her rudder off Wood End, Cape Cod, and she was taken in tow by the *Jacobs* to Provincetown. The *Jacobs* then took the *Cape Cod's* 360 passengers to Boston. Capt. Sol was always willing to lend a helping hand.

In November 1902, the *Alice Jacobs* steamed to Newfoundland for a cargo of herring and arrived back in Gloucester on December 21, with 1500 bbls. salt herring and 300 bbls. frozen herring. That herring season of 1902–03 was a record in that branch of the fisheries. Fifty-three vessels sailed to Newfoundland that season, 42 vessels from Gloucester, two from Provincetown, three from Boston, three from Boothbay, Maine, two from Bucksport, Maine, and one from Chatham. Just think of it! Today not one single American craft is engaged in this trade.

The seining season of 1903 arrived and again this grand steamer was right there banging away. On January 2, she arrived in Gloucester with a large fare of 550 bbls. fresh mackerel and 320 bbls. salt mackerel. On this trip, off Cape Negro, Nova Scotia, she passed the new schooner *Bertha and Pearl*, Capt. Joe Smith, bound home with a big fare. She was the first of the Cape Shore fleet to arrive. On August 27, 1903, she landed a fare of 35,000 lbs. fresh and 350 bbls. salt mackerel. Her stock was $10,000, share $221.

The *Alice Jacobs* arrived at Boston September 10, 1903 with 50,000 lbs. fresh mackerel and 260 bbls. salt mackerel (equalled about 900 bbls.), stocking $9,000 with a share of $185. This was the biggest trip ever landed up to that time. The vessel had been out 10 days and the fish taken 15 miles northwest of Brier Island, Nova Scotia.

Tragedy struck close to the *Alice Jacobs* that month of September, 1903, on the 16th. She was in company with the Gloucester seining schooner *George F. Edmunds* all the way up from Mt. Desert Rock. The *Edmunds* was commanded by Capt. Willard Poole, an old friend of Capt. Jacobs. Just after a heavy storm struck, and the two vessels separated. The *George F. Edmunds*, in trying to work into Boothbay, Maine, struck on Pemaquid Point and was smashed to pieces. Only two of her crew of 16 were saved. The *Alice Jacobs* rode out the storm off Portland that night.

In November, 1903, the *Alice Jacobs* again went to Newfoundland for herring and returned to Gloucester from the Bay of Islands on November 28, 1903, with 2,000 bbls. The trip was sold to Frank Stanwood. She was gone only 18 days, round trip, and this was the quickest on record up to that time. On the way she went through the Bras d'Or Lakes in a heavy gale.

The career of the *Alice Jacobs* was cut short in December, 1903, only 21 months after her launching. On the 15th while bound to the Bay of Islands for her second herring cargo of the season, she crashed on the reefs of Durant Island, to the eastward of Cape Ray, Newfoundland. A gale was blowing and the temperature was below zero. The vessel struck with such force that the engines were driven up through the deck. Mate William Hudder, a half brother of Capt. Jacobs was at the wheel. The vessel began to pound to pieces. The rescue of the *Jacobs'* crew was another story of the heroism of the Cape Ann fishermen. It was indeed fortunate that she was carrying two nests of dories. Two of these small craft were put over and both were pounded to pieces. By this time the vessel heeled over, forming a lee, and a third dory was launched successfully. Austin George succeeded in rowing to the shore, where he made a line fast to a rock. The remainder of the crew left in more dories and were pulled to safety by means of this rope. All were frostbitten. Austin George had fingers and ears frozen. His courageous act had saved his shipmates. The island on which they landed was uninhabited. A dory was dragged over the island, which was 3½ miles wide, to the main channel, separating it from the mainland. Without much difficulty they rowed to the mainland and safety. The wreck of the *Jacobs* later took fire and burned to the water's edge. A grand vessel was gone. Her value with outfits was placed at $40,000.

Capt. Edgar Brayman, the last survivor of the crew, died in 1952. A native of Point Judith, Rhode Island, he recalled quite vividly the wreck of the *Alice Jacobs*.

Capt. Sol Jacobs, the "Mackerel King," was one of the greatest mariners ever to take the wheel of a Gloucester fisherman. The fame of this son of Twillingate, Newfoundland, was known all over the globe. Tall, raw boned and strong, he possessed great courage, determination, fearlessness, judgment and ability.

He was a pioneer in the fisheries. Way back in the '80's he sent his two fine schooners, *Molly Adams* and *Edward Webster*, around the Horn to the Pacific Coast to fish for halibut and seals. In 1899 he sent the crack schooner *Ethel B. Jacobs* on a cruise for mackerel along the Irish coast. In 1900 he had built the first auxiliary schooner in the fleet, the *Helen Miller Gould*. In 1902, he had built Gloucester's first large fishing steamer, the *Alice M. Jacobs*.

Capt. Sol made and lost several fortunes, but always had the courage to go on. When it came to fighting for his rights, Capt. Sol was right there. At one time he had claims against three governments. Like all great men, he was both criticized and praised.

His success in the mackerel fishery was uncanny. Not one man could top him in this field. The old saying was, that when a vessel arrived on seining grounds, the first thing asked was "Where's Sol?" They knew right well that where Sol Jacobs was, there were fish. Capt. Sol was one of the greatest money makers out of Gloucester.

Capt. Jacobs commanded some of the finest vessels out of this port, including the schooners *Sabine*, *S. R. Lane*, *Moses Adams*, *Sarah M. Jacobs* (named for his wife), 1878; *Edward Webster*, 1881 to 1891; *Ethel B. Jacobs* (named for his older daughter), 1891 to 1899; auxiliary schooner *Helen M. Gould*, 1900–1901; steamer *Alice M. Jacobs*, 1902–03; auxiliary schooner *Victor*, 1904; auxiliary schooner *Veda M. McKown*, 1905; schooner *A. M. Nicholson*, 1906–07–08; auxiliary *Benjamin A. Smith*, 1909; schooner *Georgia* and schooner *Elmer E. Gray*, 1910; gas boat *Quartette*, 1911; steamer *R. J. Killick*, 1912; schooner *Romance*, 1913; schooner *Pythian*, 1914; steamer *Bethulia*, 1915.

Death came to this great mariner on February 7, 1922, when he was stricken with apoplexy at the age of 74. Great skippers will come and go in the Gloucester fleet, but there will never be another Sol Jacobs.

Mrs. Alice Jacobs Cox, namesake of the steamer, passed away in Rockport in November, 1967.

Gross tons, 220; length, 141.6 feet; beam, 24 feet; depth, 12 feet. Main engine vertical inverted compound, 300 indicated horsepower; smokestack, 25 feet above deck, hinged to make way for sails.

Claudia

GLOUCESTER-BUILT, AND A WHALER /
1902–1939

In 1902, the Sylvanus Smith Co., one of Gloucester's finest firms, ordered a new vessel built at John Bishop's shipyard at Vincent Street. Named *Claudia*, she was launched on September 17, 1902.

The *Claudia* was a good, medium-sized vessel of the clipper bow type, taken off the models of schooners *Yakima* and *Tacoma*. Capt. Henry Jacobs, one of the firm's best skippers and one of Gloucester's finest, was given command.

The *Claudia* sailed on her maiden trip to Newfoundland for a cargo of herring on October 9, 1902, with Capt. George Turner as skipper.

Capt. Jacobs, her regular skipper took over the wheel on the next trip. In this second trip the *Claudia* was caught in the ice at Birchy Cove with the schooners *Dauntless*, *Lewis Giles*, *Arcadia*, *Sceptre*, *Golden Rod*, *Talisman* and *T. M. Nicholson*. All were frozen in for the winter. Capt. Jacobs kept up his fine reputation as a "killer" while in command of the *Claudia*, engaging mostly in the Georges handlining and halibut fishery.

Capt. John Matheson took over the vessel in 1905, seining. In the early part of 1906, Capt. Leonard Crowell had her fresh and salt fishing, and Capt. Matheson again took over during the seining season of 1906.

Capt. Dan Grady went seining in the *Claudia* during the season of 1907. In the fall of that year, Capt. Bob Keefe took the vessel halibuting.

The season of 1909 found the *Claudia* dory handlining under Capt. Bill Wharton. Capt. Andrew Gouvreau (Black Andrew) took over the helm in the spring of 1910 and remained skipper until the spring of 1917, deck handlining and Georges halibuting. "Black Andrew" did very well in *Claudia*, keeping up with the leaders year after year.

On May 21, 1915, Capt. Gouvreau landed one of the biggest trips of its kind in years (deck handlining) hailing for 60,000 lbs. salt cod and 5,000 lbs. halibut, having been gone only three weeks. In those days when a vessel's crew shared $100 or over, it was said they rang the bell. Capt. Gouvreau rang the bell on this trip.

Capt. Fred Howard was the last skipper in *Claudia* while she was Gloucester-owned. In 1917, the great Gloucester fleet was beginning to be broken up, due to the great demand for vessels and the big prices paid for them. In

December of that year the *Claudia* was sold to Antone Sylvia of New Bedford for a whaler. In 1919 she survived a hurricane at sea in which two companion whaling schooners were lost with all hands.

The *Claudia* was one of the lucky vessels as far as loss of life was concerned. Only two lives were lost during her fishing career.

John Campbell, one of her crew, was found dead in his bunk on January 10, 1912, while the vessel was lying at Sylvanus Smith Co. wharf. Death was due to heart failure. He was 60 years old and a native of Prince Edward Island.

On March 4, 1916, the *Claudia* was boarded by a big sea, while she was lying hove-to under a double-reefed foresail in a gale. Two of the crew were on watch, a man named De-Coste and Samuel Goodwin. DeCoste saw the sea coming and jumped for the forecastle in time. Goodwin was not so fortunate. The weight of the sea drove the vessel over on her beam ends, sweeping him overboard. He was never seen again.

The crew scurried on deck and got to work on the pumps. One man jumped to the wheel and they got her off the wind and ran under bare poles for 120 miles. It took 26 hours to get the water out of the vessel. On March 6th, the wind abated and under jury sail a course was set for Halifax, 380 miles away.

On March 13th, the badly battered *Claudia* arrived in Halifax. Capt. Gouvreau reported that the last two days before reaching port, the only food they had was bread. The *Claudia* was almost a complete wreck. Her foreboom and foresail were gone. Also missing were the big mainsail and mainboom, which had been furled and crotched at the time of the disaster. Every dory and everything movable had been washed off the deck. Temporary repairs were made in Halifax and the *Claudia* arrived home in Gloucester on March 27th. Samuel Goodwin was 50 years old and a native of Woods Harbor, Nova Scotia.

After several years as a whaler out of New Bedford, the *Claudia* was placed in the Cape Verde packet service. She remained in this grueling trade for some time making many passages across the Atlantic. Two of her packet skippers were Capt. Peter Brito and Manuel Chautre.

In 1926 the battered *Claudia* returned to Gloucester, her old home.

Capt. Manuel Domingoes and Marian Cooney, purchased the old craft at auction with the intention of restoring her to a fisherman. This plan fell through, however, and the vessel remained tied up, sad and forlorn, on the east side of the S. B. Ruth (Old Steamboat) wharf for some years. The old Boston fishing schooner *Mary T. Fallon* also remained idle near the *Claudia* for some years until she was broken up. Charles Williams, old-time fisherman, later purchased *Claudia* for the "large" amount of $7.

The *Claudia* with her tall spars was a familiar sight for some years as she remained tied up in back of the North Shore theatre. Finally the old vessel fell over on her side and the spars came out. In 1939 she was broken up by W.P.A. workmen, almost in the very spot she was built, 37 years before. I believe the schooners *Claudia* and *Mary T. Fallon* were the only fishing schooners of their size and type that were broken up in Gloucester in the last 60 years. This speaks for itself the wonderful construction and the demand for use in other parts of the world for this type of schooner.

In 1941, the bones of the old *Claudia* were covered up by workmen filling in the parking space back of the North Shore theatre. Here was built and here died a great schooner.

Capt. Henry Jacobs passed away on September 30, 1905 at the age of 51. This fine mariner, in the prime of his life, had taken the schooner *Ramona* on a pollock fishing trip. He was taken ill on the trip and was landed in Gloucester, where he passed away at the hospital following an operation.

Capt. Henry was the son of Harry and Mary (Smith) Jacobs. He was of Danish descent. At the age of 19 he took command of his first vessel and served 32 years as a skipper.

Big in stature and big in heart, Capt. Henry won for himself an enviable reputation as one of Cape Ann's finest skippers. By vessel owners, fellow mariners and fishermen, he was alike beloved and respected for his ability, integrity and honor.

Although he loved the sea and spent many years on the water, his greatest love was his home and family. He was the father of 15 children, of whom 13 were living at the time of his death.

Some of his commands were the schooners *Northern Eagle, Bloomer, Della Tarr, Farragut, Belle Franklin, William H. Moody, Claudia* and *Ramona.* Capt. Jacobs, one of the few native-born skippers of his time, gained his fame in a period when every dollar was earned the hard way. The going was rough but our skippers and their crews were equal to the task. They were real builders of Gloucester.

Gross tons, 113; net tons, 79; length, 97 feet; breadth, 24.6 feet; depth, 10.4 feet.

The *Helen B. Thomas*, built without a bowsprit, revolutionized fishing schooner design, according to the author. She was a smart little sailer, too.

Helen B. Thomas

SAFER WITHOUT A BOWSPRIT / 1902–1926

Schooner *Helen B. Thomas*, the first knock-about fisherman, was one of the most famous two masted crafts ever built, a vessel whose design created a great change in fishing vessel construction; a change destined to save many lives.

Schooner *Helen B. Thomas* was built during the winter of 1902 at the Oxner and Story yard in South Essex (formerly occupied by Willard Burnham) for Capt. William Thomas, famous Down East skipper, and Cassius Hunt and others of Boston.

It was a big launching day on March 11, 1902. In Essex, steamer *Alice M. Jacobs* was launched at the Arthur D. Story yard and the *Helen B. Thomas* followed soon after at the Oxner and Story yard. The schooner *Manhassett* was launched at the Hugh Bishop yard in Gloucester on that same day.

It was difficult to launch the *Helen B. Thomas* on account of the peculiar shape of the vessel, but everything went fine and the craft slid into the water in splendid style.

The *Thomas* was a distinct departure from any craft ever before constructed for the fishing business. The knockabout rig (no bowsprit) was originated in 1892. Two small yachts, the *Nancy* and the *Jane*, were built by Higgins and Gifford at Gloucester for a Marblehead yachtsman. Stewart and Binney of Boston were the designers of these craft. Capt. Tom McManus, brilliant fishing schooner designer, created the *Helen B. Thomas*. Capt. Tom had thought up the idea several years before but nobody would take a chance on this kind of vessel until Capt. Thomas and Mr. Hunt decided to give it a try.

The new craft attracted much attention when she was brought around to Gloucester to be rigged and much criticism was passed upon her. Some people said she was designed by the man who planned Noah's Ark. Some said, "There will be more built like her." How true was this last statement!

Schooner *Helen B. Thomas* had a very crooked sheer, with long overhanging ends, especially in the bow. All her head sails were inboard, as there was no bowsprit, which proved to be a great life saver. She carried a good spread of canvas. The length of her forecastle was 27 feet. The fine little craft was named for the daughter of her skipper, Capt. William Thomas, known among fishermen as Down East Billy or Knockabout Bill, so as not to be confused with Gloucester's Capt. William H. Thomas. Boston was the hailing port of the new craft.

The trial trip was sailed on April 3, 1902, and she made the run from Gloucester to Boston in four hours. Capt. Thomas didn't push her too hard because of the many guests making the trip.

The *Helen B. Thomas* sailed on her maiden trip, shore fishing on Arpil 7, 1902, in command of Capt. William Thomas. She was forced to put into Gloucester because of a heavy gale outside. The *Helen B.* arrived at Boston with her maiden fare of 4,000 pounds fresh fish on April 13th.

The *Helen Thomas* was a very easy vessel to handle and maneuver. Fishermen who sailed her told me that you could almost turn her on a dime. She was also one of the flyers of the smaller vessels of the Boston fleet. On May 7, 1902 she beat the fast schooner *Viking* by about 8 miles on the run from Middle bank to T-wharf.

The *Helen B. Thomas*, Capt. William Thomas, was entered in the class for smaller vessels in the fishermen's race for the Sir Thomas J. Lipton Cup in August, 1907. The race was sailed in Massachusetts Bay and the *Helen B.* was beaten by the crack Gloucester schooner *Frances P. Mesquita*, Capt. Joe Mesquita. The big Provincetown schooner *Rose Dorothea* beat the schooners *Jessie Costa* and *James W. Parker* in the large class, to take the Lipton Trophy.

The little knockabout had her share of narrow escapes, the most outstanding as follows:

On March 2, 1904, she narrowly escaped sinking after striking a ledge off Minot's Light, The vessel was bound in from shore fishing. Owing to the thick fog the craft lost her bearings and brought up with a crash on one of the dangerous ledges in that locality. She pounded heavily and Capt. Thomas and his men were preparing to abandon her when she floated, leaking badly.

She headed for port but was fast settling when she fell in with the Rockport tug *H. S. Nichols* and was towed into Boston, nearly full of water.

On January 6, 1905 the *Helen B. Thomas*, Capt. Thomas, was involved in a collision in Boston Harbor with the fishing schooner *Rob Roy*, Capt. Gourley Anderson. The *Helen B.* was bound out and the *Rob Roy* inward bound from Cape Shore with a trip. The *Thomas* luffed and shot across the bow of the *Rob Roy*. The vessels came together with terrific force and the *Thomas* was nearly sent to the bottom. Her entire starboard side was raked, 14 stanchions were broken, forerigging torn away, main boom and gaff broken and her mainsail torn to ribbons. The *Rob Roy* was only slightly damaged. Both vessels were repaired in Boston.

Capt. William Thomas remained in command of the *Helen B. Thomas* until 1912 when Capt. Fred Chetwynd took over. In 1914, Capt. Ed Russell was her skipper, haddocking. An auxiliary gasoline engine was installed in 1914. The *Helen B. Thomas* was sold to the Gorton-Pew Fisheries of Gloucester in May, 1916. Capt. Dan Grady was her first skipper under her new owners and he took her seining in 1916. Capt. Al Malloch (Al Miller) took her seining in the fall of 1916 and Capt. William Price took her haddocking during the winter of 1916–1917.

Capt. Rufas (Rufe) McKay had her seining during the seasons of 1917 and '18. In 1917 during September and October, in nine trips seining, Capt. McKay stocked $38,311 and the crew shared $1171. This was probably the best stock ever made by the *Helen B. Thomas*.

Capt. William Tobey took over seining in the fall of 1918 and also had her haddocking that winter of 1918–19. The seining season of 1919, Capt. Charley Martin (Young Single Reef) was her skipper. The fall of 1919 Capt. Will Tobey again took over. Capt. John Vautier was the last skipper of the little knockabout, and he took her seining during the season of 1920.

Loss of life in the *Helen B. Thomas* was fortunately very small. Marshall Nickerson was slatted overboard and drowned while taking in the mainsail in a heavy breeze, 65 miles south of Seal Island, Nova Scotia, on April 8, 1912. He was a native of Woods Harbor, Nova Scotia, and 24 years old. Capt. Fred Chetwynd was skipper at the time.

Lee Parris dropped dead of a heart attack on the deck of the vessel while at anchor in Provincetown harbor on June 28, 1919. He was a native of Maine and a brother of Capt. Tom Parris, noted fishing skipper. Capt. Charles A. Martin was skipper of the *Helen B. Thomas* at the time.

The *Helen B Thomas* was sold by the Gorton-Pew Co. to Bermuda parties for a pilot boat in March, 1921. On March 12, 1921 she bid good-bye to Gloucester as she sailed out of the harbor, flying the British flag and bound to Hamilton, Bermuda. Capt. Don McCuish sailed her down.

I received the information from the British Registrar General that the registry of the British schooner *Helen B. Thomas* was closed on November 27, 1926. The vessel had been destroyed by fire.

I can well remember the *Helen B. Thomas* when I was a youngster. Her long crooked hull and overhanging bow were outstanding features among her sisters of the fleet. The little vessel that many thought such a freak, proved to be the forerunner of the type that was to outlast them all.

Edwin H. Oxner, builder of the *Helen B. Thomas*, passed away in Marblehead on May 8, at the age of 84. He was a native of Lunenburg, Nova Scotia. Oxner was one of the last of the old vessel builders. In 1901 he established a partnership with Lyndon Story at the old Willard Burnham yard in South Essex. From 1901 to 1907 about 52 vessels were sent down the ways of the Oxner and Story yard. Some of the finest and most beautiful fishing schooners in the fleet were built by Oxner, including the *Helen B. Thomas*, the first knockabout; *Regina*, one of the fastest fishermen ever built; *Squanto, Massachusetts, Susan and Mary, Raymah, Thomas A. Cromwell, Shepherd King, Onato, Fame, Tartar, Harmony* and *Richard*, the last vessel built at the Oxner and Story yard. Oxner takes his place with another great Nova Scotian, Donald McKay, as a great builder of wooden ships.

Capt. William Thomas (Down East Billy) passed away at Sailors Snug Harbor, New York, in February, 1951, at the age of 92. Capt. Billy was one of the great Down East fishing skippers. For many years he was one of the leaders of the Boston market fleet. Some of his commands were the schooners *Maud S., Helen B. Thomas* and *Benjamin Thompson*. He was a native of Maine.

Cassius Hunt, one of the early owners of the *Helen B. Thomas*, died May 31, 1914 in Somerville. He was a native of Duxbury and 70 years old. Hunt was for many years a leading figure in the fish business on old T-Wharf in Boston.

Gross tons, 76; net tons, 48; length, 94.2 feet; breadth, 21.6 feet; depth, 9.2 feet. Original spar measurements: mainmast (deck to cap), 64 feet; foremast, 58 feet; maintopmast, 40 feet; foretopmast, 35 feet; mainboom, 60 feet; main gaff, 34 feet; mastheads, 9.5 feet.

Stripped for action as the camera-carrying vessel in the making of the movie of Kipling's classic Gloucester story, *Captains Courageous*, the *Mary F. Curtis* looked like this.

Mary F. Curtis

TOP MACKEREL MONEY MAKER / 1903–1952

Schooner *Mary F. Curtis*, last of the famous round-bowed, or Indian head, vessels, was the holder of the world's record in mackerel seining; a vessel that carried the hailing port of Gloucester on her stern for nearly half a century.

The *Mary F. Curtis*, one of the prettiest of her type, lived a full life in the days of sail; carried on through the days of combination sail and auxiliary power, and even up to the day of her loss held her own with the modern high powered draggers.

She was built during the summer of 1903 at the Tarr and James yard in Essex for the John Pew firm of Gloucester and her skipper, Capt. Henry Curtis. The launching September 9, 1903, was marred by accident. While sliding down the launching ways the *Curtis* stopped and turned completely over on her side, throwing all the guests (25) with terrific force to the side of the vessel. Miss Alice Sartwell of Somerville, fiance of Harry Pew, received a broken collar bone. Several other guests were injured. The *Curtis* was towed around to Gloucester by the tug *Startle* September 12.

The *Mary F. Curtis* was a handsome round-bowed vessel of medium size, designed by Tom

McManus of Boston. She was a sharp vessel forward. She was named for the wife of her owner-skipper, and sailed on her maiden trip haddocking October 14, 1903.

Capt. Curtis, one of our fine mariners, sailed in the *Mary Curtis* until 1915, haddocking, shacking and seining. In 1915 and 1916 she was commanded by Capt. Leslie Cofill. During the winter of 1916–17 she was tile fishing out of New York, in command of Capt. Cofill.

Capt. Lemuel Firth, the great mackerel seiner, took over during the season of 1917 and made the highest stock ever recorded in the mackerel fishery: $82,869, with a share of $1,898 per man. During that season of 1917, auxiliary power consisting of two sixty-horse-power oil engines was installed. She was the first twin screw vessel of the Gorton-Pew fleet.

Capt. Firth made a splendid stock during the seining season of 1918: $71,477. This was the largest ever made in actual fishing in the same length of time, six months, up to that time. The crew numbered twenty.

Firth, who was seining skipper again in 1919, was a captain of unusual energy, practically tireless, with a splendid crew of hard workers. He was a close student of the habits and movements of mackerel.

The *Curtis*, in command of Capt. Firth, arrived at Gloucester November 24, 1917, with a cargo of potatoes from Prince Edward Island.

In 1920, Capt. Norman Ross had the *Curtis*, seining, and Capt. Chris Christianson took her haddocking. In 1921 it was Capt. Wallace Parsons seining and Capt. Frank Rose haddocking. In 1922–23, Capt. Percy Firth seining and haddocking; in 1924, Capt. Ben Bishop was skipper. In 1925 the captains were Frank Foote, John Seavey and Dave Keating. Incidentally, this was the last command of that great Down East skipper, John Seavey.

Capt. Dave Keating, a fine mackerel seiner, native of Newfoundland, took over the wheel in 1925 and remained in her, seining summers, for fourteen years until her sale by the Gorton-Pew Fisheries Co. Capt. George Hodgdon took her haddocking during the winter of 1931–32 and Capt. Andrew Decker was the haddocking skipper in the winter of 1932–33.

There were many interesting incidents in the life of the *Mary F. Curtis*. While seining off the Maine coast in command of Capt. Curtis in August 1904 the vessel and several others were struck by a spiteful southeaster and all lost their seineboats. They were the schooners *Seaconnet*, *Procyon*, *Etta Mildred*, *Pina*, *Annie Greenlaw*, *Ramona* and *Ralph L. Hall*.

In October 1909 the *Curtis*, in temporary command of Capt. Myles Somers, ran down the Boston schooner *Tartar*, Capt. Wilfred Roberts, in a thick fog, thirty miles west of Cape Sable, and nearly sent the *Tartar* to the bottom. The *Curtis* was bound to the eastward and the *Tartar* was bound home with a

trip. Both craft were going about nine knots. Fortunately it was a glancing blow, else the tale would have been far more serious. The *Tartar* was struck on the starboard quarter and her stern was started and the rail torn up and smashed for quite a distance. The big mainsail of the *Tartar* was torn to ribbons and her main boom, main gaff and fore gaff were broken. The *Tartar* began to leak badly, and the crew manned the pumps all the way home. The *Curtis*, with very little damage, continued on her trip after it was made certain the *Tartar* could reach home by herself.

The *Mary Curtis* came very near leaving her bones in Newfoundland in June 1914. The vessel, in command of Capt. Curtis on a shacking trip, struck a ledge three miles off Bonne Bay, Newfoundland. All hands left her and rowed and give her a try. They heaved the bait and ice overboard and hoisted the sails. The craft ashore, giving her up as a-goner. Later Capt. Curtis and his crew decided to board the craft and give her a try. They heaved the bait and ice overboard and hoisted the sails. The craft commenced to move, and slid off into deep water. She was repaired at Port Hawkesbury, Cape Breton.

On May 20, 1918, the *Mary F. Curtis*, Capt. Lem Firth, arrived at Gloucester and reported she had found three bodies from the ill-fated S. S. *City of Athens*, which was rammed by a French cruiser off the coast of Delaware May 1, 1918, when sixty-nine persons lost their lives. The bodies were found floating at sea, and with brief but impressive services were buried at sea. The seiner *Harvard* picked up one body. The *Veda M. McKown* found two, and the *Avalon* one.

While in command of Capt. Dave Keating, July 31, 1935, most of the crew were thrown into the water when their seineboat overturned. All were rescued.

The *Mary Curtis* was used in the filming of the movie *Captains Courageous* in October 1935. Commanded by Capt. Donald McCuish, she carried the cameras, film and other equipment, valued at $30,000. This cargo was probably the most valuable ever taken by a Gloucester fisherman. The *Curtis*, in company with the schooner *Imperator*, sailed from Gloucester October 17 for Newfoundland waters, where scenes for the movie were filmed. They returned to Gloucester November 22, 1935. About 38,000 feet of film were shot on the voyage. Both vessels were chartered from the Gorton-Pew Company.

The *Mary F. Curtis* was sold by Gorton-Pew in 1939 to Capt. Philip Giamanco of Gloucester. She was completely rebuilt into a dragger, and the old *Mary F.* could hardly be recognized as the onetime beauty of the fleet. A whaleback bow was added, the stern cut off, spars shortened, and a big three hundred horsepower Diesel engine installed. She was used by Capt. Giamanco for seining summers and dragging winters.

The *Mary F. Curtis* again nearly left her bones in Canadian waters when she stranded on Man O' War Rock near Canso, Nova Scotia, in November 1949. After she was abandoned by her crew she was refloated by a salvage vessel and taken to Sydney for repairs, and later returned to her owners.

When the Margaree Steamship Co. tug approached the *Curtis* the mate, Uriah Giles, thought the lines of the stranded vessel were familiar. He was correct. The mate of the *Mary F. Curtis* at the time of the filming of *Captains Courageous* was none other than Uriah Giles.

It was a stroke of fate that he should be intimately involved with the vessel when she had reached her finest hour and that he would be instrumental in saving her from an ignominious end off the shores of Nova Scotia.

The end came to the great old vessel February 17, 1952 when, in command of Capt. Giamanco, she stranded on the eastern tip of McNutt's Island, off Shelburne, Nova Scotia, in a blinding snowstorm. The schooner hit a shoal about two hundred yards from shore and her crew were forced to take to a dory. Their boat capsized about thirty yards from shore and the men had to swim through raging, bitterly cold seas to reach the beach.

After landing on shore they had to walk three miles through brush, woods and swamps to get to one of the few buildings on the island, Roseway Light. There they were cared for by the lightkeeper. The *Curtis* smashed to pieces and the only thing left was the engine. A grand old veteran of the sea was gone. Farewell, *Mary F. Curtis!*

In the crew at the time of the loss were Capt. Philip Giamanco, engineer Frank Ashburn, cook Harold Wagsatt, William Enos, Michael A. Favazza, Robert Goodick and James Harris, Jr.

Capt. Henry Curtis passed away in Gloucester June 3, 1933, at the age of seventy-five. This fine old mariner was a native of Ingonish, Cape Breton, and fished out of Gloucester for fifty-six years. Some of his best known commands were the schooners *Florence*, *Vigilant*, and *Mary F. Curtis*.

Mrs. Mary F. Curtis, namesake of the vessel, passed away in Gloucester March 17, 1930, at the age of sixty-six.

Capt. David Keating died at Rowley, Massachusetts, in January 1966 at the age of ninety. He was a native of Fortune Bay, Newfoundland. Capt. Dave was one of Gloucester's fine mackerel seining skippers.

Capt. Lemuel Firth passed away in Gloucester in May 1967 at the age of eighty-seven He was one of the greatest seining skippers, and in his younger days was one of the finest handliners out of Gloucester.

Capt. Lem was a native of Jordan Ferry, Shelburne County, Nova Scotia, the son of Capt. Uriah Firth, noted Nova Scotian skipper.

Some of Capt. Lem's commands were the schooners *Joseph E. Garland*, *Arcadia*, *Helen G. Wells*, *Claudia*, *Sylvania*, *Mary F. Curtis*, *Catherine Burke*, *Three Sisters*, and *Jean and Patricia*.

Gross tons, 121; net tons, 85; length, 101.3 feet; breadth, 24 feet; depth, 11.2 feet. Original spars: mainmast, (deck to cap), 71 feet; foremast, 67.5 feet, maintopmast, 43 feet; foretopmast, 35 feet; mainboom, 69 feet; main gaff, 41.5 (cut to 39.5); bowsprit, 29 feet (outboard); mainmast head, 10 feet.

Double trouble: the *Cavalier* lost two men astray in a dory, hence the flag at half-mast; then one day everything aloft came down in a heap, probably because a bobstay parted. She is being towed in by the Coast Guard cutter *Androscoggin*, which at that time doubled as a hospital ship for fishermen.

Cavalier

LOTS OF HALIBUT AND HARD LUCK /
1904–1932

Schooner *Cavalier* probably brought more halibut to Gloucester than any other schooner. She and Capt. Robert Porper made a pair noted for success. The vessel had her share of hard luck, too, coming home twice with broken spars.

The photo shows her being towed into Gloucester Harbor February 23, 1911, after a Grand Bank trip during which two men went astray. The flag at half mast indicates loss of life.

With a fine fare of halibut, caught on the southern edge of Grand Bank, the *Cavalier* squared away for home in a fresh southerly breeze. When the wind hauled to the northward next day, Capt. Bob decided to take in the mainsail. As the smaller riding sail was being bent on, everything aloft came down in a heap—spars, sails and all. It was a miracle no one was hurt. The crew cut away the spars dragging alongside, set up a jury rig, and again headed for home. They were about 70 miles southeast of Cape Sable.

For 11 days the vessel was buffeted by gales and carried to the southward. She was 300 miles east southeast of Cape Ann when she was sighted, flying a distress signal, by the Coast Guard cutter *Androscoggin*. After getting a line aboard with great difficulty, the cutter towed the schooner home, where hundreds examined her at the New England Fish Co. wharf. Capt. Bob, a hustler, had the damage repaired quickly and left March 9 for another halibuting trip.

The men lost were Thomas Babine, 32, native of Arichat, Cape Breton, and John Porper, 48, native of St. Francis Harbor, Nova Scotia, a cousin of the captain. They went astray January 25, 1911.

When the *Cavalier* made port December 7, 1916, with a small trip of 15,000 pounds of halibut, Capt. Porper had the grim duty of reporting two deaths. The cook, Carl Olson, 40, native of Sweden, died while aboard and his body was landed at Shelburne, Nova Scotia. Severen Hanson, 30, native of Sweden, was killed by part of the falling mainmast while homeward bound from Green Bank. His body was placed in the top dory of the starboard nest. When 60 miles southeast of Sable Island, a sea swept the dory overboard, with the body in it. To make his arrival home grimmer, Capt. Bob learned that his eldest daughter had passed away.

James Cavanaugh, 56, a native of Francis Harbor, Nova Scotia, and John Kenton, 31, a native of Gloucester, were washed overboard on St. Peter's Bank, January 4, 1913.

The *Cavalier* was launched, with little ceremony, on May 5, 1904, at Tarr and James yard, Essex. She was a beautiful schooner from a Tom McManus design, with round bow and lofty rig. The Cunningham & Thompson Company had her built for Capt. Porper after he lost his fine schooner *Anglo Saxon* on the Nova Scotia coast in 1903.

Cavalier's maiden trip was extremely long, as fish were scarce. She sailed May 23, 1904, salt banking, and returned nearly six months later, November 14, with 275,000 pounds of salt cod. That winter the *Cavalier* was sent to Newfoundland for a cargo of frozen herring, arriving in Gloucester, January 9, 1905, from Bay of Islands, with 1500 barrels of herring.

From the spring of 1905 on, Capt. Bob and the *Cavalier* went after halibut, and brought in plenty of it. He had no superior in the halibut fishery. He was not too fortunate in striking fancy prices, but he sure brought in the fish. He spent little time in port, and although the *Cavalier* was not fast, he made her sail. He had stiff competition from schooners, *Tacoma*, Capt. Dell Nickerson; *Massachusetts*, Capt. Jack Carroll; *Monitor*, Capt. Jerome MacDonald; *Squanto*, Capt. Jack McKay; and *Harmony*, Capt. Chris Gibbs.

She fished mostly on the northern banks, such as Quero, Sable Island, Burgeo, St. Pierre, the Anticosti Grounds and Green. His favorite place seemed to be the southern edge of Grand Bank. Another narrow escape was experienced in January, 1912, when she was hit by a giant sea off the Cape Shore, losing 10 dories and smashing her main boom and gaff.

Along with hard luck she had good fortune. On February 7, 1907, for example, she brought 65,000 pounds of halibut from Grand Bank, stocking $5000. On April 26, 1909, she brought 50,000 pounds of halibut from Burgeo Bank after being gone only 12 days, and sailing 1300 miles. A contrast was a fare of 12,000 pounds landed December 27, 1906, after being gone 12 weeks, on a Quero trip. In 1908 Capt. Bob was high line of the halibuters, stocking $21,248, with a share of $430. Many larger trips and greater stocks were made in the 1920's and '30's, but Capt. Bob was still the king. He commanded the *Cavalier* from 1904 until 1920. Capt. George Tufts took her salt banking in 1921. The vessel was usually painted a pretty green, with white mastheads, booms and gaffs.

Gorton-Pew Fisheries Co., Ltd., took over the *Cavalier* in 1917 when Cunningham and Thompson sold out. In 1922, the *Cavalier* was sold to the British for rum running.

She was registered out of Nassau, Bahamas Islands, in Lloyds, 1924 to 1931, and was renamed *Quistcachan*. She was sold to Chesly Boyce of Jersey Harbor, Newfoundland, and renamed *Marjorie and Eileen*, after his two daughters.

She was driven ashore in Miquelon Roads with another former Gloucesterman, schooner *Admiral Dewey*, on September 10, 1932. She had parted her chains in a heavy east northeast gale, drove up on the beach and was a total loss. She was in ballast for Sydney, Nova Scotia, to load coal for Newfoundland in command of Capt. George Yarn.

Capt. Porper, a native of Manchester in Guysboro County, Nova Scotia, where so many great mariners came from, became a master at 21, in command of schooner *Frederick Geering*. Other commands included the *Bessie Wells*, *Gladstone*, *Waldo L. Stream*, *Imperator*, *Pilgrim*, *Angie L. Marshall* and *Louise R. Sylvia*. It was said by fishermen that Capt. Porper saw more rough water than any other man fishing out of Gloucester. He died in October, 1941, at the age of 83 years. That was 19 years after the *Cavalier* rounded Eastern Point for the last time. Captain and vessel, two grand old veterans of the deep, will never be forgotten by Gloucester people.

Gross tons, 130; net tons, 97; length, 105.2 feet; breadth, 25 feet; depth, 11.2 feet. Mainmast (deck to cap), 76 feet; foremast (deck to cap), 67 feet; main boom, 72 feet; bowsprit, 25 feet (outboard); mast heads, 12 feet; main gaff, 43.7 feet; main topmast, 45 feet; fore topmast, 43 feet.

Ingomar

HALIBUTER WRECKED ON PLUM
ISLAND / 1904–1936

Schooner *Ingomar* was one of the finest and best known vessels of her day, a fast, able craft that made halibut history and died close to home on Plum Island sand.

The *Ingomar* was built by James and Tarr in Essex during the summer of 1904 and launched on September 14th of that year. She was a splendid craft designed by Capt. Tom McManus of Boston. She was of the round bow or Indian head type with a long bowsprit and mainboom and spreading a large amount of canvas.

The Cunningham-Thompson Co., of Gloucester were the owners. She was named after the big schooner yacht *Ingomar* (143 tons) which was launched in 1903, one of the finest sailing yachts under the American flag. The name *Ingomar* came from a leader of a band of half savages of the German forests, taken from a play *Ingomar the Barbarian.*

The fine new craft sailed on her maiden trip to Newfoundland for a herring cargo on September 29, 1904 in command of Capt. Wallace Parsons. She arrived back in Gloucester on November 18, 1904 with 1500 bbls. of herring from the Bay of Islands. She beat up the harbor close on the heels of the fast schooner *Independence II*, Capt. Joe Cusick. Both craft had left about the same time and made a driving passage of a little over five days, encountering on the way one of the worst gales in some time.

As the two craft came to an anchor a longshoreman was heard to remark, "I'll bet Joe and Wallace have drove them all right." "You can bet neither have slept very much," said another. And they were both right, for neither of these hustlers had their oil clothes off since they turned the high headland off Webald and drove out into the turbid waters of the gulf.

The *Ingomar* was one of the flyers of the fleet in her younger days and one of her greatest rivals was Capt. Joe Cusick's big schooner *Independence II.* The two vessels had many a friendly brush, with the honors about even. In January, 1905, Capt. Parsons and the *Ingomar* beat the schooners *Lottie G. Merchant, Ralph L. Hall, Dictator, Faustina* and *Bohemia* from the Bay of Islands to Gloucester.

Capt. Parsons remained in command of the *Ingomar* until the fall of 1909, seining and on Newfoundland herring voyages. Capt. Horace G. Wylde, one of the leading fresh fishing skippers, took over in the fall of 1909 and remained in the craft right up to November, 1917, haddocking, shacking and halibuting. From

November, 1910 to April, 1911, Capt. Wylde stocked $21,076 landing every fare at the Gloucester Fresh Fish Co.

Capt. Jerry Cook took the *Ingomar* to Newfoundland for a herring cargo in December 1907.

The *Ingomar* was taken over by the Gorton-Pew Co. when they purchased the Cunningham-Thompson Co. in 1917. In 1919 two 60 horsepower oil engines were installed. Capt. Freeman Crowell took over the *Ingomar* in November, 1917 and remained until October, 1919, haddocking and shacking. Capt. Frank Gaspa, crack Provincetown Portuguese skipper, took command from February 1920 to October 1920, haddocking, stocking $65,970. Capt. Percy Firth was skipper from November 1920 to January 1922, haddocking and seining.

The *Ingomar* was taken over by Capt. Carl Olson, great halibut skipper, in March 1922 and he remained until October 1925. Under Capt. Olson she broke all halibut records. In 1922, the stock was $56,222 with a share of $1854. In 1923 the stock was $58,834 and a share of $2124. In 1924 the *Ingomar* landed 402,000 lbs. halibut, stocking $74,847 with a share of $2713. (On February 24, 1924 she landed a fare stocking $16,250 and on March 16, 1924 landed 80,000 lbs. halibut stocking $16,928 with a share of $482.) The season of 1925 the *Ingomar* stocked $87,905 and shared $3196. (On February 24, 1925 she landed 90,000 lbs. halibut at Boston, stocking $16,250 and sharing $453). The total stock for the four seasons was $277,878 and a share of $9887 per man. This was sure making money and Capt. Carl Olson firmly established himself as one of the greatest halibuters out of this port.

Capt. Guiseppe Strescino took the *Ingomar* haddocking during November and December of 1925. Capt. "Little" Dan McDonald had her halibuting in January, February and March of 1926.

Capt. Alvaro Quadros, one of our hustling Portuguese skippers, took over, haddocking, April to September 1926 and made a splendid stock of $37,398. (Capt. Quadros was swept to his death from the Boston schooner *Mayflower* during the August gale of 1927).

The next skipper of the *Ingomar* was Capt. Horton Mason, who had her haddocking September 1926 to November 1927. Capt. Alfred Goodwin took her Rip fishing from March to December 1928 and made a fine stock of $40,547.

In 1929 Capt. Frank Palmer, haddocking and

The *Ingomar* a few hours after she ran aground in the fog with 50,000 pounds of fresh fish in her pens.

Capt. Edward Nickerson, Rip fishing were the skippers. The season of 1930, Capt. Alfred Goodwin again took her Rip fishing and in the winter of 1930–31, Capt. Frank Palmer had her haddocking. Capt. William Goodwin had her Rip fishing during 1931.

Capt. Sayward McLaren was *Ingomar's* skipper, haddocking and Rip fishing from November, 1931 to March, 1934. The season of 1934 found Capts. George Goodwin and Les Matthews in command. Capt. Albert Hines had her haddocking January to August, 1935. Capt. John Atwood took over haddocking in September 1935 and remained in her until her loss in February 1936.

Loss of life in the *Ingomar* was as follows: John Samuel Perry was drowned when his dory capsized in heavy seas 60 miles north of Magdalen Islands on May 22, 1915. His dorymate Edward Conrad was saved. Perry was a native of Nova Scotia and was 38 years old. He left a widow and six small children. Capt. Horace Wylde was skipper at the time.

Augustus (Soapsuds) Peterson was drowned on Quero when his dory upset on October 22, 1922. The body of Peterson, kept afloat by air in his oilskins, was taken aboard the dory of Capt. Wylie Rudolph and his dorymate, members of the crew of the schooner *American*, Capt. Tom Downie, who were fishing nearby. Edward Shea, dorymate of the unfortunate man, was also rescued by one of the *American's* dories. Augustus Peterson was a native of Sweden and 50 years old. Capt. Carl Olson was skipper at the time.

Murray Amero was swept overboard to his death when the vessel was hit by a heavy sea 65 miles off Boston Light on February 23, 1932. He was a native of Lower East Pubnico, Nova Scotia, and 22 years old. Capt. Sayward McLarren was the skipper at the time.

On October 22, 1927, Capt. Horton Mason reported that Caleb Conrad, one of *Ingomar's* crew, fell overboard and drowned on the way out of Boston Harbor. He was a native of Nova Scotia.

Another member of the *Ingomar's* crew came very nearly losing his life, but was rescued by his skipper, Capt. Carl Olson, at the risk of his own life. The *Ingomar* was fishing on Quero Bank on April 23, 1923 when Christopher Neilsen and Augustus Johnson were being lowered in their dory into the sea. A comber struck the dory, hurling Neilsen into the icy water, weighted down by his rubber boots and oil skins. Capt. Olson was at the wheel and when he saw what happened, dove in after him. Capt. Carl, being a powerful swimmer, managed to get one of the floating oars and shoved it ahead within grasp of Neilsen and in this way got him to the vessel, where both were taken on board. For his heroic deed Capt. Olson was awarded the William

Penn Harding medal for bravery by the Massachusetts Humane Society.

The *Ingomar* herself had many narrow escapes from destruction. On November 15, 1909 while she was tied up at the Gloucester Fresh Fish Co. wharf, two of her crew, George Nourse and Levi Muise were seriously burned in a powder explosion in her cabin. Nourse, while looking for something in Capt. Wylde's closet, lit a match which ignited a keg of powder which was stored there. Both men were removed to the hospital. The explosion wrecked the cabin near the forward bulkhead.

In August, 1931, the *Ingomar*, Capt. William Goodwin, was riding at anchor in a dense fog on Brown's Bank. Her fog horn was sounding continuously. Suddenly out of the fog came the giant White Star liner *Majestic* (56,000 tons). The liner came so close it was possible to make out her name and they could feel the rush of air caused by her speed as she raced past. Fortunately, the *Ingomar* was swung by the wind and tide in such a way that she was heading, parallel to the course of the big steamer. Lady Luck was sure smiling on *Ingomar* that day. If that giant steamer had hit her there would have been another Gloucesterman "Lost at sea with all hands."

The *Ingomar's* life ended on February 18, 1936 on the sands of Plum Island, not far from her birthplace. The vessel in command of Capt. John Atwood lost her course in a heavy sea and fog while bound to Boston with 50,000 lbs. fresh fish. She struck the beach about 2 miles north of the Plum Island Life Saving Station. The big seas cast her high and dry on the beach, breaking her back.

Capt. Atwood and 19 of his crew left the vessel in dories and landed at Boar's head, Hampton, New Hampshire. These men included Capt. John Atwood, engineer Irvin Hersey, sey, cook Ben Nickerson, Leslie Sholds, Freeman Allen, Eli Doucett, Lyman Nickerson, Manuel Catwind, Qeuter Surrette, Andrew Surrette, Samuel Boudreau, Preston Crowell, Benton Halliday, Phillip Brazier, William Kennedy, Jerry Malonson, Augustus Beridreu, Herman Walsh, Donald Christholm.

The other two crew members, Andrew White and John Whalen, decided to remain on the vessel, taking a chance in the rigging, but were taken off by the Merimac life saving crew.

For several days souvenir hunters thronged the sands looking for any movable piece of the vessel. Two days later the portside of the vessel was nearly gone and by the end of March, nothing remained. Her spars were salvaged by the owners. So ends the story of *Ingomar*, "Ingomar the Barbarian."

At the time of her loss, she was in the first stages of alteration (cut down). Her bowsprit was out, she carried a wheelhouse aft and a riding sail in place of the big mainsail.

Schooner yacht *Ingomar*, namesake of the Gloucesterman, was lost off Cape Fear, North Carolina, in February, 1931. Her crew was saved.

Capt. Wallace Parsons, known among fishermen as "Little Sol," lost his life when he fell from Davis Brothers' wharf in Gloucester on January 4, 1935. He was skipper of the schooner *Thomas S. Gorton* at the time. This able mariner was one of our great skippers in the days of sail. Small in stature, but great in deed, he was a fine seiner and one of the best in the Newfoundland herring trade. During his career he made 57 trips to his native land for herring. He learned the ropes from the great Capt. Sol Jacobs.

Some of Capt. Parsons' commands were the schooners *Pinta*, *Harry G. French*, *Nourmahal*, *Ingomar*, *Saladin*, *Thomas S. Gorton* and the three-masted *Aviator*. He was 65 years old and a native of the Bay of St. George, Newfoundland.

Capt. Horace L. Wylde lost his life in the Bucksport, Maine schooner *T. M. Nicholson*, when she was lost with all hands on a passage from Port aux Basques to Bay of Islands, Newfoundland, in January, 1924. Capt. Wylde was one of our finest fresh fishing skippers. Smart, capable, and well liked, he was always up with the topnotchers. He commanded many fine vessels including the schooners *Ramona*, *Olga*, *Dictator*, *Corona*, *Ingomar*, *John Hays Hammond*, *Corinthian*, *John J. Fallon*, *Killarney*, etc. He was a native of Port Medway, Nova Scotia. His brother. Capt. Lyman Wylde, was also a noted skipper.

Capt. John Atwood, last skipper of the *Ingomar*, died at Melrose, January 4, 1940, at the age of 64. He was a native of Argyle, Nova Scotia.

Capt. Atwood was a leader in the haddock fishery, sailing mostly out of Boston. His commands included the *Yakima*, *Fannie Belle Atwood*, *Manhassett* and *Dawn*.

Capt. Carl Olson died at Gloucester in May 1965 at the age of seventy-eight. A native of Kristainsand, Norway, he was one of our great halibut skippers and in the 1920's was the talk of the town because of his big halibut trips and big stocks.

Some of his commands were schooners *Fannie Prescott*, *Elk*, *Elsie*, *Ingomar*, *Progress*, *Raymonde* and *Oretha F. Spinney*, and the steam trawler *Seal*.

In the *Seal*, he landed one of the biggest trips of fresh fish ever landed at an American port. The fare of 475,000 fresh fish was landed at Boston on July 15, 1918.

Neils Christian Neilsen, the man saved by Capt. Olsen, passed away in Gloucester in July 1972 at the great age of 106 years. He was a native of Denmark and came to Gloucester in 1891.

I knew this little "old man of the sea" very well. Many are the tales he told me of his experiences at sea. I admired his modesty and stamina. Here was a man who cheated death at least three times; had always worked hard afloat and ashore to provide for his family. Here was a man, a living symbol of all the courage and greatness of his dorymates who had sailed on into the past. Here was Chris Neilsen, Gloucester fisherman.

Gross tons, 143; net tons, 103; length, 104.8 feet; breadth, 25.7 feet; depth, 11.4 feet. Original spar measurements: mainmast (deck to cap), 78 feet; foremast, 69.5 feet; main topmast, 47 feet; foretopmast, 42.5 feet; main gaff, 44 feet (cut to 39 feet); main boom, 76 feet (cut to 69.5 feet); bowsprit, 29 feet (cut to 22.5 feet).

Onato tacks in light air in Boston Harbor; a workmanlike vessel whose appearance belies her hair-raising experiences.

Onato

MUTINY WAS CHARGED / 1904–1919

The fine schooner *Onato*, one of the leaders in the fresh fishery, was sailed by a crack skipper; was a big producer of fish and a big money maker—and she was to end her days as a suspected murder ship.

The *Onato* was built during the spring and summer of 1904 by Oxner and Story at Essex alongside of schooner *Tartar*. A large party was on board at the time of her launching and when about to take her first dip into the briny, in some unknown manner she fell over on her side, throwing the people on board to the deck, and covering them with fresh paint. *Onato* was unkind to her guests on her christening day. She was launched successfully on August 27,

1904 and towed around to Gloucester to fit for sea.

The *Onato*, like a great many vessels of that period, carried an Indian name. She was built for Capt. J. Henry Larkin, who owned a quarter, E. A. Malone of Boston, owning an eighth, and ten other greater Boston people, including Benjamin F. Phillips and Orson Arnold.

The *Onato* was a large round bowed vessel from Tom McManus' design. Her rig was lofty and she spread a large sail area.

Capt. J. Henry Larkin, the *Onato's* skipper, was formerly in the schooner *Colonial*, and had earned a fine reputation for himself.

The *Onato* sailed from Gloucester on her maiden trip fresh fishing on September 14, 1904 and arrived back in Gloucester on October 1, 1904, with 100,000 lbs. fresh fish, of which 25,000 lbs. had been landed at Boston.

The *Onato* was a great fish producer, and always used in the haddocking and shacking game. Some of her largest trips were as follows: On June 27, 1907, she arrived at Gloucester with 200,000 shack, stocking $4,240, which was one of the largest shack trips up to that time. The summer season of 1909, she landed four trips, with a total of 840,000 lbs.

One of the trips was a record breaker. At the time, *Onato* weighed out 113,000 lbs. salt cod and 140,000 fresh cod. The trip was sold to the Slade Gorton Co. and she stocked $5,550. Her crew of 22 men made a fine share. The fish were taken on Quero Bank.

I have been told that the *Onato* was so deep on this trip that while lying at the wharf, the water was on her deck, coming in through the scuppers.

The *Onato* was having a race that season of 1909 with schooner *Thomas S. Gorton*, Capt. William Thomas. Both vessels were highline. On three of these trips that season the *Onato* stocked over $14,000. This was big money at the time.

In 1915 on one of *Onato's* shack trips she stocked $5,741. On April 26, 1916 she landed 171,000 fresh fish and 3,000 lbs. halibut at Boston. She caught this trip on Brown's Bank, and was out two weeks. Capt. Nelson Amero, one of our departed skippers, was cook on the *Onato* for over four years.

Loss of life was small in the *Onato*. Capt. Howard Morrissey, purser of the *Onato*, died of a heart attack in her cabin at the Slade Gorton Wharf, East Gloucester on March 29, 1906. He was 38 years old and a native of Pubnico, Nova Scotia. His brothers were Capts. William E., Fred, Delmar and David Morrissey. Incidentally, at that time the *Onato* had brought in the biggest trip of the season: 150,000 lbs. fresh fish.

On November 2, 1913, while the *Onato* was picking up her dories in the Channel, one of these small craft, in some unknown way, was run down by the vessel and its occupants were thrown into the water. Howard Nickerson was drowned and his dorymate rescued. Nickerson, a good swimmer, was probably hurt in the collision. He was 30 years old, a native of Woods Harbor, Nova Scotia.

The *Onato* was dismasted in 1905. She was fishing off the Nova Scotian coast when she was struck by a squall. The foremast had to be cut away, and soon after, the mainmast went over. Schooner *Muriel*, Capt. Jason Daley, took the wrecked vessel in tow and made for Pubnico, Nova Scotia. An entrance couldn't be made there because of the ice in the harbor, and the *Muriel* towed the *Onato* into Yarmouth, Nova Scotia, on March 7, 1905. The *Onato* arrived at Gloucester on March 14, in tow of the big Boston tug *Underwriter*. Her fare of 105,000 lbs. fresh fish was sold to the Slade Gorton Co. New spars were stepped and the necessary repairs made and the *Onato* again sailed fishing on April 7, 1905.

The *Onato* was never a fast sailer, but at times, like a great many vessels, put on a burst of speed. One of these incidents happened on September 26, 1909. The *Onato* was returning from Western Bank, when she was struck by a gale. Capt. Larkin, with the open sea around him, decided to run before it. She fairly flew over the water, making 52 miles in four hours.

The *Onato*, during her fishing career under Capt. Larkin, helped to save many lives. From February, 1911 to February, 1912 she picked up 14 men astray in dories from different vessels. In July, 1908, she picked up two of the crew of the Canadian schooner *Favorite* and landed them at Barrington, Nova Scotia.

The *Onato* went the way of many fine vessels of the fleet when she was sold to Newfoundland in March, 1917. E. Inkpen of Burin was the buyer.

The *Onato* while on passage from Oporto, Portugal to Burin with a cargo of salt, in March, 1919, struck heavy gales in the Gulf Stream. The American steamer *Zirkel* came upon the sinking vessel, flying the distress signal. Things didn't look just right to the officers of the steamer. There were signs of a struggle and the cook had bruises on his face. Two shots were heard by the rescuers when approaching the vessel. The body of the captain was lying across the hatch. The four survivors claimed that Capt. James Brussia, 26 years old, and his brother, the mate, Ernest Brussia, had dug a hole in the salt to free the pumps, when the vessel heeled over burying them in the salt. The bodies were buried at sea and the survivors were brought to Philadelphia, where they were charged with murder and mutiny on the high seas. They were released after standing trial and returned to their homes in Newfoundland in October, 1919.

The gallant old *Onato* went down on March 5, 1919, shortly after her survivors were taken off.

Capt. J. Henry Larkin was one of the leading figures in the fresh fishing fleet. He passed away in February, 1947. He was a native of Lower East Pubnico, Nova Scotia. Tall, quiet, modest, a born fisherman and a natural hustler, he loved the sea and was eager for fish. His ability and judgment were exceptional and he always carried a hard working gang. He started as master about 1901 and commanded many fine vessels, including the schooners *Colonial, Onato* (which he commanded 13 years), *Bay State*, and in 1921 the big Boston schooner *Mayflower*, built to race against the Canadians, but barred from racing by the absurd ruling of the Halifax Race committee, who claimed she was a yacht. He was a brother of Capt. Albert Larkin, another fine skipper of his day.

Gross tons, 140; net tons, 105; length, 101 feet; breadth, 24.6 feet; depth, 11.8 feet; original spar measurements: mainmast, 77 feet (deck to cap); foremast, 66.5 feet; main topmast, 44 feet; main boom, 72 feet; main gaff, 43 feet; bowsprit, 27 feet (outboard).

A short foremast and a tall mainmast en-
hance the yachtlike character of the *Selma*,
shown on her trial trip. Crewman Wylie
Rudolph is standing on a halyard next to
the foremast, loosening the fastenings of
the foretopsail.

Selma

SHE LOOKED LIKE A CERTAIN YACHT /
1904–1914

During the spring and summer of 1904 two fine fishing schooners were built by Arthur D. Story's yard in Essex for the Atlantic Maritime Co. of Boston. One of them, the *Selma*, was one of the handsomest vessels in the fleet.

She had a beautiful overhanging spoon bow, short foremast, tall mainmast, and carried a large amount of sail. She greatly resembled one of the big schooner yachts of that time. Although I have been unable to trace her designer, I am quite sure she was from a B. B. Crowninshield design. The *Selma* was a good, able vessel, but not speedy as lack of sufficient head sail always was a handicap. The schooner *Muriel*, her sister vessel, was almost identical in size and appearance.

The *Selma* was launched on August 17, 1904. She was rigged and fitted at Gloucester. Sails were made by the E. L. Rowe Co. A trial trip was sailed on Labor Day, September 4th, of that year. About 200 guests, many of them ladies, enjoyed a fine sail in the bay.

The beautiful *Selma* sailed on her maiden trip, haddocking, in command of Capt. Felix Hogan on September 8, 1904. It is interesting to note that 16 of the crew on that initial trip were under 21 years of age. My friend Wylie Rudolph was one. The *Selma* arrived in Boston September 20, 1904, with her maiden fare of 63,000 lbs. mixed fish, caught in the Channel.

Capt. Hogan remained in the *Selma* about a year, and then took over command of the new schooner *Raymah*, owned by the same company, in October 1905. Capt. George Steele was the next skipper of the *Selma*, haddocking. In January, 1906, Capt. William H. Goodwin took over, haddocking. During the spring of 1906, the *Selma* changed over to seining with Capt. John McKinnon at the helm and during the winter of 1906–07 she was commanded by Capt. Manuel Greer in the haddock fishery.

Capt. Frank Enslo had her haddocking in the spring of 1907 and Capt. Free Decker took over for seining in May, 1907.

Capt. Charlie Colson (Blossom) took over the *Selma* in 1907 as his first command and that great little Scandinavian skipper established a fine record in the halibut fishery, remaining as skipper during 1908–09–10, leaving her to take command of the new schooner *Elk* in January, 1911. A typical trip of Capt. Colson's was landed in January, 1910, when the *Selma*, out only 19 days landed 25,000. lbs. halibut at Portland, stocking $3276 with a share of $96.22 per man. Besides the above

stock there were $200 worth of hand line fish, which brought the returns up to over $100 per man.

Capt. Albert Saulnberg was the next skipper of the *Selma*, also using her halibuting.

Capt. George E. Heckman had her seining in the spring of 1913 and in July of that year Capt. Billy Firth took over, halibuting. In October, 1913, Capt. Robert Winslow took over haddocking. Capt. Tom Downie took over the helm in January, 1914 and the vessel was lost on his first trip.

The *Selma* was a lucky vessel as far as accidents and loss of life were concerned. However, on January 29, 1910, while under Capt. Colson's command she was lying at anchor in Gloucester Harbor, ready to sail, when the schooner *Mooanam*, Capt. Hugh Quinlan, in beating up the harbor collided with the *Selma* and carried away the latter's bowsprit. The helmsman of the *Mooanam* had misjudged his distance in passing the *Selma*. Repairs were made in Gloucester.

Only two deaths are recorded in the history of the *Selma*, both by natural causes. On March 31, 1907, Capt. Walter Whittey who had shipped as one of the crew, under his brother-in-law, Capt. Frank Enslo, died of a heart attack while hauling trawls on the Banks. He was 54 years old and a native of Port Hood, Cape Breton.

George Strahan, one of the *Selma's* crew, died at Vineyard Haven hospital on April 25, 1911. He had been landed while the vessel was at Vineyard Haven seeking bait. Strahan was 52 years old and a native of Port Mulgrave, Nova Scotia. Capt. Albert Saulnberg was skipper at the time.

The end of the *Selma* came on January 25, 1914. The vessel, in command of Capt. Tom Downie, was running for Halifax, Nova Scotia, to replace a broken mainboom when she was struck by a 40-mile southwest gale and driven ashore on Meagher's beach, Halifax. Capt. Downie and his crew were forced to leave the vessel. As the last man left, the cabin was full of water.

High seas cast the dories far up on the beach in wild disorder, filling them, while others were capsized and the men thrown into the water. When all hands were accounted for, they walked around the edge of the cove to the lighthouse where they were given shelter.

All attempts to float the *Selma* proved in vain and she was given up as a total loss.

Her crew list at the time of loss: Capt. Thomas Downie, James Burton, John Burton, John Evans, Hans Schupert, Sore Bezurren, Arthur Fraser, Alfred Steele, Octave Moulesong, David Barrett, Peter Rose, William Nickerson, Michael Bremce, Andrew Magney, Peter Steele, E. Seeton, John Maker, Frank Maynard.

Herman Spooner's beautiful photo of the *Selma* was snapped on her trial trip in September, 1904. The man on the foremast head just below the topsail is Capt. Wylie Rudolph. Wylie, who was just a lad of 19 at the time, probably set a record of his own. Starting in 1902 with Capt. John Glynn in schooner *Colonial*, Wylie sailed in 67 vessels under 70 skippers. Truly, he was a real veteran of the deep.

Known from the Bay of Islands to Cape Cod, Wylie was also quite an oarsman in his day. One of his most cherished treasures was a little silver medal, he won at the age of 13 in a dory race at his native Canso, Nova Scotia, in 1898. Gloucester's great dorymen are gone now, but in the days of sail, they took their hats off to no one.

Wylie was one of my dearest friends, a man with a great love and vast knowledge of the Gloucester fishing schooners. To me, he was Mr. Gloucesterman.

Wylie passed away in Gloucester in September 1957 at the age of seventy-two.

Capt. Charles Colson, affectionately known as "Blossom," died in Gloucester in January 1933 at the age of fifty-nine. A native of Sweden, he was one of the crack skippers in the halibut fishery. He commanded schooner *Natalie Hammond* for many years.

Gross tons, 122; net tons, 87; length, 103.2 feet; breadth, 24.5 feet; depth, 11.4 feet. Original spar measurements: mainmast (deck to cap), 76 feet; foremast, 62.5 feet; main topmast, 43 feet; fore topmast, 40 feet; main boom, 72 feet; main gaff, 40 feet; bowsprit, outboard, 25 feet; leach of mainsail, 78 feet; mastheads, 11 feet.

Waldo L. Stream

SIX DEATHS IN THREE YEARS / 1904–1924

Capt. Frank G. Stream was one of our great Scandinavian skippers. He established a fine record in his schooner *Florence E. Stream* (named for his daughter.) When this vessel was 11 years old, in 1903, she was sold to New York parties. He took over the schooner *Volant* from the John Pew firm and also did well in this craft.

In the spring of 1904 a fine vessel was built for Capt. Stream and Samuel Montgomery at the Tarr and James Yard in Essex. Each owned a half interest.

The new craft was named *Waldo L. Stream* after Capt. Stream's young son. She was launched on July 16, 1904. She was towed around to Gloucester and her spars were stepped at Burnham Brothers' shears.

The *Waldo L. Stream* was a handsome, good sized vessel of the round bow type with long bowsprit. Like most vessels of that period, she was from a Tom McManus design. As far back as I can remember, she was painted a dull green which gave her a striking appearance.

The trial trip of the new craft was sailed on Sunday, July 31, 1904. A great number of guests of Capt. Stream enjoyed the sail up the North Shore and return in a stiff southwest breeze. A fine dinner was served and all were well pleased with the handsome vessel.

The *Waldo L. Stream* sailed on her maiden trip, bound to Georges for halibut, on August 4, 1904. She arrived back in Gloucester with a maiden fare on August 26th hailing for 3,000 lbs. halibut, 25,000 salt cod, 20,000 lbs. fresh cod, 70,000 lbs. cusk and one swordfish.

The *Waldo Stream* sailed on through the years, under the able guidance of Capt. Stream, fishing on all the banks from Grand to Georges, usually halibuting and haddocking. Quero and Georges banks were Capt. Stream's favorite spots. The *Waldo Stream* was never a record breaker but always finished up each season, right up with the leaders. Her best year was 1918 when she stocked $38,955 under Capt. Stream.

On September 17, 1917, she arrived at Boston with 35,000 lbs. halibut, 35,000 lbs. cod, stocking $6,927 and sharing $255. This was the largest share made in the halibut fishery up to that time.

Samuel Montgomery sold his half interest in the *Waldo L. Stream* to Gorton-Pew Fisheries in 1911 and in 1917, Capt. Stream's half was also purchased by Gorton-Pew Fisheries Company.

Capt. Stream remained as skipper of the *Waldo Stream* until 1920 when she was commanded during that year by Capts. Daniel McDonald, and Horace Wylde. In 1921–22 Capt. Bob Porper took her halibuting.

In January 1918, the *Waldo Stream* while bound home from the Bay of Islands, Newfoundland, with 1400 bbls. salt herring, struck severe gales and freezing weather. The vessel iced up so badly she had to put into Liverpool, Nova Scotia, with her decks to the water on account of ice forming over her. She had to be steamed off before proceeding home.

While in command of Capt. Bob Porper, the *Waldo Stream* encountered the heavy gale of January 22, 1922, when about 300 miles south of Halifax, Nova Scotia. The vessel was hove down till the crosstrees were awash. Two of her crew, Duncan King and Herb Crowell, were injured when they were thrown from their bunks in the forecastle, when a big sea hit the vessel. Six of her dories and deck gear were swept over and the foresail blown to ribbons. This was the same gale in which the Gloucester schooners *Corinthian* and *Teazer* each lost two men on Brown's Bank.

Two of the crew of the *Waldo Stream*, John White and Fred Dort, had a narrow escape from death when they went astray from their craft on the eastern part of Grand Bank on May 23, 1914. Thirty-three weary hours later they were picked up by the French brigantine *Notre Dame des Flots*, one of the French banking fleet. When found the men were cold and wet to the skin from heavy seas which broke continually over their dory. Experiences of this sort could never be counted in the lives of these dorymen of Gloucester. Just think what they had to go through for what they received!

Six men lost their lives in the *Waldo Stream*. On January 30, 1910, Charles Peterson and Edward Hanson lost their lives on Quero Bank. The crew went out to haul their trawls and it came on to blow heavy while they were gone. Capt. Stream called the dories in, but the dory with Peterson and Hanson failed to return. By this time, it was blowing a living gale and it was impossible to put over a dory to search for the missing men. The gale continued all that night and the next day, and the men on the *Waldo Stream* knew that their shipmates could never stay afloat in those raging seas. Two more brave souls had gone to their last resting places. Buth men were natives of Scandinavia and each was 45 years old.

On Thanksgiving day in 1912, Patrick Smith died of a heart attack while taking his trick at

the wheel of the *Waldo Stream*, off Cape Sable, Nova Scotia. He was a native of Newfoundland and 21 years old.

The following story is one of the strangest, tragic occurrences ever recorded in the annals of the fisheries.

On Wednesday, February 26, 1908, the *Waldo L. Stream*, Capt. Frank Stream, was lying to an anchor on Quero Bank. Her dories were out hauling their trawls, when a heavy fog shut in. All the dories returned to the vessel except one, containing Sven Larsen and Augustus Johnson. The fog continued, with the vessel continually blowing her horn, and all that night, a burning torch at the mast head.

The next day, the fog was so thick the bowsprit was scarcely visible from the cabin house. There were no signs of the missing men. The sea remained very smooth and the wind light. That afternoon (Thursday) four of the crew, Paul Williams (a big rugged fellow), Alex Campbell, John Tompkins, and Sylvine Landry (a small young fellow) offered to make a search for the missing men. It had not been rough, but the fog was thick, and this they believed had prevented their mates from getting back to the vessel. Their comrades thought they could find them.

The four men left in a dory, taking along a fog horn. In a few hours they found the missing men, but by now the fog was thicker than ever and they too had lost the vessel.

They decided to anchor for the night, and the next afternoon (Friday) with the fog still thick, it was decided to divide the party. Larsen got into the dory with Williams and Landry, and they decided to make a try for the vessel.

The dory with the three men waving good-bye rowed off into the fog. This was the last ever seen of them. The remaining men decided to anchor another night. By this time the men on the *Waldo Stream* were thoroughly alarmed, and the fog horn was kept going, with a signal fire at night. On Saturday afternoon of the 29th, the fog let up and the vessel was sighted. The survivors were picked up, and for two more days the *Waldo Stream* searched in vain for her missing men. Williams and Larsen were 53 years old. Landry, a native of Tusket Wedge, Nova Scotia, was only 23. Of big sturdy Paul Williams and brave little Sylvine Landry, it can well be said, "Greater love hath no man than this, that a man lay down his life for his friends."

The *Waldo L. Stream* went the way of a great many of our fine fishing schooners when she was sold to Newfoundland in May, 1922. Richard Cramp of St. John's was the purchaser, and she was to be used as a rum runner.

The end came to the handsome *Waldo L. Stream* when she was smashed to pieces in a gale off Muskegat Island, off the southern coast of Massachusetts on December 26, 1924. She was bound to Nassau, Bahamas Islands, with 2,295 cases of liquor. Her young 22 year-old skipper, Capt. Williams Cluett was not acquainted with these treacherous waters and the *Waldo Stream* was an easy victim.

Capt. Cluett was later killed on board his Canadian rum runner, *Josephine K.*, when a warning shell from a pursuing Coast Guard cutter struck the pilot house in which he was standing.

Capt. Frank Stream passed away in Gloucester October, 1935, at the age of 75. He was a native of Gottenberg, Sweden. Capt. Frank was one of our great Scandinavian skippers. He was highly regarded by his fellow mariners and members of his crew. Always a plugger and hard worker, but economical and easy on his vessels. He was always up with the highliners, particularly in the halibut fishery. Although most of his crews were made up of men from his native Scandinavia, a great many Nova Scotians and Newfoundlanders sailed under this fine skipper.

His commands included the *Epes Tarr, Eleanora, Florence E. Stream, Volant, Waldo L. Stream* and *John J. Fallon.*

Waldo L. Stream, namesake of the vessel, died in Germany in April, 1919, five months after the signing of the Armistice. He was a band corporal in the first division of the American Army of Occupation.

Gross tons, 122; net tons, 81; length, 102.3 feet; breadth, 24.4 feet; depth, 11.4 feet. Mainmast, deck to cap, 70 feet; foremast, deck to cap, 61.5 feet; main boom, 72 feet; bowsprit, outboard, 25.5 feet; mastheads, 10.5 feet.

On their maiden trips the schooners looked so handsome and full of promise! This is the *Arthur James*, moving right along with her seineboat on deck.

Arthur James

Schooner *Arthur James*, one of the most famous vessels of Gloucester's all-sail heyday, probably was involved in more collisions than any other vessel out of the port. Withal, she was always successful and was commanded by crack skippers.

Capt. Archibald Devine had earned a fine reputation for himself in schooners sailing from the firm of M. Walen and Son of Gloucester. During the winter of 1904–05 a fine new schooner was built for him by Tarr and James at Essex.

The new vessel, through the intervention of Frank W. Lothrop, local agent of the product, was given the name of *Arthur James*, after the manufacturer of the world's greatest fish hooks, located at New York. A fine set of colors was given the vessel by the firm. During 11 months ending June 1, 1893, L. D. Lothrop handled no less than 77,500 gross of famous Arthur James fish hooks.

The *Arthur James* was launched on March 25, 1905, towed around to Gloucester by the tug *Nellie*, and immediately fitted for the southern mackerel fishery. She was a medium sized clipper bowed vessel, taken from the model of the schooner, *Avalon*, launched in 1903. The *Arthur James* carried a lot of sail and was rather straight sheered. She was a strong, able vessel and smart sailer. Capt. Archie Devine and the firm of Walen and Son each owned half.

The *Arthur James* sailed on her maiden trip in command of Capt. Devine on April 7, 1905, making a striking appearance as she sailed out of the harbor. Her maiden voyage nearly ended in disaster. On that very evening of April 7, she was run into off Nauset, Cape Cod, by the three-master *Andrew Nebinger* of Bangor, Maine. Ten feet of the fisherman's rail were smashed and her mainsail torn to ribbons. No one was hurt but in the rush to get home, she carried away the fore topmast. Repairs were made at Gloucester and she again got away on April 10th, bound to the southward. She arrived at New York with her maiden fare of 40 bbls. fresh mackerel on May 4, 1905.

The *Arthur James* was again in collision in 1907. On July 18, while jogging in a heavy fog on Georges, she was run down by the British steamer *Saxoline*, bound to Philadelphia. The vessel was struck a glancing blow on the bow, and the steamer scraped along her side, crushing in several planks. The shock of the collision swung the schooner around on her

tack. The *Arthur James* made port, where repairs were made and she soon was ready for sea again.

The next mackerel season of 1908, the *Arthur James* was again in collision. On August 5, she was run down by the four-masted schooner *Samuel Goucher* off Pollock Rip Lightship. The big coaster struck the *James* a sharp blow which started her grub beam and her cabin, and started the fisherman leaking. The fog was dense at the time. Again the *Arthur James* returned home, where repairs were made. It was a miracle indeed that in three collisions at sea, no lives were lost and no one was badly injured.

The *Arthur James* remained in command of Capt. Devine from her launching until about two months before his death in 1914. Under his able guidance she was always up among the leaders and in 1914 she was second highline of the seiners, stocking $20,017, shares $397. Capt. Devine's last voyage was a cruise to North Bay in September, 1914.

In March, 1913, auxiliary power of two gas engines was installed. In 1924 two new Lathrop 36 horsepower gas engines were installed.

The *Arthur James*, under Capt. Devine's command, always went seining summers and occasionally to Newfoundland winters for herring cargoes. In fact this was the only kind of fishing she ever engaged in.

On the death of Capt. Devine, the *Arthur James*' new skipper was Capt. John Matheson, who purchased an interest in her. He sailed in her during the seasons of 1915 and 1916 and made seining history. The season of 1916 she broke all records, up to that time, in the mackerel fishery. On October 19, 1916, she landed at Boston 125,000 lbs. fresh mackerel. On her previous trip she had landed 100,000 lbs. These two trips, taken within three days, gave her a grand stock of $17,000, which eclipsed anything heard of in the mackerel line.

On the evening of October 31, 1916, the *Arthur James*, with a total season stock of $67,225 and a share of $1,520, was overtaken by disaster. The craft had sailed from the Boston Fish Pier on another mackerel cruise, and because of heavy fog, turned back. When abreast of Castle Island, at 5:30 p.m. the big bow of the passenger steamer *Camden* sliced through the fog into the schooner, cutting her nearly in two. The steamer prow struck the vessel just forward of the fore rigging. All the crew with the exception of the cook were on deck at the time, taking in the foresail. The captain and 16 men jumped into the seineboat, before the *James* went down. The cook, Malaska Hager, who was in the fo'castle, went down with the vessel.

The steamer backed away, the gaping hole in the schooner's side filled and she went down in three minutes in 50 feet of water. The masts and the mainsail stuck up out of the water. There were two pet cats aboard at the time. One drowned, and the other climbed the rigging and was hanging to the crosstrees, when rescued by the crew.

Cook Hager, one of the best known cooks out of Gloucester, had been in the *Arthur James* since she was built. He was a native of Shelburne, Nova Scotia, and 49 years old. His 17-year-old son was one of the survivors. The body was later recovered by divers. The *Camden*, owned by the Eastern Steamship Co., was bound to Maine with 150 passengers. The wreck of the *Arthur James* was raised later and repairs were made. This was the fourth collision of the *Arthur James* and the most disastrous. Capt. Joe Lyle and William Corkum (Little Billy) were members of the *James* crew on this trip.

The *Arthur James* was taken over in 1917 by Capt. John Seavey, one of the crack Maine skippers and he remained in her seining until the season of 1923 when Capt. Wallace Parsons took command, and he remained in her through 1924. Capt. Asa Baker was the *Arthur James'* last skipper, seining in her in 1925–26.

Disaster again struck the *James* on April 29, 1925. While cruising for mackerel 40 miles southeast of Atlantic City, New Jersey, without warning the foremast head let go, carrying the mainmast with it. The craft returned home under auxiliary power. Capt. Asa Baker was skipper.

When the champion of the Gloucester fleet, schooner *Esperanto*, was lost in 1921, an elimination race was held off Gloucester to select a new defender. The *Arthur James*, with Capt. John Matheson at the helm, was entered, finishing third to the newer *Elsie* and the *Ralph Brown*. For the first time in 21 years, the spring seining list of 1927 failed to carry the name of *Arthur James*. The grand old vessel was hauled up in 1927. In April, 1928, she was sold to New Bedford for the Cape Verde trade. She was the last of the M. Walen fleet.

The *Arthur James* again made news in 1931, while running freight and passengers out of New Bedford. Found by the destroyer *Davis*, 65 days out of the Cape Verde Islands, the vessel was short of fuel and for days the only food was uncooked salt beef. Everyone aboard was in a weakened condition, owing to cold, hunger and thirst. Within 50 miles of Nantucket a terrific northeast gale struck her and drove her to sea. She was sighted by a tanker, who reported her plight to the Coast Guard and a destroyer was sent to pick her up and tow her into port. At the time she carried 9 alien passengers.

The grand old *Arthur James* finally went to a watery grave on January 11, 1937, when she foundered off the Azores with her entire 20 crew and passengers. At the time she was still under American registry.

Capt. Archibald Devine passed away in Boston on December 30, 1914, at the age of 59. He was a native of Pubnico, Nova Scotia. As a master mariner he was one of the most capable who ever sailed from Gloucester. In his early days, he was a great salt fisherman, but later changed to seining. He sailed mostly from the M. Walen firm. Capt. Devine held the record for 15 years for the largest amount of salt fish landed in a salt banking season. This was made in the schooner *Bessie M. Devine*, landing 306,480 lbs., taken in four trips. He commanded many fine vessels, including the *Edith Walen*, *Orpheus*, *Bessie M. Devine* (named for his daughter) and the *Arthur James*.

Capt. John Matheson died at Gloucester on March 26, 1940 at the age of 59. A native of North Sydney, Cape Breton, he was a great helmsman and one of the great skippers, mostly in the seining and Newfoundland herring fisheries. Some of his commands were the *Claudia*, *Dauntless*, *Arthur James*, *Saladin* and *Helena*.

Gross tons, 135; net tons, 95; length, 103.4 feet; breadth, 24.8 feet; depth, 10.6 feet. Spar measurements: mainmast (deck to cap), 75 feet; foremost, 68 feet; main boom, 73 feet; main gaff, 42.5 feet; bowsprit (outboard), 30 feet; mainmast head, 11.5 feet.

Elizabeth Silsbee

Even with a dory and two seineboats in tow the *Elizabeth Silsbee*, using sails and her 300-horsepower Standard engine, could do twelve knots.

FIRST HADDOCKER WITH AN ENGINE /
1905–1909

I consider the auxiliary schooner *Elizabeth Silsbee* one of the finest fishermen ever built, a great sailer and the first big offshore (haddocker) vessel with an engine.

With the advent of the schooner *Helen Miller Gould* in 1900, the first fishing vessel equipped with an engine, many of the firms quickly followed on with the idea. In 1901, the auxiliary schooners, *Nellie B. Nickerson*, *Victor*, and *Mary E. Harty* joined the fleet; followed in 1902 by the schooners *Saladin*, *Constellation*, and *Veda M. McKown*. All of these vessels were mackerel seiners. It was not until 1905 when the first motor driven haddocker, the *Elizabeth Silsbee*, made her debut.

The *Elizabeth Silsbee* was built by Arthur D. Story at Essex for the Atlantic Maritime Co. of Boston. She was launched in the evening of August 12, 1905. She was named after a relative of Mr. Silsbee, a stockholder in the company.

The *Silsbee* was a fine large vessel of the clipper bow type. She was designed by Starling Burgess, son of the late Edward Burgess, great American yacht designer. The *Silsbee* was very radical in design; closely resembling a yacht, with long overhangs, long pole bowsprit, and tall spars. She carried a steel exhaust stack forward of the cabin house. Her 21 foot trunk cabin, finished in sycamore, was built by Edward Perkins, master craftsman of the Essex yards.

The *Silsbee* was a most impressive vessel; long, wide and deep. Her sail area was tremendous. She was fitted with all the latest improvements including motor hoisters for sails, anchors, etc. Her 300 horsepower Standard engine made by the Standard Motor Co. of Jersey City, could drive her at a speed of 12 knots (very few of the modern draggers can boast of this speed). She carried 12 double dories and 27 men, the largest crew and most dories up to that time. The vessel was never profitable, however, as the big gasoline bills (she burned about 28 gallons an hour) and large crew ate up the stocks. Her engineers during her fishing career were Jim Morash and Jack Greenleaf.

The *Elizabeth Silsbee* besides being one of the most beautiful vessels, was also one of the greatest sailers. It is said she could beat the fleet, while towing two seineboats. She was a strong, able craft, but had one bad feature. This was a tendency to dip her long sharp bow into a sea. Fishermen who sailed in her have told me that on a passage home from the banks, it sometimes was not safe to stay on

her decks, as her bow would dip into a sea and tons of water would sweep along the deck.

The *Elizabeth Silsbee* arrived in Boston with her maiden trip on October 24, 1905, hailing for 74,000 lbs. fresh fish. Her skipper was Capt. Josh Stanley, one of the best dory fishing skippers in the business. Capt. Stanley remained in her through the winter of 1905–06. In the spring of 1906 she was taken over by Capt. Eben Lewis, seining. During the winter of 1906–07, she was commanded by Capt. Felix Hogan, haddocking.

In April, 1907, Capt. John McKinnon took over the helm, seining, and he had a successful season. On May 2, 1907, he landed at New York, 52,000 medium mackerel in count, stocking $5,110. This was one of the largest stocks made on a single trip in the history of the southern mackerel fishery up to that time.

The *Silsbee* was selected to carry the Gloucester delegation to the laying of the cornerstone of the new Pilgrim monument at Provincetown in August, 1907. In command of Capt. John McKinnon, she started across the bay on the evening of August 10, 1907, with members of the Gloucester Master Mariners' association and invited guests. At Provincetown they were cordially greeted by President Theodore Roosevelt, an ardent admirer of the Gloucester fishermen. Among the guests were Capts. John Chisholm, Jerome McDonald, James McHenry, Carl Young, Henry M. Atwood, Mayor George E. MacDonald, George H. Procter of the *Daily Times*, Benjamin Pine, Freeman D. Hodsdon, Walter Henderson, William J. MacInnis, James B. Connolly, and many others. The return trip was made to Gloucester on August 21st. This was a time to be remembered by all.

While on a seining cruise in command of Capt. Herbert C. Greenleaf the *Silsbee* struck on Aldin's Rock while entering Portland harbor on September 9, 1907. She was later floated, leaking 1500 strokes an hour. Repairs were made in Gloucester.

Capt. McKinnon again took the *Silsbee* seining during the season of 1908. In September, 1908, the vessel was taken over by Capt. John Laurie, haddocking and he remained in her until her loss in January, 1909.

Fortunately, only one life was lost out of the *Elizabeth Silsbee*.

On March 19, 1906, Eben Martin, one of her crew, was struck in the chest and killed by the fluke of the big anchor while it was being catted. Martin, a strong, powerful man and one of the best known fishermen out of Gloucester, was a native of Shelburne, Nova Scotia. He was 36 years old.

The fishing career of the *Elizabeth Silsbee* was ended on the night of January 24, 1909. The vessel, in command of Capt. John Laurie, had been fishing on Brown's Bank when it breezed up and it was decided to run to Shelburne, Nova Scotia, for harbor. A mistake was made in the light houses and she piled up on Allen's Point near Blanche, about 20 miles west of Shelburne. The night was clear and a good east south east breeze was blowing. She went on the rocks easily and hung up hard and fast. All attempts to float her were futile. The crew landed without difficulty on the beach near by.

Soon after a storm came up and the *Silsbee* began to break up. She was declared a total loss and the wreck was sold at public auction on February 5, 1909. Before sailing on her final trip, part of her engine and propeller were removed and only her sails were used. So ended one of the greatest fishing schooners ever built.

Capt. John Laurie sailed his last voyage on September 22, 1917. Capt. John was one of Cape Ann's fine mariners in the days of sail. A fine haddocker and shacker, he sailed many years from the Andrew Leighton and Gardner and Parsons firms. Some of his commands included the schooners *Gloriana*, *Indiana*, *Illinois*, *Mary A. Whalen*, and *Elizabeth Silsbee*. Capt. Laurie holds the honor of commanding the first fishing vessel to sail on a maiden trip from Gloucester in the new 20th century, the schooner *Illinois* on January 2, 1901. He was a native of Mulgrave, Nova Scotia, and was 63 years old.

Gross tons, 153; net tons, 105; length, 116.6 feet; breadth, 26 feet; depth, 11.6 feet. Original spar measurements: mainmast, 77.5 feet (deck to cap); foremast, 66 feet; main topmast, 49 feet; mainboom, 75 feet; maingaff, 50 feet (cut in 1908 to 48.5 feet); foreboom, 32 feet; bowsprit, 29 feet (outboard); mastheads, 12 feet.

Frances P. Mesquita

SMART IN FISHING AND RACING / 1905–1918

A smart little vessel was the schooner *Frances P. Mesquita*, built for Capt. Joseph P. Mesquita, one of Gloucester's outstanding men of Portuguese ancestry, a great contributor to the community, and instigator of the crowning ceremonies which became such an important religious civic activity.

The *Mesquita* was another Gloucester-built vessel and was launched on March 8, 1905, at John Bishop's yard, Vincent Cove, in the rear of the present North Shore theatre. The craft was christened by then little Miss Frances P. Mesquita, youngest daughter of the owner, who was one of the most successful of the Portuguese skippers. The trial trip came on March 19, 1905 (it didn't take long in those days to fit a vessel for sea) and there were 250 guests who enjoyed a sail to Salem and return with music for the occasion by Veator's orchestra.

The vessel was another of the Capt. Thomas McManus designs and was off the *Belbina Domingoes* model with a round bow. Her staysail, jib and jib topsail were made from the sails of Tom Lawson's famous big sloop yacht *Independence*.

Schooner *Frances P. Mesquita* sailed on her maiden trip haddocking under command of Capt. Joe on March 23, 1905 and 13 days later, April 5, 1905, landed the maiden fare at Boston.

The 92.6 foot *Mesquita* was not as large as some of the contemporary vessels. However, she was very fast in her class and frequently demonstrated her sailing ability in running to market and in brushes with other vessels. There was such a brush off Highland Light in March, 1909 when she easily outsailed the Boston schooners, *Victor and Eathan*, *W. M. Goodspeed* and *Ethel B. Penny*. In the Fishermen's Races in Massachusetts Bay on August 1, 1907 for the Lipton Cup, the *Frances P. Mesquita* won first prize in the second class over the crack Boston schooner *Helen B. Thomas*.

This smart little vessel, nearly always commanded by Capt. Mesquita, was always a big money-maker in haddocking, some shore fishing, occasionally to the eastward for fresh and salt shack, and some swordfishing. In the summer of 1907, Capt. Mesquita landed 205 swordfish, which was a record at the time.

In April, 1908, the *Mesquita* raced for Boston from Georges with the big schooner *Regina*, probably the fastest fisherman out of Boston. The comparatively small *Mesquita* put up

Schooner *Frances P. Mesquita* really was the pride of the Portuguese fleet. In keeping with Portuguese custom, her waterline, booms, gaffs and mastheads were painted white.

a great fight and was beaten only by half an hour.

On February 18, 1908, the *Mesquita* left Boston at 3 p.m., caught 19,000 pounds of fresh fish and was back at Boston in 25 hours. Capt. Freeman Crowell took her shacking in 1915.

During three winters, 1913–1916, Capt. Mesquita stayed ashore for a needed rest, and Capt. Freeman Crowell took command.

In 1918 Capt. Mesquita sold his vessel to Burin, Newfoundland, parties and she went under British registry. The vessel made one more trip to Gloucester in April 1918 bringing a cargo of 300,000 pounds salt cod. Tragedy befell the skipper on that voyage. While boarding the *Mesquita* at Rocky Neck railways, Capt. Thomas Hamilton of Burin, Newfoundland, fell overboard and was drowned. That was on April 14, 1918.

The *Mesquita* was one of the many fine vessels sunk by German U-boats during the summer of 1918 and this fine little vessel ended her days on a voyage from Newfoundland to Portugal in 1918 with a cargo of salt fish. The

members of the crew were rescued by the S. S. *Isabella*, Capt. Martin Gracia, a former Gloucester captain.

Capt. Mesquita was one of Gloucester's greatest mariners; a man of sterling character, sincere, honest and courageous. Capt. Joe (or "Smoky Joe," as he was affectionately known) commanded many fine vessels, including *Abby Snow, Almeida, Ramona, Mary P. Mesquita,* a second *Mary P. Mesquita, Joseph P. Mesquita, Francis J. O'Hara, Jr., Thomas S. Gorton* and *Herbert Parker.* He was known principally as a haddocker and shacker. A native of the Azores, he built a fine reputation during his 50 years in Gloucester, living up to the traditions of his homeland and his adopted country. Capt. Joe passed away in November, 1933 at the age of 74.

Gross tons, 105; net tons, 71; length, 92.6 feet; breadth, 23.2 feet; depth, 10.2 feet. Spar measurements: bowsprit, 27.5 feet (outboard); main boom, 67 feet; mainmast, 72 feet (deck to cap); foremast, 63 feet.

For years when a new vessel appeared in Boston Harbor an artist who signed his work A. Acores would photograph her, then paint her "portrait" in watercolor to sell to the owner or captain. This Acores painting of the *Raymah* was in the home of Captain Felix Hogan. Incidentally, the author has never seen an Acores painting in a museum; what happened to them?

Raymah

"RISING SUN" in HEBREW / 1905–1912

Raymah: The Rising Sun. This story of the *Raymah* is dedicated to the author's oldest daughter, who was named after this grand old vessel.

Schooner *Raymah* was one of the finest fishermen built. She was owned by the Atlantic Maritime Co. of Boston, and commanded by the beloved Capt. Felix Hogan.

The *Raymah* was built at the Oxner and Story yard in Essex during the summer and fall, launched on October 11, 1905, towed around by the tug *Nellie* and fitted for sea at Gloucester.

The *Raymah* was a large, powerful vessel, with a round bow, long bowsprit, and she carried a large spread of canvas. She was of the schooner *Thomas S. Gorton* type from a Tom McManus design.

The naming of these fishermen of the past was most interesting and important. Their names dominated the fishing news in the daily papers, some for only a short time, some for a great many years. They were names that car-

ried the fame and glory of the Gloucester fishermen all over the world.

Most of these craft were named for relatives of their respective owners and for famous yachts, a great many after famous and prominent local citizens. Once in a while an odd name would come along. One of these names was *Raymah*.

Capt. Felix Hogan, always obliging, gave me the full story. When the vessel was building at Essex, a Hebrew gentleman asked Capt. Hogan if he would name his new vessel after the secretary of the Hebrew Society in Boston with which he was connected, saying the lady was probably the only one in the country so named. The name means Ray (Sun), Mah (Rising) in Hebrew.

Capt. Felix liked the idea and thought it might prove lucky, so on launching day the name *Raymah* blazoned in gold on bow and stern of the fine new craft. To show their appreciation, the society presented every man of the crew a suit of oilskins and the vessel a set of colors.

Capt. Hogan was proud of his *Raymah* and he was always very emphatic about the spelling of the name. He would always say to me, "Don't forget the H on the end. It must have the H."

Schooner *Raymah* sailed from Gloucester on her maiden trip haddocking in command of Capt. Hogan on November 1, 1905. Seven days later on November 8, she arrived at Boston with her maiden fare of 43,000 lbs. of fresh fish.

Capt. Hogan was one of the kingpins of the haddock fleet. He had made a fine record in schooner *Selma* in 1904 and he started right in with the *Raymah* in keeping his name up with the leaders.

On March 19, 1908, the *Raymah* landed at Boston the largest trip of the winter, 135,000 lbs. fresh fish.

In 1909 the *Raymah* was high line of the Boston haddockers with a stock of $24,632 and a share of $550. In three weeks in October, 1910, she stocked $4,100. This was big money in those days.

The *Raymah* during her entire career under the American flag, was in command of Capt. Hogan and used haddocking and shacking. She was a fast vessel, at her best in heavy weather. Capt. Hogan once told me that the *Raymah* at one time ran all day, making 12 knots.

Raymah was a lucky vessel. Accidents and loss of life were small during her career.

Michael (Micky) McDonald was drowned on Georges on March 2, 1909. A squall hit his dory, throwing him and his dorymate, William Goslin, into the sea. Goslin hung on to the dory and was rescued in an exhausted condition by his shipmates. Micky McDonald was never seen again. He was 24 years old and a native of the Bay of Islands, Newfoundland.

He was the only man ever lost in the *Raymah*. He was one of the crew of the auxiliary schooner *Alert*, which blew up during the preceding summer of 1908 at Chisholm's wharf. He was among those who were injured.

The *Raymah* ran ashore at Wolf Island in the Magdalens on May 5, 1909, but was floated without serious damage. She was after bait at the time.

In 1908, the *Raymah* was seized off Cape North, Cape Breton, by a Canadian cutter for alleged violation of the Canadian fishing laws. She was charged with fishing within the three mile limit, taken to North Sydney, Cape Breton, held until a fine of $2,000 was paid by the owners, then released. These incidents and seizures of American fishermen, in my estimation, were absurd. Both nations were at fault. It was like a brother putting a brother in jail. Most of our fishing vessels were manned by Canadian and Newfoundland subjects.

In November of that same year of 1908 the *Raymah*, while bound to Boston with a trip, picked up the crew of four of the coasting schooner *James A. Brown* of Thomaston, Maine. They were found drifting in an open boat 60 miles east by south of Thacher's Island on November 6th. The *Brown* had gone down in a gale the day before. She was copper laden, bound from Portland, Maine, to Crome, New Jersey. Her crew had made a miraculous escape and Capt. Simmons, the last man to leave, had to climb the davits on the stern and dive far out from the vessel as she went down. The shipwrecked men were landed at Boston on November 7th. The *Raymah*, having been out for some time, was short of provisions, but no stint was put on the appetites of the shipwrecked crew. Everything possible was done to make them comfortable on the way in.

The *Raymah*, like many of the crack fishermen of her day, was sold to Newfoundland in May, 1912. Capt. Leslie Tibbo of Grand Bank was the purchaser. *Raymah* was reluctant to leave her native land, however. On sailing from Boston on May 25 she ran ashore in Boston's lower harbor, was floated the same day but had to be towed back to her loading pier for examination. She finally sailed on May 29, 1912, with a cargo of pitch for Halifax, Nova Scotia.

The *Raymah*, under her Newfoundland owners, was used in the trans-Atlantic fish trade between Newfoundland and Portugal. Her career under the British flag was short, however. On December 10, 1912, she sailed from Burin, Newfoundland, for Oporto, Portugal, with a cargo of fish. On the way across she was struck by a heavy gale. The mainmast was carried away and before it could be cut clear of the entangling rigging several holes were pierced in the schooner's hull and the dory was carried overboard. The crew worked at the pumps and kept the craft afloat until help

came. The steamer *Ardoyne* hove in sight and took off the crew of seven men. Before leaving the *Raymah* the crew set her afire to prevent her becoming a menace to navigation. As the steamer with the survivors on board got under way, the burning schooner was slowly settling beneath the waves. The *Raymah: The Rising Sun*, was gone.

The Atlantic Maritime Company was one of the finest firms of the North Atlantic. It started at Boston. The company was made up mostly of men connected with the cotton and woolen industry. Many of their vessels were named for relatives of these men. Herbert Nute was president. Capt. Henry M. Atwood, noted fishing skipper, was manager. In April, 1906, the company, as the Atlantic Maritime Company, leased the wharf at Gloucester owned by Charles Boynton, formerly occupied by S. G. Poole and Sons. Many crack schooners were owned by the company, including *Raymah*, *Georgianna*, *Muriel*, *Catherine G. Howard*, *Mina*, *Swim*, *Hortense*, *Selma*, *Elmer E. Gray*, *Fannie E. Prescott*, *James W. Parker*, *Elizabeth Silsbee*, *Susan and Mary*, *Mildred Robinson*, and *Elk*. Their last vessel was the famous *Elsie*. The Atlantic Maritime wharf was taken over by the Atlantic Supply Co. in March, 1922.

Capt. Felix Hogan passed away in Gloucester on May 30, 1951 at the age of 79. Capt. Felix, a native of Northern Bay, Newfoundland, was one of the most capable and beloved mariners of the past. He was a hustler and one of the topnotchers in the fresh fishery. I don't think there was a fisherman who ever sailed under him, who didn't admire and respect this man. Capt. Felix with his characteristic little jig and his jew's-harp made the cabin of any vessel he commanded a scene of merriment. He commanded many fine vessels, including the *Raymah*, *Elizabeth Silsbee*, *Elmer E. Gray*, *Elk*, *Somerville* (named for his home), and the *L. A. Dunton*. The *Raymah* was his pride and joy and I regret that Capt. Felix is not here to read this story, because no skipper loved his vessel any more than Capt. Felix did the *Raymah*.

Gross tons, 141; net tons, 95; length, 108.6 feet; breadth, 25.9 feet; depth, 11.5 feet. Mainmast, 75.5 feet (deck to cap); foremast, 68 feet; main topmast, 45 feet; main boom, 75 feet; main gaff, 47 feet; bowsprit, 28 feet; mainmast head, 11 feet; leech of mainsail, 86 feet.

A famous incident: the foretopmast broke while the *Rose Dorothea* was racing; this picture shows the spar dangling, before the crew lowered it and cleaned up the mess. The schooner kept right on racing and won.

Rose Dorothea

LIPTON CUP WINNER WITH A BROKEN TOPMAST / 1905–1917

In the glory days of sail the Portuguese fishermen of Gloucester and Provincetown were a very important part of the fishing industry.

The sons of Magellan and Vasco de Gama were courageous and smart fishermen. They were competitive and they took great pride in their vessels. The schooners were kept in the best of repair and paint, and some of them were the fastest in the New England fleet.

Many were the brushes between the American and Portuguese schooners on their way to and from the Boston market.

The Portuguese fleet usually fished on Brown's and Western banks to the east'ard off the Nova Scotian coast, and on Georges and the Channel off Cape Cod. Most of them were haddockers, using both single and double dories.

Two of the prettiest and fastest vessels in the Provincetown fleet were the schooners *Rose Dorothea* and *Jessie Costa*.

The *Jessie Costa* slid down the ways at the Tarr and James yard at Essex on July 13, 1905. Capt. Manuel Costa was her owner and skipper.

The *Rose Dorothea* was launched at the same yard on September 27, 1905. Capt. Marion Perry was her skipper. Both vessels were designed by Tom McManus.

The *Rose Dorothea* was a big round-bow vessel with a big spread of canvas, a very large mainsail and a mainboom about 89 feet long.

Her hull was painted black, and the booms, gaffs and mastheads a shining white which was characteristic of the Portuguese fleet. She carried twelve double dories and a crew of twenty-seven men. Her cost was $15,000. She was one of the first Portuguese vessels to install a gasoline hoisting engine.

The *Dorothea* was fitted for sea by E. L. Rowe Co. at Gloucester and on October 16, 1905 she sailed for Provincetown in a trial race across the bay with the schooner *Annie C. Perry*, Capt. Perry's former command. On board for the trip were Miss Rose Dorothea McGowan, fiancee of Capt. Perry, and A. H. Hearn and Albert Phillips, co-owners of the vessel. Miss McGowan was the pretty daughter of an Atlantic Avenue, Boston, tavernkeeper.

The *Dorothea* sailed into Provincetown in a stiff southwest breeze about fifteen minutes ahead of the *Perry*. As the vessels entered the harbor they were greeted by many foghorns and whistles.

During Boston's Old Home Week celebration in August 1907, a cup was offered by Sir Thomas Lipton for a fishermen's race in Massachusetts Bay. There was a great rivalry between Capts. Perry and Costa, each claiming his vessel the fastest, and they readily accepted the offer to race. The Boston and Gloucester "queens" were not available at the time, as they were on the banks, fishing.

The schooner *James W. Parker*, Capt. Val O'Neil of Boston, entered the race, but went along mostly for the sail, as she stood no chance with the Provincetown vessels.

The race, over a forty-two mile course, started in a light wind which developed into a smart breeze as the race progressed.

The larger *Rose Dorothea*, sailed by John Watson, a Massachusetts Bay yachtsman, got a good jump at the start. Her rival, sailed by Capt. Costa himself, hung right on, however.

The *Dorothea*, only thirty seconds in the lead in rounding the buoy marker off Eastern Point, Gloucester, heeled way over, and the great strain on her big mainsail as it swung over caused the foretopmast to snap, bringing down her foretopsail and jibtopsail. Her crew quickly cleared away the wreckage and the *Dorothea* seemed to sail much better.

The game *Costa* hung right on her back, and when they crossed the finish line trailed by only two minutes and 34 seconds. It was one of the best races ever sailed by fishermen in these waters.

From 1910 to 1916 the owner of the *Dorothea* was Joseph Crowell, Provincetown vessel owner. Capt. Joe Bragg became skipper.

In June 1913 the *Rose Dorothea*, Capt. Joe Bragg, picked up the lifeboats of the big five-master *Paul Palmer* that had burned in the bay. The boats contained Capt. Albert Allen, his wife, a woman guest and the crew of ten. They were landed at Provincetown.

The *Rose Dorothea* was sold in October 1916 to Campbell and McKay of St. John's, Newfoundland, for $14,000.

In February 1917 she was sunk by the Germans on a voyage from Oporto, Portugal to St. John's with a cargo of salt. Her crew landed at Lisbon, Portugal.

Her old rival the *Jessie Costa* was sold to Newfoundland in December 1916. She sailed for her new home port in command of Capt. Allen Dolman and was never heard of again.

So passed two of the finest schooners ever built.

The Provincetown folks were so proud of the *Rose Dorothea's* victory in 1907 that a large stone was erected in Provincetown in front of the Town Hall. On the stone was a picture cut of the *Rose Dorothea* and the words:

ROSE DOROTHEA

This stone commemorates the victory of the schooner *Rose Dorothea*, captained by Marion Perry, and crew, at the Old Home Week celebration in Boston 1907.
This cup given by Sir Thomas Lipton for the winner of this race can be seen in the Provincetown Town Hall.
This stone erected by popular subscription through the efforts of the Portuguese American Civic League.

Gross tons, 147; net tons, 108; length, 108.7 feet; breadth, 24.6 feet; depth, 12.0 feet.

Teazer

ONE OF THE TOUGHEST / 1905–1948

This is the story of the *Teazer*, one of the toughest and staunchest little vessels that ever sailed the North Atlantic. She was a money maker commanded by many fine skippers and was the survivor of many battles with the gales and the ice of northern waters. The *Teazer* was one of the few vessels ever hove down at sea that lived to tell the tale. She was appropriately named, because she sure teased the elements.

Schooner *Teazer* was built during the summer and fall of 1905 at the Tarr and James yard at Essex, and launched on October 16, 1905. She was built alongside the famous fisherman *Rose Dorothea* of Provincetown. The *Teazer* was towed around to Gloucester by the tug *Nellie*. The D. B. Smith Co. was the owner of the fine new schooner. Although not a large vessel, she was strong and fine lined, and from a Tom McManus design with a round bow.

On her maiden voyage she sailed in command of Capt. Peter Dunsky on a deck hand-lining trip. She arrived at Gloucester with her maiden fare of 25,000 lbs. salt cod on January 6, 1906. Capt. Dunsky was one of our great skippers and he had earned a fine reputation in the schooner *Hattie L. Trask*, before taking over the new *Teazer*.

It is interesting to note that R. Russell Smith, son of Benjamin A. Smith of the D. B. Smith Co., sold his champion racing dory, also named *Teazer*, to Cleveland, Ohio, parties in 1907.

Schooner *Teazer* was used in most branches of the fisheries: halibuting, haddocking, seining, drifting and she wound up her career as a sealer. Under Capt. Peter Dunsky's command from 1905 until 1916 she was very successful. He was highline of the Georges halibuters in 1909 with a stock of $24,922 and a share of $651. In 1912 his total stock was $34,596.

Capt. Dunsky sailed the *Teazer* all over the western North Atlantic in search of fish. One of his favorite spots was the Gully. He also fished a great deal on Burgeo Bank, where he was caught several times in the heavy field ice, but always succeeded in getting through to safety.

On January 29, 1911, in command of Capt. Dunsky, the *Teazer* went through an experience, that was one of the most feared by Gloucester fishermen; hove down, at sea. The vessel had been fishing in the Gully, that dan-

Even while just waiting, apparently for a dory in Boston Harbor, the *Teazer* has dignity. She met the supreme test at sea when she was hove down, and thanks to her stability, righted herself, though she did not roll all the way over as the *Helen G. Wells* did.

gerous bit of water, which made a lee shore of Sable Island bar whenever the wind blew from the north, where vessels, except in great stress of weather did not anchor. Her sets were made under sail. Bad weather of three days running forced her to anchor with 300 fathoms of cable out. The wind was blowing 60 miles an hour. All hands were below except a watch of one man on deck. He saw a big sea coming and dove for the companionway of the cabin, reaching its shelter just in time. The giant comber hit the *Teazer* amidships, parted the cable like common wrapping cord and pushed the craft down until the mast heads lay in the water. Below in the forecastle, men were thrown from their bunks and the rush of water down the companionway filled some of the bunks to leeward. The stove upset, starting a fire, which was put out by the crew. The kettles of boiling water on the stove upset when the latter overturned and landed on Charles Strobel, who had been thrown from his bunk down into the starboard corner of the galley. He was badly burned but before the craft righted his mates had him in a bunk and were doing all they could for him.

While some were looking after Strobel, others rushed to the deck to get a view of the plight of their craft. George Braggs, first man up, looked out of the companionway and gazed upon a scene few men have seen and lived to tell about. The mast began to lift as Bragg crouched in the companionway. On the cross trees of the foremast was one of the dories, 60 feet above the deck. The *Teazer* slowly staggered up to an even keel. Fishermen say the noise of a vessel righting herself after being hove down is terrific. It sounded as if she was being torn apart. But the dory stayed in the crosstrees. With each lurch of the vessel, this dory threatened to catapult into space. All but two of the other eight dories were gone or smashed to splinters. The deck was swept clean. The gurry kids and checkers were gone. The fore boom, fore gaff and main gaff were broken.

The dory in the crosstrees showed how far down the craft had been. She must have laid on her side with the crosstrees in the water.

Capt. Dunsky said that the sea that hit the vessel must have been the father of all bad ones. It was lucky the cable snapped, for had it held, that would have been the end of the *Teazer*.

With Sable Island under their lee, the crew worked feverishly to get the craft under way and get out of that danger zone. Capt. Dunsky drove her with what sail he had and all the way home she met strong gales and head winds. The craft arrived in Boston on February 6, 1911 covered with ice and looking like a floating iceberg. The injured Strobel was hurried to the hospital for treatment. That the *Teazer* came back was a credit to her builders and the seamanship of her fine skipper and crew.

On her arrival at Boston, pieces of the dory could be seen that had been chopped out of the crosstrees. In the forecastle a mustard mug could be seen stuck to the ceiling. Schooner *Agnes*, Capt. Charles Wilson, was also hove down on Quero in this same gale. She too came back.

Capt. Dunsky took the *Teazer* on an experimental trip in May, 1911. A 65 horsepower Globe auxiliary gas engine was installed. On May 1st he sailed halibuting, taking with him a "long line" as used by the English trawlers on the Iceland fishing grounds. Dories were taken along so they could set and haul trawls in the usual way, should the new plan prove unsuccessful. Capt. Dunsky was familiar with long line style of fishing. A manila ground line was used about 1½ inches in diameter. It was about two miles long, with seven foot gangings 12 feet apart. A small 5 horsepower gas engine was placed snug against the starboard rail, just forward of the pawl post. This little engine was completely housed in, and used to act as a regular winch, just like a fisherman's gurdy, used in dories for hauling trawls.

The experiment was watched with great interest, and if a success, a regular steel wire ground line would be used.

The *Teazer* arrived back in Boston from this trip on June 5, 1911 with a fine fare of 70,000 lbs. halibut and 35,000 lbs. cod, stocking $4,589 and a share of $133. This was the largest fare of the season, but the fish were caught in the usual way with dories off Anticosti, in the Gulf of St. Lawrence. The long line was used only briefly. The craft found good fishing and caught them in the usual way. The new line didn't have enough length.

The *Teazer* sailed again on June 10, 1911, and arrived home on June 29th with only 8,000 lbs. halibut and 50,000 lbs. hake and cusk. This ended the "long line" on the *Teazer*. It was considered a failure.

The *Teazer* and Capt. Dunsky had many encounters with the ice off Newfoundland, but the trip of March 1915, was the most thrilling. She was nearly lost on this trip. The *Teazer* left Gloucester on March 15, and fished on Burgeo Bank. In a few days she had 40,000 lbs. halibut on board and then started for home. She got caught in heavy field ice off Scatterie and was imprisoned for three days. The vessel was surrounded by ice with no open water in sight. Ice piled up over her rail. It looked like the end of the *Teazer*. The auxiliary engine was started and forced. For two and one half days the little craft slowly plowed through, with water pouring through her seams. It was a mighty thankful crew when open water was

sighted. Her engine had saved the gallant little vessel.

On her arrival at Gloucester, the *Teazer* plainly showed her battle with the sea. The planking on both sides was scraped bare and in some places even pierced where the sharp ice came in contact. One of her propeller blades was broken off. The *Teazer*'s escape from the ice recalled a similar experience of the schooner Quanapowitt, Capt. Dan (Little Dan) Mac-Donald, who on a trip to the Funks in July, 1913, was caught in ice and saved by her gas engine.

Peter McNally, superintendent of the Boston Aquarium and world famous long distance swimmer, died of a heart attack on the deck of the *Teazer*, at the Gorton Pew Wharf on April 10, 1915 while inspecting a baby seal that Capt. Dunsky had brought from Newfoundland on this trip. McNally had once tried to swim the English Channel.

It seemed as if Capt. Dunsky was always bringing something home. One time in the *Teazer*, he brought home 50 or 60 wooden drums of lubricating oil, picked up at sea. They had been washed off of some ship. Another time he brought home a load of lumber, also picked up at sea.

Capt. Dunsky gave up command of the *Teazer* in 1916 and from then on many skippers sailed on her.

In 1917 Capt. Wallace Walker had her seining. This was a big mackerel year, and Capt. Wallace was right up with the leaders. On one trip, he landed 20,000 lbs. fresh and 250 bbls. salt mackerel at Boston and stocked $10,037, with a share of $230. His total stock for 1917 was $41,654.

Capt. Howard Tobey was her seining skipper in 1918, stocking $26,093. The winter of 1918–19, Capts. Mansfield Conrad, John McInnis, and Jim Mason had her haddocking. The seining season of 1919, Capt. Howard Tobey was again in command, stocking $17,670. Capt. Tobey was also seining skipper in 1920, stocking $17,693. Capt. Manuel J. Goulart, Capt. Horton Mason and Capt. Larry Norris were haddocking skippers in 1921. Capt. Horton Mason and Capt. Ernest Parsons had her haddocking in 1922 and Capt. Norman Ross took over for the seining season of that year.

In 1923–24–25 she was drifting in command of Capt. Stil Hipson. Capt. Alfred Goodwin had her drifting in 1926–27. In 1926 he stocked $43,833. This was the *Teazer*'s biggest year's work. Capt. Clifford Hopkins took her drifting in 1928–29–30. In 1931 Capt. Alonzo Smith took her seining, and Capt. Stil Hipson again took over in 1932–33–34 drifting. Capt. John Placanica was her next skipper and he had her haddocking in 1934–35–36–37. Capt. John Morash went seining in the *Teazer* in 1938. From then on she was used as a freighter at

Newfoundland and the Magdalen Islands, in command of Capt. John Barry and his son, Capt. Fred Barry.

The *Teazer* was taken over by the Gorton-Pew Co. in 1906 when the D. B. Smith firm was consolidated into the Gorton-Pew Co.

An auxiliary sixty-five horsepower Globe gasoline engine was installed in 1911. This was changed in 1917 to a sixty horsepower Fairbanks-Morse crude oil engine. In 1926 she took two forty-five horsepower crude oil engines and in 1943 a big 160 horsepower C. O. was installed. In her last days the *Teazer* carried a short rig. Her bowsprit was removed, her spars shortened and a wheel house was added.

In January 22, 1922 a severe gale swept Brown's Bank, and the *Teazer*, in command of Capt. Horton Mason, lost two of her crew.

Myron Lennox was drowned when his dory upset while returning to the vessel. He was 28 years old, a native of Glouceser and left a widow and five small children.

On that same day, a heavy sea boarded the vessel, sweeping the dories and Fred Thorne, one of her crew, into the sea. Thorne was a native of Newfoundland and 37 years old. Schooner *Corinthian*, Capt. Albert Hines, also lost two of her crew that same day on Brown's Bank.

The end of the grand little *Teazer* came in 1948. The vessel, still owned by the Gorton-Pew Co. and commanded by Capt. Joe Barry, son of Capt. James Barry, was crushed in the ice in the Gulf of St. Lawrence a few miles northwest of St. Paul's Island while on a sealing voyage in March, 1948. Her Canadian crew

of 20 were saved by walking over the ice to St. Paul's Island. It was a perilous journey, with a storm raging and the temperature below zero. The *Teazer* was completely buried by the ice. She had finally been beaten by her old enemy. At the time of her loss she was carrying a cargo of seals valued at $20,000.

Capt. Peter Dunsky lost his life with one of his crew. Samuel Cole, in the sinking of the schooner *Republic*, when she was run down by the British four-master *Wellington* off Cape Sable, Nova Scotia, in February 1925.

He was one of Gloucester's great mariners, a big, sturdy man, a smart, capable fisherman and one of the leaders in the halibut fishery. He was a native of Russia and 53 years old. Capt. Dunsky, in his early days, went square rigging and he was a member of the crew of the American barkentine *Herbert Fuller*, when Capt. Charles Nash and his wife were murdered on board. Mate Bram was charged with the murder and this case attracted widespread attention at the time. Capt. Dunsky commanded the schooner *Nelson Y. McFarland*, *Hattie L. Trask*, *Teazer*, and *Republic*.

Capt. Wallace Walker, one of the very few old mariners still with us in 1972, praised the *Teazer* to the highest. Capt. Wallace was a native of Prince Edward Island.

Gross tons, 97; net tons, 59; length, 91.3 feet; breadth, 24 feet; depth, 9.8 feet. Mainmast, deck to cap, 66 feet (later cut to 54 feet); foremast, deck to cap, 62 feet (cut to 49 feet); main topmast, 38.5 feet; main boom, 65 feet (cut to 59 feet); bowsprit, 27 feet (cut to 19 feet); mainmast head, 10 feet.

For more than fifty years the *Thomas S. Gorton* sailed the North Atlantic; here she is going fishing, circa 1909.

Thomas S. Gorton

LAST OF THE ALL-SAIL FLEET; SHE HIT AN ICEBERG / 1905–1956

Schooner *Thomas S. Gorton*, the last all-sail schooner to go fishing out of Gloucester, was built during the spring and summer of 1905 and launched at the Tarr and James Yard in Essex for Capt. John Chisholm and the writer's uncle, Capt. William H. Thomas, on August 14, 1905.

Named for Thomas S. Gorton, a member of the Slade Gorton Co., of Gloucester, at that time, she was christened by Mrs. Gorton with a bottle of wine. Mr. Gorton later proved to be one of the greatest salesmen of Gloucester fish in the United States. He was vice president of Gorton-Pew Fisheries Company for 25 years.

Both Mr. and Mrs. Gorton and 255 guests made the trip around from Essex on the new schooner.

She had beautiful lines, with a round bow and lofty rig, and was designed by Thomas McManus of Boston.

On the *Gorton*'s trial on August 24, 1905 were about 100 guests, including many of the leading wholesale grocers of New England and many of the leading citizens of Gloucester. Among them were Capt. John Chisholm, Nathaniel L. Gorton, Thomas J. Carroll, John F. James, builder; Arthur E. Rowe and Allan S. Rowe of the firm of E. L. Rowe & Sons, sailmakers; Capts. Henry M. Atwood, Jerome MacDonald, Alfred Green, Lemuel Spinney, and Carl C. Young; Benjamin Frazier, Benjamin F. Cronin, Alfred P. Merchant, Hazen Follansbee, Alex J. Chisholm, John F. Perkins, Benjamin Stanley, Edwin Oxner, and many others. Entertainment was furnished by Clark's Military Band. As she was towed down the harbor by the tug *Nellie*, she was saluted by many whistles. Outside the whistler the Boston schooner *Onato*, Capt. J. Henry Larkin, was waiting to give the *Gorton* a race.

The *Gorton* sailed on her maiden trip haddocking, August 30, 1905 under command of Capt. William H. Thomas. She arrived at Boston on September 13, 1905 with 70,000 lbs. of fresh fish. The *Gorton* established a shacking fisheries record when she stocked $5,642 on a fare of 254,225 lbs. of fish taken off Cape North in May, 1910. The *Gorton* was commanded by Capt. Thomas from 1905 to 1916 and stocked $383,713, which made her one of the greatest money makers out of this port.

Capt. William Thomas was without a doubt one of the greatest skippers to sail from this port. It was always considered an honor to sail with Capt. Bill. Capt. Billy retired from the sea in 1916 to manage the Gloucester Cold Storage. The *Gorton's* last trip under the command of Capt. Billy and also the last of his career was when she arrived in Gloucester June 7, 1916 from Quero Bank with 200,000 lbs. of shack, stocking $7,500, share $189, for a grand wind-up to a remarkable career.

Capt. Thomas sold the *Gorton* to Gorton-Pew Company in June, 1916. Her various commanders while owned by this firm were Capts. Norman A. Ross, Bob Porper, Dominic Arsenault, Wallace Parsons, J. Henry Larkin, Val O'Neil, Alden Geele, Joseph Mesquita, George Nelson, "Little Dan" McDonald, William Firth and her last commander, Don MacCuish.

Two of the greatest skippers out of Gloucester met tragic deaths while in command of this vessel. On April 10, 1926 Capt. Alden Geele was found dead in his cabin at Shelburne, Nova Scotia. Capt. Wallace Parsons was drowned in Gloucester Harbor when he slipped while boarding the vessel on January 4, 1935.

Gus Amero, 40, a native of Pubnico, Nova Scotia, was knocked overboard by the balloon sheet 25 miles west of Seal Island, Nova Scotia, on July 23, 1918, when Capt. Firth was in command.

On September 2, 1929 the *Gorton*, in command of Capt. Wallace Parsons, sailed in the Fisherman's Race off Gloucester against the schooners *Arthur D. Story*, *Progress*, and *Elsie*. She finished last as the weather conditions were not in her favor.

The *Gorton*, although not a fast vessel, was a real old sea dog. She was used mostly haddocking, shacking, and in the Newfoundland herring trade. In her last years out of Glouces-ter she was used in freighting fish from the Canadian Provinces.

The *Thomas S. Gorton* was sold by the Gorton-Pew Co. in March, 1935 to Capt. Arthur Earle of Carbonear, Newfoundland. She was rebuilt at Dayspring, Nova Scotia. Her rig was cut down, a whaleback bow was added and auxiliary engine installed.

On October 7, 1947, with a cargo of lumber, she stranded on Whale Back Rock, 15 miles north of Bonne Bay, Newfoundland (the same spot the schooner *Henry Ford* was lost in June, 1928). Her crew was saved and she was thought to be a total loss. However, she floated off herself and drifted about in the Gulf of St. Lawrence for about a week when she was picked up by a Newfoundland fisherman and brought to port. Although leaking badly, her cargo of lumber had kept her from sinking.

The *Gorton* sank after colliding with an iceberg in 1956. All hands were saved. At the time she was bound to Labrador with a cargo of supplies.

I had always hoped that this great vessel would remain in Gloucester. She would have made a wonderful memorial to the great schooners and men that brought fame to Gloucester.

Thomas S. Gorton passed away in Florida on April 1, 1947, at the age of 76. A great vessel; a great skipper; and a great namesake.

Gross tons, 140; length, 106 feet; breadth, 25.4 feet; depth, 11.5 feet. Mainmast, 76 feet (deck to cap); foremast, 67 feet; main boom, 76 feet (original); bowsprit, outboard, 28 feet (later cut to 22 feet); mainmast head, 12.5 feet.

What a thing to happen on a maiden trip! The *Cynthia* was bound to New York with mackerel when she grounded on Romer Shoal. A derrick lifted her, fish and all, and she lived for eight years.

Cynthia

ADVENTUROUS AND PRODUCTIVE /
1906–1914

Schooner *Cynthia* had an adventurous and productive career after she was launched January 25, 1906 at the John Bishop yard, Vincent Cove. The writer of these stories of Gloucester vessels has a personal interest in the *Cynthia*, for her first skipper was Capt. Jeff Thomas, the writer's father.

A good sized vessel, from a Capt. Thomas McManus design, she had a round bow, long bowsprit and lofty rig. She was built during the fall and winter months of 1905–06 for Sylvanus Smith Co. Her name coincided with the firm's policy of using names ending in "ia."

Capt. Jeff was offered command of the new schooner *Cynthia* after doing remarkably well in the schooner *Arcadia*, from the Smith firm. He was highline of the haddock fleet in 1905.

The *Cynthia* got off to a bad start, for when

she was launched she snapped her checking lines, shot across the cove, and her stern crashed into a shed. Luckily, there was little damage.

The *Cynthia* sailed on her maiden trip April 12, 1906, bound to the south'ard for mackerel, and Capt. Jeff was mighty proud of his beautiful new vessel.

But the jinx had not been shaken off. On April 20, 1906, while bound for the Fulton Market, New York, with her maiden fare of 90 barrels of mackerel, she struck on the dreaded Romer Shoals in lower New York harbor in a dense fog. The vessel heeled over on her port side and began to fill. The wind was light with little sea, and an attempt to work her off in her sails failed.

The Boston schooner *Mattakeeset*, Capt. Jack O'Brien, following the *Cynthia*, also grounded on the shoals, but worked off. She took the *Cynthia's* crew to New York.

The Merritt-Chapman Wrecking Company was engaged, and tugs and the lighter *Century* (with a lifting capacity of 150 tons dead weight) were sent down to the wreck. Divers passed straps around the hull. On April 22 the vessel was lifted, water, mackerel, and all, and taken to Erie Basin. Her false keel was gone, her garboard started a little aft, stern post damaged and her main sail badly torn. Repairs were made and the schooner arrived back in Gloucester on April 27.

The Merrit-Chapman Co. sent photos to the Sylvanus Smith Co. showing the difficulty in the vessel. These remarkable photos are now in the writer's possession.

On December 18, 1906, while running up Broad Sound in Boston Harbor, she grounded and floated off shortly after, sailing on to T Wharf, leaking 500 strokes an hour.

A classic narrow escape took place January 24, 1908, when George Painter, Joe Harding and Stephen Borge were swept overboard by a giant sea. They were smart enough to grab the main sheet, which was trailing, and hold on until they were assisted back aboard.

Michael Lynch, 33, a native of Newfoundland, died of a heart attack on board, off Boone Island, March 24, 1908. The vessel was bound in. The body was landed at Boston.

This seemed to be the end of the *Cynthia's* jinx, and she sailed on through the years, driven hard by Capt. Jeff, seining, shacking, and haddocking.

Cynthia continued seining summers until 1910 when she changed over to shacking. On August 13, she arrived at Gloucester with 200,000 pounds of fresh and salt fish from Quero Bank, stocking $4,550. This was one of the biggest shack trips in some time.

In May 1911, while bound to the eastward, on a fresh bait trip, the *Cynthia* fell in with the crewless derelict *Flora* of Liverpool, Nova Scotia, southeast of Sambro light. Capt. Thomas and two of his crew boarded the hulk, and set her afire as she was a menace to navigation.

The *Cynthia*, never a fast vessel, was given up by Capt. Jeff in April, 1913, when he took command of the fast schooner *Sylvania*, owned by the Smith firm.

Capt. Chris Carrigan had *Cynthia* seining in the summer of 1913 and Capt. Marty Welch seining in the fall of that year.

On January 30, 1914, the *Cynthia* sailed from Gloucester on a halibut trip in command of Capt. Andrew Grimes. The next news of the schooner was a dispatch from St. John's, Newfoundland, saying the the crew of the sinking schooner *Cynthia* had been rescued by the cable steamer *Minia*, south of St. Peter's bank.

The vessel, battered by gales and heavily iced, had sprung aleak on February 7. Her pumps failed to work and from February 10 to 14 her deck was awash. She had been under only her foresail for eight days. Capt. Grimes had tried to make St. Pierre but failed. The *Cynthia's* crew was taken off by the *Minia* and the helpless craft was set on fire.

The survivors watched her burn through the darkness for an hour, when the flames disappeared. *Cynthia's* jinx had finally caught up with her. Nothing was saved but the crew's personal belongings, and three dories. Value of the craft was $15,000.

Few stories of miraculous escapes from death equal that of the crew of the *Cynthia*.

As a sentimental tribute to this beautiful old vessel, we named our youngest daughter after her in 1944.

John Bishop, builder of the *Cynthia*, died at Gloucester November 30, 1912. He was one of Gloucester's greatest shipbuilders in the glory days of sail. A native of Miramachi, New Brunswick, he was foreman for David Alfred Story at Gloucester and took over that yard when Story retired, under the firm name of Bishop and Murphy. Later the yard became the John Bishop yard on Vincent Cove. Bishop retired in 1911 and the yard was taken over by Owen Lantz.

Gross tons, 137; net tons, 98; length, 105.5 feet; breadth, 24.5 feet; depth, 11 feet.

This is probably the only picture in existence of the beautiful *Effie M. Prior*, according to the author. She is on her maiden trip, on the day of the San Francisco earthquake, April 18, 1906.

Effie M. Prior

SHE'D TACK IN A PINT OF WATER /
1906–1921

Schooner *Effie M. Prior* during her life of 15 years was one of the finest and prettiest vessels of the days of sail.

Capt. Elroy Prior, one of Gloucester's great mariners, had made a fine record in the schooner *Edith M. Prior* (named for his sister) and schooner *Kentucky*. In 1906, a new vessel was built for him at the Arthur D. Story yard in Essex. The new craft was built alongside the schooner *Terranova* and she was named for the wife of Capt. Prior.

The *Effie M. Prior* was a good sized vessel of the round bow type designed by Capt. Tom McManus of Boston. She carried a long bowsprit and mainboom and spread a lot of canvas. The sheer of the *Effie M.* was rather crooked and she was very deep. She was one of the prettiest vessels out of Gloucester. Capt. Prior and the M. Walen firm were the owners.

The *Effie M. Prior* was launched by Mr. Story on April 9, 1906. Tug *Nellie*, Capt. Linnekin, towed her around to Gloucester, to be rigged for sea.

The *Effie M. Prior*, Capt. Elroy Prior, sailed on her maiden trip, bound to the south'ard for mackerel on April 19, 1906. She presented a handsome picture as she sailed out of the harbor. Incidentally, at this time the great San Francisco earthquake had occurred on the Pacific Coast. The *Effie M.* returned to Gloucester shortly after, however, when a leak was discovered.

Repairs were made and the new craft again got under way on April 24. Mackerel were very scarce that season out south and the *Effie Prior* returned home to fit for the Cape Shore on May 11th. She sailed to the east'ard on May 14th.

The 1906 Cape Shore fleet, consisting of 70 vessels, was the largest in years. Three beautiful new vessels were making their debut that season, schooner *Effie M. Prior*, Capt. Elroy Prior; schooner *Cynthia*, Capt. Jeff Thomas; and the schooner *Terranova*, Capt. John Hickey.

The *Effie M. Prior* landed her first fare at Gloucester on June 24, 1906. She hailed for 6000 pounds fresh mackerel and 30 bbls. salt mackerel, selling to the Gloucester Fresh Fish Co.

The *Effie M.*, throughout her Gloucester career, was commanded by Capt. Prior, but at times when he would take a much needed rest ashore, transient skippers would take over. In December 1908, Capt. Lew Carritt had her haddocking. In November 1909, Capt. J. Henry Larkin and Tom Prior (cousin of Capt. Prior) were the skippers, haddocking. Capt. Jerry Cook took the *Effie M.* to Newfoundland for a herring cargo in December, 1910. Capt. Asa Baker had her haddocking in March, 1911.

Under Capt. Prior's command the *Effie M.* was used seining, haddocking, and shacking. On March 13, 1908 she arrived at Gloucester with 125,000 lbs. fresh fish, the largest trip of the season.

The *Effie M. Prior* was a fast vessel, but was at her best under bank sail. For a vessel of her size she was very easy to handle. Fishermen who sailed in her said, "You could tack her in a pint of water." A good demonstration of the speed of this vessel was sailed on May 10, 1906. In the forenoon of that day the *Prior* was 25 miles southeast of Block Island. At 3 a.m. of the next day she arrived off Eastern Point, Gloucester. This was pretty good sailing!

The *Effie M. Prior* in her seven years out of Gloucester led a rather peaceful life. She was a lucky vessel, but unfortunately two lives were lost out of her.

On November 10, 1910, John Muise fell overboard on Western Bank and drowned. The vessel was jogging as it was too rough to fish, waiting for the weather to moderate. Muise struck against a trawl tub and pitched over the rail. He was a native of Surrets Island, Nova Scotia, and was 23 years old.

On October 12, 1911, the *Effie M. Prior* was bound home from Western Bank under bank sail. When about 30 miles to the eastward of Cape Sable in the inky darkness of midnight, a big sea boarded the vessel, rushed along the deck sweeping the man at the wheel, Havelock Forbes, over the stern to his death. Capt. Prior, who was in the cabin, heard the man cry out, rushed on deck, but Forbes was never seen again. Forbes was a native of Argyle Sound, Nova Scotia, and was 25 years old.

The Gloucester career of the *Effie M. Prior* came to a close in November 1912. At this time auxiliary power was fast coming into favor in the fleet and Capt. Prior was having the gasoline engined *Thelma* built at Essex. The *Effie M. Prior* was then sold to Capt. S. V. Cluett and the Kearly Bros. of Belleoram, Newfoundland. She was used as a banker and fish freighter in command of Capt. Cluett.

The sale price of $6500 was one of the lowest ever brought for a Gloucester schooner of the *Prior*'s size. (Just think what a price this beautiful vessel would bring today.)

The *Effie M. Prior*, flying the British flag, made several visits to her old home port. On November 15, 1913, she arrived at Gloucester with 420,000 lbs. salt fish from Newfoundland. On March 29, 1919 she arrived from Belleoram, Newfoundland with 415,336 lbs. salt cod.

The end of the great old vessel came in October 1921, when she ran ashore at Savage Cove, Newfoundland, near the Straits of Belle Isle and was smashed to pieces. Her crew was saved. At the time she was returning from Labrador with 1300 quintals of cod. Capt. Brenton, skipper of the *Prior* when she was lost, paid a visit to Gloucester as commander of the Newfoundland motor vessel *Golden Stream* in June 1951.

Capt. Elroy Prior sailed his last voyage in June 1944. He was a native of Bremen, Maine and 81 years old. Capt. Elroy was one of Gloucester's great mariners. A smart, able all-around fisherman and one of the greatest helmsmen out of this port. Well liked and respected by his men. This great "Down Easter" was many times a helmsman on the American vessels in the International Races. Some of his commands included the schooners *Reub L. Richardson*, *Edith M. Prior*, *Kentucky*, *Thelma*, *Joffre*, *Agnes*, *Kineo* and *Elsie G. Silva*.

Capt. Tom Prior, one of the *Effie M. Prior*'s skippers, lost his life in the schooner *Ella M. Goodwin* when that vessel was lost with all hands on a voyage from Newfoundland to Gloucester in January, 1911. He was a native of Bremen, Maine and 35 years old. Mrs. Effie M. (Goodwin) Prior, namesake of the vessel, passed away at Newport, New Hampshire, in December, 1947. She was a native of Lower Sandy Point, Nova Scotia.

Gross tons, 138; net tons, 97; length, 103.4 feet; breadth, 24.6 feet; depth, 12.2 feet.

Off for Halifax is the *Esperanto*, winner of the first International Fishermen's Race, with the Canadian *Delawanna* in 1920.

Esperanto

A LEGEND IN GLOUCESTER / 1906–1921

Esperanto: A name that is a legend in Gloucester. A fine, beautiful vessel that arose from
obscurity to fame in the twilight of her life. A
vessel that carried the hopes and traditions of
her home port to victory in the first International Fishermen's Race.

Schooner *Esperanto* was another fine product
of those great shipbuilders in Essex, Tarr and
James, launched on June 27, 1906. The Orlando
Merchant firm (William H. Jordan Co.) were
the owners and Capt. Charles Harty, famous
mackerel killer, was her first skipper.

The *Esperanto* was a sturdy, good sized vessel with a round bow and a large spread of
canvas. She was designed by Tom McManus
of Boston, and taken off the schooner *Alert*
(1906) model. She resembled the schooner
Thomas S. Gorton a great deal. Her sails were
made by the S. V. Colby loft.

Esperanto was a true representative of the
glorious "Flying Fisherman." Although not as
large and yachtlike as the big racing fishermen that came after her, she had all that a
fisherman required. She was able, fast and
handsome.

The name is odd for a fishing schooner. It
means an international language.

The *Esperanto* sailed on her maiden trip,
seining on July 7, 1906, just 10 days after her
launching. She arrived at Boston with her
maiden fare of 8,000 fresh mackerel on July 20.

Capt. Harty remained only during the 1906
season as the following year he took over command of another new schooner, the *Clintonia*.
The mackerel seasons of 1907–08–09 she was
commanded by Capt. Charles Maguire. Capt.
Freeman Mason had her haddocking in the fall
of 1903. Capt. George Peeples took her to Newfoundland for a herring cargo in January 1909.
In the fall of 1909, Capt. Lem Haywood had
her shacking. In 1910 Capt. Frank Enslo had
her haddocking and shacking. The seining season of 1911, Capt. Jimmy Gannon was her
skipper and that fall, Capt. Reuben Cameron
had her shacking. Capt. Ambrose Fleet was her
seining skipper in 1912–13 and Capt. Ben
Green had her halibuting also in 1912. Capt.
Al Reynolds had her haddocking during the
winter of 1912–13 and Capt. Hugh Quinlan,
haddocking in the winter of 1913–14. Capt.
Chris Carrigan seining 1914. Capt. Asa Baker,
Peak codfishing, fall of 1914, and haddocking
the winter of 1914–15. Capt. George Heckman
seining and Capt. Chris Gibbs shacking 1915.
Capts. Davis and Ted Stewart haddocking 1916
and Capt. Ed McLean seining that year. Capt.

Dan McDonald (Little Dan) took over command, halibuting the latter part of 1916 and
remained in her during 1917–18. Capt. Carl
Dahl was her skipper, halibuting, in 1919.

Little Dan McDonald was one of her most
successful skippers. On August 24, 1917 he arrived at Gloucester from the Gully, with 30,000
pounds halibut and 115,000 pounds fresh fish,
stocking $7,100 and a share of $191. On September 25, 1917 the *Esperanto* arrived at Boston with 45,000 pounds halibut, stocking $7,278
and sharing $200. Capt. Courtney McDonald,
son of Little Dan, used to be one of his father's
crew in the *Esperanto*.

Incidentally, Courtney and Willie McKay,
son of Capt. Jack McKay, hold the distinction
of being the two youngest men ever to go in a
dory out of Gloucester. They were around 16
years old.

On December 19, 1912, the *Esperanto*, Capt.
Al Reynolds, limped into Gloucester, looking
like a wreck. Her mainmast head was gone,
her jumbo was rigged for a mainsail, her riding
sail for a foresail and tattered rags of canvas
as a jib.

The accident happened on December 17th,
85 miles west of Cape Sable Island. She was
coming along under four lowers with a fair
wind, when suddenly the mainmast snapped
off about eight feet below the head, and there
was a tangle of canvas, spars and rigging all
slatting overhead. Her crew immediately rigged
up sail to get her home.

Loss of life was very small in the *Esperanto*,
only one that's known. On March 17, 1916, off
Baccaro, Nova Scotia, John Burnham, while
standing watch, was knocked overboard by the
slatting of the mainsail, and drowned. He was
a native of Gloucester, 40 years old. Capt. John
Davis was skipper.

The *Esperanto* was sold to the Gorton-Pew
Fisheries Company in 1920, and Capt. Still
Hipson took her dory handlining that season.

In the fall of 1920 a challenge was sent to
Gloucester by the Halifax Herald, offering a
cash prize and a trophy to the winner of a race
between the fastest fishing schooners out of
Gloucester and the Canadian champion *Delawana*. That great sportsman Benjamin A
Smith of the Gorton-Pew Fisheries quickly accepted the challenge and the *Esperanto* was
chosen to represent Gloucester and Capt. Marty
Welch, great sail carrier, was selected for her
skipper.

The *Esperanto* was known to be a good
sailer, especially by the wind, and as sailing

vessels were scarce (most had been converted to auxiliary power) she was considered to be a good choice to bring the cup to Gloucester. The vessel had just returned from a salt fishing trip and extensive repairs and grooming were required to get her ready for the race. Her old skipper Capt. Charlie Harty was called upon to get the vessel in the proper sailing trim; and Capt. Charlie was just the boy who could do it. Gloucester was wild with excitement and racing fever when on October 25th the proud *Esperanto* sailed out of the harbor, bound to Halifax, as thousands of people lined the wharves to cheer her on to victory. I was a lad of 14 and watched the *Esperanto* as she was towed out by the old Halibut Wharf. What a handsome sight she made, glistening in her new paint, and with Micky Hall, her mast headsman, at the mast head!

The *Esperanto* carried a picked crew of the most able men out of Gloucester, including Capt. Marty Welch, Capt. John Matheson, mate, Isaiah Gosbee, cook, Capt. Wallace Bruce, Capt. Tom Benham, Capt. Jack Barrett, Capt. Lee Murray, Capt. Roy Patten, Raymond (Rusty) McKenzie, R. Russell Smith, Stephen Whittey, Thomas Smith, Harry Christensen, George Roberts, Ben Colby, Ben Stanley, Hugh Young, George Young, James McDonald, Michael Hall, Ernest Hendrie, Robert W. Sawtelle, Morill Wiggin, Lawrence Percival, John Batt, and James B. Connolly, noted author. Benjamin H. Colby, one of the *Esperanto*'s racing crew, helped make her sails when she was new.

The first race took place on October 30, 1920 off Halifax, Nova Scotia, over a forty mile triangular course. In this race, there was nothing to it but the *Esperanto*. She proved she could beat the *Delawana* at reaching, running, and working to windward. The gallant Gloucesterman crossed the finish line 18 minutes and 28 seconds ahead of the Lunenburger.

The Lunenburgers worked feverishly on their vessel before the second race, shifting and taking out ballast. They were taking a long chance, and praying for light winds as they knew their vessel didn't have a chance against the *Esperanto* in a heavy breeze.

The second race, held on November 1, 1920, was not such an easy win as the first. For thirty miles the *Delawana*, thanks to her altered ballast, led the *Esperanto*. But slowly and surely Capt. Marty cut down her lead. Racing history was made along the shores of Devil's Island, that day, when the *Esperanto*, facing almost certain destruction, cut through *Delawana*'s weather and went on to win the race by seven minutes and 25 seconds.

The *Esperanto*'s ability to sail by the wind was a mighty hard thing to beat.

The expert handling of the *Esperanto* by Capt. Marty Welch was responsible for the victory. R. Russell Smith, representing her owners, the Gorton-Pew Co., also had a hand in the victory, when he told Capt. Marty "To hell with the kelp and rocks, Marty, keep her to it!" Marty did.

Greater is the glory for Capt. Marty when one stops to think that this man, previous to these races, had never taken the wheel of the *Esperanto* before, and that during both races he never once left the wheel. Capt. John Matheson, mate, ably handled the head sails. The Canadians, even in defeat, especially *Delawana*'s skipper, Capt. Tommie Himmelman, displayed fine sportsmanship.

When the news of the victory reached Gloucester, the city went wild. The *Esperanto*, the able, handsome lady, had come through.

She arrived home on November 7, 1920, carrying a new broom at her foretopmast head, the signal of victory. Also on board were the trophy and $4,000 in cash, her part of the victory. What a reception she received! It was probably the greatest ever given to a Gloucester fishing vessel. There were banquets and receptions galore for the victorious crew and at the big banquet given at the Armory on November 8th, Governor Calvin Coolidge declared, "The victory was a triumph for Americanism."

At the Gorton-Pew victory dinner held at the Savoy Hotel on November 10th, each of the crew was given a fine gold Waltham watch. Raymond (Rusty) McKenzie, one of our old fishermen, proudly displayed his watch for years.

So ended the first International Fishermen's Race, the greatest ever sailed between the two nations.

The *Esperanto* sailed on a dory handlining trip in the spring of 1921, in command of Capt. Tom Benham.

On May 30th, while fishing off Sable Island, she struck the submerged wreck of the S. S. *State of Virginia*. The *Esperanto* began to fill and went down in twenty minutes in 65 feet of water. Her crew of 21 took to the dories and were picked up three hours later by the schooner *Elsie*, Capt. Alden Geele, and landed at Halifax, Nova Scotia. At the time of the accident the *Esperanto* was making for the southwest bar of the island. It was foggy and a light southeast breeze was blowing. On board were 140,000 pounds of salt cod. Only the mastheads of the *Esperanto* remained above the water after she went down.

Capt. Benham and cook Isaiah Gosbee were members of the *Esperanto* crew in the race off Halifax.

On their return to Gloucester, cook Gosbee declared, "Yes, we lost her, but Davy Jones can't take her fame away from her."

When the news of the *Esperanto*'s loss reached Gloucester, a salvaging expedition was immediately formed. R. Russell Smith and J. Norman Abbott were prominent members in financing the undertaking.

The beam trawler *Fabia*, Capt. Robert Wharton, loaded with equipment and pontoons, sailed for Sable Island on June 16, 1921. Capts. Hugh Quinlan and Donald McCuish were members of the crew. The *Fabia's* engineers were Leslie Malloch and Jim McNeil.

The *Esperanto* was brought to the surface several times by means of the pontoons, but something would happen and back to the bottom she would go again. Storms, fogs and raging tides hampered the operations, and finally lack of provisions and water forced the *Fabia* to return to Gloucester, arriving home on July 17th. A second expedition was formed and the *Fabia* was again ready to sail when the news was received on July 25th from Sable Island that the "Pride of Gloucester" was breaking up and wreckage was coming ashore on the island, including the schooner's name plate. The expedition was abandoned. Sable Island, "graveyard of the Atlantic," had claimed one of the finest.

Capt. Martin Welch, racing skipper of the *Esperanto*, sailed on his final voyage on April 16, 1935 at the age of 68. He was a native of Digby County, Nova Scotia. Capt. Marty was one of our greatest mariners. This small, rosy-cheeked veteran of the deep was one of the greatest sail carriers out of Gloucester. His skill in sailing by the wind was uncanny. He was courageous, fearless, capable, daring, yet careful. The fast schooner *Lucania* was Marty's pride and joy. His fast passages home in the *Lucania* from the Liscomb Ridges in the dead of winter, and the vessel heavily coated with ice, will always be remembered among mariners. Many fine vessels were commanded by Capt. Marty, including the *Mary A. Clark, Lucille, Titania, Navahoe, Lucania, Benjamin A. Smith, Killarney* and *Thelma*.

My father, Capt. Jeff Thomas, owed a great deal to Marty. He gave him his start as a skipper. They never made them any better than Capt. Marty. My father always thought so, and that was enough for me.

Capt. Charles H. Harty, first skipper of the *Esperanto*, passed away at Newport, Rhode Island, on May 21, 1931. He was a native of Gloucester and 80 years old. This mild mannered, smart fisherman was one of the greatest sailing masters out of the port. He probably could get more out of a fishing schooner than any man who ever lived. Capt. Charlie was one of the old highliners of the seiners. He was a participant in the first fishermen's races in 1887.

His commands included the finest vessels out of Gloucester, the *I. J. Merritt, Jr., Fredonia, Grayling, Golden Rod, Marguerite Haskins, Mary E. Harty* (named for his wife), *Clintonia, Oriole, Constellation* and *Stilletto.*

Washington Tarr, one of *Esperanto's* builders, died in Essex on December 18, 1918 at 84. He was a native of Rockport and went to Essex in 1858. John F. James passed away in Essex, March, 1920, at the age of 82. He was a native of Essex. At the time of his death, he was active head of the oldest shipbuilding yard in Essex. The year he was born, 1837, the yard was started by his father. It was known as James and McKenzie. (John James and Leonard McKenzie, Sr.) They continued in business until 1875, when the name was changed to Tarr and James. In 1913 the firm name was again changed to John F. James and Son.

Tarr and James vessels were built on honor. The builders were noted as square dealers. Some of their most famous vessels included the *Esperanto, Oriole, Independence, A. Piatt Andrew, Thomas S. Gorton, Arethusa, Cavalier* and the whaling brigantine *Viola.*

Gross tons, 140; net tons, 91; length, 107.4 feet; breadth, 25.4 feet; depth, 11.4 feet.

One of the great ones was the *Arethusa*, always productive and fast. This is the way she looked circa 1920 after her admiring owner Bill McCoy added a bowsprit and ballooner to make her sail even faster. She was probably the most famous of the rumrunners.

Arethusa

THE RUM-RUNNER FOR BILL McCOY /
1907–1929

Picturesque seems the only adequate word for the schooner *Arethusa* and her skipper for years, Capt. Clayton Morrissey, a rugged individual, able fisherman and hard worker with a heart as big as a mountain.

The tall-sparred *Arethusa* was a product of the Tarr and James yard at Essex, built during the late spring and summer of 1907, and launched in 1907. She was christened by an English actress who spent the summer in Gloucester. The craft, designed by Capt. Thomas McManus, was one of the early vessels of the knockabout type (no bowsprit).

Most of *Arethusa's* big producing was in shacking, both fresh and salt, and in salt bank trips. When she was young she carried herring cargoes between Newfoundland ports and Gloucester.

Ready in the early fall when the herring industry was in its heyday, it was quite natural for the *Arethusa* to be sent on her maiden voyage after herring at Newfoundland. Departure day on November 8, 1907 was a big event for this, the largest knockabout model of fishing craft afloat. Nothing had been spared in her construction, rigging and outfitting. Hundreds gathered at the Cunningham and Thompson wharf. The mainsail and foresail were hoisted at the wharf, and in charge of a tug, she moved slowly away amid cheers. The tug dropped the towline off Ten Pound Island and *Arethusa* stepped off under sail. For a half hour, Capt. Clayt gave his marine audience a great show as he tried the new vessel on different points of sailing. Then he headed down the harbor and around the Point to the eastward, the beginning of an eventful career.

On October 1, 1909, the *Arethusa* arrived at Gloucester from Grand and Quero banks with 430,000 pounds of salt cod. The vessel was so deep she grounded at the entrance to Harbor Cove. On her previous trip she landed 390,000 pounds of salt cod.

In 1910, in three trips, she landed a total of 826,327 pounds of salt cod, stocking $27,362. The season of 1911, she broke her own record by landing 839,716 pounds of salt cod, stocking $33,978.

Jerry Sutton, 30, native of Hermitage Bay, Newfoundland, and Thomas Foley, 30, native of Placentia, Newfoundland, were drowned on Grand Bank July 8, 1910, by the swamping of their dory.

Louis Amero, 18, native of Yarmouth, Nova Scotia, was knocked overboard by the slat of the main boom on February 18, 1914, while crossing the Bay of Fundy.

Arethusa was nearly always a big money-maker and brought thousands of pounds of fish around Eastern Point. In 1911, in two salt bank trips, *Arethusa* stocked $18,316.

Capt. Chris Gibbs had her shacking in 1917; Capt. James O'Brien shacking in 1918 and Capt. Joshua Stanley, Capt. Freeman Crowell, Capt. James O'Brien, Capt. James Mason and Capt. J. Henry Larkin also commanded the vessel.

During the early 1900's, restrictions were rigid and the law prohibiting fishing within the three-mile limit was vigorously enforced by Canadian authorities. *Arethusa*, like a good many other vessels of that time, judging from the headlines of the day, had more than one encounter with enforcement boats. One of these was in 1908, when three vessels were ordered to court. The trio set sail. Two were caught in field ice, but *Arethusa* got away. The steam cutter *Fiona* gave chase but *Arethusa* was too fast and made a spectacular getaway.

One of the most famous exploits of any Gloucester vessel was the *Arethusa's* escape from the northeast bar of Sable Island. She struck in heavy fog July 14, 1913. She worked herself off and made Canso, Nova Scotia, leaking badly, minus rudder, and with her keel torn. She was towed home by the Canadian tug *Bridgewater*.

Arethusa was sold in April, 1921 to Capt. Bill McCoy of Florida, and renamed *Tomaka*. A bowsprit was added and she carried two jibs, jumbo and jib topsail, and a lot of liquor. *Arethusa* had now become one of the rum row fleet. It was stated that she had a capacity of 6,000 cases. Capt. A. W. Coburn of Bay of Islands, Newfoundland was killed on board by a falling block at sea in December, 1922.

In 1926–1927, *Arethusa* was registered in Lloyd's as French schooner *Mistinquette* of St. Pierre. In June, 1927, the craft returned to Gloucester, lay at Chisholm's wharf and was sold to Ashbourne, Ltd. of Twillingate, Newfoundland. She was again renamed, this time *Saucy Arethusa*.

Arethusa became a total loss on Sambro ledges at the entrance to Halifax harbor on November 8, 1929, exactly 22 years after she sailed on her maiden trip. She was en route to Halifax, Nova Scotia, from Harbor Grace, Newfoundland, with a cargo of salt cod. Capt. Kenneth Oxford and the crew were saved.

Capt. McCoy, who bought her in 1921, had a great love for the vessel and after she was wrecked searched the Nova Scotia coast for the remains. He was finally rewarded and located them at Ketch Harbor, Nova Scotia, near Sambro. He brought back a piece and presented it to the Gloucester Master Mariner's Association.

An oil painting of the great vessel hung for many years over the entrance to the former Mariners' quarters in the old Wetherell block, destroyed by fire in 1946. A small model of *Arethusa* is exhibited at the Peabody Museum, Salem.

Capt. Clayt Morrissey was born in East Pubnico, Nova Scotia, of a family of great mariners, who included his father, Capt. William E. Morrissey, and two brothers, Capts. Billy and Howard, who all sailed out of Gloucester. Capt. Clayt was one of the greatest salt fishing skippers; a giant in size and deed, capable, daring and fearless. He made many records.

He became a skipper at 19 in the *Effie M. Morrissey*, and later commanded the *Joseph Rowe*, *Elector*, *Harry A. Nickerson*, *Arethusa*, the steam trawler *Walrus*, *Henry Ford*, *Imperator* and *Flora L. Oliver*. He was a participant in the international fishermen's races in schooner *Henry Ford*. He died of a heart attack at the age of 62 on board his small trawler *Nimbus* at Hyannisport, Massachusetts, July 1, 1936.

Gross tons, 157; length, 114 feet; breadth, 25.6 feet; depth, 12.5 feet. Mainmast, 79 feet (deck to cap); foremast, 74 feet; main boom, 71 feet, length of forecastle, 41 feet.

Benjamin A. Smith

SHE FISHED IN MAINE WATERS /
1907–1923

The auxiliary schooner *Benjamin A. Smith* was one of the most famous craft of her day. She was built during the summer and fall of 1907, at the Tarr and James yard in Essex for Gorton-Pew Fisheries Co. of Gloucester and Capt. George H. Smith of Vinalhaven, Maine. Launching day was on December 21, 1907.

The *Smith* was a large knockabout, with rather a straight sheer. For a vessel of her size, she was not very deep, as she was to be used in fishing along the Maine coast and her shallow draft would make her handy in entering Down East harbors. She was a fine looking and able vessel with a large spread of canvas. She was fitted with a big 85 horsepower Globe gasoline engine, but this was changed to two 65 horsepower oil engines in 1917. In September 1913, a short bowsprit was added which changed her appearance.

Thomas McManus of Boston was the designer of the *Smith* and she was from an original model. She was named for Benjamin A. Smith of Gorton-Pew Fisheries Co. Her cost ready for sea was $18,000.

Capt. George Smith of Vinalhaven, Maine, one of her owners, was also her first skipper. He was the premier hake catcher of New England, and had made a fine reputation in the schooners *Evelyn L. Smith*, *Fannie A. Smith*, and *Eglantine*. Capt. George was a hustler and wasted little time between trips. Many of his trips were landed at Maine ports and when a trip was sold at Gloucester, immediately after the fare was taken out, the vessel would sail to Vinalhaven, where the livers were sold to the Libby Oil Plant, and she fitted out at that port for another trip.

The new *Benjamin A. Smith* in command of Capt. Smith, sailed for Vinalhaven to fit out on January 29, 1908. Ira Smith, son of her skipper, was the engineer. She sailed on her maiden trip from Vinalhaven on March 13th, pollock seining along the Maine coast.

Capt. Smith caught plenty of fish while in command of the *Benjamin A*. On May 4, 1908, he caught 50,000 lbs. pollock in one set off Boone Island. A trip of 200,000 lbs. pollock was landed at Gloucester on May 18, 1908. This fare was taken on the Rips. Later that season the *Smith* changed over to shacking and on July 11, 1908 she landed at Gloucester a fine fare of 190,000 lbs. fresh fish (mostly hake). This skipper could really catch them.

The *Benjamin A. Smith* had many skippers.

Another exception to the banish-the-bowsprit trend was the *Benjamin A. Smith*, originally a knockabout; a bowsprit was added to improve her sailing qualities.

Some of the most famous mariners out of Gloucester commanded her.

Capt. George Smith remained in the vessel only during the summer and fall of 1908. His interest in the vessel was taken over by the Gorton-Pew Co. The winter of 1908–09, she sailed haddocking in command of Capt. James D. Goodwin (Little Jim). The summer and fall of 1909 the "mackerel king," Sol Jacobs, was master, and Capt. Goodwin again took over haddocking in the winter of 1909–10.

Capt. Billy Corkum (Big Billy) had her seining during the season of 1910. Capt. George Hodgdon took her haddocking that winter of 1910–11. During the seining season of 1911, Capt. Jimmy Gannon and George Hodgdon were the skippers. Capt. George Heckman was her next skipper, haddocking in the winter of 1911–12. Capt. Chris Carrigan was her seining skipper the summer of 1912. That fall and winter of 1912–13, Capt. Chris Gibbs and Capt. Tom Benham were her skippers. Capt. Dave Keating and Capt. Marty Welch had her seining in 1913. Capt. Billy Firth took her haddocking the fall and winter of 1913–14. Capt. Marty Welch again had her seining in 1914 and also in 1915 and 1916. Capt. Hugh Quinlan was her haddocking skipper during the winter of 1914–15. The winter of 1915–16 Capt. Jim Mason had her haddocking. The seining season of 1917, Capt. John Vautier was master and that winter of 1917–1918, Capt. Horace Wylde took over. The seining season of 1918, found Capt. Norman Ross in command. The fall and winter of 1918–19, my father, Capt. Jeff Thomas, had her haddocking and the following spring in 1919, Capt. Ross again took over seining. Capt. Jeff Thomas again took over in January 1920 and remained in her until April 1921.

The seining season of 1921 found Capt. Frank Hall in command. Capt. Chris Gibbs again took over that August and remained in her until August, 1922, when she was taken over by Capt. Fred Thompson, halibuting. Capt. Daniel McDonald (Little Dan) was the Benjamin A. Smith's last skipper. He took over in August 1923, and she was lost on his first trip.

The Smith was a successful vessel. Some of her outstanding trips were as follows: under Capt. Jimmy Goodwin haddocking, in four months ending in March, 1909, she stocked $16,000 with a share of $320. Capt. Goodwin liked the Smith. He said she was ideal for winter haddocking and was a home on the ocean. She was handy in working around her dories.

On March 17, 1909, he landed at Gloucester the biggest trip of that winter, 175,000 lbs. fresh fish of which 120,000 lbs. were haddock. The stock was $2,623 with a share of $60. The fish were taken on LaHave Bank and she was out 11 days. The previous trip, out only 11 days, he landed 116,000 lbs. fresh fish. Capt. Jimmy also knew how to catch them.

On October 18, 1916, the B. A. Smith, Capt. Marty Welch, landed 15,000 mackerel at Boston. She sailed again at 2 p.m. on that day, struck a big school and the next day, October 19th, she was back at Boston with a tremendous fare of 110,000 lbs. of mackerel.

The seining season of 1918 was a big one and the B. A. Smith, under Capt. Norman Ross, stocked $40,521.

The largest stocks ever made by the Benjamin A. Smith were made under Capt. Jeff Thomas. From October 10, 1918 to April 7, 1919, she stocked $61,160 with a share of $1,284 per man. From January, 1920 to April, 1921 her total stock was $94,268.

The Benjamin A. Smith had her share of accidents and loss of life. On September 16, 1912, Andy Peddle and Patrick Joy were astray in the fog, 25 miles south of Cape Sable, Nova Scotia, and were never seen again. Peddle and Joy were both natives of Newfoundland and they were both 25 years old. Capt. Chris Gibbs was the skipper at the time.

On March 4, 1916, William DeYounge was washed overboard and drowned on Brown's Bank. He was 34 years old and a native of Nova Scotia. Capt. Jim Mason was skipper.

While she was in command of Capt. Jeff Thomas, two of the crew went astray in fog off Liscomb, Nova Scotia on December 17, 1919. They were Howard Penney, 52, and John Ernst, 55. Although the vessel searched and searched for them, neither man was seen again. Penny and Ernst, two of the best known fishermen from this port, were the first men my father ever lost.

This proved to be a hard luck trip for the Smith. On her arrival at Boston and while the fish were being taken out, Will Fletcher, one of the crew, got his gloved hand caught in the hoisting winch and his left hand was torn off. He climbed the rigging unaided, jumped ashore and got into the waiting ambulance and was taken to the hospital. What courage those sturdy fellows had!

The Smith's most tragic accident occured on May 14, 1918, while in command of Capt. Norman Ross. The Smith, bound home from seining to the southward, was rammed in the fog by the Norwegian steamer Commodore Rollins. Nine of the crew jumped into a dory which overturned directly under the bow of the steamer, and six were drowned. The tragedy was needless, as the Smith was not badly damaged and she proceeded home. The accident happened about 25 miles south of Barnegat, New Jersey. The steamer saw the fisherman in time and the impact was slight. All rescue efforts proved futile.

The drowned men were Patrick Powers, 47, a native of Newfoundland; Leonard Williams, 27, a native of Green Harbor, Nova Scotia; Caesar Doucett, 40, a native of Yarmouth, Nova Scotia; Murdock Beaton, 48, a native of Port Hood, Nova Scotia; Capt. William Burbridge,

40, a native of Maine; Peter Powers, 44, a native of Nova Scotia.

The *Benjamin A. Smith* in command of Capt. Chris Gibbs, rammed the Canadian fishing schooner *Douglass Conrad* in the fog 30 miles off Halifax, Nova Scotia, on January 26, 1922. It was a narrow escape for both craft. The *Conrad* had her gaff broken and the riding sail torn off.

The end of the *Smith* came on August 3, 1923. She left Gloucester on a halibut trip on August 2, in command of Little Dan McDonald. The next day in a heavy fog she stranded on Flat Island, nine miles north of Seal Island, Nova Scotia. It was low water at the time, the vessel quickly filled and she was five feet under water at high tide. She proved a total loss. The crew of 18 made shore safely. The compass being off at the time was blamed for her loss.

Benjamin A. Smith, namesake of this grand vessel, passed away on May 7, 1923, at Gloucester, several months before the loss of the craft. He was 58 years old and a native of Rockport. He became associated with his uncle, David B. Smith, and later entered in business as D. B. Smith & Co. On formation of the Gorton-Pew company in 1906, he joined them. He was president of the Gorton-Pew Vessels Co. Mr. Smith was an authority on matters pertaining to the fishing industry. He made possible the International Fishermen's Races in 1920. Ben Smith was a man of sterling character, with a word that was his bond. My father, Capt. Jeff Thomas, often said he couldn't sail under a better man or a better firm.

Capt. James D. Goodwin, one of the *Smith's* early skippers, was of the finest skippers out of Gloucester. He was lost with all hands in his schooner *Ella M. Goodwin* while bound home to Gloucester from Newfoundland with a cargo of herring in January, 1911. Capt. Jimmy was a man whom the fishing industry could ill afford to lose. A man widely known and respected along the Atlantic seaboard. His commands were the *Edith Prior, Ella M. Goodwin* and *Benjamin A. Smith*.

Gross tons, 146; net tons, 75; length, 116 feet; breadth, 25.6 feet; depth, 10.6 feet. Mainmast (deck to cap), 77 feet; foremast, 71 feet; main topmast, 47 feet; fore topmast, 42 feet; main gaff, 45.5 feet (cut to 40 feet); bowsprit, 18 feet; main boom, 72.5 feet (cut to 66.5 feet); mainmast head, 12.5 feet.

Where people now park to go to the movies this big powerful schooner was built and launched. The *Clintonia* caught a lot of mackerel.

Clintonia

The handsome schooner *Clintonia* was regarded as one of the ablest and smartest vessels out of Gloucester.

She was built during the spring of 1907 by John Bishop and launched from his yard at Vincent Cove, at 11 a.m. on June 26, 1907. Orlando Merchant (William H. Jordan Co.) was her owner and the old reliable Capt. Charles H. Harty was her first skipper. Capt. Harty was a sailor without a peer.

The *Clintonia* was named for a yellow, bell shaped flower that blooms in the woods in June. The vessel was christened by Miss Marjorie Newell, holding a bunch of Clintonias. Miss Newell, a neighbor of Mr. Jordan on Hovey Street, used to gather these flowers in the woods and take them to Mr. Jordan for his office desk at home.

The launching of *Clintonia* was a gala affair with over 500 people attending. Mr. Merchant and many friends were on board on her initial dip into the briny. The *Clintonia* was a large semi-knockabout round bow vessel. She was from an original design by Tom McManus of Boston. Schooner *Oriole*, built the following year, was taken from the lines of the *Clintonia*.

I am fortunate to have in my possession the original construction plan of the *Clintonia*, given to me by Charles McManus, son of the famous designer.

The *Clintonia* spread a great sail area and she was one of the smart sailers in the fleet. Few vessels could pass this great vessel.

The *Clintonia* sailed on her maiden trip seining in command of Capt. Charles Harty on July 3, 1907, at 7:30 p.m. Capt. Harty hustled to get the vessel ready to sail before the Fourth of July. She arrived at Boston, with her maiden fare on July 13, 1907 having 400 barrels salt mackerel and 100 barrels fresh mackerel. This was a spendid start for the new craft. Capt. Harty was well pleased with his new command. He stated he had given her a good try, under various conditions and said, "She is just right."

Many fine skippers commanded the *Clintonia* during her nine years out of Gloucester. Capt. Charles Harty finished the seining season of 1907 as her skipper. Capt. James Vannamberg took her to Newfoundland for a herring cargo during the winter of 1907–08. Capt. Ralph Webber, that great seiner from Down East was her skipper during the mackerel season of 1908. Capt. Ben Spurling, another crack Down Easter, took her south in 1909 and Capt. Ambrose Fleet took her to North Bay for

mackerel in the fall of that year. The great Capt. Tommie Bohlin made a herring voyage to Newfoundland during the winter of 1909–10. Capt. Webber again took over the *Clintonia* for seining in March, 1910, and remained in her for the seining seasons of 1911 and 1912. During the winter of 1912–13, Capt. Lyman Wylde had her haddocking. Capt. Fred Carritt took her seining in 1913 and that winter of 1913–14 Capt. Lyman Wylde again took over in the haddocking game.

The mackerel season of 1914 found Capt. William Bissett as *Clintonia's* skipper. In the fall of that year, Capt. Eli Beck took her to North Bay.

Capt. Lou Wharton, great salt fisherman, took *Clintonia* to Newfoundland in December, 1914, and went dory hand lining in 1915.

In command of Capt. James Vannamberg, she left Bay of Islands, Newfoundland, with 30 American and Canadian vessels. She arrived in Gloucester on January 14, 1908 with 2,200 barrels herring, making the passage in five days, and beating the whole fleet home. Schooner *Arkona* was the first to leave, followed by the *Saladin*. The fast *Clintonia* passed the *Saladin* off of Canso. The *Arkona* arrived five days later.

When in Capt. Ralph Webber's command the *Clintonia* made herself known in the fleet. This smart skipper could almost make her talk. The *Clintonia* was pride and joy. The handsome vessel, with her cloud of sails, could often be seen eating her way through the fleet bound for market.

Loss of life was small in the *Clintonia*. While she was under command of Capt. Lyman Wylde in January, 1913, Stephen Muise and Simon Merchant failed to return from their trawls off Liscomb, Nova Scotia. A heavy gale set in that night and they were never seen again.

In October, 1914, George Colson was killed by a falling gaff aboard the *Clintonia*, off Souris, Prince Edward Island. Capt. Eli Beck was the skipper at the time.

In the years of World War I, Gloucester vessels were much in demand at Newfoundland. Many of their vessels had been lost and they were paying high prices for the Gloucestermen. The schooner *Clintonia* was of the fine vessels sold. She was bought in March, 1916, by Campbell and McKay of St. John's. She carried a cargo of kerosene to her new home port. The *Clintonia* was highly regarded by the Newfoundlanders. I have been informed that while owned there, she carried two crotches for her large main boom. She could carry 4,500 quintals of salt fish.

The *Clintonia* went to her last resting place in November, 1921, when she was abandoned, dismasted, in the North Atlantic, while on a passage from Placentia Bay, Newfoundland, to Oporto, Portugal, with a cargo of salt cod. Her crew was rescued by the Newfoundland three-master *Jean Wakely*, which, incidentally, was built in Essex for Newfoundland owners.

Before closing the story of the *Clintonia*, a few words might be said of another *Clintonia*. This schooner was launched in March, 1908, at the Smith and Rhuland yard of Lunenburg, Nova Scotia. Her captain was Emiel (Paddy) Mack. She was also designed by Tom McManus, off the model of the Gloucester *Clintonia* and named after her. She was identical in size, rig, and sail plan, and she proved one of the fastest vessels in the Lunenburg fleet. The Canadian *Clintonia* visited Gloucester on September 1, 1908, with 300,000 lbs. salt cod for Gorton-Pew Fisheries. On June 2, 1910, Capt. Mack brought the *Clintonia* into Gloucester direct from Quero Bank with 200,000 lbs. salt cod. He decided to try the Gloucester market instead of Lunenburg.

The Canadian *Clintonia* was later sold to the Kearley brothers of Belleoram, Newfoundland, and she was abandoned on fire off Sable Island in January, 1923, just 15 months after the loss of her namesake. Thus ended two grand vessels.

Capt. Ralph Webber passed away in Gloucester in February, 1940, at the age of 68. Capt. Ralph was one of the finest men and ablest seining skippers out of Gloucester. Although long handicapped by a persistent illness, he proved always up with the leaders in the mackerel game. Probably no other skipper out of this port was liked any better than Capt. Ralph. He was a native of Bremen, Maine. His first command was the schooner *Richard Lester* in 1899, followed by the *Hattie A. Heckman*, *Edith Prior*, and then from the William H. Jordan and Orlando Merchant firm in the *Marguerite Haskins*, *Clintonia*, *Lottie G. Merchant*, *Stilletto*. His last commands were the *Beatrice K.* and *Florence K.* (named after his wife). He retired in 1934. Capt. Ralph never lost a vessel or a man. Truly a remarkable record. Men of his type are not easily found today.

Gross tons, 147; net tons, 105; length, 109 feet; breadth, 25.1 feet; depth, 11.9 feet.

John Hays Hammond

NAMED FOR A CELEBRITY—AND LUCKY /
1907–1917

Schooner *John Hays Hammond*, one of Gloucester's most famous vessels and biggest money makers, was what the fishermen call a "lucky vessel." Most every skipper who commanded her did well.

She was owned by Capt. Lemuel E. Spinney, leading mariner and independent owner. Built during the winter and spring of 1907 by Tarr and James in Essex, the fine new craft was launched upright and glided gracefully and easily as could be wished into the waters of Essex Creek on June 25, 1907.

Capt. Spinney, Mrs. Spinney, and a large party were on board, including Mrs. Alonzo Smith, Capt. Jerome McDonald and Capt. Peter Grant.

The *Hammond* was a handsome vessel of the round bow type, designed by Tom McManus of Boston. Her bowsprit was long and she carried a good spread of canvas named for Gloucester's most distinguished citizen. A few days before she sailed on her maiden trip, Mr. Hammond paid her a visit, accompanied by two distinguished gentlemen, Major Frank F. Burnham and ex-Governor Thomas of Colorado. Capt. Spinney showed them all over the craft, and they were delighted with her.

Mr. Hammond on behalf of Mrs. Hammond presented the vessel with a set of colors and then himself presented Capt. Spinney with a first class chronometer.

The sails were made by E. L. Rowe and Sons.

The *John Hays Hammond* sailed on her maiden trip halibuting in command of Capt. Spinney, July 17, 1907. Capt. Spinney sailed the new craft back and forth off the Hammond estate at Freshwater Cove, as Mr. Hammond greatly desired to see her under sail.

The fine craft arrived in Gloucester with her fare on August 27, 1907. She hailed for 30,000 lbs. halibut, 65,000 fresh cod and 20,000 lbs. salt cod, taken on Baccalieu Bank, 150 miles east by north of St. John's, Newfoundland. The *Hammond* started right from the beginning as a leader in the fleet.

While homeward bound on the maiden trip, a little seal was observed swimming near. It chased the vessel for miles, and continually nosed the side as if it wanted to be taken on board. At last some of the crew got a rope and flipped him on deck, where he was right at home. On the vessel's arrival at Gloucester this

Named after an internationally known mining engineer who lived in Gloucester, the *John Hays Hammond* was, like her namesake, a big money maker; the first halibuter to carry dories right side up in cradles, and one of the first to use a power hoister.

seal and a 40 pound halibut were given to Mr. Hammond.

During the *Hammond's* career out of Gloucester, she was mostly under Capt. Spinney's command, but at times he would remain ashore to handle his business affairs and the vessel was taken over by crack skippers. Some of them were Horace Wylde, Archie MacLeod, Chris Gibbs, Will McClure, John Olson, and Fred Thompson. Capt. Richard Wadding took her for a trip or two in March, 1912.

The *Hammond*, in command of Capt. Spinney, was highline of the halibuters in 1909 with a stock of $30,352. In 1911, the *Hammond's* total stock was $36,572. In that year Capt. Fred Thompson, in command for a few months, stocked $13,624 and Capt. Spinney for six months stocked $22,948.

This was the greatest year's work in the halibut fishery up to that time. Capt. Spinney had broken his own record of $31,350, made in the schooner *Dictator* in 1901.

Capt. Archie MacLeod made a splendid year's work in the *Hammond* in 1913 when he stocked $35,078 with a share of $750.

The *John Hays Hammond* was a credit to her name. She paid a flattering compliment to the prosperous citizen for whom she was named.

The *Hammond*, although a lucky vessel, had some narrow escapes. While in command of Capt. Horace Wylde, she arrived at Boston on December 23, 1908 after a hard drive home from the Cape Shore. She reported that she had a mighty close shave from being wrecked almost in sight of home.

The vessel had made up in Massachusetts

Bay, with a 40-mile-an-hour wind, blowing clouds of vapor driving mast head high and flying spray freezing when it struck. Capt. Wylde, wishing to make sure where he was, climbed to the masthead to have a look around. Suddenly, directly ahead through the scudding mist, he made out the great grey tower of Minot's Light. The vessel was sailing straight for destruction on the dreaded ledge. Capt. Wylde shouted a warning. The craft answered her wheel quickly and swung around on another tack and reached safe water.

In December, 1909, the *Hammond* was on Quero Bank, and Hilton Acker, one of the crew, was on watch. A big sea came over the bow, swept along the deck and struck Acker full in the back. It hove him hard down on the checker boards, dislocating his shoulder, and then right out over the rail. The sea carried him quite a distance from the vessel and quickly he began to swim for her with all his might. This rugged Nova Scotian was a powerful swimmer and in spite of his oil clothes and heavy boots managed to gain the side of the vessel. The craft had been listed over by the sea striking and just as he got there, she was shaking herself clear, and the rail was coming out of the water. In spite of his badly injured shoulder he reached the same damaged arm out of the water and grabbed the rail. The pain was intense and how he hung on he didn't know.

As the craft rose, he came up with it and still clinging on with the injured limb, managed to reach up the other arm and haul himself on board. Acker was landed at Louisburg, Cape Breton, for medical treatment. Seldom has a more remarkable escape been recorded. It was a great demonstration of the courage and endurance of these great fishermen of the Canadian Maritimes.

On April 16, 1912 the *John Hays Hammond*, in command of Capt. Spinney, was rammed during a heavy fog by the Nova Scotian salt banker *Uranus*, 40 miles west of Sable Island. The *Uranus* immediately began to fill and seven of her crew leaped on board the *Hammond*. The crafts separated, and the *Uranus* drifted off in the fog. The *Hammond's* crew cleared the wreckage away forward, where her bowsprit had been torn off. Capt. Spinney sailed her about several hours looking for the *Uranus* but without avail and then reluctantly started for home. On her arrival at Gloucester with the seven men of the *Uranus* crew on board, it was learned that the remaining members of the *Uranus* crew had rowed in their dories, 100 miles to Liscomb, Nova Scotia. The *Uranus* went to the bottom shortly after the collision. She was in command of Capt. Coolen, and there were 13 Coolens in the crew, all belonging to Hubbards and Fox Point, Nova Scotia.

The *John Hays Hammond* was fortunate in loss of life. Only once was her flag at half mast and this was for Peter Ryan. On December 20, 1907, Ryan and his dorymate were taken off the bottom of their overturned dory, to which they were clinging. They were brought on board but Ryan died soon after of shock and exposure. He was 45 years old and a native of Aquiforte, Newfoundland. His body was landed at Liscomb, Nova Scotia, and sent home for burial. Capt. Horace Wylde was skipper.

The *Hammond* was known by the fishermen as a "tender" vessel. She couldn't carry a mainsail too well and would heel very easily. In spite of this fault, she carried a fine crew.

My old friend Charlie Downie, native of Jordan, Nova Scotia, and fisherman out of Gloucester for more than 35 years, well remembered his days in the *Hammond* under Capts. Spinney and MacLeod. Charlie passed away at Deerfield, New Hampshire, in July 1971. He was a real veteran fisherman and sailed under many of the great Boston and Gloucester skippers. He was ninety-five when he died.

The *John Hays Hammond* was considered a fair sailer. She was at her best when running before the wind. Capt. Archie MacLeod once told me that the *Hammond*, while under his command, left Gloucester on a Friday noon and went through the Gut of Canso on the following Sunday. This was pretty good sailing and her hustling young skipper must have driven her.

A gasoline deck hoister was installed on the *Hammond* in the spring of 1915. This was a blessing to her crew as before this event, all sails and the anchor cable were hoisted by hand. She was the first halibuter to be equipped with one of these hoisters.

The *Hammond* was also the first halibut catcher to carry dories in wooden cradles bolted to the deck. Previous to this they were carried bottom up in nests or stacks on deck.

A fine model of the craft was given to Mr. Hammond by the Gloucester Day Committee in 1916. This model, built by Tom Irving, famous Gloucester shipbuilder, is now on exhibit at the Cape Ann Historical Association museum in Gloucester.

During World War I many of Gloucester's fine vessels were sold to foreign countries at fancy prices and the *Hammond* was one of those to go. She was sold in December, 1916 to David W. Simpson, shipbroker of Boston, who in turn sold her to Newfoundland parties. The grand old vessel didn't live long under her new owners for on July 27, 1917 she was sent to the bottom by a German submarine, 360 miles off the Irish coast. Her crew was turned adrift; they were later picked up by a British destroyer. The *Hammond* at the time was in command of Capt. Joe Bonia, one of Gloucester's

famous skippers, and carried a crew of Newfoundlanders. She was bound from Iceland to Queenstown, Ireland, with a cargo of salt cod.

Capt. Lemuel E. Spinney passed away in June, 1942, at the age of 76. He was a native of Argyle, Nova Scotia. Capt. Lem was a fisherman par excellence. A leader in the halibut fishery and one of the greatest independent owners of fishing schooners out of Gloucester, he was always careful of his men and vessels and always up with the leaders in the halibut fishery. Some of his commands, many of which he owned, were schooners *Gladiator*, *Arbitrator*, *Dictator*, *John Hays Hammond*, *American* (built 1891), *Natalie Hammond*, steam trawlers *Seal* and *Gloucester*, schooner *Oretha F. Spinney* (named for his wife) and the *Clara and Hester* (named for his daughters). Capt. Spinney was truly a builder of Gloucester's prosperity.

Capt. Christopher Gibbs, one of the *John Hays Hammond*'s skippers, died at Chelsea Marine hospital in March, 1939. Capt. Gibbs was one of the leaders in the halibut fishery, smart, capable and well liked by his crews. He was a native of Rocky Bay, Nova Scotia, and 67 years old. Many fine vessels were commanded by this great skipper, including the *James W. Parker*, *Esperanto*, *Benjamin A. Smith*, *John Hays Hammond*, *Grand Marshal*, *Governor Marshall*, *Harmony*, and *Joffre*.

John Hays Hammond, namesake of the fine craft, passed away at his estate, Lookout Hill, Gloucester on June 8, 1936. He was a native of San Francisco, California, and was 81 years old. Mr. Hammond was one of Gloucester's most distinguished citizens, a famous mining engineer, author, and at one time the highest salaried man in the country. He had charge of Cecil Rhodes' interest in Africa. Mr. Hammond bought the Hovey estate at Freshwater Cove, Gloucester in September 1902. In 1908, he became a citizen of Gloucester. He was always a friend of the Gloucester fishermen, and always took a great interest in any matter that promoted their wellbeing. In 1912, through his generous assistance, a memorial stone to the dead fishermen was erected at Beechbrook Cemetery in West Gloucester. A plot of land was given to the fishermen for their last resting place by Mr. Hammond. He was also a life member of the Gloucester Fishermen's Institute.

Gross tons, 132; net tons, 92; length, 101.9 feet; breadth, 24.5 feet; depth, 11.8 feet. Mainmast (deck to cap), 75 feet; foremast (deck to cap), 66 feet; main topmast, 45 feet; fore topmast, 40 feet; main boom, 72 feet; main gaff, 41 feet; bowsprit, 27 feet (outboard); mainmast head, 13.5 feet.

While the long, lean hull of the *Richard* sat unfinished in Essex the planks dried and shrank and the seams opened. To make her tight before launching—she's ready to slide in this picture—water was pumped into her, swelling the planks.

Richard

UNFINISHED AND UNSOLD FOR A YEAR / 1907–1917

Schooner Richard, a good sized round-bowed vessel, with tall spars, long bowsprit and a good spread of canvas, was considered one of the handsomest vessels in the fleet.

The birth of the *Richard* was rather unusual.

The vessel was started at the Oxner and Story Yard in South Essex and for some reason was not finished in the usual time of building. She laid on the stocks almost completed for a year or so and was sold at receiver's sale in August, 1907 to Manuel Simmons, Gloucester sailmaker, for $3750. The vessel was then finished and named Richard in honor of the young son of Lyndon Story, one of her builders. The vessel had laid so long on the stocks that she dried up, and before the launching, the Essex hand tub pumped her full of water to swell her up. She was launched successfully on September 21, 1907.

Schooner Richard sailed on her maiden trip haddocking in command of Capt. Johnnie Keefe on Nov. 5, 1907 She arrived at T Wharf, Boston with her maiden fare of 30,000 lbs. fresh fish on November 19, 1907. Capt. Keefe remained in command during the winter of 1907–08. She was taken over by Capt. Dan McCuish in the spring of 1908 when he took her to the Peak. Capt. Dan always had a high regard for the Richard, and he claimed she was the fastest vessel that he commanded.

Capt. McCuish remained as skipper through 1908 and into 1909. During 1909 the Richard was commanded by Capt. Manuel Perry of Provincetown.

Capt. Miles Somers was skipper during the winter of 1909–10 and in the spring of 1910, haddocking and shacking. In September 1910, Capt. Lovell (Lov) Hodgdon, one of the great "killers" of the '90's came out of a 10-year retirement to take the Richard shacking. In October, 1910 the Richard, Capt. Hodgdon, ran ashore at Cape Negro, Nova Scotia, and the vessel was saved only after 50,000 lbs. fish and ice were thrown overboard to lighten her up. Incidentally the Richard was the last command of this great mariner.

Capt. Aneas McPhee had the Richard haddocking in December, 1910. Capt. Peter Tobin took over in January 1911. Capt. William (Little Billy) Corkum took command in the spring of 1911 and remained as skipper until September 1914, haddocking and shacking. Capt. Corkum proved to be the Richard's longest skipper and one of the most successful. On May 20, 1912 he arrived from Cape North with 200,000 lbs. shack, stocking $4,347 and sharing $94. In May 1913 on a shack trip he stocked $4,750 with a share of $108 per man. One of Capt. Billy's trips in 1913 was a combination Cape North cod and Quero halibut trip.

Capt. Free Decker took over command, haddocking in September 1914. Capt. Will Chetwynd had the Richard, drifting in 1915. Capt. John Olson also commanded the Richard at one time.

The only loss of life in the Richard happened on December 29, 1911 when Rupert Isner, one of her crew, was swept overboard to his death by a monster sea that boarded the vessel taking him over the rail while crossing the Bay of Fundy. Isner was a native of Nova Scotia and was 49 years old. Capt. Billy Corkum was skipper at the time.

The Richard went the way of many of our great vessels when she was sold to Newfoundland during World War I. Simmons sold her to the Holletts of Burin in April 1916. The handsome vessel did not last long under her new owners, however, as she was abandoned in latitude 40 degrees 42 minutes N, longitude 52 degrees 21 minutes W on February 5, 1917 while on a passage from Cadiz, Spain to Burin, Newfoundland, with a cargo of salt. The vessel had been raked by severe storms, her sails were gone and she was out of food. Capt. Cecil Lake and his crew of seven men were rescued by a British steamer.

Capt. William Corkum, the Richard's longest skipper, died at Gloucester in September 1953 at the age of 91. Little Billy Corkum was one of our great mariners, and commanded many fine vessels in the glorious days of sail including the schooners Vera, Romance, Richard and Vanessa. He was a native of Chester, Nova Scotia.

Capt. Donald (Dan) McCuish, one of the Richard's skippers, passed away in Gloucester, December 10, 1947 at the age of 74. He was native of the Bay of Islands, Newfoundland. Capt. Dan was one of our fine mariners of the past, capable, honest, well-liked and a good navigator. He had the enviable record of never losing a man or a vessel. His commands included the Dictator, Gossip, Elmer E. Gray, Tacoma, Massachusetts, Lucinda I. Lowell, Richard and Thomas S. Gorton. Capt. Dan also commanded many vessels freighting fish and, in his last days afloat, was the skipper of yachts. He delivered several vessels to their new owners in foreign countries.

Manuel Simmons, owner of the Richard, was one of Gloucester's great sailmakers. He also was the independent owner of several vessels. Simmons moved his sailmaking business to Marblehead in 1916. He passed away at Marblehead in February 1930 at the age of 71. He was a native of Fayal, Azores.

Richard Story, namesake of the vessel, a native of Essex, made his home in New York.

Lyndon J. Story died at Essex December 15, 1931 at the age of 74. A native of Essex, he started in business with Edwin Oxner at the old Willard Burnham yard in South Essex in 1901.

Edwin Oxner, builder of the Richard, died at Marblehead May 8, 1952, at the age of 85. A native of Lunenburg, Nova Scotia, he and Lyndon Story started the Oxner and Story shipyard in South Essex in 1901 and in five years built fifty-two vessels. He was foreman at the William A. Robinson shipyard in Ipswich,

Massachusetts, during World War II. After the war he operated a yacht yard at Marblehead.

Gross tons, 134; net tons, 90; length, 103 feet; breadth, 25 feet; depth, 11.6 feet. Original spar measurements: mainmast (deck to cap), 75.5 feet; foremast (deck to cap), 68 feet; maintopmast, 45 feet; foretopmast, 40 feet; mainboom, 73 feet; main gaff, 44.5 feet; fore boom, 29.5 feet; bowsprit, 25.5 feet; masthead, 13 feet.

Cover girl: in the author's opinion the schooner *Oriole* was the most beautiful of them all, even including the yachtlike racers that came later. She was a typical fisherman, but there was something special about her, even the set of her sails, that made her truly what the fishermen called her, "the beautiful *Oriole*." Here she is about to make a passage, all sails set, seineboat on deck.

Oriole

QUEEN OF THE FLEET / 1908–1916

One of the fastest and most beautiful vessels out of Gloucester was the schooner *Oriole*, of the great Orlando Merchant, or William H. Jordan, fleet. She lived from 1908 until 1916, when she was rammed and sunk by a steamer.

She carried a long mainboom of about 76 feet and spread one of the largest mainsails of any Gloucester fisherman. She was the queen of the Gloucester fleet while afloat, and few vessels could match her in speed.

The *Oriole* was built during the spring of 1908 by Tarr and James at Essex and launched at 7:45 p.m. on June 24, 1908. Over 500 people attended the launching, including William H. Jordan and Orlando Merchant, her owners; Capt. Thad Morgan, the office force of Jordan's, and many ladies, some from New York, New Jersey, Missouri and two from Virginia, the home of Capt. Morgan. Mr. Fenn, the well-known magazine illustrator, was there. All the guests enjoyed the trip around to Gloucester.

The excellent photograph by Herman W. Spooner clearly shows the beauty of this vessel.

The *Oriole* was designed by Tom McManus of Boston. She was quite similar to the schooner *Clintonia*, launched the year previous and also owned by this firm. The *Oriole* was a large, able vessel, with a tremendous sail area. She was of the round bow, semi-knockabout type. Sails for the new schooner were made by Benjamin Colby.

The *Oriole* sailed on her maiden trip, seining, on July 2, 1908 in command of Capt. Thad Morgan, that great skipper from Virginia. Capt. Morgan was one of our great seining skippers and was one of the very few captains out of Gloucester who came from the south. Most of our skippers were from Maine, Newfoundland, Nova Scotia, Scandinavia, and Portugal.

The *Oriole* arrived at Gloucester on her maiden trip July 11, 1908 with 10,000 lbs. of fresh mackerel which were sold to the Gloucester Fresh Fish Co. The fare was taken on the Rips.

The following mackerel season of 1909, the *Oriole* was commanded by Capt. Charles Harty and Capt. Peter Tobin. Capt. Tommy Bohlin took the *Oriole* to Newfoundland for a herring cargo the following winter, and was the first of the whole fleet to arrive back in Gloucester, arriving on January 24, 1910. Capt. Tommy drove her all the way.

Capt. Charles Maguire took the *Oriole* seining during the season of 1910. In 1911 she was taken over by Capt. Lew Wharton, for dory handlining, and Capt. Wharton remained in command during 1911–12–13–14, using her for dory handlining and Newfoundland herring voyages.

Capt. Ambrose Fleet made a herring voyage in the *Oriole* in November, 1914.

Capt. Daniel McDonald was her skipper, taking over in 1915 for halibuting and remaining in her until her loss in 1916.

In May, 1909, the *Oriole* was tied up at Merchant's wharf. Word came that the mackerel were schooling off Long Island. Capt. Charlie Harty immediately started getting the vessel underway, but at the time there was no wind. This hustling skipper couldn't let a litttle matter like this stop him; so he engaged the services of the local tug *Eveleth*, and on May 18, left Gloucester in tow of the tug. The *Oriole* was towed clear to Highland Light, Cape Cod, when a fresh northeast breeze came up, and she was let go, and dusted for the fishing grounds off Long Island. The great skippers of those days were pretty hard to stop, wind or no wind.

On the evening of January 17, 1911, the George Perkins and Son plant, situated between the Pew wharf and Orlando Merchant's, was swept by fire. The plant was a total loss, with damage of $175,000. The schooner *Eugenia*, lying at the foot of the Perkins wharf, and the *Oriole*, at Merchant's wharf, were both aground at the time, the tide being low. Both vessels were threatened with destruction. Neither could be moved. The crews, which were up street, heard of the fire, came down, and helped soak the sails with buckets of water until the factory was leveled. The sails had caught fire several times. When the tide came up, the schooners were hauled into the stream, and to safety.

On January 16, 1914, the *Oriole*, Capt. Lew Wharton, arrived at Gloucester from Bay of Islands with 1400 bbls. of herring (70 bbls. in her cabin). She reported that on January 15, while lying becalmed on Georges, she witnessed a steamer rescuing the crew of a burning five master. The crew of the *Oriole* watched for several hours, but could not get near enough to learn the identity of either vessel. It was learned later that the five-master was the

Fuller Palmer, one of the famous Palmer fleet. The sinking vessel had been fired, after her crew were taken off.

The end of the beautiful *Oriole* came on the evening of August 12, 1916, when she was rammed and sunk by the Norwegian steamer *Borghild*, 40 miles west southwest of Seal Island, Nova Scotia. It was a thick fog and the schooner was bound home with a fare of 27,000 fresh halibut and 6,000 lbs. salt fish. The steamer's whistle could be heard in the distance and all hands were called on deck. Before anything could be done, the big bow of the steamer sliced into the vessel just forward of the main rigging, cutting her almost in two. Capt. McDonald shouted for every man to look after himself and there was a mad scramble for the rigging, dories, and buoys. Nine of the crew were saved in dories, two saved from trawl buoys which they grabbed, one from a dressing tub that was keeping him afloat. The remaining survivors climbed the rigging to the steamer. Just as Capt. McDonald jumped from the mainmast to the steamer's deck, the mainmast snapped, halfway down, and fell on the steamer deck. Frank Doucette, in the rigging at the time, was probably stunned by the fall and drowned. Charles Strople, Robert Boudreau, and Edward Moriarty were dragged down by the suction. The doomed *Oriole* went down in four minutes. Capt. McDonald's young son, Courtney, was one of the survivors. The steamer, after searching for the missing men, proceeded to Halifax, Nova Scotia, where the survivors were landed.

The steamer was libeled at Halifax and later at the Admiralty Court in that city, the steamer was found at fault, and ordered to pay damages.

Capt. Thaddeus Morgan, first skipper of the *Oriole*, returned to his native Virginia in 1915, and died in Norfolk in July, 1931, at the age of 70.

Capt. Lew Wharton lost his life when the schooner *Columbia* was lost off Sable Island in August, 1927, with all hands. He was a native of Liverpool, Nova Scotia, and a brother of Capts. Robert and Newman Wharton.

Capt. Daniel McDonald (Little Dan) passed away in Dorchester, Massachusetts, April 30, 1932, at the age of 75. A native of Cape Breton, he commanded some of our finest vessels, including the *Mooween, Quanapowitt, Squanto, Elizabeth Howard,* and *Benjamin A. Smith.*

Gross tons, 145; net tons, 104; length, 115.5 feet; breadth, 25 feet; depth, 12 feet.

Rex

RUN DOWN BY A LINER; 15 MEN LOST / 1908–1925

Schooner *Rex*. Her story is not a pretty one. Many Gloucester folks remember this vessel and her tragic loss with 15 lives in 1925. She was a victim of one of the worst disasters in the history of the Gloucester fisheries.

The *Rex* was a noted vessel in the fleet, sailed by fine skippers and good crews, but hard luck seemed to follow in her wake.

The *Rex* was one of the many fishing schooners built by Arthur D. Story in Essex and put on the market for sale, after they were launched. She was launched unnamed in the summer of 1908 and brought around to Gloucester to await a buyer. She was later purchased by the Fred L. Davis firm of Gloucester and given the name of *Rex.*

The *Rex* was a good sized, deep vessel of the round bow type, with her jumbo carried out to the stem (most of the vessels built at this time were of the semi-knockabout type). Although not so pretty and fast as some of her sisters, she was able and in the 17 years of her existence took plenty of punishment. The length of her forecastle was 35 feet. Two auxiliary oil engines were installed in 1919.

The *Rex* sailed on her maiden trip, haddocking, in command of Capt. John Grady (formerly in the schooner *Lena and Maud*) on November 7, 1908. She arrived at Boston with her maiden fare of 90,000 lbs. fresh fish on November 27, 1908.

An interesting incident took place while under Capt. Grady's command. On December 13, 1909, the incoming vessels from the eastward all reported the hardest kind of windward buck from Cape Sable to port. Many vessels were forced to sail over twice the actual number of miles between the two points in order to reach port. The *Rex* was fishing about 130 miles to the eastward of Cape Sable on Western Bank, so that she was about 350 miles from port. The log was put out when she left for home and was hauled off Eastern Point. It registered 748 miles, this being the actual number of miles the vessel had sailed over in her effort to cover the 350 miles between her starting point and Gloucester.

Capt. Grady remained in command of the *Rex* until January, 1912 when she was taken over by Capt. Lyman Wylde, haddocking. The winter of 1912–13 Capt. Asa Baker had her haddocking and the summer of 1913 he took her shacking. The winter of 1913–14, Capt. Delbert Lyons had her haddocking. In March,

1914, Capt. Augustus Hall, one of our great old time mariners, took over halibuting.

On Capt. Hall's first trip in the *Rex*, he landed a trip of 50,000 lbs. halibut at Portland, Maine, on April 3, 1914, stocking $4,205 and sharing $99 per man. In 1915 he was high line of the halibuters with a stock of $30,500 and a share of $740. Capt. Hall remained in command until 1919. In her last six years afloat she was commanded by Capts. Andrew Decker, Albert Williams and Tom Downie, haddocking, shacking and halibuting.

Capt. Free Decker took the *Rex* to Newfoundland for a herring cargo in November, 1916.

Nineteen lives were lost in the *Rex* during her career. On March 25, 1911, Bert Hunt and John Williams were drowned when their dory capsized on Georges. The overturned dory was sighted by the schooner *Elsie*, another of the haddocking fleet that was fishing nearby. Hunt was a native of Lockeport, Nova Scotia, and 43 years old. Williams was a native of Green Harbor, Nova Scotia, and 30 years old. Capt. John Grady was skipper at the time.

On June 20, 1914, Capt. Gus Hall nearly lost half his crew. The *Rex* was fishing in the "Gully" between Green and Grand banks when a heavy fog shut in. Only Capt. Hall and the cook were aboard. Before her crew of 20 men in 10 dories could return to the vessel, the stock came out of the anchor and she began to drift. The vessel drifted 10 miles before 12 men succeeded in reaching her. Four dories failed to show up and all the next day couldn't be found. The missing men were Andrew Strickland, Martin Blagdon, F. Broussard, Peter Lake, Joseph Young, Paul Simmons, John Malcom and Joseph Arsenault.

The *Rex* arrived at Portland on June 27th and reported the loss of eight men. After being adrift 29 hours, three of the missing dories landed at the little town of Branch, Newfoundland. The dory containing Malcom and Arsenault was never heard of again. Paul Malcom was a native of Caribou Cove, Nova Scotia, and 40 years old. Joseph Arsenault, a native of Prince Edward Island, was 35 years old.

The *Rex* herself had a narrow escape from destruction in 1918. She left Grand Bank for Gloucester in company with the schooner *Robert and Richard*, Capt. Bob Wharton in July, 1918. The *Rex* being the slower of the two craft was soon left astern. The *Robert and Richard* never reached port, as she was sent to the bottom on Cashes by a German U-boat. The slowness of the *Rex* had saved her from the same fate.

On June 17, 1925 the *Rex* in command of Capt. Tom Downie sailed from Gloucester on a routine halibut trip to the eastward. Her crew was comprised of 23 of Gloucester's finest fishermen. The next news of the *Rex* came in a wireless message on June 28th from the Cunard

An ordinary vessel when this picture was taken at the F. L. Davis Wharf, the *Rex* became famous two years later when she was run down at anchor, and fifteen died, including the cook's young son.

liner *Tuscania* to the Fred L. Davis Co., owners of the vessel. The grim message stated that the *Rex* had been run down by the liner and sunk with a loss of 15 lives. The nine survivors were picked up by the *Tuscania*'s lifeboats.

On Sunday morning of June 28th the *Rex* was lying at anchor in a dense fog on Quero Bank. All the gang were on deck baiting up their trawls, to be ready when the fog cleared. Charles Firth, little 10 year old son of cook Austin Firth, who was enjoying his summer vacation at sea, was asleep in his father's bunk in the forecastle.

Suddenly out of the fog came the gray form of a liner, bearing down on the vessel. Before anyone had a chance to say boo, the great knifelike bow of the 17,000-ton Cunard liner *Tuscania* sliced into the *Rex*, on the port bow near the cathead, and cut through the vessel, her bow coming out of the starboard side just forward of the main rigging. The foremast was ripped out of the vessel and ground into small pieces of wood. Forty tons of ice in large cakes came floating out of her hold and those men who were in the starboard side of the vessel were thrown into the water among the ice and they never had a chance to save themselves. The heavy cable holding the anchor was chewed into small strands so small it looked like common sewing thread after the liner had cut her way across the deck.

When cook Firth saw the steamer coming he jumped down into the forecastle to save his son, but neither was seen again.

The *Tuscania* was going so fast, it was some time before she was brought to a stop and lifeboats put over. Nine of the *Rex*'s crew were picked up, including James O'Brien, Alfred Dornet, Edgar Meuse, Dan Grady, Ralph Clayton, Capt. Thomas Flannagan, Edward Fralick, Edward Surrette, and engineer Albert Roberts. The body of Capt. Tom Downie, who probably died of a heart attack in the crash, was the only one recovered.

After searching amid the wreckage for hours, the *Tuscania* proceeded to New York with the survivors and the body of Capt. Downie.

The 15 victims in the sinking of the *Rex* were Capt. Thomas Downie, Austin Firth (cook), Charles Austin Firth, 10-year-old son of the cook, George Johnson, Joseph Dalton, Angus D. McDonald, Angus Smith, Clyde Larkin, Samuel Tibbits, Charles Goodick, William Roach, William Turner, Archie Hill, Oscar Williams, Charles Wieball.

Capt. David Bone, skipper of the *Tuscania*, was deeply overcome by the tragedy and did all he could to make the survivors comfortable. Capt. Bone was one of the veterans of the Cunard Line.

Four of the victims, Archie Hill, Sam Tibbits, George Johnson, and Joseph Dalton had been members of the crew of the schooner *Republic*, which was sunk in collision February 15th of the same year, with the loss of three of her crew.

Gloucester and the Maritime Provinces were deeply shocked over this sea tragedy.

The little lad Charles Firth, who lost his life in the collision, was I believe the only youngster lost in a Gloucester vessel at sea in the past 50 years. His name rightfully belongs to "Gloucester's Sailor Dead."

Edward Surrette was badly injured in the crash, receiving a fractured skull and broken jawbone. Eddie was taken off the floating booby hatch.

Eddie Frelick, grand old veteran of the deep, survived five shipwrecks: *Virginia* in 1902, *Selma* in 1914, *Juno* in 1916, *Rex* in 1925 and *Dawn* in 1943. Eddie was sure an iron man. James (Jimmy) O'Brien, probably the last survivor of the *Rex* disaster, died at Gloucester at the age of eighty-one in August 1970. He was a native of Gloucester.

Capt. Tom Downie, who lost his life in the *Rex*, was one of the finest and best liked skippers in the Gloucester fleet. He followed the sea in most all branches of fishing. Capt. Tom never had any difficulty in shipping a crew. His command's included the *Dauntless, Selma, Muriel, Elsie, Rex,* and *American.* He was a native of Jordan Ferry, Shelburne County, Nova Scotia, and fifty-one years old.

Capt. Augustus Hall passed away at his home in Portland, Maine, July, 1923 at the age of 77. Capt. Gus was one of the great mariners of the past, commanding many fine vessels including, schooner *Anna B. Cannon, Annie C. Hall, Faustina, Miranda, Thomas A. Cromwell, Imperator, Rex* and *American.* He was a native of St. George, Maine. He was a brother of Capt. Frank Hall, another great skipper of the past.

Gross tons, 134; net tons, 93; length, 102.5 feet; breadth, 24.4 feet; depth, 12 feet. Original spars: mainmast, deck to cap, 75 feet; foremast, 68 feet; main topmast, 44 feet; fore topmast, 40 feet; main boom, 73 feet; main gaff, 44 feet; bowsprit, outboard, 28 feet; mastheads, 12 feet.

This businesslike vessel in Boston Harbor, the *Georgia,* broke records for catching pollock.

Georgia

SHE BROKE RECORDS FOR POLLOCK / 1909–1918

In the fine knockabout schooner *Georgia*, Capt. Charles Forbes and crew made history in 1911 by landing the largest trip of pollock ever recorded at a New England port. The vessel also did well in halibut fishing with Capt. John G. Stream in command.

She was built at Arthur D. Story's yard in Essex, during the winter and spring of 1908–09 for Capt. Alonzo Frank Cahoon, of Chatham, and was launched in April, 1909.

The vessel was towed around to Gloucester to be fitted and rigged for sea. Her sails were made by E. L. Rowe and Son. The *Georgia* was a handsome, medium sized knockabout (no bowsprit) from a Tom McManus design. Her forecastle of 42 feet was one of the longest of any fisherman up to that time. Her port of registry was Boston.

The *Georgia* sailed on her maiden trip to the southward, seining, on May 6, 1909, in command of her owner, Capt. Cahoon. She sailed across the bay and put into Chatham, her skipper's home. There a party of friends was taken aboard and a trial trip was sailed to Monomoy Point and return.

The *Georgia* got off to a great start in her fishing career when she arrived at Newport, Rhode Island, on May 17, 1909 with 30,000 pounds of fresh mackerel.

Capt. Cahoon sailed in the *Georgia* during the season of 1909–10. In October of that year, the great mackerel king, Capt. Sol Jacobs, took her to the Cape Shore on a seining trip. Capt. Sol, however, found very little mackerel that trip. It was the worst mackerel season in 40 years.

Capt. Charles Forbes, another crack skipper, took command of the *Georgia* in 1911–12.

In May, 1911, pollock had struck in on the Rips off Cape Cod and many of the seining fleet sailed in pursuit of this fish. Capt. Forbes had made a remarkable record in this branch of the fisheries in the schooner *Thomas J. Carroll* during the season of 1910, and he started right in again in the larger *Georgia*.

On May 3, 1911, she landed at Gloucester 50,000 pounds of fresh pollock. On May 10, she landed 210,000 pounds of pollock, which was the largest trip of pollock ever landed at a New England port. On this trip, she carried 43,000 pounds of fish on her deck. The vessel stocked $2,621 with a share of $93.85. Cunningham and Thompson Co. purchased the fare. On May 16, she landed 160,000 pounds of pollock and on May 23, 175,000 pounds of pollock. On June 4, she arrived with 120,000 pounds of pollock. This made a grand total of 715,595 pounds of pollock, all taken within a month. This record has never been broken.

The *Georgia* was sold to Capt. John G. Stream, the great Georges halibut skipper, in the spring of 1913 and her home port was changed to Gloucester. An auxiliary gas engine was installed. Capt. Stream made many fine trips halibuting in the *Georgia*, catching most of his fish on Georges during 1914–15. In the winter season of 1914–15, Capt. Stream took the craft snapper fishing in southern waters.

Capt. Ernest Parsons took command of the *Georgia* after he lost the schooner *Pontiac* in October, 1915. In about nine weeks he stocked $11,200, using fourteen single dories.

In 1916, the *Georgia* was sold to the Gorton-Pew Fisheries Company of Gloucester and a Fairbanks-Morse 60 horsepower Diesel oil engine was installed. This was the first of the Gorton-Pew fleet to be fitted with an oil engine. She sailed seining under her new owners in command of Capt. Almon Malloch, one of Gloucester's great skippers.

On July 21, 1916, the *Georgia* in command of Capt. Malloch, took off the crew of five of the British schooner *Albertha* off Monomoy Point. The coaster was drifting helplessly and rudderless and was in a sinking condition. She was bound from Ship Harbor, Nova Scotia, to New Jersey with a cargo of lumber.

The end of the *Georgia* came on July 11, 1918 when she was rammed in a dense fog, six miles north of Great Round Shoal Lightship by the steam collier *Bristol*. The *Georgia* was on a seining trip in command of Capt. Percy Firth. The vessel was struck on the port side between the fore and main rigging and practically cut in two. Her crew of 17 jumped into a seineboat and rowed to the steamer. The vessel sank in four minutes in 13 fathoms of water. Nothing was saved but the seineboat and a dory. The steamer, bound to Boston from Norfolk, Virginia, with a cargo of coal, was not even scratched. It was a miracle that the *Georgia's* crew were all saved.

Capt. Alonzo Frank Cahoon, of Chatham, *Georgia's* first owner and skipper, died in April, 1938. He was one of the last of the great Cape Cod fishing skippers.

Capt. Charles M. Forbes, who made pollock history, died in New York in February, 1933. He was a native of Argyle, Nova Scotia.

Capt. Percy Firth, the *Georgia's* last commander, passed away in March, 1935, at the age of 51. He was a native of Jordan Ferry, Shelburne County, Nova Scotia. He was a brother of Capt. Lemuel R. Firth.

Mainmast, 67 feet; foremast, 64.5 feet; main boom, 67 feet; main gaff, 38 feet; fore boom, 22 feet; fore gaff, 23 feet; main topmast, 38 feet; fore topmast, 36 feet. Gross tons, 102; net tons, 65. length, 105.8 feet; depth, 10.2 feet; breadth, 22.6 feet.

The lovely *Elsie* is racing, probably off Gloucester in an open race in September 1929. She sailed very well, putting up quite a fight against the big new Canadian *Bluenose* after the American *Esperanto* was lost. Later the *Elsie* was a trial horse with other American racers.

Elsie

ONE OF THE VERY GREATEST / 1910–1935

Schooner *Elsie* was smart, able, beautiful and a very famous vessel. Originally of Boston, she became, in Gloucester, one of the big money makers of the salt fishing fleet, a contender and trial horse in the International Cup Races, and in the twilight of her career, the pride of the Newfoundland fleet.

Schooner *Elsie* was built alongside of schooner *Premier*, during the winter and spring of 1910 by Arthur D. Story in Essex for the Atlantic Maritime Co. of Boston. She proved to be the last vessel built for this great firm. Launching day was May 9, 1910.

The *Elsie* was a handsome round bow, semi-knockabout of medium size, designed by Capt. Tom McManus of Boston and taken off the model of the schooner *Oriole*. She was somewhat smaller, however, than that famous craft. The *Elsie* carried a short bowsprit, long mainboom, large mast heads and spread a good sail area. The length of her forecastle was 35 feet.

The fine new craft sailed from Gloucester on her maiden trip dory handlining in command of Capt. William Forbes on May 31, 1910. She arrived back in Gloucester from St. Peter's Bank with her maiden fare of 286,800 lbs. salt cod on August 23, 1910, stocking $10,400 for the banner stock of the season. Capt. Forbes remained in command until September, 1910, when he took over command of the schooner *Muriel*. The *Elsie*'s next skipper was Capt. Tom Downie and he remained at her helm from the fall of 1910 through 1913 haddocking and halibuting. One of this fine skipper's trips was landed on May 29, 1913 when the *Elsie* arrived in Gloucester from the Natasquam Grounds with 60,000 lbs. salt cod, 50,000 lbs. fresh cod, 10,000 lbs. flitched halibut and 10,000 lbs. fresh halibut.

Under Capt. Downie's command an interesting incident occurred. The little two-man fishing sloop *Helena* was caught in a heavy storm off Eastern Point, Gloucester, on January 6, 1912. Epes Tarr, who was on board the sloop, was rescued with great difficulty by Capt. Nelson King and the Dolliver's Neck Lifeboat Station crew. Fred Tarbox, the other member of the sloop's crew, was out in his dory hauling the trawls and when the storm struck was unable to reach the sloop. After being afloat a few hours and suffering from the cold, he was picked up by the *Elsie*, bound into Boston. Both men were mighty lucky to be rescued.

The summer of 1914 found Capt. Al Reynolds, skipper of the *Elsie*, shacking, and that fall of 1914 Capt. Will French took over the helm and remained through 1915 haddocking and shacking. In 1916 Capt. Fred Thompson and Carl Olson had her shacking and halibuting.

In October, 1916, the Atlantic Maritime Co. sold the *Elsie* to Capt. Alden Geele, great dory handliner, and the Gorton-Pew Co. Gloucester. In the *Elsie*, Capt. Geele broke all records in the salt fishing business. He had landed larger trips in the big schooner *Tattler* but the *Elsie*'s stocks were larger. A glance at the records shows that this great skipper had no peer as a dory handliner. Three trips were landed during the season of 1917 and the *Elsie*'s stock was $44,871. In 1918 her stock was $37,368 (two trips). In 1919 two trips were landed with a stock of $40,889, making a grand total stock of $123,128 for three years. During that 1918 season the *Elsie* arrived in Gloucester in June with 342,215 lbs. salt cod, stocking $22,768. On September 13, 1919, the *Elsie* landed at Gloucester 335,000 lbs. salt cod, stocking $21,385 with a share of $519. These were two of the largest single stocks in the history of the salt fishery.

In October, 1919, Capt. Geele sold five-eighths of the vessel to the Gorton-Pew Co. Her registry was then transferred to the W. C. Smith Co. of Lunenburg, Nova Scotia, and went under the British flag. In 1921 her registry was again changed to Gloucester. In 1922 the controlling shares of the *Elsie* were purchased by the Frank C. Pearce Co. of Gloucester.

An auxiliary 100 horsepower oil engine was installed in 1924. Under the ownership of F. C. Pearce the *Elsie* was commanded by Capts. Joseph Sears and Morton Selig (his first command) in the fresh fishery. Capts. Wallace Parsons, Don McCuish and William Nickerson (Billy Nick) also commanded the *Elsie* in the Newfoundland herring trade and freighting fish from the Provinces, in her last days out of Gloucester.

It was the *Elsie*, Capt. Alden Geele, that picked up the crew of the schooner *Esperanto*, stranded on Sable Island in May, 1921. The shipwrecked men were landed at Halifax.

With the loss of the champion *Esperanto*, a new defender had to be selected and the *Elsie*, known to be a fast vessel, was entered in an elimination race sailed off Cape Ann on October 12, 1921. Capt. Marty Welch was chosen and this great skipper skillfully sailed the *Elsie* to victory over the schooners *Ralph Brown, Arthur James, Elsie G. Silva,* and *Phillip P. Manta.*

After this victory the *Elsie* sailed to Halifax Nova Scotia where on October 22, 1921 she sailed against the big, new schooner *Bluenose,* pride of the Nova Scotians. After getting off to a beautiful start the *Elsie* was finally beaten in this race by about 12 minutes. During this race the *Elsie* snapped her foretopmast under the strain. Six men in charge of Harry Christensen, rigger, went out on the bowsprit to haul in the balloon jib, when the vessel dove headlong into a wall of sea, and shoved them all under completely out of sight.

The second race held on October 24th, saw the *Elsie* again start off beautifully, only to go down to defeat by her larger rival. She was beaten in this race by about 10 minutes. Capt. Marty stated after the final race that the windward work of the *Bluenose* was the chief factor in her winning the cup. Being longer and deeper she could hold closer to the wind while the *Elsie* kept constantly falling off. Regardless of the result, Capt. Marty and the *Elsie* put up a great fight, as Gloucestermen could do.

The *Elsie* again turned to racing when she sailed in a race off Gloucester in September, 1929 against the *Arthur D. Story* (ex-*Mary*), *Progress* and *Thomas S. Gorton.* Capt. Norman Ross was skipper of the *Elsie.* The little *Progress* won this race by very skillful handling, with the *Elsie* finishing third. Although the *Progress* sailed a great race, she would never have beaten the *Elsie* when that vessel was in her prime.

In 1931, the *Elsie* was used as a trial horse to tune up the schooner *Gertrude L. Thebaud.* Naturally, she was not in it with the larger and newer *Thebaud.*

The *Elsie* was chartered for use as a Sea Scout training vessel for several months in 1931. When the F. C. Pearce Co. was purchased by the Gorton-Pew Co., the *Elsie* went with the sale. Her auxiliary engine was removed about 1930 and she went back to sail.

In March, 1934 the grand old vessel was sold to Capt. Levi Kearley of Belleoram, Newfoundland. She was regarded very highly by the Newfoundlanders. My friend Capt. Sam Walters of Fortune Bay, Newfoundland, once told me that the *Elsie* was one of the finest vessels that ever sailed out of Fortune Bay.

In December, 1934, the *Elsie,* Capt. Kearley, brought a cargo of Newfoundland herring to Gloucester. On January 13, 1935, she sailed for her home port, Belleoram. She was five days getting to the Gulf of St. Lawrence and on the morning of the 18th she began to leak. The pumps were put to work, but on the following morning the vessel opened up forward near the stem. Capt. Kearley and his crew of six men worked at the pumps for nine hours, but at 9 o'clock the night of January 19 they saw the task was hopeless and it was decided to abandon ship. Heavy seas and a strong northerly wind added to their peril, but the men in two dories set out for the land. After rowing for 48 hours they finally arrived at St. Pierre on the night of January 21.

In a letter written by Capt. Kearley to his old friend, Capt. Wylie Rudolph of Gloucester, full details of the loss of the *Elsie* and the hard fight of her crew to reach land were given. Capt. Kearley stated that all his men except one suffered from frozen limbs and that Horatio Kearley, nephew of the skipper and later lost, with all hands in schooner *Margaret K. Smith,* was taken to the hospital suffering from exposure. Capt. Kearley himself suffered from badly frozen feet and it wasn't until the following August that a shoe could be put on.

Many faster vessels than the *Elsie* were built, but none any more able.

Gross tons, 135; net tons, 90; length, 106.5 feet; breadth, 25 feet; depth, 11.5 feet. Spars: mainmast (deck to cap), 76 feet; foremast (deck to cap), 68 feet; main topmast, 45 feet; fore topmast, 43 feet; mainboom, 75 feet; main gaff, 44 feet; bowsprit, 24.5 feet (outboard); leech of mainsail, 84 feet; mastheads, 13 feet.

When powerful engines were installed in schooners designed to be propelled by sails, the practice was to remove topmasts and reduce the sail area, using the greatly reduced sails for steadying, as shown by the *Rhodora*, circa 1914.

Rhodora

SHE WORKED FOR FORTY-THREE YEARS / 1910–1953

The knockabout schooner *Rhodora*, a fine, medium-sized vessel, sailed out of Gloucester for 29 years, then went to Newfoundland, where, renamed *Mettamora*, she worked for 14 years more.

She was built by Arthur D. Story in Essex during the winter of 1909–10 and launched shortly before noon on March 12, 1910. She was christened with a bottle of wine by Miss Helen Proctor of Gloucester, before a large crowd.

She was designed by Tom McManus and named for a beautiful flowering shrub of the heath family, native to the bogs and wet hillsides from Newfoundland south to New York. She was first owned by Cunningham and Thompson Co. of Gloucester and Capt. John A. McKinnon. Her forecastle was 34.6 feet long.

The *Rhodora* sailed on her maiden trip seining, April 4, 1910 in command of Capt. McKinnon. The mackerel season of 1910 was the poorest in years and the *Rhodora* cruised with little success. In the fall of 1910, Capt. Charles Forbes took over the helm, and remained in her for about a year. Capt. McKinnon sold his share of a quarter of the *Rhodora* to Cunningham & Thompson in December 1911.

In command of Capt. Forbes, the *Rhodora* in October 1910 made a fast run from Seal Harbor, Nova Scotia, to Thacher's in 17 hours, a distance of about 230 miles.

Capt. Gus Peterson was the next skipper of the *Rhodora* and remained in the craft, halibuting, from 1912 to 1918. He purchased one-quarter of the schooner in January, 1912 and sold his share in March 1919 to Gorton-Pew.

Capt. George Marr in 1917, and Capt. Al Roberts in 1918, commanded the *Rhodora* for short periods.

The *Rhodora*, in command of Capt. Gus Peterson, was involved in a tragic accident, right in the middle of Gloucester harbor in September, 1913. About 2:30 a.m., on Sunday the 28th, the vessel, bound up the harbor with a trip of halibut, rammed and sank the small motor boat *Abbie E.*, of Beverly. Three of the motor boat's company were drowned and two were saved. The accident happened off Ten Pound Island, when the helmsman of the *Abbie E.* misjudged distance and crossed the path of the *Rhodora*. The weather was clear. Two dories were put over by the schooner and the survivors picked up. As is customary on entering a harbor, all hands were on deck, with Capt. Peterson the forward lookout. The wreck was later raised and the bodies recovered. The *Rhodora* was found not at fault for the unfortunate collision.

When the Cunningham & Thompson firm was taken over by the Groton-Pew Co., in January 1917, the *Rhodora* came under their ownership. An auxiliary 60 horsepower oil engine was installed. Capt. John Stream, that great Georges halibuter, took command of the *Rhodora* in 1919 and he started off with a bang. In 1919 he stocked $42,000 and in 1920 his stock was $64,570, and the share $1,959 to a man. These were the *Rhodora*'s two greatest years.

Capt. Stream remained as skipper until 1930, when he retired. Capt. Still Hipson in 1929 and Capt. Ernest Engstrom in 1927 and 1930 were transient skippers. Capt. Frank Santos was *Rhodora*'s skipper in 1930 and 1934. In 1935 Capt. Ross Locke took over and remained until her sale in 1939. In her last years out of this port, she carried two 45 horsepower oil engines.

In April, 1939, the *Rhodora*, like many fine vessels before her, was sold to Newfoundland, the Southern Fisheries of Bay of Bulls, and renamed *Mettamora*, after a former Boston schooner that had been sold to Newfoundland. This famous vessel, incidentally, was a great favorite in Newfoundland. She was the first Newfoundland banker to be equipped with an engine.

The old *Rhodora*, under the new name, called at St. John's in 1953 to take on a cargo of barreled oil for the south coast of Newfoundland. She was then owned by Thomas Garland of Galtois, Newfoundland and was finally lost at Point Ridge, Newfoundland in 1953.

Gross tons, 116; net tons, 70; length, 103.9 feet; breadth, 23.5 feet; depth, 11 feet. Spar measurements: mainmast, 68.5 feet (deck to cap); foremast, 63.5 feet (cut to 59 feet); main topmast, 40 feet; fore topmast, 36 feet; main gaff, 32 feet; main boom, 60 feet.

Bound to the southward to hunt and seine schools of mackerel is the *Stilletto*, pretty and fast.

Stilletto

A VERSATILE VESSEL / 1910–1930

Schooner *Stilletto*, built in 1909–10 at the John Bishop shipyard, Vincent Cove, was a round-bowed, semi-knockabout type from an original design by Capt. Thomas McManus. She was a beautiful craft with graceful lines, a very fast sailer.

Built for Orlando Merchant, *Stilletto* was launched May 11, 1910. She was named for a fast yacht. She was the last vessel built for this firm, which later became the William H. Jordan Company, one of Gloucester's outstanding firms, noted for crack vessels, well kept and commanded.

She sailed on her maiden trip May 21, 1910, seining off the Cape Shore, in command of Capt. Charles H. Harty.

Capt. Harty had no superior when it came to bringing out the sailing qualities in a fishing vessel, and usually commanded new Jordan vessels. *Stilletto* cruised with the fleet in Nova Scotian waters for about a month, landing a few fish at Louisburg, Cape Breton.

The Cape Shore fishery was a failure, and *Stilletto* returned to Gloucester on July 24 without a fare. It was the worst mackerel season in 40 years.

Stilletto was commanded by many able skippers. In the fall of 1910 she was shacking in command of Capt. Lewis Carritt, the winter of 1910–11 haddocking, in the summer of 1911 seining under Capt. Carritt.

In the summer of 1913 Capt. Will Grady took her halibuting. The winter of 1913–14 Capt. Ambrose Fleet took her to Newfoundland for herring cargoes. Capt. Lyman Wylde had her Cape North shacking in 1915, and also had her haddocking during the winter of 1915–16.

Capt. Ralph Webber, one of Gloucester's great mackerel skippers, took over her helm in the spring of 1917 (when an auxiliary engine was installed) and remained until the spring of 1924, when Capt. Howard Tobey took command. During the winter of 1923–24 Capt. Stephen Post also had her haddocking.

Capt. Tobey had command from 1924 until her loss. While bound south on a spring mackerel trip, the *Stilletto* stranded in a light fog, on a sand bar, one mile off Fork River, New Jersey, April 4, 1930. She was four miles off her course. The schooner's keel was pounded off, and she was a total loss. Her crew of 15 were saved, and her seine and seineboat. At the time she was owned by Capt. Tobey.

Over a span of 20 years, this craft engaged in every branch of the fishing business: mackerel seining, shacking, halibuting, haddocking and freighting bulk herring cargoes from Newfoundland in winter months during the heyday of this branch of Gloucester's fishing activity.

John Bell, 43, native of Port LaTour, Nova Scotia, fell overboard and drowned when attempting to board the *Stilletto* at Perkins Wharf, Gloucester, March 31, 1915. He was one of the few Negroes shipping out of Gloucester in sailing days, and was well liked as a shipmate.

Gross tons, 136; net tons, 91; length, 105.7 feet; breadth, 24.8 feet; depth, 11.7 feet; length of forecastle, 36.5 feet.

The author is enthusiastic over the virtues of the *Sylvania;* fast, able, a great producer, and lucky—until she was caught in the great German U-boat raid on the North Atlantic fishing fleet, August 21, 1918.

Sylvania

ICE DIDN'T SINK HER, U-BOAT DID /
1910–1918

Schooner *Sylvania* was one of the finest and handsomest fishing schooners of the past; fast, able, lucky, and one of our greatest producers. The *Sylvania*, commanded by Capt. Lem Firth and my father, Jeff Thomas, proved herself one of the greatest sail carriers out of Gloucester. She was driven hard, summer and winter, by these two great mariners and never lost a life.

Sylvania was built during the spring of 1910 at John Bishop's Yard on Vincent Street, Gloucester. The Sylvanus Smith firm of Gloucester was the owner and the *Sylvania* was the last vessel built for this firm.

She was named for a Cunard steamer, and like most of the Smith vessels, carried the traditional "ia" on the end of her name.

The *Sylvania* was launched at 12:25 p.m. on September 6, 1910. The only persons on board at the time were M. H. Perkins and his grandson, Franklin.

Sylvania was a large, handsome, round bow vessel of the semi-knockabout type. She was taken off the model of the schooner *Stilletto*, which was designed by Capt. Tom McManus and launched several months previous.

The fine new craft spread a lot of canvas and her mainsail with its 76 foot main boom was one of the largest out of Gloucester. Her 15-foot mast heads were the largest of any fisherman at that time.

The length of the *Sylvania*'s forecastle was 38.4 feet.

The *Sylvania* sailed on her maiden trip to Newfoundland for a cargo of herring in command of Capt. Walter Doucette. She returned to Gloucester on December 14 of that year, from the Bay of Islands with 1600 bbls. herring.

Capt. Lem Firth, one of the smart young skippers, took over command of the *Sylvania* in the spring of 1911, mackerel seining. The *Sylvania*, Capt. Firth, was the second Cape Shore vessel to arrive, when she landed 35,000 large fresh mackerel at Boston on June 9, 1911, receiving 16 cents per pound.

On this trip from Sambro, Nova Scotia to Gloucester (a distance of 340 miles) the *Sylvania* made the last 300 miles in 23 hours—a 13-knot average.

The *Sylvania* and Capt. Firth shifted over to dory handlining in the summer of 1911 and arrived in Gloucester on November 7, 1911 with 260,000 lbs. salt cod. She was then fitted and sailed to Newfoundland to pick up a herring cargo, in command of Capt. Firth.

On January 13, 1912, news was received in Gloucester that the great herring fleet had been trapped in the ice at the Bay of Islands, Newfoundland and at Bonne Bay 30 miles to the north.

The *Sylvania* was one of the vessels caught in Bonne Bay. Her companions were the schooners *Oriole*, *T. M. Nicholson*, *Smuggler*, *Bohemia* and *Gossip*.

The Bay of Islands fleet consisted of 25 vessels: *Aloha*, *Saladin*, *Athlete*, *John R. Bradley*, *Senator Gardner*, *Veda M. McKown*, *Alert*, *Arthur James*, *Miranda*, *Massachusetts*, *Lottie G. Merchant*, *Theodore Roosevelt*, *Essex*, *Arkona*, *Oregon*, *Maxine Elliott*, *James A. Garfield*, *Margie Smith* and *S. P. Willard*.

On receipt of this alarming news, great anxiety was felt in the city. The vessels, all loaded with herring, were in great danger of being frozen in for the winter. Furthermore, the vessels would be seriously delayed in refitting and getting ready for the spring fishing.

Never before had the American herring fleet faced such a condition.

It had not been an uncommon thing for two or three vessels to get caught inside by the heavy ice and on one occasion there were eight that were hemmed in at Bonne Bay and Bay of Islands for the winter. With 25 American craft there, it meant not only the loss of cargoes, as most of the fleet had full loads, but the loss of time and service in the spring salt bank fishery, which was an important and vital part of the local fishery.

The American cutters *Androscoggin* and *Gresham* were dispatched to the aid of the stricken vessels.

On January 17th the Bay of Island fleet took advantage of a southeast wind that drove the ice field off the coast, and started for home.

With the assistance of the Newfoundland mail steamer *Portia*, the fleet at Bonne Bay, including the *Sylvania*, was freed from the ice about the 20th and started for home, with the exception of the *Bohemia*, Capt. Percy Firth (brother of Capt. Lem) who was forced back into Bonne Bay by the heavy ice, where she remained for the winter.

Capt. Lem Firth gave me the real story of the *Sylvania*'s escape from the ice at Bonne Bay, how she fairly flew down the Gulf of St. Lawrence, along the Cape Shore, across the Bay of Fundy and home. How after leaving Bonne Bay, a full two days after the Bay of Islands fleet had sailed, she overtook and passed every one of these craft, in her mad dash down the coast.

She passed the big, fast *Massachusetts*, one of the best sailers in the fleet, off Shelburne, Nova Scotia, and nailed the last one, the *Lottie G. Merchant*, on Cashes.

Capt. Firth also told me that the *Sylvania* would probably be beaten by the *Oriole* and *Clintonia* (queens of the fleet) in sailing by the wind; but give the *Sylvania* a little sheet and she would show her stern to the best of them. The *Sylvania* arrived in Gloucester on January 25, 1911, after her escape from the Newfoundland ice. She hailed for 850 bbls. frozen herring.

The *Sylvania* and Capt. Firth started mackerel seining in the spring of 1912, and on April 18, 1912 landed a fine fare of 400 bbls. large mackerel at Lewes, Delaware. She again changed over to dory handlining during the summer of 1912 and the winter of 1912–13 turned her attention again to the Newfoundland herring trade.

The *Sylvania* in command of Capt. Firth arrived in Gloucester on January 1, 1913 from Bonne Bay with 1415 bbls. herring for her owners the Sylvanus Smith Co.

In April, 1913, the *Sylvania* was taken over by Capt. Jeff Thomas. Capt. Jeff had made a fine record in the schooner *Cynthia* from the Smith firm, but this vessel was far too slow and the fast *Sylvania* was just what he needed. He purchased one-quarter of the vessel in 1913 and another quarter in 1917.

Capt. Thomas always used the *Sylvania* shacking summers and haddocking winters and year after year was right up with the highliners. Some of the outstanding trips of the *Sylvania* under command of Capt. Thomas were as follows:

The *Sylvania* sailed haddocking on October 17, 1913, fished in the South Channel and arrived at Boston on October 20th with 41,000 lbs. mixed fish (three days), stocking $1930 and the crew sharing $44. This was some hustling for a vessel without power.

On January 15, 1914, the *Sylvania* arrived at Boston with the largest trip of the winter, hailing for 100,000 lbs. fresh fish, stocking $4,226 and sharing $100. This trip was taken five miles off Liscomb, Nova Scotia, and she was only two weeks out. In approaching Boston, the craft, badly iced, was struck by a gale, which drove her 100 miles out to sea. This trip was the best ever made up to that time by a double doried vessel.

On June 26, 1914, the *Sylvania* arrived from Cape North with 140,000 lbs. salt fish and 20,000 lbs. fresh fish. She arrived from Pearce Bank on August 13, 1915, with 200,000 lbs. shack.

The *Sylvania* had a splendid year in 1916 when she stocked $49,850, the crew sharing $1150 per man, haddocking and shacking. One of her biggest trips that year was on July 5th, when she landed 250,000 lbs. shack from Cape North, stocking $7006.

The *Sylvania* arrived in Gloucester on August 7, 1917 with a splendid fare of 240,000 lbs. fresh fish and 4000 lbs. halibut from Quero Bank. On this same day ten shackers landed almost 2,000,000 lbs. of fresh and salt fish at Gloucester. This was probably the biggest shack day in Gloucester's history.

The *Sylvania*, Capt. Jeff Thomas, had the biggest fare, 244,000 lbs., schooner *Joseph P. Mesquita*, Capt. Joe Mesquita, 200,000 lbs.; *A. Piatt Andrew*, Capt. Wallace Bruce, 230,000 lbs.; schooner *Kineo*, Capt. Ralph Silva, 151,-500 lbs.; schooner *Mary P. Golart*, Capt. Antone Goulart, 177,000 lbs.; schooner *Elsie Silva*, Capt. Manuel Silva, 178,000 lbs.; schooner *Flora L. Oliver*, Capt. Tony Brown, 171,000 lbs.; schooner *Leonora Silveira*, Capt. John Silveira, 160,000 lbs.; schooner *Murial*, Capt. Tom Downie, 159,000 lbs.; schooner *Adeline*, Capt. John Goulart, 141,000 lbs. All the trips were taken on Quero Bank. The *Sylvania* on this trip stocked $5861 with a share of $150.

On March 20, 1918, the *Sylvania* landed a fare of 85,000 lbs. fresh fish at Boston, stocking $7860 and sharing $231 per man. This was the highest double dory share ever made up to this time.

On July 8, 1918, the *Sylvania* landed 200,000 lbs. fresh fish at Gloucester, stocking $7573 with a share of $207. The trip was caught at Quero.

In August 1918 the *Sylvania* landed a trip of shack at Gloucester. She stocked $7160 and shared $187 per man. This was her last trip.

Most of the skippers had their favorite fishing spots and one of Capt. Jeff's was the Cape North grounds.

The Cape North shackers would fit out about the middle of April and would be gone on a trip from three to six weeks. These vessels carried 10 or 11 double dories. Twenty five to 50 hogsheads of salt for salting down the first part of the trip would be taken on at Gloucester. Ice was taken at Canso or some other Nova Scotian port and bait was secured at the Magdalens, Souris, Prince Edward Island or St. Pierre. The shackers took a chance on securing their bait, but it usually turned out in their favor.

Most of the fish were taken on two baitings, but at times a lucky vessel would get a trip with one baiting.

The vessels fished within sight of land (outside the three mile limit) off Cape North, which is the northern tip of Cape Breton.

It was a hard place to fish, because of the strong tides, but the fine codfish trips that were taken there made it worthwhile.

Many skippers fished the Cape North grounds, but the greatest producers were Capt. Jeff Thomas, his brother, Capt. Billy Thomas, Capts. Henry Larkin, Wallace Bruce, Robertson Giffin (Strings); Joe Mesquita, Horace Wylde, Hugh Quinlan, Billy Corkum (Little Billy) and Henry Curtis.

Mishaps were few in the life of the *Sylvania* and no men were ever lost. On January 26, 1914 the *Sylvania*, while making harbor to get out of a storm, drove up on White Shoal, entrance to Sheet Harbor, Nova Scotia. The crew stood by and floated her after a few hours. She was leaking badly and was towed to Halifax for repairs. It was found that almost her entire keel was torn off. It was very lucky the *Sylvania* floated, for she hit the shoal hard, sailing at a seven-knot clip under four lowers.

The *Sylvania* and Capt. Jeff had the honor of being one of the first vessels to take out a trip at the opening of the new South Boston Fish Pier on March 30, 1914. She landed a fine fare of 95,000 pounds fresh fish. On that eventful day, 19 vessels landed over 1,500,000 pounds of fish.

On February 4, 1918, the *Sylvania* and schooner *Kineo*, Capt. Ralph Silva, landed fares at Boston. That evening they sailed for Gloucester for necessary repairs, but were forced to anchor off Ten Pound Island, because of the heavy ice. During the night the vessels were frozen in tight. The crews were able to walk ashore the next day.

Not since 1875 had the harbor been frozen so badly. Hundreds of people walked out to the breakwater.

Capt. Jeff wasn't goinng to let some ice stop him. Six of the *Sylvania's* crew hauled a pung from Pavilion Beach to the imprisoned vessel, where the vessel's wind-torn sails were picked up and hauled back to shore for repairs. A horse and sleigh went out to the vessel with provisions, and on February 11th, the tug *Blanche* broke out the vessel and she cleared for fishing. She had fitted out while in the ice without coming near a wharf.

The end of the *Sylvania* came on August 31, 1918 when she was caught in the great U-boat raid on the fishing fleet.

The *Sylvania*, with 35,000 pounds fresh fish on board, met her end 90 miles off Sydney, Nova Scotia. The doomed craft was overhauled by the Canadian steam trawler *Triumph*, which was manned by a prize crew from the German U-boat 156. Capt. Jeff and Emery Doane, one of his crew, rowed over to the *Triumph* with his papers after being ordered to do so by Oberleutnant J. Knoeckel of the captured trawler. The *Sylvania's* crew were given 10 minutes to leave the vessel. German sailors came aboard and placed time bombs in the hold of the *Sylvania* and shortly after all had left, the beautiful vessel was sent to the bottom. As Capt. Jeff left the *Sylvania* he saw the U-156 on the surface about two miles' distant.

The crew of the *Sylvania* landed at various points along the Nova Scotian coast. The dory containing Capt. Thomas landed at his birthplace of Arichat, Cape Breton. This dory was equipped with an outboard motor, which was in charge of Fred Thomas, cousin of the skipper. (This was Fred's first experience with an engine. He later rounded out 26 years as engineer of the schooner *Adventure*.) The value of the *Sylvania* when lost was $28,000.

Wally MacLeod, of Gloucester, was a young lad enjoying his school vacation on the last trip of the *Sylvania*. Wally at the time received quite a thrill from this experience. He was more concerned in rescuing the graphophone from the *Sylvania's* cabin than he was in Germans. Wally can truly boast of this experience. Few persons in Gloucester have had such an experience.

The crew list of the *Sylvania* when sunk by the Germans:

Capt. Jeffrey Thomas, Frank Thomas (cook) cousin of skipper. Peter Thomas, brother of the skipper, Fred Thomas, cousin of skipper, Emery Doane, Howard Penney, Richard Burke, Arthur L. Goodwin, Lindley McComiskey, Samuel Ernst, George F. Meuse, Peter Doucette, Thomas Delorey, Harry Fletcher, Robert Devine, Arthur Meuse, Moses Deveau, Arthur Surrette, Reuben Babine, Alexander T. Muise.

I have always had a personal interest in the *Sylvania*. She was the first vessel that I can remember and many happy days of my youth were spent aboard her while she was in port.

Through her I came to know and love the great vessels of her time and those that followed.

It seems as if I can see the *Sylvania* now, pulling into the Sylvanus Smith wharf, deeply laden with one of her big shack trips. Her sails were neatly furled; her crew lined along the rail, clad in their bright heavy shirts, exchanging greetings with those on shore.

When she was made fast and the trip ready to be taken out, I would climb up on the big main gaff, or shinny out on the bowsprit and lie down on the furled jib, where I could get a fine view of all that was going on. Everything was thrilling to me, the towering spars with their big black mastheads, the deck and cabin top, piled high with gear, the big coil of cable and the big anchors up forward, the nests of dories; even the loud noise of the big deck hoister was music in my ears.

All this is gone now, but hardly a day goes by, but what I wish it was all back again.

The *Sylvania* while in command of my father was driven for all she was worth; and she could take it. This vessel was one of the fastest vessels out of this port. Many fine vessels of the fleet were beaten by the *Sylvania*, including the *Elsie*, *Stilletto*, *Gov. Foss*, *John Hays Hammond*, *A. Piatt Andrew*, *Thomas Gorton*, *Massachusetts*, *Onato*, and many others.

Capt. Jeff was a great sail carrier and when the going was the hardest, he was right there on deck to handle things.

A little story once told to me by Capt. Wylie Rudolph, I think, characterizes the *Sylvania* and her skipper.

Capt. Rudolph was hand with Capt. Bill Thomas in the schooner *Thomas S. Gorton*.

The *Gorton* was hove to in a gale off Gloucester. A vessel could be seen approaching, bowling along under a good spread of canvas. The *Gorton*'s crew all wondered what craft this could be carrying all that sail, while they were hove to. Capt. Billy after sizing up the approaching craft turned to one of his crew and with a broad grin said: "There's only one damn fool carrying all that sail and that's Jeff."

It was the *Sylvania*, all right and she sped by the *Gorton* like a greyhound. She was bound to market and a little wind couldn't stop Capt. Jeff.

Gross tons, 136; net tons, 99; length, 105.6 feet; breadth, 24.8 feet; depth, 11.6 feet. Original spar measurements: mainmast (deck to cap), 77 feet; foremast (deck to cap), 70 feet; mainboom, 76 feet; main gaff, 45 feet; foreboom, 28 feet; foretopmast, 40 feet; maintopmast, 45 feet; bowsprit (outboard), 22 feet; mastheads, 15 feet. Sails were made by Ben Colby.

Gov. Foss

ONE OF THE LUCKY ONES / 1911–1920

In our great fleet of vessels of the past, many
were lucky and many not so fortunate. Some
rolled up big stocks year after year. Others,
misfortune seemed to follow wherever they
sailed. Many craft lost a lot of men. Others
lost very few if any. One of the lucky ones
was schooner *Gov. Foss*, a great vessel with a
distinguished name.

Schooner *Gov. Foss* was built during the
winter and spring of 1911 by James and Tarr
in Essex. Capts. Fred Thompson and Lemuel
Spinney were the owners.

The *Gov. Foss* was a handsome, good sized
vessel of the round bow, semi-knockabout
type. She carried a short bowsprit and large

sail and her forecastle was 41 feet long. She greatly resembled vessels of the *Elk, Elsie, Premier* type. Capt. Tom McManus of Boston was her designer.

The fine new craft was named after Eugene Foss, Democratic governor of Massachusetts at that time. Foss was born in West Berkshire, Vermont, in 1858.

Launching day on May 2, 1911, was intended to be a gala day in Essex, as Gov. Foss was invited to witness the new craft's initial dip into the briny. School children were dismissed from their classes. The Governor failed to put in an appearance, however. The launching party included Capt. Lemuel Spinney, Mrs. Spinney and son Russell Spinney, also Mrs. Thompson and son Fred Thompson, Jr. There was no sponsor. The tug *Eveleth* towed the new craft to Gloucester.

Schooner *Gov. Foss* in command of Capt. Thompson sailed on her maiden trip halibuting, May 18, 1911. She returned with her maiden fare of 28,000 lbs. halibut, 20,000 lbs. salt fish and 35,000 fresh fish on June 9, 1911.

The *Gov. Foss* was a money maker right from the start. In her first year she stocked $40,000. Her second year's stock was $41,000 and the third year's, $49,000. Phenomenal stocks and quick trips by Capt. Thompson became bywords in the fleet of halibuters and haddockers. His three year grand total stock of $130,000 was unsurpassed up to that time.

During brief vacations by Capt. Thompson the *Foss* was skippered by Capt. Lem Spinney in the fall of 1913 and Capt. Albert Saulnberg in December, 1915. Capt. Thompson sold the *Gov. Foss* to the Gorton-Pew Co. of Gloucester in the spring of 1916.

When the craft was taken over by Gorton-Pew, Capt. Joe Mesquita took the wheel, one trip shacking.

During August and September of 1916, Capt. Albert Rose was the skipper. Capt. Al Reynolds took over haddocking October, 1916 to March, 1917. Capt. Henry LeBlanc had her salt banking from April to July in 1917, then changed over to shacking up to November, 1917. Capt. Lyman Wylde had her haddocking December, 1917 to March, 1918. In April, 1918, Capt. Ed Brayman took her haddocking, one trip, and from April, 1918 to July, 1918, her skipper was Capt. George Marr.

The *Gov. Foss* was placed under the British flag in 1918. Her port of registry was St. John's, Newfoundland and her owners listed as the Bay of Islands Fish Co. She was placed in the transatlantic fish carrying trade between Newfoundland and Portuguese ports.

Although the *Foss* was not a fast vessel, she made a good run of 15 days from Port Union, Newfoundland, to Oporto, Portugal in October 1919.

The year 1922 saw the *Gov. Foss* again under the American flag, and owned by Capt. Tom Benham of Gloucester. Capt. Benham used the vessel dory handlining from 1923 to 1926.

Capt. Benham kept up his reputation as one of our great dory handliners, in the *Gov. Foss*. On June 16, 1924 he arrived in Gloucester with 320,000 lbs. salt cod, stocking $14,338 with a high line share of $395. In 1925 two dory hand line trips were landed with a total stock of $28,600.

Auxiliary power, consisting of two 60 horsepower oil engines was installed in the *Gov. Foss* in 1927. The craft was then sent seining in command of Capt. George Hodgdon. Capt. Free Crowell took her haddocking in the fall of 1927.

Loss of life was very small in the *Gov. Foss*. On September 27, 1915, William J. McCarthy was swept overboard to his death in a heavy gale off Shelburne, Nova Scotia. McCarthy was assisting in reefing the foresail when a giant sea struck the craft, washing him overboard and far beyond the reach of his mates. The *Gov. Foss* was swept clean of dories and everything movable on deck. William McCarthy, the unfortunate man, was a native of Fortune Bay, Newfoundland. He left a widow and five children. Capt. Fred Thompson was skipper at the time.

Capt. Lyman Wylde, skipper of the *Gov. Foss*, was found dead in his boarding house at Gloucester on March 10, 1918. Death was caused by escaping gas, while he was asleep. Capt. Wylde was one of the best liked skippers out of Gloucester. He was 50 years old and a native of Port Medway, Nova Scotia. He was a brother of Capt. Horace Wylde.

The North Atlantic gave the *Gov. Foss* quite a drubbing in December, 1924. The craft in command of Capt. Garrett Hickey was returning home to Gloucester from the Bay of Islands, Newfoundland, loaded with 1300 bbls. herring. She was struck by a howling easterly and when 30 miles off Thacher's Island on December 6, her mainmast suddenly snapped and crashed over the side, followed shortly by the foremast. When the foremast went over, it took the bowsprit with it. Patrick Murphy and Patrick Abbott, two of the crew, rushed out on the bowsprit to free the wreckage when the vessel suddenly dipped into a sea throwing both men overboard. They were rescued by their mates with great difficulty. Abbott when brought aboard was unconscious as he had been hit in the head by the bow of the *Foss* in the struggle for his life.

A riding sail was rigged and she drifted helplessly on the ocean for four days. She was finally sighted 55 miles off Portland Lightship by the Portland schooner *Benjamin Thompson*, Capt. William Thomas, and was towed into that port, by the *Thompson*. She arrived home in Gloucester on December 11 in tow of a Portland tug. Salvage of $3000 was awarded to Capt. Thomas and crew of the *Thompson*.

The crew of the *Gov. Foss* at the time of the accident was Capt. Garrett Hickey, Patrick Abbott, Patrick Murphy, William Sullivan, Ellick Merchant, John Welch, Angus McPhee and James Sears.

When the seining season of 1929 rolled around, the *Gov. Foss* was all slicked up for the cruise south. She sailed from Gloucester in command of Capt. Tom Benham on March 30, 1929.

On April 2nd while entering the harbor of Cape May, New Jersey, in a south southwest breeze, she struck the ledges on the east side of the entrance. The crew left the vessel in the seineboat. The next day her bowsprit was gone and several holes were stove in her planking. She was given up as a total loss. The only things saved were the seineboat, seine and a quantity of running gear.

Capt. Fred Thompson sailed on his last voyage on November 9, 1928.

Capt. Fred was one of our most successful mariners, especially in the halibut fisheries. He commanded many vessels, including the *Elsie Smith, Dictator, Niagara, Gov. Foss, John Hays Hammond, Florence,* named for his daughter, and *Alden,* named for a son. He was a native of Norway.

Capt. Garrett Hickey passed away in February 1935. He was a native of Placentia, Newfoundland.

Capt. Thomas Benham died in October 1964 at the age of eighty-six. He was a native of Lockport, Nova Scotia. Capt. Tom was one of the greats of the salt fishermen. He commanded many fine vessels, including the *Emma Wetherell, Athlete, Esperanto, Gov. Foss* and *Ruth Lucille.* He was captain of the famous *Esperanto* when she was lost on Sable Island in 1921.

Ex-Gov. Foss died at Boston in September 1939.

Gross tons, 130; net tons, 88; length, 105.9 feet; breadth, 24.6 feet; depth, 10.8 feet. Original spars: mainmast (deck to cap), 76 feet; foremast, 67 feet; main topmast, 43 feet; fore topmast, 40 feet; main boom, 71 feet; main gaff, 41 feet; bowsprit, outboard, 18 feet; mastheads, 13 feet.

Laverna

FOR LOOKS, FEW VESSELS SURPASSED HER / 1911–1936

Capt. Albert Larkin made a fine reputation for himself in the schooner *Natalie J. Nelson* and *Valerie* during the early years of the century and in 1911 the fine schooner *Laverna* was built for him by James and Tarr in Essex.

The *Laverna* was a good sized vessel of the round bow, semi-knockabout type, designed by Tom McManus. She was taken off the moulds of the schooner *Valerie*, with some improvements. She carried a great spread of canvas, was able, and as for looks, few vessels surpassed her.

The new craft made her maiden dip into the waters of Essex Creek on July 8, 1911. There was no sponsor. On July 25th, she rounded Eastern Point bound to the eastward on a shack trip in command of her proud owner, Capt. Albert Larkin. She arrived home with her maiden fare on September 12, 1911, in company with the schooner *Cynthia*, Capt. Jeff Thomas. The *Laverna* hailed for 150,000 pounds salt cod, caught on Quero Bank. Capt. Larkin and his crew were loud in praise of their "fine" new craft. On this trip the *Laverna* spoke the schooners *Lucinda I. Lowell* and *Smuggler* on Quero and the schooner *Lottie G. Merchant* off Halifax, Nova Scotia.

Capt. Larkin did very well in the *Laverna* and remained in command haddocking and shacking until November, 1913, when he was forced to retire from the sea because of illness. The vessel was then sold to the Cunningham-Thompson Co. and the veteran skipper, John McInnis, took over the helm. Capt. John took advantage of the rising prices of fish due to World War I and while he was skipper of the *Laverna* was right up with the highliners, year after year.

On January 1, 1918, Capt. John landed a trip of groundfish at the South Boston Fish Pier, consisting of 138,235 pounds, stocking $8,396 and the crew of 23 sharing $199.90 each. This was the biggest check paid out to a vessel by the Fish Exchange for a trip of groundfish up to that time. The trip was caught on the Cape Shore.

On December 28, 1913, while under Capt. John McInnis' command the *Laverna* nearly came to grief in Boston Harbor. The vessel was running to port with the biggest trip of the season. A mistake was made in the harbor lights and she bid up with a heavy thud on Ram Head Bar in Broad Sound. At low water the craft listed heavily to port. A hole 28 inches in diameter was discovered in her port

side and her hold was full of water. Later the tugs *Mercury* and *Vesta* succeeded in swinging her around but could not release her. After 30 hours on the bar she was successfully floated by the wrecking lighters *Salvor* and *Admiral* and the tugs *Confidence* and *Mercury* and was towed to Boston for repairs. It was Capt. McInnis' second trip in the craft. Within 48 hours a second fishing schooner, the *Juno*, struck on the same Ram Head Bar, but was quickly floated with little damage.

The *Laverna* was a lucky craft in loss of life. Only two men lost their lives in this vessel, both while she was commanded by Capt. John McInnis. On January 5, 1918, William E. Welsh, one of her crew, was drowned by falling overboard while boarding the vessel at the South Boston Fish Pier. He was 33 years old and a native of Bay of Bulls, Newfoundland.

Timothy McDougall was washed overboard and drowned on Georges on February 20, 1918. It was rough and blowing a heavy gale at the time. McDougall was coming out of the forecastle when a heavy sea broke across the vessel, carrying him overboard to his death. He was a native of Aspey Bay, Cape Breton, and 36 years old.

Capt. McInnis remained in the *Laverna* until September, 1918, when she was taken over by Capt. Bob Wharton, halibuting. The *Laverna* was sold in December, 1918, to Capt. Lovett Hines.

Capt. Wiley Ross became her skipper in 1919, and in January, 1920, she was sold to S. Harriss of Grand Bank, Newfoundland. A fancy price was paid for the handsome craft. On December 23, 1920, the *Laverna*, flying the British flag, paid a visit to Gloucester. She came from the Bay of Islands, Newfoundland, with 1308 barrels herring.

The *Laverna* when she sailed out of Gloucester was considered a smart sailer, although she couldn't carry a mainsail too well. Capt. Albert Larkin once told me that she was the fastest craft he had ever commanded. In Newfoundland waters she kept up her fine reputation, and was greatly admired by the Newfoundlanders.

My friend Capt. Sam Walters, Newfoundland skipper, claimed that the *Laverna* at one time, left St. John's in command of Capt. C. Rose at 4 p.m. on a Friday. Capt. Rose became ill and the vessel put into Grand Bank on the southern coast of Newfoundland. She was delayed there about two hours and sailed in command of Capt. Charles Amstay. She came to anchor at the Bay of Islands on the west coast at 4 p.m. on Sunday. This was pretty smart sailing.

The end came to the handsome *Laverna* on September 9, 1936, when she drove ashore in a gale at Salmon Bight Passage, Labrador. Her crew was saved. Capt. Frank Thornhill was her skipper at the time.

Capt. Albert Larkin sailed on his last voyage in December, 1948, at the age of 69. Capt. Albert was one of our great mariners. Smart, capable, well liked and a gentleman from the word go. He came from a family of great mariners. Capt. Albert started his career at sea as a boy of 14 when he was taken as deck boy for his uncle, Capt. Fred Morrisey. He became a skipper in 1902 when he took over the schooner *Helen G. Wells*. Later he commanded the *Natalie J. Nelson*, *Lizzie M. Stanley*, *Valerie* and *Laverna*, Illness forced him to retire in 1913. He was a fine haddocker, shacker and seiner.

I owe much to Capt. Albert Larkin for his encouragement and help in the early days of assembling these stories of our great vessels.

In spite of a lingering illness, Capt. Albert's great enjoyment was a day spent with his fellow skippers at the Master Mariners. His brother, Capt. Henry Larkin, was also one of our great mariners. He was a native of Lower East Pubnico, Nova Scotia.

Capt. John McInnis, affectionately known as "Whipsaw," was a great mariner; a great fisherman. I doubt if a tougher, more rugged man ever sailed the North Atlantic than Capt. John McInnis. He was an expert in all branches of the fisheries and commander of many fine vessels, including the schooners *Charles Barrett*, *John W. Bray*, *Henry W. Longfellow*, *Effie M. Morrissey*, *Belle Franklin*, *Talisman*, *Aloha*, *Independence II*, *Norma*, *Pilgrim*, *Elizabeth Howard*, *Killarney*, *Columbia* and *Desire*. Books could be written of the exploits of this great skipper. He was one of the last links with our great past of great vessels and great men. Capt. John was a native of West Bay, Cape Breton.

Gross tons, 141; net tons, 95; length, 106 feet; breadth, 25.2 feet; depth, 12 feet. Spar measurements: mainmast (deck to cap), 77.5 feet; foremast, 68 feet; main topmast, 46 feet; fore topmast, 41 feet; main boom, 74 feet; main gaff, 45.6 feet; bowsprit (outboard), 22 feet; mast heads, 14 feet.

A. Piatt Andrew

A MONEY-MAKER, SUNK BY A U-BOAT / 1912–1918

Schooner *A. Piatt Andrew*, a splendid vessel, was named for a distinguished gentleman and commanded by a great skipper. Although her life was short (six years) she was one of the great money makers of the past, and she never lost a life.

The *A. Piatt Andrew* was another product of that great shipyard of Tarr and James in Essex. She was built during the winter and spring of 1912 and launched on April 20, 1912.

The firm of Capt. John Chisholm and her skipper Capt. Wallace Bruce were the owners. The *Andrew* was a good sized, round bow vessel of the semi-knockabout type, with a short bowsprit. Her spars were tall and she spread a lot of sail. She was one of the prettiest vessels of the fleet.

I was informed by Capt. Bruce that the *Andrew* was taken from the lines of the schooner *Valerie* (1910) and the *Laverna* (1911). Both of these vessels were designed by Tom McManus.

The *A. Piatt Andrew* was an able vessel, but not exceptionally fast. She was at her best in heavy weather.

Schooner *A. Piatt Andrew* was named for one of Gloucester's distinguished citizens. At the time of the launching of the new vessel, he was assistant secretary of the treasury in Washington, D. C. Mr. Andrew was a great friend to the Gloucester fisherman. On April 17, 1912, 54 members of the Gloucester Master Mariner's Association were guests of Mr. Andrew at his home at Eastern Point, where they were most cordially received and entertained.

The *Andrew* sailed on her maiden trip in command of Capt. Bruce, on May 9, 1912, bound to Cape North, shacking. The fine new vessel presented a picturesque appearance as she sailed out of the harbor. Capt. Bruce swung her in opposite "Red Roof," the Eastern Point home of Mr. Andrew, where flags and bunting were flying in honor of the sailing, after which she squared off and put to sea.

The *A. Piatt Andrew* arrived in Gloucester, June 16, 1912, with her maiden fare: 80,000 lbs. fresh fish and 80,000 lbs. of salt fish, taken off Cape North. On that day five other large trips were in from the Cape North grounds. The *Rex*, 160,000; *Arabia*, 135,000; *Massachusetts*, 200,000; *Conqueror*, 100,000; and *James W. Parker*, 170,000 lbs.

The schooner *A. Piatt Andrew* is posing for admirers gathered at nearby Red Roof, the Eastern Point home of the man named A. Piatt Andrew, who became a high government official, founder of the American Field Service in France, and congressman.

On October 21, 1912 the new schooner was inspected by Mr. Andrew, Miss Caroline Sinkler, a summer resident, and Mrs. Jack Gardner of Brookline. All enjoyed their visit very much, after inspecting the vessel from stem to stern.

The *A. Piatt Andrew* was a big producer and money maker right from the start, and Capt. Wallace drove her all the way. She was a lucky vessel and paid for herself many times over. From January to December 10, 1913 her stock was $36,400.

From September, 1914 to September, 1915 her stock was $46,000, with a share of $853.00. From January 1, 1915 to April, in eight trips, she landed 665,000 lbs. fresh fish, and by September of that year she had landed a grand total of 1,313,000 lbs. of fish. This hustling skipper made them all take notice. On one of these trips she landed at Boston on February 3, 1915, 100,000 fresh fish, making the highest stock of the winter, $4050, with a share of $90.00.

The *Andrew* arrived at Gloucester from Perce Bank on July 17, 1915, with 215,000

shack caught in seven days fishing. The salt fish was kenched on deck.

The season of 1916 Capt. Bruce broke all records in the fresh fishery when he stocked $53,395, nosing out the schooner *Sylvania*, Capt. Jeff Thomas, who had a $50,000 stock. This was money making in those days. On one of these trips that season of 1916 the *Andrew* left Gloucester on Saturday afternoon, October 7, and on Tuesday, October 10, landed 31,000 pounds of fresh fish at Boston. The hustling skippers of those days didn't need big engines in their vessels to make quick trips. All they needed was wind enough to fill those big "white wings."

Capt. Bruce took a vacation ashore during the winter of 1917–18 and Capt. Tom Downie, another smart skipper, took command of the *Andrew*. In five weeks he stocked over $10,000.

The *A. Piatt Andrew* never had auxiliary power, but in September, 1914, an automatic hoister was installed.

Mishaps were few in the career of the *Andrew*. No lives were lost, but on November 15,

1914, she was rammed in a haze in the South Channel by the Boston haddocker *Mary*, losing 15 feet of her starboard rail. The *Mary* lost her bowsprit.

This great vessel's career was cut short in August, 1918, when she was caught in the great U-boat raid on the fishing fleet. On August 21, 1918, the *A. Piatt Andrew*, while fishing 55 miles south of Canso, Nova Scotia, was hailed by the Canadian steam trawler *Triumph*. This craft had been captured by the German U-boat 156. A prize crew had been put on board and the craft converted to an armed raider. Capt. Bruce was ordered to row alongside the trawler with his papers. He then learned the identity of the trawler and that his vessel was about to be sunk. Three of the Germans boarded the fisherman's dory, and carried time bombs aboard the *Andrew*. While this was going on, the Gloucester schooner *Francis J. O'Hara, Jr.*, Capt. Joe Mesquita, observed two vessels to the eastward. Both appeared to be fishing, and a beam trawler was steaming up between them. He decided to run over and find out how the fishing was. He received a hail from the trawler ordering him to heave to. Capt. Mesquita thought the whole thing a joke until four shots were fired across his bow. He, like Capt. Bruce rowed over to the raider and returned with three Germans and time bombs. The crews of both vessels were told to gather their belongings and take to the dories. After muffled explosions, both the *O'Hara* and the *A. Piatt Andrew* went to the bottom. The crews were picked up and landed at Canso, Nova Scotia, on August 25. While all this was going on, the U-156 remained lurking in the distance. The third fisherman sunk in this group was the Canadian *Una A. Saunders*. The next day, August 22, Capt. Bruce's old rival, the schooner *Sylvania*, skippered by his chum, Capt. Jeff Thomas, met the same fate at the hands of the raider *Triumph*. It seemed as if the Germans knew how to pick them, for they nailed three of the highliners of the Gloucester fleet. After sinking the *Sylvania*, the Germans, having no more use for the *Triumph*, sank her with bombs.

The *Andrew* carried a complement of 26 men at the time of the sinking. They were as follows:

Capt. Wallace Bruce, Phillip Bonia, Ambrose LeBlanc, Raymond Amero, John R. Muise, Benjamin White, James L. Doucett, Archie Hubbard, Charles Hubbard, Edmund Carter, Benjamin Doucett, Sylvania Amirault, Edgar Muise, Ambrose Doucett, William Newell, Clyde Devine, Winfred A. Brown, Jeffrey Robbins, John F. White, Isaiah Meuse, Ernest Lartey, Joseph Amero, Walter Muise, Robert Wilson, Simon Muise.

The German U-boat 156, in command of Kapitan-leutnant Von Oldenburg, on returning home to Germany, struck a mine in October, 1918, in the North Sea and was lost with all hands. She was about 200 feet long, carried two 5.9 inch guns and a crew of 77 men. She was the most destructive of the U-boats that raided our coast, having sent 33,582 tons of shipping to the bottom.

Col. A. Piatt Andrew, namesake of the grand vessel, passed away at his home "Red Roof," on July 3, 1936. He was a native of LaPorte, Indiana, and 63 years old. During World War I, he was the organizer and leader of the American Field Service, and was decorated by three nations for his brilliant war service. It was a strange coincidence that at the time of the schooner *A. Piatt Andrew*'s sinking, the news came from Europe, that Col. Andrew had been injured in an automobile accident but was recovering. Col. Andrew was U.S. Congressman from the Sixth District from 1921 to the time of his death. He was always a friend of the Gloucester fisherman.

Capt. Wallace Bruce, a native of Guysbro, Nova Scotia, was one of the finest skippers who ever trod the decks of a Gloucester fisherman. A hustler, smart, and in my estimation, having one of the greatest virtues a skipper could have, being liked and admired by his gang. Every old fisherman I have conversed with has the same words to say of Capt. Wallace: "a swell fellow." He commanded many fine vessels including the *Arabia*, *Valerie*, *Joffre* and steam trawler *Roseway*.

Capt. Wallace Bruce passed away at Sailor's Snug Harbor, New York, in October, 1954 at the age of 75.

Gross tons, 141; net tons, 92; length, 105 feet; breadth, 25 feet; depth, 11.8 feet. Original spar measurements: main mast (deck to cap), 78.5 feet; foremast, 68.5 feet; main topmast, 44 feet; main boom, 73.4 feet; main gaff, 43 feet; fore boom, 29 feet; bowsprit (outboard), 22.5 feet; mainmast head, 14.5 feet.

Bay State

CRUDE OIL ENGINES DROVE HER /
1912–1927

In the fall of 1912, two vessels were built off the same moulds for the New England Fish Co. for halibut fishing in the North Pacific.

Schooner *Knickerbocker*, built by A. D. Story at Essex, sailed 16,000 miles to Seattle via Cape Horn, in command of Capt. Bob Lathagee in the spring of 1913. She proved unsatisfactory, however, for fishing in the Pacific and was later sold for a freighter.

Schooner *Bay State* was built by Owen Lantz at Vincent Cove, Gloucester. She never made the Pacific voyage, but instead turned out to be one of the finest vessels and greatest producers of the local fleet.

The *Bay State* was a large, powerful vessel of the knockabout type, designed by Capt. Tom McManus of Boston. Her hailing port was Portland, Maine. She and her sister ship, the *Knickerbocker* were fitted with two 100 horsepower Blanchard oil engines, the first vessels in the fleet with this kind of power.

These engines burned crude oil, and the operating cost was cut about three quarters. Oil at that time cost about 6 cents per gallon and gasoline 20 cents a gallon. This type of engine proved unsuccessful. It wasn't until 1915 that the Boston schooner *Manhasett* came out with a Nelseco diesel, the first successful oil engine for fishermen. I have been told that when they were trying out the new *Bay State*'s engines at the wharf, all you could see was heavy black smoke.

Launching of the *Bay State* took place on October 26, 1912. Owen Lantz, her builder, was faced with a most difficult task. He had to launch a vessel 126 feet over all into a cove 180 feet across. These great old shipbuilders were always equal to the occasion and after seeing that the new vessel had good checking lines, he let her go at 10:25 a.m. About 500 spectators lined the cove and adjacent buildings. The launching was one of the prettiest and most successful that ever took place at Vincent Cove.

Lantz told me that the checking lines held and the *Bay State* came to a stop within three feet of a building on the opposite shore of the cove. He said that the roof of this shed was crowded with people, and when they saw the *Bay State* heading straight for them, he never saw folks scatter so fast. I believe the *Bay State* was the largest vessel ever built at Vincent Cove.

On October 28, her spars were stepped at

An important place on the waterfront was the Gorton-Pew Machine Shop, where the *Bay State* is tied up. Astern is the three-masted schooner *Marne*, built in Essex for freighting and sold to Newfoundland.

Burnham's shears. The vessel was completely outfitted by E. L. Rowe and Co. Her sails were made by this firm. Her forecastle was 39.3 feet long. The *Bay State* proved to be a fair sailer, especially running before the wind.

The *Bay State* sailed on her maiden trip halibuting, in command of Capt. Norman A. Ross, one of Gloucester's great mariners on May 29, 1913. She returned with her maiden fare of 18,000 pounds halibut on July 10, 1913. The fish were caught on Grand Bank. Capt. Ross reported the vessel worked well, but difficulty was experienced with the oil which continually bothered the pistons.

The *Bay State*, Capt. Norman Ross, landed the first fare of halibut at the new South Boston Fish Pier on March 31, 1914. (The pier opened the previous day.) This fare consisted of 40,000 pounds halibut, taken on Grand Bank. The *Bay State* left the bank on Friday, March 27th at 8 p.m. and she sighted Thacher's at 11 p.m. on Monday, March 30th. (1000 miles in three days).

Capt. Ross remained in command of the *Bay State* until August 1914, when she was taken over by Capt. Archie MacLeod, formerly in the schooner *John Hays Hammond*.

Capt. Archie arrived from Quero with his first trip on September 17, 1914, hailing for 20,000 pounds halibut, 80,000 fresh, 12,000 salt cod.

Capt. MacLeod sailed in the *Bay State* halibuting until October 1915, when he took over his new schooner *Catherine*. (Incidentally 35 halibuters sailed out of Gloucester in 1915.)

One of these trips in August 1915, while in command of Capt. MacLeod proved very eventful. Howard Feener, one of the *Bay State's* crew, was drowned in the Gulf of St. Lawrence. On a calm day in some unknown way, Feener disappeared out of his dory. It was thought he probably fell and hit his head on the dory. He was a native of Liverpool, Nova Scotia, and 28 years old.

On this same trip Angus (Hungry) McEachern and Jim McNeil went astray in the fog and six days later were picked up 145 miles off Cape Race, Newfoundland, by the liner *Ormidale*. They were landed at Montreal, Canada. The men while astray had only a few biscuits to eat.

This was Jim McNeil's second experience in being astray. In September, 1912, Jim and Capt. Tom Flannagan, his dorymate, went astray from schooner *Conqueror* on Georges, and were later picked up.

Capt. Charles Goodick, a Sandy Point, Nova Scotia boy, was the next skipper of the *Bay State*. He had her haddocking during the winter of 1915–16, shacking, during the summer of 1916 and haddocking the winter of 1916–17.

In August, 1917, the *Bay State* was sold to Capt. Lemuel Spinney, who in turn sold her in October of that year to the Atlantic Coast Co.

The Gorton-Pew Fisheries Co. of Gloucester, bought the vessel shortly after and a 100-horsepower Fairbanks-Morse oil engine was installed.

Capt. Henry Larkin now took over command of the *Bay State*, and this great fisherman made a wonderful record in her. Capt. Larkin was skipper from February 1918 to March 1921, haddocking and shacking. In 1918, he stocked $109,578. In 1919, $73,881, and in 1920 he stocked $76,122, a remarkable record.

While in command of Capt. Larkin, one of The *Bay State's* crew, Simon Goodwin, 50 years old, dropped dead in his dory while hauling trawls off of Isaacs Harbor, Nova Scotia.

Capt. Jeff Thomas was skipper of the *Bay State* from April, 1921 to March, 1922, halibuting and haddocking, stocking $45,222. In August 6, 1921, the *Bay State* in command of Capt. Thomas, arrived from Grand Bank with 40,000 lbs. halibut and 55,000 lbs. salt cod. The halibut was sold to the Interstate Cold Storage at Rockport. I had the pleasure of making the trip to Rockport in the *Bay State*. She steamed right up to the Cold Storage wharf, where the trip was taken out. I wonder how many folks can remember the *Bay State*, taking out her trip of halibut at Rockport? It seemed odd indeed to see a big fishing schooner steaming up Rockport harbor.

Capt. Emery Doane, one of Capt. Jeff Thomas' crew, took command of the *Bay State* for one trip in March, 1922. Capt. Fred Thompson was the skipper in 1922 halibuting stocking $34,844. Capt. Chris Gibbs was in command in November, 1922 and Capt. Charles Goodick in December, 1922. Capt. Ralph Jensen took over in 1923–24 halibuting and haddocking. The summer of 1925, Capt. Eric Carlson was skipper. The winter of 1925–26, Capt. Leo Doucett, took over haddocking and stocked $28,569. From March, 1927 to October, 1927, Capt. Doucett stocked $44,585 halibuting. Capt. Horton Mason was the *Bay State's* last skipper.

Felix Boudreau was washed overboard in November 1925. He was a native of Nova Scotia. Capt. Leo Doucett was skipper at the time.

The end of the *Bay State* came on December 13, 1927. The vessel in command of Capt. Horton Mason, stranded on the bar at Liverpool, Nova Scotia and became a total loss. The *Bay State* was trying to make port in a heavy southeaster. The southeast wind sent her high over the bar and she soon began to break up. One side was battered out. She was valued at $25,000. The *Bay State* at the time of her loss, had 12,000 fresh fish on board.

Capt. Norman Ross, one of the great mariners, who carved a name for himself in the pages of Gloucester's history, passed away January 30, 1939. He was a native of Riverside, Guysboro County, Nova Scotia, and was 68 years old.

Capt. Norm, big, powerful, capable and well-liked, commanded some of our finest vessels including the *Lewis H. Giles, Golden Rod, Veda M. McKown, Monarch, B. A. Smith, Elsie, Kineo,* and many others. In his late days Capt. Ross commanded many large schooner yachts including the *Zodiac* and *Blue Dolphin.* In the *Zodiac,* he was a participant in the ocean race of 1928 for the King's Cup. Capt. Ross engaged in most branches of the fisheries, but was at his best seining and the Newfoundland herring trade, in which he had no superior.

Owen Lantz, builder of the *Bay State,* was a native of Mahone Bay, Nova Scotia. He located in Essex in 1901. His first job was building the stem of the big fisherman *Massachusetts* at the Oxner and Story yard. Lantz took over the John Bishop yard at Vincent Cove, Gloucester, in April 1912. There he built many fine vessels, including the *Elsie G. Silva, Bay State, Lucia, Bettina,* etc. He moved to Essex in 1917, and there, at the old Oxner and Story yard, built schooners *Rush, Yukon, and Florence,* and several three-masters. Owen Lantz died at Gloucester in October 1956 at the age of eighty-five.

Gross tons, 159; net tons, 109; length, 112.7 feet; breadth, 25.4 feet; depth, 12.3 feet. Mainmast, deck to cap, 78 feet; foremast, 71 feet; main boom, 65 feet; main gaff, 37 feet; mastheads, 12 feet.

This pretty little vessel starred in some of the best schooner sailing pictures ever taken, in the author's opinion. The schooner was the *Shirley C.*, previously named the *Pilgrim*, originally christened *Leonora Silveira*, shown in Boston Harbor with a man climbing the rigging. The film was *The World in His Arms*.

Leonora Silveira

BEAUTIFUL SAILING IN THE MOVIES / 1912–1951

Schooner *Leonora Silveira*, one of the beauties of the great Portuguese fleet of the past, lived three full lives as the *Leonora Silveira, Pilgrim, and Shirley C.*; a vessel that came back from the sands of Cape Cod and the rugged shores of Cape Breton to finally round out her life as a "movie queen."

Schooner *Leonora Silveira* was a handsome round-bowed vessel of the semi-knockabout type with tall spars, short bowsprit and a good sail spread. Fishermen called her a big little vessel. She was named for the daughter of her skipper, Capt. John Silveira, who was one of the owners. Boston was her port of registry. The new craft was similar in model and appearance to the schooners *Progress*, *Russell*, and *Ralph Brown*.

The *Leonora Silveira* was built during the winter of 1911–12 at Arthur D. Story's yard in Essex. She was christened by Miss Leonora Silveira, launched on April 5, 1912 and towed to Gloucester to be rigged, by the tug *Mariner*. The fine new vessel sailed from Gloucester on her maiden trip haddocking on May 7, 1912 in command of Capt. Silveira. With all her colors flying she presented a handsome appearance as she sailed out of the harbor. She arrived in Boston with her maiden fare of 62,000 lbs. fresh fish on May 22, 1912.

Capt. Silveira, who was one of our fine Portuguese mariners, did well in the *Leonora*, remaining in command about nine years, haddocking and shacking.

A 100 horsepower gasoline engine was installed about 1918.

On October, 1921, Capt. Laurance Lawler took over command of the *Leonora*, haddocking. On November 2, 1921, the vessel while bound to Boston market with 40,000 lbs. fresh fish struck on Peaked Hill Bar, Cape Cod in a raging fifty-mile gale. Three of her crew, Mike Clark, Charles Langer, and Esau Manuel, volunteered to go for help. They left the vessel in a dory, but the little craft upset when it hit the sand, spilling its occupants into the sea. They made land, however, and set out for Provincetown for help. Meanwhile, Capt. Lawler and the remainder of the crew took to the rigging of the vessel, where they were forced to cling for their lives while heavy seas pounded across the deck.

One of the crew, Sylvine E. Muise, lost his grip and was swept into the sea and drowned.

The wrecked craft was sighted by the beach patrol and the crew taken off in a breeches buoy by the combined crews of the Highland and Peaked Hill stations.

The body of the unfortunate man, Sylvine Muise, was picked up a few days later and his body was sent home to Sluice Point near Tusket, Nova Scotia. He was 27 years old.

The *Leonora Silveira* was purchased from the insurance company by Capt. Ben Pine of Gloucester. Capt. Pine and his men filled the craft with barrels of all kinds, more than five hundred filling the holds, cabin and forecastle. Tugs then pulled her into deep water and she was towed to Gloucester. Her keel was gone and she was found to be badly strained. The *Leonora* was lucky indeed, as few vessels ever escaped from this dreaded region.

Capt. Mike Clark, a member of the crew of the wrecked vessel, was still with us as this was written.

Capt. Pine renamed the vessel *Pilgrim* and her second life got underway. Many skippers commanded the craft, in all branches of the fisheries, while she was owned by Capt. Pine. Only sails were used for a year and a half. In 1922 Capt. Dan Nelson had her halibuting. Capt. John McInnis, halibuting in 1923. In 1924 Capts. John McInnis, Bob Porper, and Dan Nelson were her skippers. In 1926 Capt. Waldo Carrigan had her seining. Capts. Dexter Goodwin and Albert Grimes had her halibuting in 1927. Capt. Val O'Neil, halibuting 1930–31–32. Capts. Cecil Moulton and Jack Grant commanded her in 1933 and Capt. Moulton had her halibuting in 1934.

Capts. Harry Gillie, Ed Lasley, Forman Spinney, Chris Gibbs, also commanded the *Pilgrim* at various times.

While in command of Capt. John McInnis, a 60 horsepower oil engine was installed in 1923.

One of our great deeds of heroism took place while the vessel was commanded by Capt. Chris Gibbs. In February 1930 she was at anchor during a raging gale on Green Bank.

A big sea hit, sweeping Jimmy Dober, one of the crew, overboard. Tom Cove, a shipmate, immediately jumped in with a buoy line tied to his waist. Two hundred fifty fathoms of line had almost run out when Cove reached Dober, who was held afloat by the air in his oilskins. He was knocked unconscious when he went over the side. Cove was almost cut in two when the men were hauled back to the vessel. It was difficult to get them over the rail.

Oldtimers still talk of this brave deed and of the remarkable circumstances that Cove was a short man and Dober a big six-footer. Tommy Cove received a Livingstone Medal for his bravery.

Arthur Carter and Jack Hanrahan, two members of the crew at the time, were still with us in 1972. Hanrahan received a broken leg when the sea hit the *Pilgrim*.

In May 1934 the *Pilgrim*, in command of Capt. Cecil Moulton, ran ashore at North Sydney, Cape Breton, and was given up as a total loss. She was stricken off the American Register. But the Canadians went to work on her, floated her and sold her to Twillingate, Newfoundland.

She began her third life as the schooner *Shirley C.* and was used for years in the Labrador fishery.

In August 1951 the *Shirley C.* was chartered by Universal-International Motion Picture Studios for use in the movie *The World In His Arms*, starring Gregory Peck. The vessel, whose tall spars and bowsprit were still intact, was refitted with topmasts at Lunenburg, Nova Scotia. The *Shirley C.*, in company with a Lunenburg vessel, was used in many scenes shot off Lunenburg. The sailing scenes in this movie were some of the most beautiful ever taken.

After her work in the movie was finished the *Shirley C.*, in command of her owner, Capt. William Hancock, sailed for North Sydney, Cape Breton, where she took on a load of coal for Wesleyville, Newfoundland. Her engine failed off St. Pierre, and on October 21, 1951, she grounded and sank, becoming a total loss. The crew landed at St. Pierre. The old *Leonora Silveira* had finally gone to her last resting place.

Capt. John Silveira died August 29, 1948, at the age of seventy-four. He was a native of Pico, Azores. He commanded many fine vessels, including the *Flora Sears, Leonora Silveira,* and *A. Piatt Andrew* (built 1922).

Mrs. Leonora Silveira Goodick, namesake of the vessel, still resided in Gloucester in 1972.

Gross tons, 107; net tons, 52; length, 94.3 feet; breadth, 23.4 feet; depth, 11.4 feet. Original spars: mainmast (deck to cap), 73 feet; foremast, 65 feet; main topmast, 43 feet; fore topmast, 39 feet; main gaff, 42.5 feet; main boom, 63 feet; fore boom, 24 feet; bowsprit, outboard, 21 feet; leech of mainsail, 75 feet; mastheads, 12 feet.

A very impressive looking vessel, the *Catherine*, with a reputation for being great in sailing off a lee shore. Here she is on her maiden trip.

Catherine

EVERYTHING ABOUT HER WAS BIG /
1915–1933

Everything about the schooner *Catherine* was big. She was the biggest knockabout fishing schooner out of Gloucester. She carried a big crew, spread a big sail area, was a big producer of big fish and was commanded by a man big in heart, courage, character, and ability, Capt. Archie A. MacLeod.

The *Catherine* was built by Arthur D. Story at Essex during the summer and fall of 1915 and launched on October 8, 1915. She was modeled by Mr. Story off the schooner *Bay State*, but lengthened out in the bow and given more sheer. The *Bay State*, incidentally, was designed by Thomas McManus. The *Catherine* was named after Capt. Archie MacLeod's mother and wife.

She was a beautiful, big vessel, with a long overhanging knockabout bow and graceful stern. She had the longest forecastle of any Gloucester fisherman, 53 feet. She carried 12 and 13 double dories. Her cost was $16,500. The *Catherine* was an impressive vessel. I can remember her when I was a youngster. She seemed to loom up over the other vessels, with her tall spars and black mastheads.

Catherine's owners were Capt. MacLeod, who owned 8/16, Capt. Fred Thompson, 4/16, Gorton-Pew Fisheries, 3/16, and the Atlantic Maritime Co., 1/16. Later Capt. MacLeod bought out the other shares, making him the sole owner.

The *Catherine* sailed on her maiden trip haddocking November 4, 1915, and arrived at Boston on December 6 with a dandy fare of 150,000 fresh fish, consisting mostly of cod, taken off Scateri. The maiden stock was $3100 with a share of $53 each for her crew of 26. From November 4, 1915 to May 6, 1916, her haddocking stock was $28,364, with a share of $539, a fine start for the new vessel.

The *Catherine* went halibuting summers and haddocking winters. She probably brought in more big halibut trips than any other vessel out of this port. Some of her greatest achievements were as follows: in the year 1918 her total stock, halibuting and haddocking, was $123,000. In 1922, she landed 425,000 lbs. of halibut; in 1923, 388,000 lbs. of halibut, and that year she was high liner of the fleet.

On March 8, 1927 she arrived at Boston with 120,000 halibut, stocking $15,900. She was gone three weeks on this trip. In August, 1929, she landed a trip of 115,000 halibut at Boston. In May, 1930, a dandy fare of 90,000 halibut was landed at Boston, stocking $11,450 with a share of $247. On September 6, 1932, she landed at the Producers Fish Co., Gloucester, 120,000 lbs. of halibut. This was the largest halibut trip at Gloucester in many years. She pulled in to the wharf shortly before 10 a.m. and the trip was out before 6 p.m.—208 boxes of 500 lbs. each were shipped.

A 100 horsepower auxiliary oil engine was installed in the *Catherine* in 1921, and later this was changed to a 250 horsepower crude oil engine.

The *Catherine* was a great sailer, especially in heavy weather. She could stand up with the best of them and was probably the fastest of all knockabout fishermen. At one time she met the great knockabout *Arethusa* in command of Capt. Josh Stanley and gave her a trimming. I have been informed by Capt. MacLeod that the *Catherine* was a great vessel for clawing off a lee shore, and he said that "Wherever you pointed her, she would go."

Catherine during her career took part in three rescues at sea. In December, 1916, off the Nova Scotia coast, she came upon the sinking Nova Scotia two-master *Lena F. Oxner*, and took her crew off with great difficulty, the rescue made in one of *Catherine's* dories. The *Oxner*, bound to Halifax from New York with a cargo of coal, sank shortly after the rescue. The survivors were landed at Boston on January 2, 1917.

On December 22, 1918, she towed into Liverpool, Nova Scotia, the helpless and battered French yawl, *Quo Vadis*. The yawl, bound to St. Pierre from Martinique with a cargo of salt and with a crew of Caribbeans, was found drifting helpless and storm wracked, and her crew was suffering from cold and exposure. One of her crew was dead in the cabin.

In August, 1929, she came upon the British tanked *Mina Brea* that was on fire 20 miles off Canso, Nova Scotia. The crew of the tanker was picked up in two lifeboats by the *Catherine*. Capt. MacLeod stood by the burning tanker for 24 hours, and then he transferred the rescued men to a Nova Scotian vessel. The burning tanker was later towed into the Strait of Canso by another vessel.

The *Catherine* was very fortunate in loss of life. No men were ever lost in dories, but two men were swept from her deck and lost.

One of these men, Peter Peterson, was swept to his death on May 9, 1917, near Brazil Buoy, off Barrington, Nova Scotia.

Albert Kenney, native of Bay of Bulls, Newfoundland, fell overboard and drowned off Boston Lightship February 23, 1917.

The mighty *Catherine* met her doom in 1933. Bound to Canso, Nova Scotia, for harbor, she piled up on Bald Rock Shoal at the entrance of Canso harbor on December 31, 1933. The crew of 29 men left the schooner in nine dories, and after bucking heavy drift ice for three hours landed at Canso. The *Catherine*, soon after the last men had left, toppled over and the galley stove, in which a roaring fire was burning, because of the intense cold, upset. The flames licked hungrily at the vessel, and finally reached the oil tanks, causing explosion after explosion. On New Year's day the tall mast fell into the sea and she burned to the water's edge. Thus ended one of the finest fishing schooners ever sailing out of Gloucester.

The story of the *Catherine* would not be completed without a few words about Jack Arthur. This grand old veteran of the deep sailed in the *Catherine* during her entire existence. It seemed as if he were part of her. At the time of her loss he was 78 years old and still as able as the best of them. Jack was typical of those great "Prosperity Builders" who gave so much and asked for so little. Well liked, widely known, this native of Liverpool, Nova Scotia, was a fisherman out of Gloucester for nearly sixty years. This type of iron man is slowly fading from the local scene. Jack Arthur passed away on February 15, 1934, just 13 months after *Catherine's* loss.

Capt. Archie passed away in July, 1967, at

the age of 84. He was a native of St. Peters, Cape Breton. He was skipper of some of Gloucester's finest vessels, starting in the schooner *Electric Flash* in 1910. Also the *Agnes, John Hays Hammond, Hortense, Louise R. Silva, Georgianna, Bay State, Gertrude L. Thebaud, Dawn, Arthur D. Story and Marjorie Parker.*

He will go down in the history of the Gloucester fisheries as the last halibuting and dory trawling skipper to sail from this port. He was one of the great halibut skippers of the past, and there were many of them, including Capts. Robert Porper, Bob Wharton, Jack McKay, Jerome McDonald, Tommy Bohlin, Little Dan McDonald, Andrew McKenzie, Dick Wadding, Fred Upshal, Del Nickerson, Peter Dunsky, Charlie Colson, John Stream, Frank Stream, Jack Carroll, Jim Mason, Carl Olson, Iver Carlson, Chris Gibbs, Charles Flygare, Albert Flygare, and Lemuel Spinney.

For those who followed the halibut fishing there was no mystery attached to the tides and bergs and great ice fields of the Funks and Baccalieu; no terror to the fogs of the Grand Bank; the sudden gales on Quero and in the Gully with the "Graveyard of the Atlantic," Sable Island, under their lee. These were old stories to them.

It is fitting that no finer man and greater skipper should carry the honor of being the "last of the old school," Capt. Archie A. MacLeod.

Gross tons, 159; net tons, 103; length, 120.6 feet; breadth, 25.2 feet; depth, 12.4 feet. Spar measurements: mainmast (deck to cap), 78 feet; foremast (deck to cap), 72.5 feet; main topmast, 47 feet; fore topmast, 42 feet; main boom, 77 feet; fore boom, 27.5 feet; main gaff, 46 feet; mainmast head, 13.5 feet.

This big crew on the *Elsie G. Silva* worked for the fun of it; she was racing in a contest off Gloucester to pick a schooner to take the place of the lost *Esperanto* in a race to be sailed in Canadian waters.

Elsie G. Silva

A PRETTY PORTUGUESE KNOCKABOUT / 1915–1927

Schooner *Elsie G. Silva* was one of the fastest and prettiest vessels of the great Portuguese fleet of the past.

The *Elsie Silva* was built for Capt. Manuel Silva and others of Gloucester by Owen Lantz of Vincent Cove. She proved to be the last big craft of her type built in Gloucester.

Capt. Silva had done well in his schooner *Clara Silva* but a larger craft was needed. The *Elsie G.* made a splendid addition to the fast growing Portuguese fleet. She was a knockabout, taken from the lines of the schooner *Adeline*, which was a Capt. Tom McManus design.

The *Elsie Silva* had a very straight sheer, with plenty of overhang to her bow and stern, which gave her a handsome appearance. The length of her forecastle was 33.4 feet. She carried a good spread of canvas.

Launching day came on June 28, 1915, and in the forenoon of that day, little Elsie G. Silva, daughter of Capt. Silva, smashed a bottle of champagne on the bow of the new craft as she made her initial dip into the waters of Vincent Cove.

The *Elsie G. Silva* in command of Capt. Manuel Silva sailed on her maiden trip shacking on July 23, 1915. She arrived at Boston 12 days later on August 4th with a splendid fare of 110,000 lbs. fresh fish and 3,000 lbs. halibut. Capt. Silva certainly started the new craft well.

The *Elsie G.* was commanded most of her career by Capt. Silva, haddocking (single dory) and shacking, fishing mostly on the Shore and Quero, Brown's and Western banks.

Capt. Elroy Prior, one of Gloucester's great mariners, took the *Elsie Silva*, Cape Shore seining in May, 1924. She proved to be the last vessel commanded by this great skipper. During the seining season of 1925, Capt. John McKinnon, another of our great mackerel skippers, took over the helm.

Loss of life was small in the career of the *Elsie Silva*. In April, 1924, the vessel arrived at Sandy Point, Nova Scotia, and reported that one of her crew had been drowned at sea. John Zinch, 40 years old and a native of North Sydney, Cape Breton, lost his life by the capsizing of his dory.

Another of the *Silva*'s crew came very near to having his name added to the long list of "Gloucester fishermen lost at sea." On August 6, 1918, a vessel arrived in Gloucester with Charles Fernandez, one of the *Elsie Silva*'s crew who had been picked up at sea after being

astray ten days. Fernandez had a hard struggle for his life and had been ten days in his dory with barely anything to eat or drink when he was sighted on August 4th. All he had in his dory when he went astray was a small bottle of water and this was soon exhausted during the long vigil of his first few days of his trying experience. He had a few matches in his pocket and managed to start a fire in the bottom of his dory and with this he cooked a haddock. It came up rough several times during the ten days and more than once the little dory narrowly escaped being swamped in the heavy sea.

Fernandez was pretty badly used up when he was rescued and the chances were that he could not have held out much longer.

It is certainly remarkable what our sturdy fishermen of the past went through to earn their living from the sea. Yes, in those days we didn't have to look elsewhere for heroes, we had plenty of them here.

I believe Charles Fernandez holds the record of being astray the longest of any single dory fisherman from Gloucester. Just think of it, ten long days lost at sea and all alone at that!

An auxiliary gasoline engine was installed in 1918.

The Portuguese of Gloucester and Massachusetts Bay always kept their vessels in tiptop shape. They were always well painted and the standing and running rigging and equipment were frequently overhauled to keep them in the best of condition. These industrious people took great pride in their vessels, especially in their sailing qualities and there was always keen rivalry among the fleet. Many friendly brushes were sailed from their home ports to the fishing grounds or on the return trip to market.

The *Elsie Silva* was considered one of the flyers of the Portuguese fleet. In December, 1916, Capt. Silva reported the vessel made the run from the Graves Light to Eastern Point in one hour, 10 minutes.

The *Elsie Silva*, Capt. Manuel Silva, entered in the elimination race off Gloucester on October 12, 1921, to select a successor to the lost *Esperanto*. At the starting gun she was far to leeward and made a poor getaway. She was hopelessly outclassed by the schooners *Elsie*, *Ralph Brown* and *Arthur James*.

Capt. Silva turned his attention to halibut in the fall of 1921. The Portuguese did not usually engage in this branch of the fisheries. On October 5th of that year, he landed at Gloucester a fine fare of 45,000 lbs. halibut, 10,000 salt fish, stocking $7,522 with a share of $186. The fish were taken on Quero.

The *Elsie Silva* had her share of mishaps. During the night of June 22, 1920, the *Elsie Silva*, Capt. Manuel Silva, and the *Natalie Hammond*, Capt. Charles Colson (Blossom), grounded in a dense fog in Gloucester Harbor. The *Hammond* grounded on Pavilion Beach about fifty yards off shore and the *Silva* struck the rocks close inshore on the western side of the canal. If she had been a few yards to the eastward she would have sailed right up the Annisquam River.

The unusual sight of two big vessels hard aground so close to each other attracted many people to Western Avenue, but most of the time the fog hung so thick it was almost impossible to see more than the bare outlines of the stranded craft. Both went aground about the same time. The *Silva* was in the more dangerous position.

The *Natalie Hammond* was bound from Boston with 50,000 lbs. fresh fish, and the *Silva* was bound here direct with 130,000 lbs. fresh fish. The *Hammond* was floated by tugs on the next tide. The *Elsie Silva* was freed without assistance, the engine being used as soon as flood tide floated the craft to back her into deep water.

On January 14, 1926, the *Elsie Silva*, while jogging on Georges, was hove down by a sudden northeast squall. Both masts were snapped off and the main boom broken, besides starting her stern. The foremast snapped off at the deck and toppled over the port side. The mainmast, left without stays for support, soon followed, crashing down across the stern and listing the vessel over. Capt. Silva and his crew worked feverishly and cleared the rigging, let the masts free and the craft righted herself. The engine was started and the vessel then headed for the nearest land, which happened to be Plymouth, 285 miles away, reaching there on January 18.

On the way into Plymouth she had to push through considerable floating ice which broke off one of the propeller blades. The disabled craft reached Gloucester in tow of the Boston tug *Juno* on January 20th. She was re-rigged with new pole masts (without topmasts).

Thirteen months later the *Elsie G. Silva* went to her doom on the sand bars of Cape Cod. On the night of February 14, 1927, she struck a sand bar one mile south of Pamet River, Cape Cod, during a blinding northeast snow storm. Fifteen of her crew left in dories and rowed 6 hours for 15 miles before they were rescued by Wood End Coast Guardsmen.

Capt. Silva and five of his crew remained on the stranded vessel until forced to leave in a dory. They reached the Pamet River Station safely.

The *Elsie Silva* was pounded to pieces. Within four or five hours there wasn't a piece of her left. At the time of her loss, she was bound to Boston with 80,000 lbs. fresh fish.

My friend Harry Eustis, veteran fisherman still with us in 1972, vividly recalled this wreck of the *Elsie Silva*, as he was one of her crew at the time.

Leander Williams, another of her crew at the time of the disaster, was twice a wreck victim in less than a year. Williams was one of the crew of the schooner *Helja Silva* when she was lost off Shelburne, Nova Scotia, during the fall of 1926.

Capt. Manuel Silva, long one of the top-notchers of the Portuguese fleet, died at Gloucester in May 1956 at the age of eighty-two. He was a native of the Azores. Some of his commands were the *Clara G. Silva*, named for his wife; *Elsie G. Silva* and *Mildred Silva*.

Mrs. Elsie G. Silva Donnellan passed away in Gloucester in August 1961.

Gross tons, 104; net tons, 59; length, 101.9 feet; breadth, 22.8 feet; depth, 10.3 feet.

One of a kind was the *Gaspe*, with her whaleback bow and round steamer-style stern with rail.

Gaspe

THREE-MASTED FREIGHTER, MOVIE WHALER AND RUM-RUNNER / 1917–1930

The three-masted schooner *Gaspe* was used as a freighter and brought in some of the largest cargoes of salt fish ever brought to this port by a Gloucester vessel. She was a vessel with a most interesting career: as a fish freighter, movie vessel and rum runner, sailing under three names and four flags.

Schooner *Gaspe* was built by Arthur D. Story in Essex during the spring and summer of 1917 and launched on July 26 of that year. Her owners were the Gorton-Pew Fisheries Co.

The *Gaspe* presented an able, unique appearance and made a splendid addition to the Gloucester fleet. Originally intended for a steam trawler, she was probably the only vessel of her type ever built. She was designed by Capt.

J. D. S. Nickerson (Doane) who was in charge of rigging for Gorton-Pew. The vessel was named for the famous Gaspe peninsula in Quebec.

The *Gaspe* was a three-master with topmasts. She had a raised forecastle deck forward (similar to the whaleback bow used on the modern draggers), with no bowsprit. Her quarter or poop deck was raised, with a rail around it. The cabin was much higher than the usual fisherman style. The stern was rounded like a steamer, and she was painted black with white rail and trimmings. Two 100 horsepower crude oil engines were carried for auxiliary power. She had a crew of nine men.

The *Gaspe* sailed on her maiden trip to Labrador and Newfoundland for a cargo of salt fish on September 7, 1917, Capt. Richard Wadding, one of our great old mariners, was skipper.

The *Gaspe* arrived back in Gloucester on October 20, 1917, from Newfoundland ports with 960,000 pounds salt cod, consigned to her owners. This was the largest cargo of salt fish ever brought to Gloucester by a local vessel up to this time.

The *Gaspe* certainly brought in some big cargoes. On January 26, 1918, she arrived from Newfoundland with 400,000 pounds salt cod and 433 barrels salt herring; on May 10, 1918, she landed a cargo of 800,000 pounds salt cod at Gloucester. On January 27, 1919, she arrived from Newfoundland with 780,000 pounds salt cod.

In her role as a fish freighter, the *Gaspe* took salt fish cargoes, picked up in Newfoundland and the Canadian Provinces, to many ports along the Atlantic coast. On June 13, 1919, she sailed from Gloucester to Sweden with a load of barrelled herring.

Many fine skippers sailed in command of the big Gaspe, including Capts. Dick Wadding, Gus Dunsky, Forman Pothier, Wallace Parsons and Henry Atwood.

Gloucester received a big scare on November 8, 1918, when the *Gaspe*, Capt. Gus Dunsky, arrived from Provincial ports with a cargo of salt fish and one of her crew, George McLean, with a case of smallpox. The crew was vaccinated and the *Gaspe* towed to quarantine on the Pancake Grounds off the breakwater where she remained a week and then was released. The vessel had landed two of her crew at Halifax, Nova Scotia, supposed to be suffering from influenza. She was fumigated and allowed to clear, but after she left, the illness of the two men was pronounced as smallpox.

In February, 1922, the *Gaspe* was chartered for use in the making of the whaling movie *Down to the Sea in Ships* (silent version). In command of Capt. James A. Tilton, old time whaling captain, she sailed from Gloucester on

February 4, 1922, for New Bedford, where she was fitted, taking on apparatus and equipment for a real whaling voyage south. Wooden davits with whaleboats were fitted on her sides, a crow's-nest or lookout on her foremast and in fact the *Gaspe* looked like a real old New Bedford whaler.

The *Gaspe* returned to Gloucester on May 1, 1922 after a very successful voyage in Caribbean waters. Many movie scenes were taken and four whales were caught, one of them a big fellow yielding 100 barrels of whale oil.

The Gloucester career of the *Gaspe* came to a close when she was sold by Gorton-Pew Co. to parties in Palermo, Sicily, in July, 1923. She sailed from Gloucester on her long voyage across the Atlantic, flying the Italian flag, on August 2, 1923. Capt. Henry M. Atwood was skipper and Capt. Fred Thompson mate.

It wasn't long, however, before the *Gaspe* was back off Cape Ann, this time as a rum runner and known as the *Beatrice*, flying the French flag. The *Beatrice* became one of the most notorious rum carriers on Rum Row off the New England coast. According to my records, the *Beatrice* was listed among the rum runners off this coast more than any other vessel.

It was reported in December, 1925, that Capt. Charles Lemeros of Fecamp, France, skipper of the *Beatrice*, took his own life by jumping overboard off Cape Cod. The mate, Steve Burranger, brought the vessel into Lunenburg, Nova Scotia.

The *Beatrice* was later sold to John R. Burdock of Belleoram, Newfoundland, in 1928, and renamed *Chapel Point*, after a point of land near Belleoram. She was now flying the British flag (her fourth) and was used as a fish freighter and rum runner. Capt. Kenneth Fudge, one of the famous Fudge brothers of Belleoram, was skipper.

The career of the old *Chapel Point*, ex-*Beatrice*, ex-*Gaspe*, came to an end on December 9, 1930, when she was destroyed by fire off of Cape Colonet, Mexico.

Capt. Forman Pothier, one of the *Gaspe's* skippers, lost his life in the wreck of the fourmaster *Grace Pendleton* at the mouth of the Elbe River, Germany, on November 16, 1923. He was a native of Yarmouth County, Nova Scotia.

Capt. Jonathan D. S. Nickerson, designer of the *Gaspe*, died in Gloucester on April 16, 1932 at the age of 75. He was a native of Marblehead. Capt. Nickerson came to Gloucester when he was nine years old. At 18 he was a fishing skipper. One of his best known commands was the schooner *Herald of the Morning*. When he retired, he went into the rigging business and also vessel designing. Some noted vessels this fine old mariner designed were the schooners *Killarney*, *Corinthian* and *Gaspe* and the steam trawlers *Walrus* and *Seal*. Capt. Doane made small miniature models in his later days.

Gross tons, 262; net tons, 176; length, 122.6 feet; breadth, 28.8 feet; depth, 10.4 feet. Original spar measurements (the three masts were called fore, main and mizzen; the sails on the mizzen, or third mast, were called spanker sails); foremast (deck to cap), 57 feet; mainmast (deck to cap), 62 feet; mizzen mast (deck to cap), 64 feet; fore boom, 27 feet; main boom, 27 feet; spanker boom, 46 feet; fore gaff, 27 feet; topmasts, 39 feet; mastheads, 10 feet; length of forecastle deck, 24 feet; length of poop deck, 50 feet.

A schooner that lived to become an exhibit at the Mystic Seaport Museum in Connecticut is the *L. A. Dunton*. This is how she looked when she was fishing out of Grand Bank, Newfoundland, in the 1940's. Her bowsprit had been removed, her masts slenderized to poles with no provisions for topmasts, her stern squared, a wheelhouse added.

L. A. Dunton

STILL AFLOAT AT MYSTIC MUSEUM / 1925–

Very few of the old American sailing fishing schooners are still in existence. Those that are are mostly museum vessels in ports along the coast. The *L. A. Dunton* is located at Mystic Seaport, Mystic, Connecticut.

Others are the *Roy M.*, formerly the *American*, now a restaurant at Cape May, New Jersey; the *Lettie G. Howard*, formerly of Beverly, Massachusetts, a floating exhibit at the South Street Seaport Museum in New York City; the *Virginia*, a museum at Pensacola, Florida.

The *Carrie B. Welles*, ex-*Seaconnet*, is featured at Sponge-orama tourist attraction, Tarpon Springs, Florida.

The *Adventure* is still in commission as a cruise ship out of Camden, Maine.

The *Ernestine*, ex-*Effie M. Morrissey*, as far as known is still in service in the Cape Verde islands in Europe.

This is the story of Mystic Seaport's *L. A. Dunton*.

Capt. Felix Hogan of Boston sold his schooner *Somerville* to Newfoundland in 1919, and two years later a new vessel was built for him by A. D. Story at Essex. The new vessel was named *L. A. Dunton*, after Louis A. Dunton, a noted sailmaker of Boothbay, Maine, who was one of the stockholders.

The *Dunton* was a fine looking schooner off a Tom McManus design (schooner *Joffre*), with a round bow, good sheer, rather high stern and ample sail spread.

Although built at the time of international fishermen's racing, the *Dunton* was of the conventional type and not classed with the big racing vessels built as contenders.

The *L. A. Dunton* was launched at the Story yard on March 21, 1921. She was towed to Gloucester to be fitted for sea.

At the time of the *Dunton's* debut the big new schooner *Mayflower* was also being fitted for fishing, having been built at the nearby James yard in Essex. The Starling Burgess-designed schooner was built as a contender for the International Cup, and her Boston owners had great hopes for her and gave her plenty of publicity. As it later turned out the great speed of the vessel, and so much publicity, scared the hell out of the American and Canadian committees, with the result she was barred from international competition with the absurd ruling that she was a yacht.

When it came time to sail for the fishing grounds Capt. Henry Larkin of the *Mayflower* and Capt. Hogan of the *Dunton* agreed to a trial race to Nova Scotian ports, where they were to pick up ice and bait.

The trial proved very one-sided, as the smaller *Dunton* was no match against the big speedy *Mayflower*. On the run from Gloucester to Shelburne, Nova Scotia, the *Mayflower* won by seven hours. While at Shelburne, a dance at the Odd Fellows Hall was given in honor of the two new vessels. I have heard much about the fishermen's dances at Shelburne. Sometimes they got a little out of hand, but usually a grand time was had by all. Many of the American crews were relatives and friends of the Shelburne folk.

The second lap of the race, Shelburne to Canso for ice, was also an easy victory for *Mayflower*. The third lap, Canso to the Magdalen Islands in the Gulf of St. Lawrence, where the vessels were to pick up their bait, was won by the *Mayflower* by about ten miles.

I have heard my father speak so much of the Magdalens. It was a long sail from Gloucester, but the vessels usually went there in the spring for bait. The schooners did not go in the harbor; the bait was brought out to them. Sometimes they took two baitings. Sometimes as many as twenty-five or thirty American and Canadian vessels were there at one time.

In October 1922 Capt. Hogan entered the *Dunton* in the elimination races off Gloucester to select a challenger for the International Cup. Again the *Dunton* was badly beaten by the new schooner *Henry Ford*, Capt. Clayton Morrissey. She lost the first race by thirty-seven minutes and the second by thirty-nine minutes. Capt. Hogan knew he had no chance, but always the good sport, said, "The more the merrier."

One of my dearest friends, a fisherman who sailed with Capt. Hogan for some years, told me that the *Dunton* was a good, comfortable fisherman, but she was a very poor sailer. After all, she was not built for racing.

Capt. Hogan used the *Dunton* halibuting summers and haddocking winters. In 1925 an auxiliary crude oil engine of one hundred horsepower was installed.

No lives were ever lost out of the *L. A. Dunton*. Capt. Felix retired from the sea and the *Dunton* lay in the mud of the Atlantic Supply wharf in Gloucester for some time. In 1955 she was sold to Aaron F. Buffett of Grand Bank, Newfoundland. On May 17, 1934, she sailed for her new home port in command of her Newfoundland skipper, Capt. Clarence Williams.

The *Dunton* paid a return visit to Gloucester in 1947 with a cargo of salt herring. While owned in Newfoundland she was rebuilt. Her bowsprit was taken out, short pole spars were put in, her stern was squared off, and a wheelhouse added. One would never recognize the old *L. A. Dunton*.

In 1953 the *Dunton* was halibuting in command of Capt. "Arch" Evans of Grand Bank. In 1955 the vessel was sold to Erik Piercy of Grand Bank, to be used as a coaster.

In 1958 a group was formed called the *L. A. Dunton Associates*, of which I was a member, with hopes of bringing the old vessel back to New England. Edmund F. Moran, a seafarer from East Boston who once had sailed on the *Dunton* and fell in love with her, was the originator of the Associates. For some years Ed Moran kept plugging, and through his efforts the *L. A. Dunton* was purchased in 1963 by the Marine Historical Association, Mystic, Connecticut.

The *Dunton* was brought to Mystic Seaport, where she was again rebuilt and restored nearly to her original appearance. At the seaport she has been one of the main attractions. It is understood that further repairs are to be made on the vessel, and when completed the old *L. A. Dunton* will look like she did on that race to the Magdalens so many years ago.

Aaron F. Buffett, Newfoundland, owner of the *L. A. Dunton*, died in January 1948 at the age of seventy-one. He was long connected with the fishing business under the firm name of G. and A. Buffett, Ltd., of Grand Bank, Newfoundland.

Gross tons, 134; net tons, 94; length, 104.3 feet; breadth, 25 feet; depth, 11.6 feet. Mainmast above deck, 75 feet; foremast, 68 feet; maintopmast, 45 feet; foretopmast, 41 feet; mainboom, 74 feet; bowsprit, 18.5 feet (outboard).

The brand new *Henry Ford* bid up on Wingaersheek Beach when a tow line parted as she was being taken around to Gloucester for rigging. No one watched her that night and she floated and drifted close to rocks. Rescued, she sailed very fast, though some observers said she was better on one tack as a consequence of her night on the beach.

Henry Ford

SHE ACTUALLY BEAT THE BLUENOSE / 1922–1928

This story of the *Henry Ford* is dedicated to Dana Story, one of the last Essex shipbuilders, and son of Arthur D. Story, greatest builder of the flying fishermen.

The *Ford* was Dana's favorite vessel, and was one of the famous contenders in the International Fishermen's Races.

The American schooner *Elsie* was defeated in 1921 by the new Canadian schooner *Bluenose*. During the following winter and spring two big vessels were built at Essex with high hopes of bringing the cup back to the United States.

Schooner *Puritan* was built at the James yard and the *Henry Ford* by Arthur D. Story, for Capt. Clayton Morrissey.

The *Ford* was designed by the veteran Capt. Tom McManus. She was a big vessel with spoon bow, an ample beam carried well aft, and a very wide stern. She was a pretty vessel and her very long spars gave her a noble, tall appearance.

Racing fever had struck Gloucester, and the building of the two vessels created much excitement in the old Fish Town.

The owners of the *Ford* were listed as Bessie Morrissey, Frank C. Pearce, F. Wilder Pollard, Jonathan Raymond and Arthur D. Story. Pollard and Raymond were Gloucester summer residents. Her skipper was Capt. Clayton Morrissey, one of Gloucester's great mariners.

The *Henry Ford* was launched on April 11, 1922. She was christened by Miss Winnie Morrissey, daughter of the skipper, before a huge crowd.

The jinx that seemed to follow these racing schooners hung right on to the *Ford*, right from the very start. While towing down the Essex River on her way to Gloucester her tow line snapped and she bid up on the sand at the mouth of the river. Efforts were made to try and float her, but she would not budge. As she was not in a dangerous position it was decided to float her the next day.

With no one to watch her, she floated again at full tide and drifted over on Wingaersheek Beach, close to the rocks near the Hawkes estate. She floated during the night of April 12 and turned over on her port side. For several days on the full tides tugs tried in vain to pull her off. Fears were now beginning to mount as it was thought she would be badly strained.

The *Ford* was finally floated on April 16 by the local tug *Eveleth* and the Boston tugs *Juno* and *Neptune*. She was towed around the Cape

to Gloucester, where she was given a big reception.

She was immediately put on the railways, where it was found she was not seriously damaged. She had won her first battle with the judges. I have been told by oldtimers, however, that after her accident she was one-sided, and sailed better on one tack.

The new schooner was rigged by Harry Christensen and the sails were made by the United Sail Loft.

According to the international rules the *Ford* was over her time in getting away to the fishing grounds. Extra time was granted and the beautiful new vessel sailed on her maiden trip salt banking on June 2, 1922. She was towed out of the harbor by the converted subchaser 247, owned by the designing firm of Burgess and Paine, designers of her rival, *Puritan*.

Then *Henry Ford* arrived in Gloucester August 5 with her maiden fare of 225,000 salt cod. Her skipper and crew were all pleased with the sailing abilities of the new craft. They reported fish scarce, and the trip taken on the Scateri, Grand Bank and Sable Island grounds.

Prior to the *Ford's* arrival there was anxiety in the city because a Canadian vessel had picked up the *Ford's* name-board twelve miles off Canso, Nova Scotia. Capt. Morrissey said the board had been ripped off during a rough spell on August 1 when a sea tore off part of the bulwarks on the starboard side. Losing nameboards was a common experience for these vessels.

In early October 1922, elimination races were held off Gloucester to pick a challenger to race for the International Cup. The *Puritan* was lost on Sable Island in June and Gloucester hopes were now in the *Ford*.

The first race was won by the *Ford* over the Boston schooner *Yankee*, Capt. Mike Brophy, by about sixteen minutes. The fast *Elizabeth Howard*, Capt. Ben Pine, was forced to withdraw with a broken maintopmast head. The schooner *L. A. Dunton*, Capt. Felix Hogan, trailed far astern.

The ballast in the *Ford* was changed, as she seemed sluggish in the first race, and repairs were made to the *Howard*. The *Ford* beat the *Howard* in the second race by five minutes, twenty seconds, and was chosen to meet the Canadian champion, *Bluenose*, Capt. Angus Walters.

The *Ford's* troubles were beginning. All the arguments and confusion that were to haunt the International Races began in this 1922 series.

On the eve of the first race the committee notified Capt. Morrissey his sails, according to the rules, had to be cut about 437 square feet. Imagine . . . a fisherman cutting his sails! Although this meant a delay. Capt. Clayt was game and decided to comply with this absurd rule. A gang of sailmakers worked all night, but the next morning the sails were not quite ready and the first race was delayed. Her crew worker feverishly, bending the big sail as she was being towed out. After the sail was cut it did not reach within four feet of the boom and gaff. No one knew how this would affect her sailing.

The first race started, but the skippers of both craft didn't know the race had been called off, due to lack of wind. There was much confusion, the committee not properly notifying the skippers of the postponement. The vessels sailed on and when they crossed the finish line, with the Ford ahead by about a mile, there was no committee boat. The race had been called off.

This was bad enough, but that night the committee said another eighty feet would have to come off the mainsail. The Ford's crew refused to sail, but after much persuasion by the owners, finally consented to race.

The first official race was sailed on October 23 over a forty-mile course, and the Ford beat the Bluenose a little less than three minutes. The second race went to Bluenose by seven minutes, 23 seconds; the last leg, a dead beat to windward, with Bluenose at her best.

On October 26 the Bluenose won the third and final race by seven minutes, fifty-one seconds. The Ford near the finish carried away her foretopmast head, losing the use of two of her sails. Her chances were gone.

The 1922 races should have ended in a tie. The Ford was like a gull with clipped wings. She proved she had the better of Bluenose running before the wind, but was no match in beating against the wind with the Canadian.

The Henry Ford must have been a tender vessel. During the races she was frequently hove down until the solid water came up to the lee hatch coamings, or about nine feet inboard, and the sheer poles of her rigging eight feet above the deck were buried.

On August 31, 1923, the Henry Ford beat the schooner Elizabeth Howard by fifty seconds, and the new schooner Shamrock of Boston by almost fifteen minutes. The race was sailed off Cape Ann during Gloucester's 300th Anniversary, and raced for the Sir Thomas Lipton Cup. The new schooner Columbia did not compete in this race as she had been damaged in a collision with a French trawler and had been towed into St. Pierre, Miquelon.

When the time came in October 1923 to select a challenger to race for the International Cup the Henry Ford was still out on a trip.

Extra time was granted, and the Henry Ford finally arrived with her trip of fish.

Topmasts were set up and the vessel was hastily prepared to meet the other contenders.

The elimination race was sailed on a Sunday in a very light breeze with the Columbia leading all the way. The vessels did not finish within the time limit but the committee decided that the Columbia would be the American representative. The Ford and the Elizabeth Howard had been badly beaten, but it is my guess that Capt. Morrissey was pretty well fed up with international racing.

To keep up with the times, Capt. Clayt decided to install a hundred horsepower crude oil engine in the Ford, in January 1924. Capt. Morrissey stayed ashore and Capt. Lem Spinney took command, halibuting, in March and April 1924. For the next few years it was halibuting summers and haddocking winters with Capt. Clayt at the wheel.

In 1926 Capt. Steve Post had the Ford a few trips and in March of that year, while under Capt. Post's command, one of her crew, Raymond Babine, was drowned when his dory capsized on Georges. His dorymate, Simon Meuse, was rescued, but Babine was weighted down by his oilskins and boots. He lived in Sluice Point, Nova Scotia, and left his widow and seven children. This, I believe, was the only man lost from the Henry Ford.

Several years passed with no racing, but the Fish Town was still in the grip of racing fever. Capt. Morrissey, meanwhile, still thought his Ford a better vessel than the Columbia. The international committees were still arguing over measurements and rules and were showing little interest in racing.

In October 1926 the Henry Ford met the Columbia in two races in a Fishermen's Open Race sailed off Gloucester for the Frank E. Davis Cup. The first race, sailed on October 11, was won by Columbia, Capt. Ben Pine, by one minute, twenty seconds. It was a close and exciting race, but the Ford was again beaten in windward work.

The second and final race was also won by Columbia in a little under five minutes. This proved to be the last race ever sailed by the Henry Ford. At least her last one was a real fishermen's race, sailed under conditions suited to fishermen.

The unlucky Ford's life ended in 1928. In June of that year, while cruising for halibut off Newfoundland's rugged west coast, during a thick fog, she struck the sunken ledges of the "Whale Back" off Martin's Point. A heavy sea was running and the bottom was pounded out of her. All hands quickly got away from the doomed vessel, saving practically nothing. She slid off the rocks and sank in eleven fathoms, with only her mastheads above water. The crew landed at the settlement of Gull's Marsh, close by.

At the time of her loss she had on board 40,000 pounds halibut. Value of the vessel was $45,000.

The Whale Back was a narrow ridge of rocks about a mile long lying parallel to the coast.

The *Henry Ford* was lost not far from where the Reid-Newfoundland passenger steamer *Elthie* was wrecked nine years previous. In December 1919 she became a total loss on Martin's Point. When this happened there were ninety-eight men on board. They owed their lives to the sagacity of a Newfoundland dog who secured the line thrown from the ship, enabling the rigging of a breeches buoy by which means all were safely brought to land despite the terrible cold and terrific seas pounding the ship.

In the short period of six years, two of the finest fishing schooners that ever sailed out of Gloucester were gone and with them, high hopes and deep pride. One on the treacherous sands of Sable Island, and one on the ugly teeth of the Whale Back.

Gross tons, 155; net tons, 90; overall length, 138 feet; breadth, 26 feet; depth, 12 feet. Mainmast, above deck, 88 feet; foremast above deck, 77 feet; mainboom, 76 feet, maintopmast, 52 feet; bowsprit, outboard, 18 feet; sail area, 9,640 square feet.

Oh what a thrill when she started to heel and go, recalls the author, who was the guest farthest forward in this photograph of the *Puritan's* trial trip more than fifty years ago. His father, Captain Jeff Thomas, was at the wheel. The *Puritan* was *so* fast that she was tricky, and she lived only one hundred and one days.

Puritan

Designed for speed, with the tallest mainmast in the Gloucester fleet, the schooner *Puritan* proved fast, indeed, but she lived only three months and had only one race, and that informal, before she sailed right over the northwest bar of Sable Island, landing a wreck in shallow water.

When the Gloucester schooner *Elsie* was defeated by the Canadian schooner *Bluenose* at Halifax, Nova Scotia, in October, 1921, a group of Cape Ann people got together and formed the Manta Associates. They vowed to have a new vessel built and bring the International Fishermen's Cup back to Gloucester. The associates were named after Philip P. Manta of Boston. Members of this group were Capt. Jeffrey Thomas, his brother, Capt. William H. Thomas, Capt. Robert Wharton, Capt. Charles C. Colson, Capt. James Mason, Philip P. Manta, Marian J. Cooney, Capt. Benjamin Pine, George E. Roberts, Herbert W. Wennerberg, Alexander McDonald, Carmello Capillo. Charles F. Fuller, Charles A. Steele and J. Norman Abbott. Each owned 1/16 of the vessel with the exception of the skipper, Capt. Jeff Thomas, who held a 3/16 share.

W. Starling Burgess, the great yacht designer, was commissioned to draw the lines of the new schooner. Mr. Burgess was a genius in getting the utmost speed out of a vessel without sacrificing in the slightest degree her utility. Schooner *Elizabeth Silsbee* in 1905 and *Mayflower* in 1921 were from his board.

The *Puritan* was launched on March 15, 1922, at the J. F. James & Son Yard in Essex, before a huge crowd.

Her giant spars, made by George E. Thurston, were stepped the next day. Capt. Thomas had placed five dollar gold pieces beneath each mast for good luck. The new vessel was rigged by George E. Roberts. Her sails were made by the United Sail Loft of Gloucester, of which Marian J. Cooney was the manager.

The *Puritan* was a big, handsome schooner with a spoon bow and short bowsprit and very lofty rig. She carried 11 dories and crew of 25 men. She was named after the America's Cup defender in 1885.

Her 89-foot mainmast was the tallest (above deck) of any Gloucester fisherman. Her registered length of 123.9 feet made her the longest fishing schooner out of this port.

Capt. Jeff Thomas, my father, the skipper of the *Puritan*, was one of the greatest sail carriers out of Gloucester. He was schooled by the great skipper Capt. "Marty" Welch, and what these two did not know about sailing a vessel was not worth talking about. Capt. Jeff could drive a vessel for all she was worth but still he never lost a man on a passage. He was a driver, hard worker, and extremely modest. His crews were made up of Gloucester's finest and in those days a skipper had to have a good crew. They were the makings of him. If the *Puritan* had lived, I feel quite sure that the cup would have remained in Gloucester. The combination of the *Puritan* and Jeff Thomas would have been mighty hard to beat.

The *Puritan* proved to be a ghost on the water. It was nothing for this great schooner to reel off 15 knots. She was a real flying fool, tricky and hard to handle. You just could not hold her down. In fact, her own speed carried her to her destruction. She was at her best in heavy weather, but in Capt. Thomas' own words, "any breeze would do."

The *Puritan* sailed on her maiden trip halibuting on April 17, 1922. She was towed out of Harbor Cove by the converted sub-chaser S. C. 247, owned by F. C. Paine, of the firm of Burgess and Paine, the designers. A great send-off was given the new schooner. Whistles screamed from the gill netters and the Cape Ann Cold Storage, and a cannon salute of three shots was fired from Lufkin and Tarr's wharf. Off Ten Pound Island the schooner was let go and she sailed out of the harbor bound for Edgartown for bait. Off the breakwater, the sub-chaser, logging 11 knots, tried to overhaul the *Puritan*, but could not do so. The *Puritan* harbored in Provincetown overnight and next day she continued her trip to Edgartown. Off the Cape she was met by the big Boston schooner *Mayflower*, Capt. J. Henry Larkin, who was itching for a race. The *Mayflower* was soundly beaten. This proved to be the only vessel the *Puritan* had a chance to race.

The *Puritan* arrived in Boston on her maiden trip, May 8, 1922, with 25,000 lbs. of halibut, having been gone three weeks. She stocked $3,200. On the afternoon of May 12, 1922, she sailed on her second trip. A few guests were taken along as far as Thacher's where they were taken off by Mr. Paine's sub-chaser. I was fortunate to be aboard at the time, and I think it was the greatest thrill of my life. Many fine photos were taken of the *Puritan* by Robert W. Phelps from the sub-chaser. She arrived at Boston from her second trip on June 10, 1922 with a fine fare of 40,000 lbs. of halibut and 11,000 lbs. of salt fish, stocking $5,100 with a share of $116.

On the evening of June 16, 1922, a radio concert was given on board at the Gloucester Cold Storage wharf. It was given as a demonstration to vessel owners. The vessel was jammed with people to witness this demonstration. The *Puritan* was the first Gloucester fisherman to be equipped with a radio receiving set.

At about 4:30 p.m. on June 17, 1922, the *Puritan* sailed on her third trip. Capt. William H. Thomas, George E. Roberts and J. Kenneth Ferguson went along to Boothbay, Maine, where bait and ice were taken aboard. Capt. Thomas telephoned that same evening, reporting that *Puritan* sailed from Thacher's to Boothbay in five hours, seven minutes, averaging 14 1/4 knots. I do not believe this record has ever been equalled. She fairly flew over the water.

The next news was a dispatch from William H. Dennis, publisher of the *Halifax Herald*, on June 24, 1922, stating that he had word that the *Puritan* was a total loss on the northwest bar of Sable Island. The fate of her crew was unknown.

The vessel, sailing at 12 knots under full sail, had struck the northwest bar of Sable Island at 7:30 p.m. on June 23, 1922. She sailed right over the bar and landed in shallow water beyond. The rudder jammed up through the wheel box and part of the keel floated up near the vessel. The fog was dense and there was a heavy swell running, with a strong southerly breeze. Capt. Jeff was at the wheel. This vessel was so tricky she had overrun her course by 20 miles. Heavy seas were breaking over her and there was a mad scramble to leave the vessel. The first dory over capsized and Christopher Johnson was drowned. The other occupants of the dory were saved.

Fifteen of the crew got away in dories and headed for the Nova Scotia coast. Capt. Thomas and the seven remaining members decided to make for Sable Island. The skipper and Israel Larkin jumped into a dory. A breaker carried the dory upon the rail of the vessel and the deck wash swept the skipper overboard. Fortunately, another wave swept him back on board. Capt. Jeff and Larkin finally succeeded in getting their dory clear and they joined the other two dories that had left ahead of them. The skipper and his seven men landed on the island and were there for several days when they were taken off and brought home by the Coast Guard cutter *Tampa*.

The 15 survivors who had headed for Nova Scotia were picked up after they had rowed 50 miles by the LaHave schooner Coral Spray, Capt. Roger Wambach. The value of the *Puritan* was $33,000 with outfits.

A poem by J. D. Logan, in memory to the lost *Puritan*, appeared in the *Halifax Herald* in June, 1922, as follows:

To the Puritan

A gallant Ship of Speed that swept the sea,
Fearless, confident, and proud and free!
O hapless Ship of Beauty that had no flaw,
Too soon a prey to Ocean's avid maw.
We sorrow that an envious, ruthless Fate
Marked thee to be the Esperanto's mate;
And meet the self-same, swift unworthy doom
Where Sable's treacherous waters loudly boom!
Had Ocean spared thee and thy gallant crew,
We should have seen thee come into thy due—
Speed champion of the waters, or win fame,
And add new glory to thy Gloucester's name!
But Hearts Courageous still in Gloucester
    dwell;
Their souls are brave, their wills undauntable;
Another "Puritan" will rise at length,
And ride the seas with greater speed and
    strength.

Capt. Jeffrey Thomas died of a heart attack at the wheel of his schooner *Adventure*, 90 miles off Halifax, Nova Scotia, in March, 1934. A native of Arichat, Cape Breton, he was 59 years old. He had been a skipper for 30 years and a commander of 13 vessels.

Everett James, builder of the *Puritan*, passed away January 1, 1936, at the age of seventy-two. A native of Essex, he was the son of John F. James, one of Essex's greatest shipbuilders.

His father took him into the business in 1914 and the firm name was changed to John F. James and Son, which name was held until Everett's death in 1936.

Some of the finest vessels in the New England fleet were built by Everett James, including the schooners *Puritan*, *Oretha F. Spinney*, *Mayflower*, *Governor Marshall*, *Mary Sears*, *Adventure*, *Marechal Foch*, *Radio* and *Falmouth*.

Gross tons, 149; net, 96; length, 123.9 feet; breadth, 25.7 feet; depth, 11.8 feet. Original spar measurements: mainmast (deck to cap), 89 feet; foremast, 77 feet; main topmast, 51 feet; fore topmast, 45 feet; main boom, 75.6 feet; main gaff, 46 feet; fore boom, 31 feet; fore gaff, 31 feet. The leech of her mainsail was 100 feet and total sail area was 8,988 square feet.

No wonder men thrill to the big sailing vessels! In this photograph you're visually aboard the great schooner *Columbia*, close-hauled on the starboard tack, doing about fourteen knots. The occasion is an elimination race with the *Henry Ford* off Gloucester in 1923. The *Columbia* won, and accordingly raced the Canadian *Bluenose*. That race wound up in a snarl characteristic of international fishermen's competition.

Columbia

FAST, FAMOUS AND ILL-FATED /
1923–1927

Schooner *Columbia* was one of Gloucester's most famous fishing schooners. *Columbia* was famous in many ways. She was one of the American contenders in the International Fishermen's Races; she was the last vessel to sail salt fishing from Gloucester; and she carried more men at one time to a watery grave than any other vessel out of this port.

Schooner *Columbia* was built by Arthur D. Story at Essex, during the winter and spring of 1923, to replace the schooner *Puritan*, lost in June, 1922 on Sable Island. She was launched shortly before noon on April 17, 1923. The beautiful craft was christened with champagne by Miss Gertrude Carey of Lawrence, before a large crowd of spectators and towed around the Cape to Gloucester by the Boston tug *Confidence*.

Columbia was owned by the Columbia Associates, Inc. of Gloucester. Several members of this group, including Capt. Benjamin Pine, Marian Cooney, Kenneth J. Ferguson, George Roberts, and George Fuller, had owned shares in the ill-fated *Puritan*.

The *Columbia*, like the *Puritan*, was designed by W. Starling Burgess of Boston, one of the greatest designers of sailing vessels of the 20th century. She was a handsome vessel of the spoon bow type, carrying a lofty rig, short bowsprit, and she swung one of the longest mainbooms out of Gloucester. The *Columbia* was slightly smaller than the *Puritan*, but she had a more graceful stern. Although not as fast as the speedy *Puritan*, she was probably the fastest of all our contenders in the International races. The new craft, named after two famous cup defenders of the same name, was painted gray with a white rail. This was changed in October, 1923 to the more practical black, which I thought gave her a more handsome and larger appearance.

Columbia arrived in Gloucester about 4 p.m. on her launching day and exactly 3½ hours later George Roberts, her rigger, had her spars stepped, and work on the rigging begun. This was a record, as it usually took about six hours to step a fisherman's spars.

The *Columbia*, while being made ready for sea, was a mecca for hundreds of spectators at the Atlantic Supply wharf. She was being fitted for dory handlining under Capt. Alden Geele, one of the greatest skippers in this branch of the fishery.

The beautiful *Columbia* sailed on her maiden trip on April 26, 1923. She was bound to Shelburne, Nova Scotia to pick up her dories and some of her crew. On this trip she carried only her main topmast, and a riding sail, instead of the mainsail. The *Columbia* arrived back in Gloucester with her maiden fare of 324,000 lbs. salt cod on June 27, 1923. The fish were on Sable Island bank and the craft was gone only two months, which was fully four weeks ahead of any salt trip. Her maiden stock was $12,693, with a share of $261.

On July 4, 1923, Capt. Geele sailed on his second salt trip. The *Columbia* made a pretty picture as she sailed out of the harbor. This was her first trip under full sail, as she was carrying the mainsail of the *Elizabeth Howard*.

Now the jinx that was following these fisherman racers began to go to work. In July, 1923 the *Columbia* was rammed by the French steam trawler *La Champlain*, off the northeast bar of Sable Island. The schooner was hit on the port side, carrying away her forerigging and breaking her bowsprit and rail. The trawler towed her into St. Pierre, where temporary repairs were made. The *Columbia* arrived home from this, her second trip, on September 14, 1923, with a fare of 225,000 lbs. of salt cod, stocking $9,011 with a share of $166.

Work was immediately begun in preparing her for the International Races to be held in a few weeks. An elimination race was held off Gloucester on October 21, 1923. The *Columbia*, sailed by one of her owners, Capt. Ben Pine, easily showed her superiority over the schooner *Henry Ford*, Capt. Clayton Morrissey, and the schooner *Elizabeth Howard*, Capt. Harry Gillie. It was a poor day for racing, and the vessels could not finish within the 5½ hours time limit. When turning the third buoy, the *Columbia* led the *Ford* by 18 minutes and 40 seconds, and the *Elizabeth Howard* by 26 minutes and five seconds. The race committee on the U. S. S. *Bushnell* that followed the racers decided that the *Columbia* would go to Halifax to race the Canadian schooner *Bluenose*.

On October 22, 1923 the jinx hit out again, when the *Columbia*, on leaving for Halifax, Nova Scotia, struck a ledge outside Great Round Rock off the breakwater and had to return to Gloucester to go on the ways to ascertain if any damage had been done. The damage was a splintering of the shoe, and repairs were quickly made.

The *Columbia* sailed for Halifax on October 25, and made a fine run of 38 hours. The first race for the International Fishermen's Cup was held off Halifax, Nova Scotia, on October 29, 1923. The Canadian schooner *Bluenose*, Capt. Angus Walters, defender of the cup, won over the *Columbia*, Capt. Ben Pine, by one minute and 20 seconds.

The second race, sailed on November 1, 1923, was also won by the *Bluenose*, beating the *Columbia* by two minutes.

The races were never finished. The first race was protested, and awarded to Capt. Pine. (The *Columbia* had been fouled by the *Bluenose* in this race.) Capt. Walters ordered his crew on board and sailed for home. The committee awarded the trophy to *Columbia* but Capt. Pine, showing great sportsmanship, declined to accept.

After the 1923 fiasco, the *Columbia* returned to Gloucester and made a trip to Newfoundland after herring in command of Capt. Al Malloch. In 1924 the *Columbia* made two salt banking trips in command of Capt. E. O. Fudge, great Newfoundland skipper. She arrived in Gloucester on June 2, 1924, with 260,000 lbs. salt cod, stocking $9,000 with a share of $135. On October 30, 1924, the *Columbia* arrived at her second salt bank trip of 358,000 salt cod, making the fine stock of $18,573 and a share of $360 per man.

The *Columbia* was tied up during the whole of 1925, and in January, 1926, she was sold to Benjamin Pine, Marian Cooney, Miss Ray Adams and Alexander J. Chisholm. She was fitted for dory handlining in command of Capt. John McInnis in 1926 and sailed on April 20, but again the jinx struck. On April 25, 1926, the *Columbia* ran ashore near Canso, Nova Scotia. The schooner was floated but the stores and salt were spoiled. A bad leak was opened up and she was towed to Halifax for repairs. The *Columbia* arrived back in Gloucester in July of that year with a small fare of 85,000 lbs. of salt fish. Fish was scarce and valuable time had been lost because of her mishap at the beginning of the trip.

The racing fever had again struck Gloucester about this time and a match was again arranged between the *Columbia* and *Henry Ford*. On October 11, 1926 the *Columbia* won over the *Ford* by one minute and 30 seconds and on October 12 she was again the winner, this time by four minutes and 55 seconds. This proved to be the last of racing for the *Columbia*. In November, 1926 the *Columbia* was sent to Newfoundland after herring, in command of Capt. Mat Critchett, a Newfoundland skipper. She arrived back in Gloucester on January 3, 1927 with 1400 bbls. herring. She refitted and sailed again on January 17, 1927, and returned with a cargo a month later.

The *Columbia*, in the spring of 1927, was fitted for dory handlining in command of Capt. Lew Wharton and sailed early in April. She arrived in Gloucester June 27, 1927, with 350,000 lbs. salt cod. The fare was sold to Gorton-Pew Co. and taken out at the Slade Gorton wharf. This proved to be the last fare of salt fish, caught by a Gloucester vessel and taken out at a Gloucester wharf.

On July 3, 1927, the *Columbia*, in command of Capt. Lew Wharton, sailed on her second dory hand line trip. Little did the folks of Gloucester realize at the time that here was sailing the last salt fisherman out of this port. In the year 1909, there were 35 dory handliners out of Gloucester. This vessel, one of their greatest, was never to return to this port.

On October 20, 1927 headlines in the *Gloucester Times* carried the sad announcement. "No Hope Now for *Columbia*—Lost With All Hands in Gale of August 24th off Sable Island." On this day the owners had given the gallant vessel up. With her went Capt. Lew Wharton and 21 brave fishermen to a watery grave. The *Columbia* put into Liverpool, Nova Scotia on July 15, put out the same day and never returned to port again. She was last seen on August 23 by the Gloucester schooner *Herbert Parker*, Capt. John Car-

rancho, about 50 miles north of Sable Island. Capt. Wharton informed Cap. Carrancho that the fishing was poor, and he had little fish. The schooners *Uda R. Corkum* and *Joyce Smith*, two of the Lunenburgers lost in the great gale, were anchored close by. The next day August 24th, a great gale swept the banks. Nothing was heard of the *Columbia* again. On September 12, 1927, five battered dories marked *Columbia* were washed up on Sable Island. Considerable wreckage was reported in the vicinity. The cutter *Tampa* was sent out to search for the missing craft with no success. On October 27, 1927, the haddocker *Mary Sears* returned to port with *Columbia*'s dory No. 11, which proved beyond any doubt that the *Columbia* had gone to her final resting place.

What really happened to the *Columbia* will never be known. Among the fishermen the most logical cause of her destruction was that she was caught unaware by the gale and hove down, or that she was in collision with one of the Lunenburgers, and both vessels were lost.

The great gale of August 24, 1927 was one of the worst in the history of the North Atlantic fisheries. Beside the loss of *Columbia* with 22 lives (this was the most lives lost in any one vessel out of Gloucester) four Canadian vessels went down with 85 men. They were the schooner *Uda R. Corkum*, Capt. Will Andrews; schooner *Joyce Smith*, Capt. Edward Maxner; schooner *Mahala*, Capt. Warren Knickle, and the *Clayton Walters*, Capt. Selig.

A curious coincidence is worthy of note at this time: Vernon Goodick, one of the *Columbia*'s crew, had shipped on her final voyage, but at the last minute, changed his mind, took off his dunnage and shipped in another vessel. Way back in 1911, this same Vernon Goodick had shipped in the schooner *Ella M. Goodwin* for a herring trip to Newfoundland. Just before the craft sailed, he changed his mind and left her. The *Ella Goodwin* was lost with all hands. Fate was sure kind to Vernon Goodick.

The crew list of the lost *Columbia*: Capt. Lewis Wharton, Rubert Bragg, cook, of Dorchester; Arthur Firth, of Shelburne, Nova Scotia; James MacAloney, of Parsboro, Nova Scotia; Isaac Gould, of Gloucester; Colin Hawley, of Gloucester; William Colp, of Bucksport, Maine; Leo White, of Bucksport, Maine; James McLeod, of Liverpool, Nova Scotia; Foster McKay, of West Green Harbor, Nova Scotia; Clayton Johnson, of West Green Harbor, Nova Scotia; Joseph Mayo, of Halifax, Nova Scotia; Thomas Hayden, of Shelburne, Nova Scotia; Carroll Williams, of Liverpool, Nova Scotia; Frank Dedrich, of Shelburne, Nova Scotia; Addison Firth, cachee, 17 years old, of Shelburne, Nova Scotia; Samuel Belong, of Green Harbor, Nova Scotia; Robert Sewart, of Liverpool, Nova Scotia; George H. Mayo, of Halifax, Nova Scotia; and Charles L. Huskin of Green Harbor, Nova Scotia.

On Sunday, November 13, 1927, services to the memory of Capt. Lewis Wharton were held in Trinity Church at Liverpool, Nova Scotia. Capt. Lew, a native of Liverpool, was one of Gloucester's great mariners. Tall, big, fearless, but careful, Lew Wharton commanded many vessels of the fleet, including the *A. R. Crittenden, Latona, Mondigo, Lizzie Stanwood, Harvard, S. P. Willard, Carrie Babson, Oriole, Lottie G. Merchant, Clintonia.* His brothers, Capt. Newman Wharton and Capt. Bob Wharton, were also great skippers out of this port. At the time of his death he was 57 years old.

Capt. Alden Geele, first skipper of *Columbia*, was found dead in the cabin of his schooner *Thomas S. Gorton* in April, 1926. A native of Shelburne, Nova Scotia, he was 62 years old. Capt. Geele was one of the greatest dory handliners out of Gloucester. Some of his commands were the *Sigfrid, Emma Wetherell, Maxine Eliott, Tattler, Elsie,* and *Columbia.*

At about 2 a.m. on New Year's day, 1928, the Canadian beam trawler *Venosta,* Capt. G. M. Myrhe, while dragging about 40 miles west southwest of Sable Island, got her gear entangled in wreckage. With powerful engines and winches of the trawler pulling the taut cables, there slowly emerged from the sea, like a phantom ship, two masts with no topmasts. Slowly the form of the vessel came into view, rolling and pitching but on an even keel. The crew of the trawler were in danger of having their sides battered in by the wreck, but suddenly the steel cables holding the wreck snapped and she slowly sank from sight. While the vessel was afloat, the powerful floodlights of the trawler were thrown on the derelict. An eerie sight greeted the watchers. No signs of humans could be seen. The vessel seemed in good condition, the major portion of her rigging was intact, but no sign of a name could be made out. The rough seas prevented any attempt in keeping the vessel afloat and to ascertain if any bodies were in the cabins. All aboard the steamer seemed to think she was the *Columbia*, but this fact will never be known. Several vessels went down in that gale off Sable Island.

So ends the story of *Columbia*, the Gem of the Ocean, or perhaps we should say, the Flying Dutchman, ship of disaster.

Arthur D. Story, the builder of *Columbia*, passed away in Essex on March 5, 1932. He was a native of Essex and 76 years old. Arthur Dana was one of the greatest Yankee shipbuilders that ever lived. He was the son of Job Story, and came from old New England stock. After learning the shipbuilding business with his father, he entered partnership with Moses Adams and was with him for eight years. In 1880 he started in business for himself and continued on successfully until the time of his death. Over 400 vessels were sent down the ways by this great shipbuilder. Some of his greatest were the *Benjamin F. Phillips, Carrie Phillips, Catherine, Elsie, Henry Ford, Columbia* and the *Gertrude L. Thebaud.*

Gross tons, 152; net tons, 96; length, 123.9 feet; breadth, 25.8 feet; depth, 12.4 feet. Spar measurements: mainmast (overall), 93 feet; foremast (overall), 83 feet; main boom, 78 feet; main gaff, 49 feet; main topmast, 47 feet; fore topmast, 42 feet; sail area, 9,300 square feet.

Schooner *Adventure*, the author's favorite, looked traditionally handsome under sail when she was young, and she looks even more handsome now, with topsails, carrying vacationing passengers along the Maine coast. But the author chose to illustrate his story of her life with this view of her as many remember her, a super successful dory trawler using sails only for steadying. She's bound out of Boston Harbor in 1940, double dories stacked on deck, carrying twenty-five or twenty-six men, who were getting along in years. The grand old lady didn't wear out, her crew wore out.

Adventure

LAST DORY TRAWLER, SHE'S SAILING AGAIN / 1926–

One of the most famous fishing schooners ever built is the *Adventure*, last of the American dory trawlers. She's probably the greatest producer and money maker in the history of the North Atlantic fisheries.

The fame of the *Adventure* is genuine, not gained through publicity as a racer or showboat but through hard, long years on the banks, battling storms and hard weather, piling up tremendous stocks, year after year.

Right from the very start it has been hard work for this gallant craft, experiencing fame, shipwreck, prosperity and death. Even in this present generation she ·has held her own and fared far better than the modern draggers and beam trawlers.

Many stories have been written about the last of the dory trawlers. None has ever carried her whole true story. This is the story of her entire career. A career in two parts, under two skippers, Capt. Jeffrey Thomas and Capt. Leo Hynes.

Her story is very personal to me. I am proud indeed that her very being was conceived and carried out by my father, Capt. Jeff Thomas; that her name was created by myself; that the little girl who christened her to begin her adventurous life afloat was my sister. Also, many members of the Thomas family have sailed on this vessel. In this schooner my father's life came to an end.

The real beginning of the *Adventure* came in the spring of 1926. My father decided to have a new vessel built, and several skippers and businessmen joined him in the idea.

The firm of Everett James in Essex was engaged and the keel was laid in April 1926. She was taken off the design of the Gloucester schooner *Oretha F. Spinney*.

The origin of the name of this vessel, like many of her sisters, is interesting and I would like to tell how it all came about.

Capt. Jeff was undecided on a name for his new craft. At this time I had quite a few pencil drawings that I had made of imaginary fishing vessels, all of which carried names created by myself. One night my father requested to see these drawings, with the hope a name would be found.

Two were considered: "Indian" and "Adventure." After some serious thought my father picked "Adventure."

He said, "I think 'Adventure' is the best, because fishing is an adventure and I don't believe there was ever a vessel out of Gloucester with that name." As it turned out, what better name could she have carried!

Adventure's launching day came on September 16, 1926. Miss Natalie J. Thomas, youngest daughter of Capt. Thomas, broke a bottle of champagne on the bow of the new vessel as she began her maiden dip into the briny.

Robert and Richard Wharton, young sons of Capt. Bob Wharton, were guests on the vessel when she was launched. Because of strong winds and tides, several days passed before *Adventure* could be towed to Gloucester to be rigged.

The *Adventure* is a good-sized vessel of the knockabout type, of very able construction, as were all the James vessels. When new, she carried tall spars with four lower rails. An aux-iliary 120-horsepower Diesel oil engine was installed.

Several years later the spars were shortened, a wheelhouse was added and a larger engine installed. When ready for sea the *Adventure* was as fine and expensive a schooner as ever sailed out of Gloucester. In fact, with the exception of the *Eleanor Nickerson* (1927) and *Gertrude L. Thebaud* (1930) she was the last vessel of this type built at Essex. The owners of the new craft were listed as Schooner Adventure, Inc., Capt. Jeffrey Thomas, principal owner.

The *Adventure* sailed on her maiden trip, haddocking, on October 16, 1926. She arrived in Boston with her maiden fare on October 25, hailing for 70,000 pounds fresh fish.

Capt. Jeff, as was his usual custom, did very well in the *Adventure*, halibuting summers and haddocking winters. On October 3, 1927, he landed a mammoth fare of 100,000 pounds halibut at Boston, stocking $11,770, with a share of $276. This stock would have been much larger if there had not been as many gray fish in the trip. It proved to be Capt. Jeff's largest stock in the *Adventure*.

The *Adventure*'s flag was half-masted for the first time on May 15, 1928, in memory of my mother, who passed away on that day. The vessel sailed for the banks on that day in command of Emery Doane, one of her crew.

The *Adventure*'s flag was again half-masted on May 16, 1931. Again it was for a member of my family. My uncle Freeman Thomas, older brother of my father, was found dead in his bunk at sea when, at daybreak, he was called to take his trick at the wheel. The trip was cut short and the vessel headed for Boston, where the body was landed. Death was due to natural causes. Uncle Freeman was a native of Arichat, Cape Breton, and fished out of Gloucester for years.

Things went well for the *Adventure* for the next few years until December 1933, when a jinx boarded the craft and did not depart until after the vessel was nearly wrecked and her skipper's life ended.

The *Adventure* was leaking badly and Capt. Thomas was running for harbor, the nearest port being Sheet Harbor, Nova Scotia. She struck on a rock (White Shoal) entering the harbor and began to pound heavily. The crew started to leave the apparently doomed vessel, but the skipper was determined she could be saved, and saved she was. She was finally pulled off by the tug *Coalopolis* after a day and a half on the rocks.

Over 40,000 pounds of fish had to be thrown overboard to lighten the vessel. She was taken in tow for Halifax, where she was repaired. Her rudder was gone and part of her keel torn off. Incidentally, this was the second time that Capt. Jeff had been ashore on White Shoal. Nineteen years previously his schooner *Sylvania* had piled up on this dreaded rock in a blinding snowstorm, and after some difficulty was floated.

The jinx hung right on to the *Adventure*. On February 27, 1934, while bound to market, she lost her rudder forty-five miles off Eastern Point, Gloucester, and was towed to Boston by the Coast Guard cutter *Frederick Lee*.

The jinx dealt its greatest blow when on March 24, 1934, the *Adventure*'s skipper, Capt. Jeff Thomas, died of a heart attack at the wheel, eighty miles off Halifax. The dories were hauling their trawls. The vessel was heavily iced up and Capt. Jeff was engaged in chopping some of it from the rigging. He then went into the wheelhouse and was taken with a heart attack which proved fatal. The vessel was immediately headed for Halifax, where the body was landed.

While at Halifax, on March 28, 1934, another member of the *Adventure*'s crew, Andrew Stahre, passed away in the hospital. Stahre was fifty-six years old and a native of Stormstad, Sweden. He had sailed out of Gloucester for thirty-three years.

The *Adventure* resumed her fishing trip in command of Capt. Emery Doane. When the trip was completed the vessel was brought to Gloucester to await a new skipper.

Capt. Leo Hynes, a smart and capable Boston skipper, was chosen to command the *Adventure*, and a new part of her life began. A new life that smashed all records in the fisheries.

Adventure's new life was not all in making money, however. Capt. Hynes tried his hand at beam trawling for a short while in 1938 and the vessel was taken over by Capt. Frank Mitchell. In August 1938, while under Capt. Mitchell's command, the *Adventure* ran down one of her own dories off Shelburne, Nova Scotia, and Theodore Babine was drowned. His dorymate, Raymond Hubbard, was rescued. Babine was forty-seven years old.

On March 13, 1939, the *Adventure*, Capt. Leo Hynes, was hit by a huge sea on the northern edge of Georges Bank and two of her crew were swept overboard to their death. The craft was jogging in a heavy storm when a big sea smashed down on her, carrying away the wheelhouse, sweeping over the unfortunate men, William Nolan and Alexander Muise, and injuring several other members of the crew.

The injured men were removed to the hospital when the craft arrived at Boston. Considerable damage was done to the stern of the *Adventure*. Nolan was a native of Newfoundland, and Muise, a native of Nova Scotia. Six children were left fatherless in the tragedy.

Four of *Adventure*'s crew went astray in the fog off Cape Sable, Nova Scotia, in April 1940. Gerald Hynes, brother of the skipper, and Frank Mouzer were picked up by the schooner *Lark*, Capt. Ernest Parsons, after they were adrift seven hours. Max Benfield and James

Miles were picked up by a freighter after forty-two hours adrift.

A strange coincidence involving the *Adventure* occurred on March 20, 1943. The *Adventure*, Capt. Leo Hynes, rammed and sank the auxiliary schooner *Adventure II*, Capt. Michael O'Hearn, in a dense fog in Boston Harbor. The *Adventure*, bound into Boston with a trip, rammed the *Adventure*, formerly *Mary P. Goulart*, sheering off the latter's stern. Her crew had hardly time to take to the dories when she went down. The shipwrecked men were taken aboard the *Adventure* and landed in Boston. Both vessels were owned by the same owners.

Death again struck *Adventure*, this time in March 1947. Stanley Conrad, one of her crew, was swept overboard and drowned in a storm on Brown's Bank. He was sixty-two years old and a native of Nova Scotia.

The *Adventure* made the headlines in 1948. On April 20 the vessel sprang a leak in a heavy southwest breeze about forty miles off Cape Cod, and for several anxious hours it was a question whether she would reach port or join her many sisters in Davy Jones' Locker. The cutter *General Greene* finally reached the leaking craft and took her in tow for Boston. It was a mighty close shave for the *Adventure*.

Now for the brighter side of the *Adventure*'s ledger. The prosperity of this great vessel is phenomenal. All previous records in the haddock fishery, and in fact any fishery, have been smashed by the *Adventure* and her able skipper, Leo Hynes. Capt. Leo used mostly twelve dories, with a crew of twenty-seven men.

During the month of January 1938 she landed seven trips and stocked $13,000. Each of the crew shared $308. Her total stock for 1940 was $132,000, with a share of $2,900 per man. The total stock for 1943, which proved to be her greatest, was $364,000. Just think of it!

Capt. Hynes stated that his poorest stock since taking over the *Adventure* was $96,000. His total stock for the nineteen years that he commanded her was close to $3.5 million. I believe this is the most money ever made by any type of vessel on the entire Atlantic coast.

The career of *Adventure* as a dory trawler came to a close in 1954. She was the very last of a glorious era. The vessel herself could have gone on, but her crew was wearing out and there were no new men to take their places.

Adventure had more than held her own in this modern age. Her life had been hard, prosperous and sad. The passing of this great vessel ended a glorious era. An era of great vessels and great men; men from all corners of the North Atlantic, to man the dory trawlers: dory men from Nova Scotia, Newfoundland, Scandinavia, Portugal and New England, whose daring, heroism and hardship brought everlasting fame to the great fishing ports of Gloucester and Boston.

When the old "Queen" tied up for the last time and the last of her dories were put ashore, we could all gaze upon her proudly and say, Well done, *Adventure*!

Capt. Jeffrey Thomas, first skipper of the *Adventure*, was one of the greatest mariners out of Gloucester. He was one of the greatest sail carriers and biggest producers in the days of sail. He was smart, capable and respected by his crews. He was skipper of the great schooner *Puritan* (1932), probably the fastest fishing schooner ever built. He also commanded many fine vessels including the schooners *Arcadia, Cynthia, Sylvania, Benjamin A. Smith, Marechal Foch, Bay State, Elmer E. Gray, Corinthian, Falmouth, Oretha F. Spinney* and *Adventure*. He was a brother of Capts. William H., John, and Peter Thomas. Capt. Jeff was a native of Arichat, Cape Breton.

Capt. Leo Hynes, last skipper of the *Adventure*, was one of the finest, most capable skippers who ever took the wheel of a haddocker. It is fitting that this son of the rockbound coast of Newfoundland is the last of the dory trawlers. No finer man deserves this great honor.

Some of Hynes's commands were the schooners *Mary E. O'Hara, Shamrock, Corinthian* and *Gertrude L. Thebaud*. He is a native of Bay L'Argent on Newfoundland's south coast.

The *Adventure* was sold in 1954 to Donald Hurd of Portland, Maine, to be used in the windjamming passenger business. Her engine was removed, her galley enlarged, and fish pens became staterooms for her passengers. The rest of the vessel remained intact. For the next ten years the *Adventure* was a familiar sight off the Maine coast during the summer seasons.

In 1964 she was sold to Capt. Jim Sharp of Camden, Maine. She has sailed in the windjamming trade under his able command up to the present time.

Shortly after purchasing the vessel Capt. Sharp changed the color of the hull to white. He put in longer spars that gave her a loftier rig. Later a maintopmast and topsail were added.

Capt. Sharp has done a great job in keeping the vessel in excellent condition. Now her fifty passengers, who come from all over the world, get the thrill of their lives as they cruise the Maine coast.

I had the pleasure of sailing on the *Adventure*'s last cruise of the 1971 season. One day on this trip, a spanking breeze came up and Capt. Sharp turned the wheel over to me.

What a thrill! I was amazed how easily she handled and how fast she was sailing—twelve knots!

Standing there at the wheel of the *Adventure* my thoughts kept roaming back into the past. Here was the very same wheel that my father had steered by so many times. Here was the last dory trawler, and last schooner of her type in commission on this side of the Atlantic. Here was the very last of the beautiful schooners that I loved so much.

Gross tons, 130; net tons, 62; length, 107 feet; breadth, 24.5 feet; depth, 11.1 feet.

Gertrude L. Thebaud

LAST OF THE ABLE, HANDSOME
LADIES / 1930–1948

Last of the able, handsome ladies. Last of the long line of fishing schooners that brought fame and glory to Gloucester.

The *Gertrude L. Thebaud* was the last vessel of her type built in Essex and for the Gloucester fisheries, although not the last all-sailing vessel, as the *Columbia* of 1923 holds that honor.

The *Thebaud*, as she was most always known, was the most publicized and most photographed vessel out of this port. She went many miles as a fisherman show boat, Arctic exploration vessel and marine ambassador. The *Gertrude L.* also holds the honor, and a most important one, in being the last Gloucesterman built with tall spars, topmast and a bowsprit.

Through the generosity of Louis Thebaud, a French-American summer resident of Gloucester, this fine new fishing schooner was built during the winter of 1929–30 at the Arthur D. Story Yard in Essex. Mr. Thebaud contributed $30,000. His wife, for whom the new craft was named, gave $10,000; Robert McCurdy, son-in-law of the Thebauds, $5,000; Bassett Jones, $5,000; Wetmore Hodges of General Seafoods, $5,000; Chandler Hovey of Boston, $5,000. Capt. Ben Pine and Joseph Mellow were the managers and the firm name was Gertrude L. Thebaud, Inc.

Mr. and Mrs. Thebaud were great admirers of the Gloucester fisherman and it was hoped the new craft would bring the International Fishermen's Cup back to Gloucester.

Before a large crowd the *Gertrude L. Thebaud* was launched on March 17, 1930. She was christened by Elizabeth Hovey, daughter of Chandler Hovey of Boston, with a bottle of 35-year-old champagne given by her builder. She was immediately towed around to Gloucester to prepare for sea.

The *Thebaud* was a large, yachtlike craft, of a semi-knockabout type, with tall spars, a sharp dory bow and a short bowsprit. She was designed by Payne, Belknap and Skene, noted yacht designers.

She was a fine sturdy looking craft, but not so pretty under sail as her predecessor, the *Columbia*. One of the principal features of the *Thebaud* was the cut of her mainsail. It was different than that of any previous vessel. It consisted of a short main boom, long gaff, peaked high in the air, and a leach (outer edge of sail) of 93 feet. Only one other fisherman surpassed the *Thebaud's* mainsail leach in length; that was the big *Mayflower* (1921) with 104 feet.

Except while in the U. S. Coast Guard, the *Thebaud* was always painted black. She was fitted with a 180 horsepower auxiliary oil engine. The new craft was given a trial in Massachusetts Bay on April 27, 1930. About 75 guests of Capt. Pine and Joe Mellow were on board. On the way home, she put into Marblehead harbor, circled it and headed back to sea. Her new engine worked well and she carried a riding sail (in place of mainsail), a foresail and jumbo.

On April 29th she went to Boston to get supplies and sailed that day on her maiden trip, haddocking, in command of Capt. Freeman Crowell, one of the old dory trawling skippers. The *Gertrude Thebaud* arrived at Gloucester with her maiden fare on May 13, 1930, with 130,000 pounds of fresh fish.

The *Thebaud*, although one of our best known vessels, was not considered successful as a fisherman. However, this was made up in her spreading of Gloucester's fame as a floating ambassador to various parts of the country.

During her fishing career she was commanded by Capts. Freeman Crowell, Jimmy Abbott, Archie MacLeod, Mike Clark, and Cecil Moulton.

Capt. MacLeod landed some big trips of halibut. In June 1934 he landed 70,000 pounds. In July 1934, he again landed 70,000 pounds. On July 8, 1935 he landed 80,000 pounds halibut at Gloucester, stocking $6,871, with a share of $111. This trip sold to the Gorton-Pew Co. and Davis Bros. At this time she carried 31 men and 14 double dories which was a record. In October, 1935, Capt. MacLeod landed 70,000 pounds.

While in command of Capt. Jimmy Abbott the *Thebaud* was hit by a big sea September 9, 1932, off the Highland, Cape Cod, and two of her crew, Edward Zinck, 29, and Austin Snow, 50, were swept to their deaths. Zinck was a native of Lunenburg, Nova Scotia.

The *Thebaud* represented the fishing industry, particularly Gloucester, in April 1933, when she sailed with a large delegation of those prominent in the industry, including veteran fishermen, from Gloucester to Washington, D. C., to emphasize to President Roosevelt D. Roosevelt the plight of the fishing industry, then at a very low ebb. President Roosevelt himself went down to the pier to greet Capt. Pine and his crew. With the President was Prime Minister Ramsay MacDonald of Great Britain. Among the famous Gloucester skippers on board on this voyage were Capts.

Probably the most famous Gloucester schooner of all time was the *Gertrude L. Thebaud*, built with racing in mind. In the author's opinion she was not a very handsome vessel: she had a short foretopmast, her main gaff was too high-peaked, her sides were high; she was the least pretty of the great racers. But she won the admiration of many, and lived a varied and distinguished life.

Clayton Morrissey, Joe Mesquita, Val O'Neil, William Nickerson, Norman Ross, Jim Mason, Jimmy Abbott, Don MacCuish, Jack Carroll and Al Malloch.

On July 27, 1933 the *Thebaud* sailed from Gloucester, in command of Capt. Pine, as Massachusetts' exhibition in the World's Fair at Chicago, going by way of the St. Lawrence River and Great Lakes. I believe this was the first time a Gloucester fishing schooner sailed down Lake Michigan. Capts. Wallace Bruce and Jack Carroll, two of our old great mariners, made the trip. On board were many models of fishing vessels, loaned by the Cape Ann Historical Association, which has a museum at 27 Pleasant Street in Gloucester.

The *Thebaud* proved to be a great drawing card at the fair, averaging 2,500 visitors daily. Her racing rival, schooner *Bluenose*, was also at the fair representing Canada. The *Thebaud* returned home October 22, 1933.

Commander Donald B. MacMillan, noted Arctic explorer, chartered the *Thebaud* in the summer of 1937 for his sixteenth annual expedition and took her far north to Frobisher Bay, a voyage which came close to wrecking the schooner in an experience with the terrific drop in tides.

The *Thebaud* left Gloucester on June 24, 1937, in command of Capt. Jack Crowell, a former Gloucester boy and noted Arctic skipper, who became a lieutenant colonel in the United States Weather Service stationed in Greenland and retired to an island on the coast of Maine. On this voyage to the Arctic, the *Thebaud* carried a crew of 37, including seven college professors, 23 college students and seven of the regular crew. Eight thousand miles were covered before she returned home.

The *Gertrude-Thebaud* and the Canadian schooner *Bluenose* attended the dedication exercises of the State Fish Pier at Gloucester on October 12, 1938.

The *Thebaud* experienced both victory and defeat during her racing career.

In October, 1930 the *Thebaud*, in charge of Ben Pine, sailed against the *Bluenose*, Capt. Angus Walters, off Gloucester and easily defeated the Canadian champion in two straight races; the first, on the 9th, by about fifteen minutes and the second, the 19th, by eight minutes. Capt. Charley Johnson was skipper of the *Thebaud* in the second race. The International Cup was not at stake. *Bluenose* suffered her first defeat in nine years.

On October 12, 1931 the *Gertrude Thebaud* sailed from Gloucester, bound to Halifax, Nova Scotia, to meet the *Bluenose* in a series of races off that port. Under the able guidance of Capt. John Matheson, she made a record breaking run of thirty hours. Roy Parsons, editor of the *Gloucester Daily Times*, was a guest on board and wrote excellent reports of the passage and races for the *Times*.

The crew of the *Thebaud* in the races of October, 1931 included: Capt. Ben Pine, Capt. John Matheson, Mate; Capts. Edward Proctor, Nelson Amero, Jack Barret, Roy Patten, Colin Powers, John Sparrow and William (Billy Nick) Nickerson; also Mickey Hall, Charles Landry, Forrest Bickford, Harry Christensen, Franklin DeRoach, Louis Francis, Walter Hansen, Wetmore Hodges, James Hallett, John Hackett, Hjalmar Johnson, Bill LeCases, Henry Lapeau, Lawrence McEwen, Hilary McKinnon, James Parsons, George Roberts, Charles Stewart, Joseph Young, Nathan B. McCloud, and William Clark.

The *Thebaud* put up a poor showing and lost to the *Bluenose* in two straight races. The cup remained in Nova Scotia.

Several years later, in October, 1938, the final races for the International Fishermen's Cup were sailed off Gloucester. The Canadian *Bluenose*, Capt. Angus Walters of Lunenburg, Nova Scotia, won over the *Gertrude L. Thebaud*, Capt. Ben Pine of Gloucester, in three races out of five and thus retained the championship of the North Atlantic.

On October 9th the *Thebaud* won the first race by two minutes, 50 seconds. On October 13th *Bluenose* won the second race by twelve minutes, 10 seconds. Followed ten days of fog, calm, and the retirement of Capt. Pine through illness to give command to Capt. Cecil Moulton, her regular skipper.

On October 23, *Bluenose* won the third race by six minutes, 37 seconds. On October 24th the *Thebaud* evened up the series when she won by two minutes, 44 seconds. The fifth and deciding race was held on October 26th, 1938 and the *Bluenose* won by two minutes, 50 seconds. Thus ended the last race between fishing schooners in the North Atlantic.

Several new records were established in this series. Eighteen days were necessary to run off five completed races. In a nine-and-one-half mile reach in a 15 knot breeze on the first leg of the fourth race, on October 24, *Bluenose* attained a speed of 14.15 knots, the fastest time ever made over a fixed course by a canvassed vessel. The *Thebaud* on this leg logged 13.87 knots.

During World War II the United States Coast Guard chartered the *Thebaud* and made her the flagship of their famous Corsair Fleet, used in patrolling the coast. In the spring of 1944 she was returned to her owners. She now carried a wheelhouse and she was minus her bowsprit.

The *Gertrude L. Thebaud* was sold to William H. Hoeffer of New York in August, 1944, for use as a freighter in Caribbean and South American waters. She sailed from Gloucester for the last time on May 29, 1945. As her tall spars disappeared over the horizon an era ended! Grand, glorious era of great schooners and greater men.

The end came to the *Gertrude L. Thebaud* in February, 1948, when she was smashed to pieces on the breakwater at LaGuaira, Venezuela, during a storm. Her great rival, the Canadian *Bluenose*, went to her doom on the coast of Haiti in January, 1946.

Capt. Benjamin Pine, racing skipper of the *Thebaud*, had been a leading waterfront figure in Gloucester for years. He was a participant in more races with the Canadians than any other skipper out of Gloucester.

Capt. Pine died in Feb., 1953 at Gloucester, at the age of 70. He was a native of Belleoram, Newfoundland.

Mrs. Gertrude L. Thebaud, namesake of the vessel, passed away at her home in Morristown, New Jersey, in November, 1930. On the news of her death, various vessels in Gloucester harbor had their flags at half mast in respect to her memory.

Gross tons, 137; net tons, 93; length, 115.8 feet; breadth, 25.2 feet; depth, 12.2 feet. Mainmast (deck to cap), 85 feet; foremast, 75 feet; maintopmast, 42 feet; main boom, 71.2 feet; main gaff, 48.6 feet; bowsprit, 17.5 feet (outboard); leach of mainsail, 93 feet; mainmast head, 14.5 feet.

CAPTAIN REUBEN (REUB) CAMERON, one of the best all around skippers out of Gloucester; at his best mackerel seining.

Some of his best known commands were the *Joseph Rowe*, *Grayling*, *Mary E. Harty* and *Marguerite Haskins*.

A native of Clark's Harbor, Nova Scotia, he died in January 1950 at eighty-six.

CAPTAIN LEMUEL (LEM) FIRTH broke all records in the mackerel seining fishery in 1917. One of the most capable skippers out of Gloucester, he was at his best mackerel seining and on Newfoundland herring voyages.

Among his best known commands were schooners *Rob Roy*, *Mary F. Curtis*, *Sylvania* and *Catherine Burke*.

A native of Jordan Ferry, Shelburne County, Nova Scotia, he died in May 1967 at eighty-seven.

CAPTAIN ALDEN GEELE, greatest of all dory hand-line skippers, landed more big trips of salt fish than any other skipper on this side of the Atlantic. His best known commands included schooners *Maxime Eliott, Tattler* and *Thomas S. Gorton.*

A native of Shelburne, Nova Scotia, he died in April 1926 at sixty-two.

CAPTAIN SOLOMON (SOL) JACOBS, King of the Mackerel Seiners and a pioneer in the history of the New England fishery. He also excelled in Newfoundland herring voyages.

Some of his best known commands were schooners *Sarah Jacobs, Ethel B. Jacobs* and *Helen Miller Gould* and the steamship *Alice M. Jacobs.*

A native of Twillingate, Newfoundland, he died February 7, 1922 at the age of seventy-four.

CAPTAIN THOMAS F. MCMANUS was the greatest of all fishing schooner designers.

Captain Tom had no superiors when it came to designing a fishing schooner. His creations were handsome, fast and able. He was always striving to bring new design into the fleet that would save more lives, bring more speed in getting the fish to market, and at the same time create schooners that were the most beautiful ever built.

He was the son of John H. McManus, Boston's most noted sailmaker, born in the North End of Boston in 1856. In his younger days he worked with his father in sailmaking, later turning to the fish business, located on Atlantic Avenue.

Tom's thoughts, however, were on designing, and he was given much help by D. J. Lawlor and Edward Burgess, Boston's most famous designers.

In 1892 he designed the schooner *James S. Steele* for George Steele of Gloucester; the most radical design up to that time. She was very sharp forward, had a flush deck and proved very fast.

He kept improving and in 1902 came out with the first vessel without a bowsprit, schooner *Helen B. Thomas*. This proved the greatest change and greatest lifesaver in the design of fishermen. This also proved to be the rig carried by fishermen to the very end of the sailing era.

In 1898 McManus introduced the first round-bowed vessel, the *Mattakeesett*. The early vessels of this type were called Indian headers, as most of these schooners were named after Indians.

In 1901 Captain Tom designed the big *Regina*, a great clipper bowed speedster carrying an eighty-foot mainboom.

One of his last big vessels was the big schoo-ner *Henry Ford*, one of the contestants in the International Races in 1922. Captain McManus also designed many vessels for the Nova Scotian fleet.

The great designer passed away at his home in Milton, Massachusetts, at the age of eighty-two, November 14, 1938.

Some of his most famous creations were the schooners *James S. Steele, Richard Steele, Helen B. Thomas, Regina, Mattakeesett, Mettamora, Mooween, Rose Dorothea, Jessie Costa, Esperanto, Arethusa, Massachusetts, Clintonia, Oriole, Elsie, Conqueror, Stilletto, Sylvania, Ingomar, Thomas S. Gorton, Elizabeth Howard* and *Henry Ford*.

CAPTAIN JOSEPH MESQUITA, highline skipper, one of the pioneers of Gloucester's Portuguese fishermen, and one of the city's most respected citizens. He introduced the famous religious crowning services in 1902. At his best haddocking and shacking.

His best known commands were the two *Mary P. Mesquitas, Frances P. Mesquita, Joseph P. Mesquita* and *Herbert Parker.*

He sailed his last voyage in November 1933 at the age of seventy-four.

CAPTAIN ENOS NICKERSON was one of the greatest skippers out of Boston; at his best haddocking.

Best known commands, schooners *Pontiac, Frances Grueby, Isabelle Parker* and *Eleanor Nickerson.*

A native of Woods Harbor, Shelburne County, Nova Scotia, he died March 27, 1922 at sixty-seven.

CAPTAIN ROBERT (BOB) B. PORPER was one of the greatest halibuting skippers who ever sailed out of Gloucester; a capable hard-driving sail carrier.

Best known commands included schooners *Bessie M. Wells*, *Masconomo*, *Anglo Saxon* and *Cavalier*.

A native of Manchester, Guysboro County, Nova Scotia, he died at eighty-three in October 1941.

CAPTAIN ELROY PRIOR, one of the finest of the Down East skippers, at his best in market fishing and mackerel seining.

Some of his best known commands were the schooners *Edith M. Prior*, *Kentucky* and *Effie M. Prior*.

A native of Bremen, Maine, he died in June 1944 at eighty-one.

CAPTAIN NORMAN ROSS, one of Gloucester's greatest mariners, rugged, capable and a fine navigator. At his best in mackerel seining and Newfoundland herring voyages.

Some of his best known commands were the schooners *Golden Rod, Bay State, Benjamin A. Smith* and *Kineo.*

A native of Riverside, Guysboro County, Nova Scotia, he died in January 1939 at sixty-eight.

ARTHUR D. STORY, greatest builder of fishing vessels, was born in Essex, Massachusetts, in 1854, son of Job Story, a noted Essex shipbuilder.

In 1872 Arthur Dana Story formed a partnership with Moses Adams that lasted until 1880, when both men started their own yards.

From 1880 to 1932 Arthur D. Story built 425 ships. In 1901, his greatest year, eighteen vessels slid into the Essex River.

A. D. Story built many vessels on speculation, some unnamed, during lean years, in order to keep his men working. He was one of Essex's most respected citizens and at one time a member of the Massachusetts legislature. Tall, powerful, and a real Yankee right to the core.

The Story shipyard is still in operation today, now run by his son Dana, also a famous shipbuilder. The Story shipyard is the very last of the birth places of the finest two-masted wooden schooners ever built.

Some of Arthur D. Story's most famous vessels were the schooners *Carrie E. Phillips, Benjamin Phillips, Tattler, J. J. Flaherty, Yosemite, Maggie E. McKenzie, Iceland* (built in six weeks), *John E. McKenzie, Rob Roy, Catherine and Ellen, Elizabeth Silsbee, Elsie, Imperator, Ralph Brown, Elk, Catherine, Hesperus, L. A. Dunton, Henry Ford, Columbia* and *Gertrude L. Thebaud.*

He died at seventy-eight in 1932.

CAPTAIN JEFFREY (JEFF) F. THOMAS, one of the greatest shackers and haddockers out of Gloucester. Rugged, capable and one of Gloucester's greatest sail carriers.

Some of his best known commands were schooners *Cynthia, Sylvania, Puritan* and *Adventure.*

A native of Arichat, Cape Breton, he died at sea at fifty-nine in March 1934.

CAPTAIN WILLIAM (BILLY) H. THOMAS, one of the most picturesque and commanding figures in the New England fisheries. A great sail carrier. Probably the greatest haddocker who ever sailed from Gloucester. It was considered an honor to sail with this great skipper.

Noted commands included schooners *Horace B. Parker, Elmer E. Gray* and *Thomas S. Gorton.*

A native of Arichat, Cape Breton, he died at sixty-seven in June 1925.

CAPTAIN MARTIN (MARTY) WELCH, winner of the first International Fishermen's Races, and one of the greatest sailing masters out of Gloucester. At his best mackerel seining and haddocking.

Some of his best known commands, *Navahoe*, *Lucania*, *Killarney* and *Esperanto*.

A native of Digby County, Nova Scotia, he died in April 1935, at seventy.